INVADERS AS ANCESTORS

On the Intercultural Making and Unmaking of Spanish Colonialism in the Andes

Since pre-Incan times, native Andean people had worshipped their ancestors, and the custom continued even after the arrival of the Spaniards in the sixteenth century. Ancestor worship, however, did not exclude members of other cultures: in fact, the Andeans welcomed outsiders as ancestors. *Invaders as Ancestors* examines how this unique cultural practice first facilitated Spanish colonization and eventually undid the colonial project when the Spanish attacked ancestor worship as idolatry and Andeans adopted Spanish political and religious forms to challenge indigenous rulers.

In this work, Peter Gose demonstrates the ways in which Andeans converted conquests into relations of kinship and obligation. They worshipped Christianized and racially 'white' spirits after the Spaniards invaded, though the conquering Spaniards prevented actual kinship bonds with the Andeans by adhering to strict rules of racial separation. Gose goes beyond the usual colonial resistance narratives, describing instead a creative form of transculturation under the agency of the Andeans. *Invaders as Ancestors* is a fascinating account of one of the most unusual transcultural encounters in the history of colonialism.

(Anthropological Horizons)

PETER GOSE is the Chair of the Department of Sociology and Anthropology at Carleton University.

ANTHROPOLOGICAL HORIZONS

Editor: Michael Lambek, University of Toronto

This series, begun in 1991, focuses on theoretically informed ethnographic works addressing issues of mind and body, knowledge and power, equality and inequality, the individual and the collective. Interdisciplinary in its perspective, the series makes a unique contribution in several other academic disciplines: women's studies, history, philosophy, psychology, political science, and sociology.

For a list of the books published in this series see page 381.

PETER GOSE

Invaders as Ancestors

On the Intercultural Making and Unmaking of Spanish Colonialism in the Andes

UNIVERSITY OF TORONTO PRESS
Toronto Buffalo London

© University of Toronto Press Incorporated 2008
Toronto Buffalo London
www.utppublishing.com
Printed in Canada

ISBN 978-0-8020-9876-4 (cloth)
ISBN 978-0-8020-9617-3 (paper)

Printed on acid-free paper

Library and Archives Canada Cataloguing in Publication

Gose, Peter
    Invaders as ancestors : on the intercultural making and unmaking of
Spanish colonialism in the Andes / Peter Gose.

    (Anthropological horizons)
    Includes bibliographical references and index.
    ISBN 978-0-8020-9876-4 (bound).   ISBN 978-0-8020-9617-3 (pbk.)

    1. Spain – Colonies – America – Administration – History.   2. Ancestor
worship – Andes Region.   3. Andes Region – Religious life and customs.
4. Spain – Colonies – America – Religious life and customs.   5. Acculturation – Andes Region.   6. Andes Region – History.   I. Title.   II. Series.

F2212.G68 2008   980'.013   C2008-903991-2

This book has been published with the help of a grant from the Canadian
Federation for the Humanities and Social Sciences, through the Aid to
Scholarly Publications Programme, using funds provided by the Social
Sciences and Humanities Research Council of Canada.

University of Toronto Press acknowledges the financial assistance to its
publishing program of the Canada Council for the Arts and the Ontario
Arts Council.

University of Toronto Press acknowledges the financial support for its
publishing activities of the Government of Canada through the Book
Publishing Industry Development Program (BPIDP).

To the memory of Elliott Gose

Contents

List of Illustrations   xi

Acknowledgments   xiii

Note on Orthography   xvii

1 **Introduction**   3

Theorizing Colonial Power   7
Andean Ancestral Cultures   14
Early Modern Spanish Ancestral Culture   21
Theorizing Interaction   27

2 **Viracochas: Ancestors, Deities, and Apostles**   36

Brief Chronology of the Spanish Invasion   37
Conquest or Alliance?   43
Spaniards as Viracochas   48
Viracocha as Apostle   71

3 **Diseases and Separatism**   81

The Taqui Oncoy, 1564–65   82
Vilcabamba   85
The Rediscovery of 1569   91
The Taqui Oncoy, 1569–71   94
Aftermaths   106

4 *Reducción* **and the Struggle over Burial**   118

Reducción: Settlement Consolidation as Holistic
    Civilizing Project   119
Reducción as a Mortuary Regime   123
Crisis and 'Corruption'   128
Struggles over Burial   139
    Aullagas, 1588: An Inquisitorial Quasi-Ethnography   140
    Mangas 1604–05: Power Struggles within an *Ayllu*   145
    Huachos and Yauyos, 1613–14: Circulating Cadavers   149
    Checras, 1614: Baptizing the Ancestors   152
Syntheses of the First Campaign   155

5 **Strategies of Coexistence**   161

Reducción as a Spatial Regime   161
Ayllu Landscapes   165
Chinchaycocha   174
Pachacuti Yamqui and Guaman Poma: Updating
    Myths of Coexistence   181
Reducción and the Second Anti-Idolatry Campaign   190
More Struggles over Burial   196

6 *Ayllus* **in Transition**   207

Cajatambo, 1656   212
Santiago de Maray, 1677–1724   227
The *Ayllu* Eroded   237

7 **The Rise of the Mountain Spirits**   239

Yauyos, 1607–60   244
Canta, 1650–56   251
Cuzco, 1596–1697   262
Huamanga–Huancavelica, 1656–1811   264
Arequipa, 1671–1813   268
Analysis   272

8 **Ancestral Reconfigurations in the Ethnographic Record**   282

Differentiating the Ancestral: Mountain Spirits and *Gentiles*   283
The Ethnographic Mountain in Historical Perspective   294
The Ethnography of Death   307

Conclusion   321

Notes   331
Bibliography   349
Index   369

Illustrations

1.1 Trustee of the Spanish Crown as Inca 9
1.2 Schematics of Colonial Power 12
1.3 *Ayllus* and Founding Ancestors of Hacas 19
1.4 Ancestor Worship 22, 23
2.1 Geography of the 'Conquest' 38
2.2 Quotidian Spanish Violence 47
2.3 Viracocha Analytics by Source 50
2.4 Alliance and the Denial of Conquest 53
3.1 Geography of the Taqui Oncoy 83
4.1 Portraits of Corruption 131
4.2 The Callan Clan 147
5.1 Pariacaca: His Subdivisions and Descendants 170
5.2 Ancestral Dispersions from Chinchaycocha 175
5.3 Peru as 'Upper' and Spain as 'Lower' Moieties 189
6.1 Cajatambo, Chinchaycocha, and Chancay 213
7.1 Location of Case Studies in Chapter 7 244
7.2 Mountain Spirit Analytics over Time 280

Acknowledgments

Standard research grants from the Social Sciences and Humanities Research Council of Canada during 1992–95, 1995–98, and 2001–04 financed the archival work that underwrites this book. I am grateful for this generous support and could not have begun, continued, or finished this research without it. A project so long in the making incurs many debts, the first of which was to Juan Ossio for recruiting Teresa Vergara Ormeño to be my research assistant in Lima during the years 1992–98. Teresa's paleographic and transcription skills, her willingness to engage with my research and deploy her archival knowledge to find relevant documents got this project off to a far better start than it deserved. I look forward to having her as a colleague for many years to come and will always appreciate the kindness she and her family showed me when I was hospitalized in Lima. My gratitude also goes to Paco Quiroz for the work he did with Teresa in Lima, Arequipa, and Sevilla for me. This project also benefited immeasurably from the practical and moral support I received from Laura Gutierrez Arbulú, director of the Archivo Arzobispal de Lima. Her unrivalled paleographic skill and intimate knowledge of that key archive, but above all her fierce dedication to preserving its riches in the face of so many challenges, are all exemplary and deserve the deepest thanks.

The Archivo General de Indias in Sevilla is the other major repository on which this study draws. I thank the very professional staff and the wonderful community of researchers who work there for timely help and stimulating conversation over many years. In an era when neo-liberal policies eroded public scholarly institutions worldwide, Spain's enduring support for the Archivo General de Indias and Escuela de Americanistas in Sevilla and the Biblioteca Nacional and Archivo Histórico Nacional in Madrid were evident, enviable, and most welcome. I would also like to thank Det Kongelige Bibliotek in Copenhagen for permission to reproduce in this book figures from Guaman Poma's *Nueva corónica y bien gobierno* (1615 [1936]).

During 2000–01, I was a fellow at the Davis Center in Princeton and, thanks to the wonderful facilities, colleagues, and unfettered research time I enjoyed there, began serious work on this manuscript. I particularly thank my hosts there, Anthony Grafton and Ken Mills, for sharing their enormous learning and good humour with me. Of all the scholars whose work bears on this project, Ken is perhaps the most familiar with the sources I use, and the one with whom I most wanted to have the long conversations we shared during that time. I also thank Anthony and Ken for permission to reprint material from Gose (2003) in chapters 2 and 4 of this book.

Most of this book, however, I researched and wrote during my years at the decidedly less glamorous University of Regina. Its strongly anti-essentialist message owes a great deal, both positively and negatively, to that environment, where settler-aboriginal coexistence is an immediate and evolving question. I salute Blair Stonechild, Jan van Eyck, and other faculty at First Nations University of Canada for their courage and integrity in standing up for academic freedom under very difficult circumstances. Even more, I thank the members of my own moiety, the colleagues I had in the Anthropology Department over the years: Marcia Calkowski, Frances Slaney, Blair Rutherford, Vern Eichhorn, Carlos Londoño, Danny Rosenblatt, and the many outstanding students we taught in that small but wonderfully vibrant program. The good work we did together has outlasted the unmentionable administration under which we laboured. Tekla Eichhorn, Annette MacDougall, David Wood, Dan Holbrow, and Monica Dalidowicz were my research assistants there at different phases of this project. I thank you all for your help, company, and inspiration.

Several of my new colleagues at Carleton (some of whom were old colleagues at Regina) have read this manuscript in whole or part and offered useful suggestions. They are Frances Slaney, Blair Rutherford, Xiaobei Chen, and Amina Mire: my thanks to them and exculpations for what they could not persuade me to change, or tactfully decided to ignore. Ken Mills gave the penultimate draft of this book a rigorous critical reading that helped me improve many arguments and pushed me to reach out beyond the Andes more than I otherwise would have. My deepest thanks go to him and to to two anonymous reviewers, who also suggested valuable improvements to this book.

Finally, it is fitting that a book about ancestor worship should be dedicated to my father, Elliott Gose, who died during its final stages but helped refine an earlier draft. Like his Andean ancestral counterparts, my father was a pioneer who came to a new country and inaugurated a new way of life. Unlike them, however, the novelty of his path lay in renouncing warfare for learning. I am proud to worship at his shrine, drink to his memory, let him speak through me, and regret that only figuratively do I dance with him on my back.

Note on Orthography

Neither Spanish nor Quechua had standardized orthography when most of the primary sources for this study were written. A compelling reason to impose such a standardization here is to help the generalist reader follow the argument. Against it one must weigh the various kinds of evidence (dialectological and otherwise) that textual fidelity may preserve. Moreover, even when it is possible to normalize colonial orthography reliably to modern standards, the effect of doing so is to minimize iconically the differences between these colonial languages and their modern counterparts. Since this book centrally argues that important changes in Andean culture occurred during the collapse of colonialism, I emphasize temporal distinctions by using a standardized colonial orthography for recurring and unproblematic elements of the colonial lexicon, and a modernized orthography for their modern counterparts. In the rare cases where the two overlap, such as with *ayllu*, the text explicitly discusses the changing historical significance of the term in question. Where any substantive point may be at stake, I have tried to use original orthography for the sake of accuracy, which results in occasionally variable spellings of names or terms. This is the best resolution of competing and incompatible demands that I could manage.

When words such as *viracocha* and *quipucamayoc* occur in what I construe to be their original Quechua sense, I italicize them. When they become proper nouns, I capitalize them. In an attempt to be even-handed, I capitalize not just major figures in the Christian pantheon but also the Sun and Viracocha as putatively comparable Andean deities. Such parallel treatment appropriately calls attention to the complex colonial transculturation processes at work between Christian and Andean pantheons. Finally, I normally use *extirpation* in lower case to designate Spanish attacks on Andean 'idolatries,' but use *the Extirpation* to designate the organized institutional form (somewhat similar to the Inquisition) that those attacks eventually acquired.

INVADERS AS ANCESTORS

On the Intercultural Making and Unmaking of Spanish Colonialism in the Andes

1 Introduction

When Spaniards successfully invaded the Andes in 1532, Andean people responded much as they had to previous intrusive outsiders: by treating them as their ancestors. This book explores that incorporative strategy and its attempts to recast Spanish colonialism as inter-cultural alliance. Spanish responses to that overture also figure centrally, from the acceptance of religious dialogue and indirect rule to assertions of hard racial boundaries. The result is a study in the conflicted nature of colonial power. On the one hand, Spaniards accepted ancestral incorporation as the easiest path to colonial ascendancy. On the other, they resented the dependence on Andean institutions, sociability, and 'idolatry' that it entailed. Torn between the expediency of indirect rule and a profound will to reform Andean society, Spanish colonialism never achieved political coherence. Thus, when Andean commoners soured on their indigenous rulers during the eighteenth century, they could cite earlier Spanish attempts at reform to repudiate the worship of mummified ancestral bodies that bound them to their erstwhile lords. In so doing, they challenged colonial governance and extraction, reinventing their communities in the Christianized, egalitarian, and republican form they now have. The irony is double: not only did colonial reformism eventually undercut colonialism itself, but it did so by inciting Andean commoners to revolt against traditional forms of Andean sovereignty. By exploring colonialism's complex inter-cultural character, I will explain these apparent paradoxes and highlight how they challenge distinctions between inside and outside, self and other, indigenous and foreign that characterize contemporary liberal identity politics.

Beyond whatever intrinsic interest it may possess, this story deserves telling for at least two interrelated reasons. First, treating invaders as ancestors is not uniquely Andean but a worldwide indigenous strategy. Mexican apprehensions of Cortes as Quetzalcoatl (see Gillespie 1989: 158–201, Carrasco 1982: ch. 4) are strikingly similar. As Tylor noted long ago (1871: 91–2) and recent ethnographic research confirms,[1] indigenous peoples in Africa, Australia, and Melanesia also took European intruders for their ancestors. Hawaiians' celebrated reception of Captain Cook as their returning ancestral deity Lono (Sahlins 1981, 1985) particularly bears on this study. The second point is that this global indigenous appropriation of colonizers as ancestors disrupts liberal understandings of colonialism. While I accept and develop standard modern assumptions that colonialism was about violence, racism, and servile labour, this global indigenous view highlights inter-cultural kinship as colonialism's most salient and memorable feature. Instead of dismissing this dramatically divergent view, I take it as a politics of connection that first colonialism and then obligatory national separation successively attacked. Recent explorations of colonialism through questions of cultural representation and identity largely continue this disjunctive emphasis and so become part of the problem. From their perspective, this native view of colonialism as inter-cultural coexistence and recognition is a scandal, one that is even greater than when the natives want to 'be like us' (Ferguson 2002). Yet perhaps these deluded colonial subjects correctly see that the dominant post-colonial script has missed something important about what colonialism was, and how we might still understand and respond to it. Such, at least, is the premise of this book.

Several reasonable objections to this project are foreseeable. The most obvious is that current imperialist revivals make any discussion of post-conquest reconciliation premature and dangerous. Several more technical observations follow: the ancestral appropriation of colonizers may be an ex post facto manoeuvre, one that rewrites an earlier history through the power relations of a colonized present. To that extent, these appropriations would be a poor guide to indigenous understandings during pre- or proto-colonial encounters, and would emerge only after colonialism took hold. Indigenous ancestral treatment of colonizing Europeans would then make the best of a bad bargain, obsequiously legitimating the European colonial presence. We might ask what interests it served and particularly if it helped salvage indigenous elite privileges for relations of indirect rule. Finally, we could doubt that indigenous people were ever the real authors of the idea that Europeans were their ancestors. As Obeyesekere (1992) argued against Sahlins, it may have been Europeans, not Hawaiians, who identified Captain Cook with the returning ancestral deity Lono. If so, the ancestral attribution would be a particularly odious colonial ideology for its ventriloquized implication that indigenous people volunteered their own submission. All these suspicions are at least partly warranted, and I will explore them extensively at appropriate moments in this study. Against them, however, we must weigh some equally salient if less morally self-assured considerations.

Even if the treatment of colonizing Europeans as indigenous ancestors wholly served colonial power, that would not justify its analytical suppression. If indigenous collaboration played a larger role in establishing colonialism than contemporary nationalist sensibilities can accept, then maybe the latter need revision. Early casualties would include Ranajit Guha's writings on colonial India (1983, 1989), which deny that colonialism had any hegemonic basis and allow revolt as the only admissible subaltern response. However edifying this analytical stance might be, it comes at a high ideological cost. For if colonialism did not depend on indigenous collaboration, it must have been what racist historiography tells us it was: a unilateral assertion of European superiority and might. In the Andean case, we would have to endorse one of the more extreme versions of the European superman myth: that a band of 170 Spaniards 'conquered' an empire of more than ten million people. A more plausible and dignified explanation of the so-called conquest is that disaffected Andean people allied with the Spaniards to defeat the Incas. In the process, they portrayed the Spaniards as primordial ancestors (*viracochas*) who had returned to restore the sovereignty of local polities that the Incas had overrun. This inter-ethnic collaboration led into a system of indirect rule through indigenous lords (*curacas*), whose power over their own subjects initially increased under the Spaniards and remained crucial to the colonial order. By allying with the Spaniards and treating them as their ancestors, Andean people rejected Inca colonialism for what eventually became Spanish colonialism but initially resembled provincial sovereignty. Their appropriation of intrusive Spaniards both challenged and generated colonialism, and defies reduction to either tendency alone.

In exploring why modern anthropologists under-report and analytically avoid Melanesian convictions that white people are their ancestors, Leavitt (2000: 305–6) adds important new considerations to this general argument. Such notions embarrass us, he suggests, because we assume that Melanesians could identify with their colonizers only by internalizing white supremacist ideologies. Here the ostensibly indigenous belief that (white) ancestors are the source of 'cargo' uncomfortably approximates Western developmentalism and related ideologies of white technical superiority. Yet our principled discomfort is not only misplaced but itself constitutes a refusal to listen. What Melanesian cargo practices really do, Leavitt suggests, is to deny that white people are racially separate and to subject their wealth to indigenous social claims. Thus, Leavitt shows that Melanesians treat whites as ancestors not to deify them but to make them responsible (even when they return to their countries of origin) for Melanesians' well-being (2000: 305, 311). Far from an internalized racism, this ancestral treatment of whites articulates a politics of connection. Indeed, such ancestral appropriations look like a deliberate, counteracting response to racism in their demand for intergroup solidarity. If so, we must turn the argument around: the primary obstacle to understanding this indigenous strategy is a racist conviction that Europeans could not possibly assume kinship or ancestral obligations towards the people they colonized. By challenging this conviction, from which so much European colonizing itself proceeded, these ancestral appropriations question colonialism's moral foundation and are therefore anti-colonial in character. Moreover, by insisting on a politics of recognition, solidarity, and reconciliation, these strategies affirm values that have proven elusive in our post-colonial age of nationalist essentialism and unconstrained neoliberalism. Now more than ever, I would argue, such appropriations of whiteness have critical value for the quiet challenges they pose to globalized Eurocentric liberalism.

An important general point follows from these arguments: colonial incorporation was (and still remains) a two-way street. Colonizers subsumed the colonized by definition, but the reverse was no less true. European colonists depended on indigenous practices to recruit labour and to govern, but also in domestic and conjugal matters. Such practices were not just sites of colonial power but also points of European vulnerability, where indigenous people could encompass them with their own sociability and assimilate them to their own institutional norms. Converting intrusive colonists into indigenous ancestors was an attempt to domesticate their power and make it serve indigenous interests. The Andean representation of Spaniards as ancestors entailed (and still entails) a moral economy whereby the peasantry offers tribute to the state in return for its recognition of communal land tenure. At various moments, Andean peasantries have forced their colonial and post-colonial states to conform to this 'pact of reciprocity,' which exerts an indigenizing pressure on those states. From a possessive individualist perspective, Andean peasantries' voluntary and at times aggressive rendering of tribute (see Platt 1982, Serulnikov 2003) appears as irrational surrender. Within the sacrificial logic of Andean divine kingship, however, it becomes an act of regulative control whereby the subaltern materially reconstitute, program, and direct the powers to which they are subject. Through this strategy of connection, Andean people have defined and pursued their interests at least as effectively as any subaltern group working within the liberal idiom of freedom and autonomy. Perhaps they have done so more effectively because their strategy is inherently hegemonic and aims to transform power rather than merely replicate its received form in a separate jurisdiction. We will explore these issues at length and in many registers below. For now, the point is that we should not let the conciliatory appearances of this strategy mask its hegemonic intent.

Theorizing Colonial Power

Since post-colonial criticism has recently and influentially articulated the main notions of colonial power I am arguing against, let me briefly discuss the issues at stake. I take Said's emphasis on the binary differentiation of colonizer and colonized (1978) to be a necessary but insufficient characterization of colonialism. Without this differentiation, power ceases to be colonial in form, yet the practicalities of colonial rule, extraction, and sociability require collusions that partially blur and undermine the distinction between colonizer and colonized. Although Said himself did not discuss this counter-tendency, it gives his analysis renewed urgency: colonialism demands binary discursive oppositions between colonizers and colonized precisely because the practices of colonial rule may actually challenge those oppositions. This supplement to Said parallels Bhabha's discussions of mimicry and hybridity (1994) and shares with them the notion that cultivated similarity necessarily challenges colonial discourses of binary difference. Similarities between Andean ancestor worship and the Catholic cult of the saints were particularly troubling in this regard, as we will see extensively below. Nonetheless, this study departs from Bhabha's view of mimicry and hybridity as secondary subversions of colonial power (understood as binary differentiation) by insisting that they also constituted that power itself (as ruling practices). Furthermore, mimicry was bidirectional: not only did Andean elites imitate their Spanish counterparts, but Spaniards necessarily inserted themselves into Andean political-economic frameworks to benefit from them. Figure 1.1, in which Andean tributaries carry a trustee of the Spanish Crown about in a litter as if he were an Inca, makes this point in shorthand. Official discourse worried about Spanish colonial power's 'feral' tendencies even more than native mimicry, which at least confirmed Spanish cultural codes and convictions of superiority. By ignoring this bidirectionality, Bhabha anticipates Spivak's celebrated but problematic arguments about colonialism as discursive erasure and assimilation of the colonized (1988). A similar treatment of the indigenous as an absence also characterizes 'the new historicism' (e.g., Greenblatt 1991: 7), and is arguably the lowest common denominator of literary approaches to colonialism.

Ostensibly the result of colonialism itself, this erasure of the indigenous actually derives from the sort of discourse analysis these studies deploy. Guha (1983: ch. 2) and Spivak (1988: 283–5) identify 'power' as the distinctive feature that creates a binary colonial differentiation of elites from the subaltern, whose only consistent trait is their relative powerlessness. Thus, the colonizer's power becomes the positivity that defines the colonized negatively, by their lack. These analyses guarantee the erasure of the colonized, who are by definition disempowered and silenced. By reducing the subaltern to a negative space in a power-obsessed Saussurean exercise, these analyses erase the colonized from their own history as a point of method, and to an extent that far exceeds colonialism itself (Thomas 1994: 56–8; Sahlins 1995: 116, 197–8). Since the erasure of indigenous agency in these studies occurs through the reification of colonial power, its remedy must address that problem. By exploring the events that constituted colonial power in the Andes, I will show that colonialism did not arrive full blown as a unitary 'discourse' but rather as a compromised, conflicted, and contingent project that drew on indigenous power relations (cf. Ortner 2006: 46–9). The agency behind Spanish colonialism in the Andes was never exclusively Spanish but necessarily included Andean functionaries. Andean social relationships, tributary practices, and political institutions remained central to colonial rule throughout. Spanish colonialism was permanently torn between using these Andean frameworks on the one hand and trying to replace them with Iberian civic and religious institutions on the other. The ensemble of ruling practices that formed colonial power in the Andes was therefore culturally diverse, although it re-

Figure 1.1 Trustee of the Spanish Crown as Inca

sulted in a generalized supremacy of Spaniards over Andean people. To disassociate Spanish supremacy from social relations with Andean people and take it at face value, as post-colonial theory does when it reduces colonial power to a diacritic in an identity game, is thus an analytical blunder. These authors thoroughly beg the question of colonial power and reveal (despite all verbal indications to the contrary) that it does not really interest them.

By contrast, this study takes the formation of colonial power as a serious question. Even in its most consolidated forms, colonial power was heterogenous, most obviously in its ethnic hybridity. Throughout Spanish America, colonial rule began by pairing indigenous political authorities with conquistadores who acted as trustees (*encomenderos*) of the Spanish Crown. The jurisdictions thus created were therefore essentially parasitic on pre-Hispanic polities, which continued to exist (with many transformations) well into the colonial period. To administer such a jurisdiction effectively, and above all to profit from it economically, an *encomendero* had to ally with his indigenous counterpart, who had the social position and cultural skills to make binding demands on the aboriginal tributaries they jointly directed (Stern 1982, ch. 2, Spalding 1984: 108, Lockhart 1992: 28–30). Such relations often devolved into rivalry when *encomenderos* tried to appropriate Andean sumptuary markers such as the litter depicted in figure 1.1 or the *taqui* (a song and dance in praise of ancestral political authority) to realize their seigneurial aspirations without the mediation of Andean officials (see Estenssoro 2003: 160), but the power they sought only became more hybrid in the process. Nonetheless, most successful colonists still depended (however unwillingly) on alliances with indigenous rulers well into the eighteenth century, which suggests that an effective grasp on power still eluded them.

Even more fundamentally, Spanish colonial power was heterogenous because its various elite projects were internally conflicted and ultimately contradictory in nature. On the one hand, this power was supposed to derive from conquest and so escape the various dependencies on the indigenous that actually characterized it. In this mode, Spanish colonial power asserted an absolute binary differentiation from the colonized, as in post-colonial theory. On the other hand, Spanish colonialism was founded on a missionary imperative that made the conversion and full Christianization of Indian subjects the measure of imperial legitimacy. This second goal was assimilative. Its realization undermined the first by removing the religious grounds that morally distinguished Indians (as non-Christians) from Spaniards and rationalized their conquest and tributary subjugation (cf. Thomas 1994: ch. 4). It is no wonder, then, that Spaniards endlessly called their own missionary effort into question (Estenssoro 2003: 141–4), since to admit its very real successes would be to remove the basis for colonial rule and extraction.

This basic contradiction pitted various Spanish colonial interests against one another, most notably missionaries against *encomenderos*, which in turn only heightened the importance of alliances with the colonized, now in a mediating role. A minimally adequate schema of Andean colonial power thus requires a triad of conquest, conversion, and alliance relations (see figure 1.2b), whose interactions largely define this colonial discursive field. Figure 1.2c shows how any two of these relations could interact to generate specific political initiatives (discussed in subsequent chapters) that were at least potentially antagonistic towards the third relation they excluded, which typically responded with its own critique or initiative. Such interactions generated most of the colonial discourse this book will analyse, and explain why it did not take the simple binary form of post-colonial criticism. This schema further suggests that because colonial power was not monolithic but conflicted and decentred, it was also ultimately vulnerable in ways that post-colonial criticism typically fails to admit.

Never was Spanish colonialism more vulnerable than when it sought to dispense with indirect rule through Andean functionaries and institutions. Thus, without neglecting other permutations of colonial power, this study will particularly focus on the collusion of conquest and conversion to reform Andean society through settlement consolidation (*reducción*) and the 'extirpation of idolatry.' These reforms tried to undermine Andean *curacas*' power by promoting Iberian civic and religious institutions. For over a century after their inauguration in 1570, these reforms continued to be debated, withdrawn, modified, and reimposed without definitively changing the Andean character of colonial society and its power relations. By the eighteenth century, these debates had largely exhausted themselves in official circles, yet only then did the real crisis of colonial power begin. Relations of political obedience between indigenous lords and their peasant subjects, the backbone of indirect rule, slowly eroded, and peasantries ultimately rejected collective mummy worship, the primary ritual expression of paternalistic solidarity. *Curacas* lost their moral authority as Andean

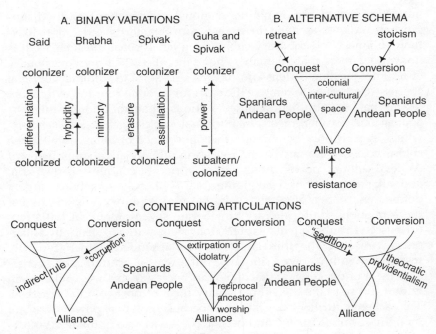

Figure 1.2 Schematics of Colonial Power

peasantries belatedly accepted this fundamental demand of the 'extirpation of idolatry.' Andean commoners began to bypass their lords and interacted directly with the colonial state through egalitarian community-based forms of authority. When the colonial state failed to incorporate these emergent forms, Andean society became ungovernable, leading to the Tupac Amaru rebellion of 1780–81, from which relations of colonial rule never recovered. In short, attempts to dispense with indirect rule and to assert unmediated colonial power were destabilizing, and ultimately cost Spain its Andean colonies. Far from proclaiming the discursive omnipotence of colonial power, then, this study explores its frailty and celebrates the death blow that Andean people gave it when they critically revised their own cultural tradition. Their ancestral appropriation of outsiders did not end, however, but found rearticulation in a republican landscape of 'white' mountain spirits, whose historical and political significance forms this study's concluding note.

To understand the intricacies of colonial power and the complex inter-cultures they produced, we must first consider Andean and Spanish cultures separately. Thus we can identify the specific colonizing agendas and indigenous strategies in play, and the ruling practices from each tradition that came into colonial alignment. Only by attending to these issues can we avoid the reduction of colonialism to the discursive policing of a binary contrast and the attendant problems discussed above. This alternative implies a largely realist approach to Andean and Spanish cultures. It suggests that each had its own repertoire and dynamics before their colonial superimposition, that neither came to this encounter as a blank slate but rather with prior orientations that shaped their reactions to each other. Since inter-cultural understandings, interactions, and solidarities quickly emerged, I do not present each culture separately to make their differences seem absolute. The first step in exploring these developments, however, is to acknowledge relative cultural difference as a point of departure, not just a post-hoc construct of colonial power/knowledge relations.

This approach has the notorious problem that pre-Hispanic Andean societies were non-literate and did not leave their own documentary record. Since all history requires such discursive raw materials, we rely on Spanish accounts to reconstruct Andean social and cultural life. Yet such accounts already presuppose the colonial distortion and silencing of the indigenous practices they purport to describe. Only in the late sixteenth century, after the Spanish policy of settlement consolidation (*reducción*) took effect, could parish priests 'discover' provincial ancestor worship and inscribe it in the historical record. The same transformations that made mummy worship visible to Spaniards also changed how Andean people practiced it. Colonial discourse analysis's suspicion that such processes both silenced and reconstituted the indigenous is warranted yet exaggerated. Documentary traces of the colonized may be scant, filtered, and diffuse, but so are those of the colonizers, as even Spivak notes (1985: 339–40). Thus, I place colonizers and colonized in a single interpretive field (cf. Mills 1997: 4), and challenge the double standard by which power/knowledge analyses treat colonial discourses as real and knowable but take a corrosively anti-realist stance towards any reconstruction of the colonized. This refusal to 'assimilate' the colonized into Western power/knowledge relations (Spivak 1988: 292) incoherently conjures up the same romantic and relatively pristine subaltern subject for which Spivak chides Foucault and Guha (1988: 272–5, 283–6). A better power/knowledge analysis would affirm colonial power's hybridity, that it partially comes from below and so is not an entirely alien grid of intelligibility. But the goal here is to challenge, not reform, that style of analysis. Thus, I argue that certain forms of colonial power such as indirect rule largely inhibited systematic observation. Those that promoted it, moreover, failed to form a stabilized epistemic field. Instead a myriad of contending colonial discourses transected the subaltern, each leaving specific traces and remainders that allow critical assessment in relation to others. Pitched hegemonic struggle among these discourses provides multiple points of entry, so I adopt a hermeneutical pragmatism suited to their plurality. I particularly hold that Spanish priests' overt competition for control over dead bodies made them acute (if not wholly reliable) observers of Andean ancestor worship in ways that no post-colonial critic, lacking practical interest in such matters, could ever be (Gose 1995a). As Mallon (1994), and Mills (2004) both differently argue, the colonial encounter and its discursive heterogeneity significantly exceed post-colonial criticism's narrow expectations. Its archival diversity includes multi-perspectival legal disputes that feature indigenous testimony, not all of which we can dismiss as colonial ventriloquism. The following sketch of pre-Hispanic ancestor worship draws heavily on such sources. When we reach the appropriate chronological moment, I will discuss these sources critically as aids to reconstructing the pre-Hispanic past. Meanwhile, I provide this sketch as a heuristic baseline, begging the reader's indulgence until it can be more fully justified.

Andean Ancestral Cultures

Before, during, and after the Inca empire, Andean society consisted of localized ancestor-worshipping polities called *ayllus*.[2] Zuidema (1973: 16) and Conrad and Demarest (1984: 89–90) rightly describe the cult of mummified ancestors as the core of Andean religion, but it was equally a political and economic phenomenon. Isbell serviceably defines the *ayllu* as a descent group that worshipped a founding ancestor who gave it a corporately held resource base (usually land) and a genealogical reference point for calculating rank within the group (1997: 98–9). Descent-based ranking coincided with territorial subdivision to create a segmentary system, in which larger *ayllus* hierarchically incorporated smaller *ayllus* as components (Isbell 1997: 115). Dual organization, by which the polity consisted of 'upper' and 'lower' divisions, was the most common pattern. Tripartite divisions also occurred, and more rarely polities might subdivide into five or ten territorial components

(Zuidema 1964). Like the whole of which they were parts, these subdivisions might also be called *ayllus*. They in turn recognized internal subdivisions between settlements that were also called *ayllus*. Thus, *ayllu* designated units of varying size within a system of recursive segmentary distinctions (Gose 1993, 1996a). To these territorial groupings corresponded a ranked hierarchy of political offices, one of which was paramount in the polity as a whole. Each of these offices gave its holder a specific title, but the Incas usually called them all *curacas* ('elders'). In some areas, however, the term *curaca* applied only to higher-ranking officials, as opposed to *camachicos* who presided over units smaller than a regional polity's primary territorial subdivisions.

Class will play an important role in this history, so we need to know how such grandees distinguished themselves. As a first approximation, they did so by exempting themselves from tributary labour and directing that of their peasant subjects. As representatives of the 'higher unity' of their communities, they oversaw internal affairs such as the formation of domestic groups, the allocation of land, public works, dispute resolution and ritual, and external affairs such as diplomacy and warfare. By controlling these key mediations in group life, *curacas* established a form of power that was largely governmental and collectivist in idiom but nonetheless conferred significant personal privileges on the office holder. Various administrative, military, and priestly positions proliferated around the office of *curaca*: all with some exemption from tributary labour. Either the *curaca*'s immediate kin or talented commoners might occupy them, which could exacerbate or ameliorate the class-like nature of the distinction between *curacas* and their subjects. The balance struck here varied but seldom excluded commoners entirely. Notions of shared descent from, and dependence on, ancestral deities undoubtedly contributed to notions of a common good that inhibited the development of class sensibilities. Yet that same ancestral ideology simultaneously underscored the *ayllu*'s internal hierarchy.

Sumptuary markers were also key to internal differentiation, and some also helped constitute *curacas*' class position as governors and recipients of their subjects' tributary labour. Foremost among them was *curacas*' exclusive right to polygynous marriage. To the extent that *curacas* extracted labour tribute through the Andean model of *mink'a*, they had to give commoners food and drink in return, which presupposed control over large amounts of land but also over large quantities of female labour to transform foodstuffs into rank-generating forms of consumption. Polygyny was one way that *curacas* secured access to this female labour, and control over unmarried women was another (Gose 2000). Sponsorship of ritual was also crucial. The living *curaca* was a direct descendant of, and privileged intermediary with, the founding ancestor. Dead rulers' mummified bodies also formed a mediating chain that linked the group to its founder. When a ruler died, potential successors could lay claim to his office by overseeing his mummification and funerary rites. In so doing, they performatively assumed his directive role and right to dispose of collective resources under the unimpeachable moral cover of bereavement and duty. On assuming office, the successor was himself invested with a degree of divinity. Two aspects of that investiture stand out. First, the *curaca* received a stool of office (*tiana*) and other insignia, which he used for the first time during his installation. By publicly displaying these prerogatives of office, the inductee became the incumbent. Second, all present at the induction recognized this change in status by performing *mocha*, a worshipful gesture of obeisance to the inductee. People also did *mocha* when approaching their ancestral deities, so it sacralized the new *curaca* and connected his office to the ancestors' power and related notions of peace, justice, and prosperity (Martínez Cereceda 1995: 129, 198–9, 201, 204–5). With differences only in pomp and expenditure, the same ceremony inducted the humblest *curaca* and the mightiest Inca sovereign (Martínez Cereceda 1995: 48–55). The privilege of being carried in a litter marked the elite end of this spectrum, and applied to both living rulers and ancestors, thereby further equating them (Martínez Cereceda 1995: 91–101). Thus, divine kingship was a basic cultural model of sovereignty for Andean political units of all sizes.

Both the ideology of divine kingship and the segmentary form that characterized these polities allowed them to expand or contract in scope, according to their military fortunes and diplomatic alliances. Isbell's important study argues that *ayllu* organization originated in the highlands of what is now northern Peru starting around AD 200, slowly spread south, and arrived in the Titicaca region in AD 1000 or later (1997: ch. 6). During periods of imperial centralization, maximal *ayllu* groupings became 'provinces,' semi-autonomous administrative units subordinate to an encompassing state. When centralized states collapsed, however, as did Wari and Tiwanaku from AD 800 to 1000, and the Inca empire following 1528, *ayllus* were the quasi-governmental units that persisted. Yet *ayllus* also initiated new expansionist episodes, such as those that caused chronic warfare in the late intermediate period (AD 1000–1400) and ultimately led to the Inca empire.

They also played a central if unacknowledged role in Spanish colonization of the Andes. In short, *ayllu* organization quickly became the bed-
rock of the Andean political order. It not only survived but frequently
generated the turbulent history of Andean states into the colonial era.
Thus, the ancestral polity was a basic organizational form in the
Andean world, and is the primary point of departure for the historical
transformations this book discusses.

Whereas structure-functionalist studies of ancestor cults (i.e., Radcliffe-Brown 1952: 163–5) typically emphasized their role in defining
lineages as bounded corporate groups, this one will emphasize their
role in establishing intergroup alliances. Andean ancestor worship had
a Durkheimian orientation towards social cohesion, but groups and
their membership did not necessarily arrive as pre-given entities to the
act of worship itself. Rather, worship performatively established group
boundaries and membership. Thus, belonging to an *ayllu* was less
about a genealogical relation to an ancestor than it was a willingness to
offer sacrifice and so express dependency on an ancestor for controlling
the circulation of life into and out of a specific locality. These performative membership criteria underscore *ayllus'* fluidity as political groupings.

Ayllu organization's flexible and scalable character prevented any
absolute distinction between the inside and the outside of political
units. *Ayllus* were not so much 'basic political units' as distinctions on a
continuum of alliances and differentiations. Structural relativity was
endemic to this political system. It enabled and registered the cycles
of expansion, contraction, and subsumption that Andean political units
underwent. When one group superimposed itself on others through
conquest, it might also revise its genealogy to subsume them. Similarly,
when two groups struck a politico-military alliance, they might seal
it by recognizing a common ancestor or engaging in reciprocal ancestor worship. Andean ancestral narratives and rituals abundantly
registered the shifting facts of conquest and political alliance in the
pre-Columbian Andes. Genealogical relations between various *ayllus'*
founding ancestors were one important segmentary idiom. Hence, jun-
ior levels of the ancestral hierarchy corresponded to minimal *ayllus* in
their most localized and differentiated form, whereas senior ancestors
encompassed these distinctions and articulated various degrees of regional and supra-regional unity. Typically, however, narratives of ancestral journeys and emergence onto the earth's surface expressed
political segmentation most concretely.

Local polities in the pre-Columbian Andes usually described their origins through the journey of a founding ancestor or cohort of ancestors. Such narratives existed in several forms. Ballad-like songs (*taquis*) were probably the most prominent, particularly in ritual commemorations of ancestors and their exploits. Their basic format was an itinerary, starting in Lake Titicaca or the Pacific, where the primordial ancestors of all Andean localities came into being and began their journeys towards the localities they were to colonize. Places where ancestral cohorts rested or dispersed on these journeys were *pacarinas* (dawning points), a notion that equates the ancestors' emergence on the surface of the earth with the rising sun. As these journeys continued, ancestors divided into progressively smaller groups that fanned more evenly and thinly across the landscape, emerging in *pacarinas* of diminishing importance until they arrived at the localities they were to populate singly, in male-female pairs, or father-son groupings. In journeys that were otherwise subterranean or celestial, *pacarinas* were places on the earth's surface where ancestors emerged from underground or were deposited by lightning strike. They not only punctuated these journeys but were ritual sites where living descendants could establish contact with the upper or lower realms from which their ancestors came. On arrival in a locality, 'some came out of caves, others from mountains, others from springs, others from lakes, and others from the feet of trees.'[3] From such terminal *pacarinas*, ancestors built settlements and agricultural infrastructure or conquered other groups already in the area. Thus, they created a patrimony to sustain the localized descent groups (*ayllus*) they established. With these exemplary deeds accomplished, they ended their days as human beings by turning into stone, an act that signified deification and a permanent accumulation of life, not ordinary mortality.

Generally, residents recognized that more than one such wave of ancestral colonization occurred in their localities, and viewed them cumulatively. San Pedro de Hacas, for example, experienced no fewer than five such episodes (Duviols 1986 ch. 5, see figure 1.3). Newly arriving ancestral cohorts necessarily conquered and partially displaced previous groups and their ancestors. The Huarochirí narratives (Salomon and Urioste 1991) are the classic and most detailed example of this phenomenon. These and many other cases prove that ancestral orders did not derive from 'an indefinitely remote sacred time, now sealed off,' as Doyle (1988: 260) claims, but changed historically with shifting political relationships in a locality. Conquest did not neces-

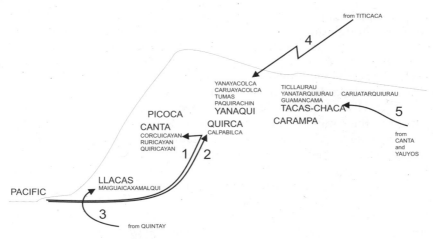

Figure 1.3 *Ayllus* and Founding Ancestors of Hacas

sarily imply ethnic cleansing or the complete dispossession of the vanquished, only an obligation to share their agricultural resources and
women with the conquerors. People would then revise ancestral
accounts, both to register this intrusion and to articulate the peaceful
coexistence that followed. In this regard, Andean ancestral narratives
differed remarkably from modern nationalist regimes in that memories
of conquest do not appear to have perpetuated a sense of grievance.
Rather, conquest became a pretext for agrarian cooperation and an ideology of complementary differentiation in *ayllu* formation. This was the
political script that underwrote Andean peoples' treatment of Spaniards as ancestors.

Most Andean polities recognized two categories of ancestors: *huaris*
and *llacuazes* (see Duviols 1973). *Huaris* were a locality's original inhabitants who created its agricultural infrastructure, whereas *llacuazes*
were intrusive pastoralist-conquerors who subsequently imposed
themselves on the *huaris* but became sedentary under their influence
(see Duviols 1986: 120). The *huari-llacuaz* distinction is thus a variant of
Andean moiety opposition between 'upper' and 'lower' groups, and
represents them as conqueror-pastoralists and vanquished aboriginal
agriculturalists, respectively (see Gose 1996a). It could operate within[4]
or between[5] localized residential divisions of an *ayllu*, and might characterize the maximal segments of an ethnic polity. Undoubtedly the

occupational identity, political status, and putative history of such groups were more complex than these traditions suggest. Their primary goal, however, was to transform military conquest into hierarchical complementarity between the two groups through reciprocal ancestor worship, a process that culminated in semiannual agrarian fertility rituals (see figure 1.4), in which each group had a specific role.[6] Once established, this hierarchical incorporation involved significant intergroup reciprocity and symmetry in which the vanquished still retained a degree of sovereignty most clearly expressed in periodic ritual battles that deployed continuing intergroup antagonism to fertilize the earth sacrificially (cf. Platt 1988). As we will see below, this moiety logic quickly subsumed the Spaniards, and only sometimes in the conquering 'upper' position.

As an indigenous political idiom, the ancestral origin narrative significantly shaped Andean responses to Spanish colonialism. First, it normalized the notion of intrusive conquest, and so made the Spaniards' remote origins and colonizing agenda intelligible in Andean terms. Spaniards did not introduce empire and colonization to the Andes: these were indigenous phenomena fully developed and comprehensible within Andean culture. More important still, ancestral narratives did not treat the localized *ayllu* as a primordial, bounded, and self-contained entity along nationalist lines. On the contrary, they emphasized the ancestors' distant origins and their exteriority to the local orders they founded. Ancestors mediated with the outside world and were valued for their ability to intercede with distant sources of fertility such as large bodies of water (Gose 1993). Their distant origins were also key to the politics of alliance. A political unit could make or renew the alliances it needed to remain locally viable by ritually acknowledging the *pacarinas* beyond its boundaries it shared with other groups. The kinds of unity that mattered politically occurred in maximal units or federations of semi-autonomous *ayllus*, not these constituent units in themselves. In most key senses, *ayllus* derived from their relation to the outside, which the founding ancestor who came from afar personified. Andean appropriations of Spaniards as ancestors simply built on this foundation.

This external orientation did not preclude fission and separatism, as we will discover in chapter 3. When an *ayllu* wished to stress its autonomy from another, it merely had to state that they came from different *pacarinas*. Andean people used this mechanism to differentiate themselves from Spaniards and blacks during the colonial period (Arriaga 1621: 219–20). Like any segmentary system, *ayllus* allowed both fusion and fission, and like any cultural tradition, this stranger-king complex could articulate a full range of political responses to various situations. Still, this form of divine kingship was not a neutral framework any more than is modern liberalism. Rather, it consistently favoured certain orientations over others. It necessarily promoted an 'open' stance to the outside through its basic cosmology and rituals, as well as the specific set of empowerments and interests it bestowed on the subject-position of *curaca*. These were to surface decisively during the so-called Spanish conquest of Peru.

Early Modern Spanish Ancestral Culture

For invading Spaniards, notions of descent and ancestry also mattered. Their cult of the saints, with its circulation of grace between Christians in heaven, earth, and purgatory, made relationships between the living and the dead as important as they were for Andean people. The standard articulation of this basic Christian doctrine of the communion of the saints was universalist: all Christians in all three realms participated in it. In early modern Spain, however, many transformed the idea that saints transmit grace to the living into a proto-racist ideology of 'purity of blood' (*limpieza de sangre*). This ideology expressed the religious nationalism that emerged during the final phases of the Christian reconquest of Spain from the Moors. It distinguished 'old Christians,' whose ancestors were also Christians, from 'new Christians,' the recently converted, whose ancestors were Jews or Moors. The former could expect to share grace with their ancestors, whereas the latter could share only religious error with theirs. By extension, old Christians had 'purity of blood,' whereas new Christians inherited the 'stain' of their ancestors' infidelity and suffered a nearly insurmountable sacramental deficit. For those in the grip of this ideology, conversion was problematic and unreliable. Thus, sources from the first half of the fifteenth century state that the newly converted (*conversos*) received the water of baptism only 'on their skins, but neither their hearts nor their wills' (Carrillo de Huete 1946: 523), and that they were incapable of receiving Christianity, which 'they frequently vomit, rashly judaizing' (Alonso 1943: 359). Old Christians might deny that *conversos* could be anything more than 'baptized Jews' (see Benito Ruano 1957: 337), and reject them as alien to the faith and the nation in both body and soul. In short, 'purity of blood' racialized religious orientation, and so made ancestry matter.

Figure 1.4a Ancestor Worship

Figure 1.4b Ancestor Worship

These developments came to a head in the Toledo rebellion of 1449, which produced a civic statute denying public office to any converts from 'the perverse lineage of the Jews' (Alonso 1943: 362). Although it was quelled within the year, the Toledo rebellion articulated a surprisingly modern language of race and nation that shaped Spanish society for the next four centuries. The Toledo rebels referred to race through such terms as *generación, género, estirpe, linaje, nación,* and *ralea* (see Alonso 1943, Benito Ruano 1957), but by the sixteenth century, *raza* predominated. Thus, a notorious *limpieza* document from 1546 refers to 'old Christians without race [*raza*] of Jews nor Moors.'[7] Such phrases became standard in official documents from the middle of the sixteenth century to the end of the eighteenth. Race could explicitly denote sectarian deviation, as in a priest's claim that his parents 'were old Christian nobles, pure, without race [*raza*] of Moors nor Jews nor of any other sect.'[8] Thus, Catholicism became the universal, unmarked background against which race emerged as defective particularity. Militant old Christians not only considered Jews and Moors to be races but 'lineages' (*linaxes*) and 'castes' (*castas*),[9] which further emphasized that religion was a matter of descent, heredity, and even a degree of endogamous closure. In contrast to contemporary usage, this notion of race referred directly to religion, not to skin colour or other bodily traits. Nonetheless, religion acted as a typifying, group-defining feature that one generation carnally transmitted to the next within a bounded collectivity: in short, it was racialized.

Limpieza's most intransigent theorists declared a person's descendants infamous in perpetuity should any trace of heresy or infidelity appear at the remotest point in their ancestry (Sicroff 1960: 225). Even those who allowed more finite periods of infamy (such as four generations) utterly condemned intermarriage with the newly converted: 'There is no plague in the world as contagious, and the slightest wind of it is enough to infect, and where the stain enters it cannot leave: a small bit of yeast corrupts the entire dough' (Sicroff 1960: 203f). The first *converso* complaints about racial discrimination date to 1437 and concerned the refusal of old Christians to intermarry with them, out of fear that such unions would allow *conversos* to appropriate their wealth and offices and defile their 'pure blood' (Netanyahu 1995: 977, 516). As this passage illustrates, old Christians judged their own purity to be less robust than *converso* impurity and saw the threat of degeneration as omnipresent.

Purity of blood was not a passive concept but the rallying cry of a social movement to cleanse Spain's body politic by converting or expelling non-Christians. This movement aimed to exclude new Christians from public office in government, the military, and the Church through *limpieza de sangre* statutes (see Netanyahu 1995, Sicroff 1960, Kamen 1965). With the emergence of the Spanish Inquisition in 1480, the *limpieza* movement found a powerful institutional sponsor that promoted and standardized this racist doctrine. From this point onward, concluding that the *limpieza* movement's triumph was absolute is easy but wrong. Kamen (1997: ch. 11) shows that surprisingly few Spanish institutions followed the Toledo rebels of 1449 in passing such statutes and that even fewer actually enforced them, in part because their underlying racism was still controversial in Spanish society. Salutary as these observations are, they only qualify and do not change the basic historical fact that within a few short decades, the *limpieza de sangre* movement transformed itself from a rebellion against the Crown into the Inquisition, an institution with royal backing and significant jurisdictional autonomy. Since the Inquisition's persecution of new Christians often damaged royal interests, we must suspect that it was a concession to plebeian mobilization and that its racism did speak for large sectors of Spanish society.

Under the Inquisition's patronage, the notion of *limpieza* further extended into law. By the mid sixteenth century, *limpieza* had come to denote a specific juridical procedure whereby all candidates for public office, promotion, or ordination theoretically had to prove through witnesses their genealogical 'purity.' This meant that their ancestors not only had to be old Christians but that they had to be born in wedlock, an interesting nuance that underlines the sacramental quality of this notion of race. A further requirement of *limpieza* was that a person's background had to include no punishment from the Inquisition. Perpetual infamy marked those who had penitential garments (*sambenitos*) hung in any church, or had ancestors who had worn such garments, which were renewed when they rotted, to keep the memory of heresy alive. Thus, proof of *limpieza* required a multidimensional examination of witnesses and church records. New Christians in good social standing in their communities might circumvent this process, as could others by judicious bribes, but none of this challenged *limpieza*'s gate-keeping role in public life.

As Manrique (1993) argues, the religious nationalism that arose during the Christian reconquest of Spain, including this emphasis on *limpieza de sangre*, continued seamlessly into the colonization of the Americas. Conquistadores and subsequent colonists frequently described Indian temples as synagogues or mosques,[10] implicitly equating the conquest of Peru with the reconquest of Spain. This formula pervaded the conquistadores' behaviour and cast Andean people as religious adversaries to be combatted, not understood or recognized. With only minor modifications, they applied emergent theories of *limpieza de sangre* to colonized peoples. As new Christians, Indians and blacks automatically failed the test of *limpieza*, as did *mestizos* and *mulatos* by extension (Castañeda and Hernández 1989: 69). Although Spaniards saw idolatry, not Judaism or Islam, as the prime cause of impurity among Indians and blacks, they also considered it a hereditary defilement of the soul. Indeed, Spaniards routinely accused Jews of idolatry (Netanyahu 1995: 362–3) and often lumped all religious 'errors' together under this heading.

Theologically, idolatry was ideally suitable as a racializing principle. By inappropriately deflecting worship from the absolute to the contingent, idolatry spawned degenerate particularity in contrast to Catholic universality. Thus, the Jesuit intellectual José de Acosta reconfigured Iberian theories for colonial consumption, first by defining idolatry as a dangerous disease or poison comparable to Judaism and Islam: 'This pestilence is the greatest of all evils. As the Wise One says, it is the beginning and end of all evil; it makes war on the true religion in all ways. It is one of the most deplorable factors in the human condition; there is no other venom that, once drunk, penetrates the innards more intimately' (Acosta 1576: 247). He then portrayed the disease of idolatry as congenital and racialized among Peruvian Indians: 'one would have to think that we are dealing with an hereditary illness of idolatry which, contracted in the mother's very breast and nursed upon suckling her very milk, made robust by paternal example, and familiar and fortified by long-standing custom and the authority of public laws, has such vigour that it cannot be cured except by the very abundant sprinkling of divine grace, and the assiduous and indefatigable work of the evangelical doctor' (1576: 255). For Acosta, communion was the privileged antidote to this accumulated disgrace (1576: 383–419). As a Jesuit, Acosta belonged to the order that most resisted the notion of *limpieza* in Spain. Although he stressed redemption over racialization, his successors decisively reversed that emphasis. Arriaga (1621: 195) echoed only his racializing arguments, as did the jurist Solórzano de Pereyra (1648: 443–5). Pedro de Villagómez (1649: 38), the archbishop of Lima who presided over the longest and most controversial extirpation of idolatry campaign in that jurisdiction, similarly believed that 'the bad customs of the parents and ancestors become converted, in a certain manner, into nature, so that they continue by inheritance in their children' (1649: 46). In short, this selective reading of Acosta became authoritative and shaped colonial policy.

Important as this tendency to racialize idolatry was, a more fundamental imperative ultimately tempered and subordinated it. Alexander VI's papal bull of 1493 made Spanish conquest rights in the New World conditional on converting the natives to Catholicism (Levillier 1919: 7–22). With this responsibility, the pope delegated many of his powers in ecclesiastical law to the Spanish Crown in an arrangement known as *patronato real*. The official position of Church and Crown was that the Indians were neophytes who could not be as culpable as Jews and Moors, for they lacked long-term exposure to the true faith and had not historically rejected it (Pagden 1982: 38, 102–3). Accordingly, they were to be patiently evangelized and slowly transformed into Christians over generations. This analysis made Indians exempt from the Inquisition, but it did not necessarily amount to a tabula rasa view of their spirituality or preclude further debates over the status of their idolatries. Las Casas and his followers viewed them as approximations of the true faith that resulted from the exercise of natural reason without revelation. Others saw them as worshippers of Satan, who took refuge in the New World after the gospel came to the Old. Precisely because of Satan's desire to be worshipped as God, however, even his previously unchallenged dominion could become providential preparation for the true faith's arrival. Others inside and outside the Church took a less sanguine view, and argued that Indians' 'vehement inclination toward idolatry' proved their descent from lost tribes of Israel (Villagómez 1649: 52), a position that Acosta (1590: ch. 23) refuted, but not to the satisfaction of other influential churchmen. As we will see more fully in the next chapter, other interpretations of native idolatries also existed, and Spaniards sustained lively debates over the matter. Hard-line positions against native idolatries repeatedly took form but ultimately foundered on Christian universalism: if Indians were spiritually irredeemable it would imply the imperfection of God's creation (Pagden 1982: 50), an ideologically inadmissible conclusion. The political fact that Spanish colonialism justified itself in missionary terms, however, was what made this theological limit real. In conclusion, Spanish ancestral understandings were conflicted: they racialized religious others on the one hand and tried to incorporate them through conversion on the

other. These opposed tendencies and their selective application generated a complex field of cultural debate in which racism could never
fully break free from the Catholic universalism it transgressed.

Theorizing Interaction

What happened when these two different ancestral orders collided, one
based on segmentary divine kingship and the other on a racializing circulation of religious grace and disgrace? For all their differences, these
ancestral traditions appropriated and worked through each other to a
surprising degree. Andean ancestors and Catholic saints had much in
common, from their hagiographies to their mummified physical
remains. While traditionally conceived cultural differences remained
salient in early colonial situations, they were never absolute and ceased
to be given once interaction began. Thereafter, issues of cultural difference and similarity became political. People redrew ethnic boundaries
using new criteria, and groups lost their initially given character as the
stuff of the traditions that once defined them shifted and became relative (Barth 1969). The result was an ongoing process of cultural redefinition, in which cultural 'elements' no longer necessarily signified their
origins. As much ethnohistoric and ethnographic work on the Andes
shows, Catholic logic came to organize indigenous content and vice
versa (Abercrombie 1998, Gose 1994, Platt 1987). We must therefore approach this situation with a relative form of cultural relativism that
allows cultural differences to exist and persist over time, but not as
absolute barriers to communication, interaction, or even political solidarity. Initially such communication was far from perfect, and the alliances it facilitated often required that neither party fully understood or
shared the motives of the other. Out of such interactions a pidginized
inter-culture nonetheless grew, in which ancestral themes played a particularly important bridging role. They articulated solidarity without
demanding consensus (Kertzer 1988). Once established, however, this
inter-culture also became an arena of debate, in which various parties
engaged with one another's interpretations as they understood them
more fully. The superimposition, interaction, and partial transformation of these emergent meanings and agendas will be the substance of
this book. A brief theoretical discussion of these issues is now in order.

Anthropology has long discussed such topics as 'syncretism.' A
recent example is Marzal (1985), who follows Redfield (1941) in treating
syncretism as a mechanical admixture of elements derived from either

Spanish or indigenous traditions. Even when they recombine, such elements still signify their traditions of origin as ongoing collective identities, which become definitive cultural syntheses frozen in time. The same assumptions hold in discussions of 'acculturation,' which have the bearers of one tradition progressively accept elements from another but still retain some of their own traits, perhaps as a kind of 'cultural resistance' (Marzal 1985: 109–14, 120–6). These narratives differ from 'syncretism' only in attributing direction or purpose to the mixture of origin-bound elements. Handler (1988) rightly derives this objectivist approach to culture from possessive individualism, in which nations and cultures inalienably 'own' their constituent elements. This peculiar vision converts the routine and banal fact that cultures interactively transform each other into 'syncretism' and its derivatives. Several varieties of contemporary identity politics, ranging from therapeutic memory and trauma discourses (see Antze and Lambek 1996) to minority 'strategic essentialisms' (see below), share this grounding in liberal ideology and institutions, and thus join syncretism in treating cultures as primordial, trans-historical collective individuals.

More recently, cultural studies has reversed this emphasis by celebrating 'hybridity' for its alleged subversion of imposed or received cultural identifications. If, following Said (1978), colonialism worked through discourses of binary cultural difference, then any hybridization that spans those binary divisions would also mock or challenge them. Mimicry destabilizes colonial discourse's fixed subject positions (Bhabha 1994), and impurity becomes a key potential for post-colonial futures. Yet hybridity thus conceived founders on the assumption that colonialism necessarily and exclusively worked through discourses of binary difference. The issue here is not merely that hyridity ultimately preserves the essentialisms it initially opposes (Young 1995) but that it fundamentally misconceives the nature of colonial power. I argue that in relations of indirect colonial rule, cultural hybridity played a constitutive (not subversive) role. It established the pidginized understandings and working relations that made colonialism work. Far from a secondary parody of a primary discourse of cultural separation, hybridization was colonial power's primary dynamic. Once we allow that differentiation and purity are not the sole mechanisms of colonial power, it no longer follows that hybridity equals subversion. In summary, both 'syncretism' and 'hybridity' oscillate between an essentialism of the element and an essentialism of the system (i.e., 'culture' or 'discourse') when colonialism itself was far more flexible. To avoid such problems, I turn to the concept of hegemony, which normalizes cultural appropriation and resignification and more adequately situates them in colonial power dynamics.

Hegemony assumes that people articulate varying understandings of the world from their positions in diverse social practices and relationships (Gramsci 1971: 6, 60, 331). To the extent that one contending articulation of a practice or relationship reorganizes others, it defines an emergent subject position whose strategic 'interests' take form only through a selective orientation. Such articulations always address 'objective conditions' but never derive from them causally: they are not objectively decidable but strategic orientations that generate their own paths of action (Laclau and Mouffe 1985: ch. 3). A hegemony arises when one emergent subject position begins to mediate and incorporate others, guiding their internal formation with its strategic terms of reference, actively modifying them when necessary. Such overdetermination is inherently a structuring and even a colonizing process but one that is always partial and provisional. Like the metaphoric seeing of one thing through another, hegemonic articulations can never overcome difference entirely, nor need they try. They allow alternative understandings and merely reorient, neutralize, or compartmentalize them. This irreducible pluralism differentiates hegemony from postcolonial theory's understanding of 'discourse.' Insofar as one perspective organizes others, a shared 'common sense' emerges and becomes provisionally normative. Yet it cannot prevent heterogenous subaltern experiences and other destabilizing political developments from arising. An existing hegemony either meets and subsumes these challenges or it fails to do so, and its claims to universality consequently diminish.

Thus conceived, hegemony encompasses various theoretical orientations that converge on this field of study. In Foucauldian terms, it combines archaeological identification of discursive formations with genealogical awareness of contingency. By extension, hegemony incorporates post-colonial theory's insights into the centrality of colonial discursive subsumption without requiring that it be all-embracing. It recognizes indigenous agency and forms of colonialism (such as indirect rule) that do not entirely redefine it but are merely parasitic on it. Instead of seeing the indigenous as an essential and unchanging 'identity,' however, a hegemonic analysis understands it as an only partially autonomous product of iterative reformulation under colonialism: a subject position whose retention necessarily implies some degree of transformation. Hegemony almost axiomatically includes subaltern resistence, which among other things explains the persistence of indigenous subject positions from below. If resistance were the only subaltern response, however, it would become the mere symptom of power that Guha (1983: ch. 2), Scott (1985, 1990), and Abu Lughod (1990) take it to be. Yet several factors offset and complement the purely negative dynamic of resistance, starting with the subaltern's partial incorporative transformation by the orders they may oppose. More important still is the grounding of subaltern subject positions in specific social practices that, even if they do not articulate an emergent hegemony of their own, remain more than a mere negation of elite positions. Such practices have an irreducible positivity that fosters non-binary cultural elaboration. Crucially, they articulate specific cultural projects (Ortner 2006: ch. 6) that Saussurean analyses cannot describe. Thus, practice theory promotes a more Hegelian approach to subalternity, one that includes resistance but not at the expense of world-constitution, which defies reduction to an impoverished model of phonetic opposition.

Hegemony is especially important as an alternative to the 'strategic essentialism' that dominates contemporary identity politics in general and attempts to theorize resistance and subalternity in particular. Here I use the phrase not in the technical sense that Spivak initially proposed[11] but in the more influential sense she later gave it in arguing that the critiques of essentialism and universalism are both necessary and unsustainable in practice, so minorities must resort to the essentialisms or universalisms that will empower them (1990: 11–12). Revealing this argument's theoretical source, Spivak notes that: 'the most serious critique in deconstruction, is the critique of something that is extremely useful, something without which we cannot do anything' (1989: 129–30, 134–5). Inexorably, the broader political judgment follows that it is in bad taste to question minority essentialisms that are, after all, just playing by the rules of the game. Similar anti-anti-essentialist thinking is now commonplace, for example that essentialisms vary in their political effects depending on who deploys them and how (Thomas 1994: 187–8). These well-intentioned arguments become pernicious when they surreptitiously normalize the assumption that subaltern politics amount to nothing more than deployments of essentialism. This study rejects that dismal conclusion. It not only shows that alternative strategies exist but seeks to foster them and overcome their marginalization. The hope is that sympathetic cultural analysis might broaden the inter-cultural space of recognition in which they exist and so extend their influence. Such appreciations cannot spring from the same ground as the strategies themselves, so they need Western identity politics and power/ knowledge analyses to relax their hermeneutics of suspicion towards outsider commentary. If we are really to advance Spivak's professed goal of 'building for difference' (1989: 128), we must make a greater intellectual effort to recognize and cultivate, as the notion of hegemony does, options that fall outside routinized common sense or stem from unfamiliar sociocultural groundings.

Most discussions confine hegemony to the internal relations of a cultural tradition, principally that between a shared core of elite-driven 'common sense' and a periphery of discordant subaltern formulations. However, the process is arguably even more important and visible in inter-cultural situations, where difference more obviously forms the point of departure, and shared understandings are even more tenuous. Colonialism's invasive dynamic, through which one perspective enters, mediates, and reorganizes others to secure its own supremacy, is paradigmatically hegemonic. Yet Guha denies its applicability by arguing that the colonial state had no grounding in Indian society, was imposed despotically as an absolute externality, and could appear as hegemonic only through a duplicitous historiography that emphasizes consent and collaboration by excluding resistance (1989: 228–32, 274, 296–9). This view derives less from colonial reality than Guha's own implicitly nationalist need for 'resistant' allegorical subjects. He reduces hegemony to 'legitimacy' through a zero-sum opposition to coercion, when, as Gramsci (1971: 12, 55f, 80f, 229, 258–9) argues, coercion only partially opposes hegemony: they also interact. Coercion may intervene in a hegemonic process by policing the boundaries of common sense and defining the limits of the possible, just as normative pronouncements may accompany the use of force. Thus colonialism can be hegemonic.

Fernando Ortiz' notion of transculturation usefully develops the interaction between coercion and consent in colonial situations. It explores how people, practices, and products are stripped from their contexts of origin and reintegrated into new situations with a cultural logic of their own (1940: 97–103).[12] Ortiz acknowledges that violent uprooting is involved, but that those upheavals also create new perspectives and points of departure, not just traumatic memories, through which their survivors and heirs experience the present. Transculturation, then, like hegemony, explores how new subject positions emerge through historical rearticulation. Colonial regimes interactively superimpose cultural repertoires and generate many strategic possibilities, only some of which involve resistance in the sense of defending a predefined 'indigenous' subject position against external encroachment. More important are the possibilities of manoeuvre and innovation, the opportunity for both colonizers and colonized to resituate and even redefine themselves within a ferment of mixed, matched, and remotivated elements. Once we abandon the notion of colonialism as a monolithic and unilateral 'discourse' of ethno-racial domination, and view it instead as a selective coordination of specific intrusive and indigenous practices (Kaplan and Kelly 1994: 144), transculturation emerges as a central concept. It foregrounds all this study's major themes: indirect rule, the cultural adjustments it involved for both groups, and the ambivalence it created in indigenous people towards 'their' culture.

Not surprisingly, those with strong theoretical commitments to resistance reject transculturation for its neglect of colonial power. For example, Lienhard finds it misleadingly optimistic and prefers diglossia, since national cultures have not transcended colonial hierarchy and still racialize different practices as European or indigenous (1997: 68–72). Similarly, Beverley denounces it as a de-politicizing fantasy, a nationalist trope that suppresses the reality of ongoing elite-subaltern conflict (1999: 43–7). These points are well taken, particularly if transculturation implies a definitive resolution of previous colonial conflicts rather than their displacement onto new ground. But they too are problematic if they imply that new incorporations and points of departure never emerge and that strategic essentialist politics are the only ones possible. Like Gilroy (1993), I emphasize the much-neglected cosmopolitan face of subaltern politics and how the colonized strategically embraced the dislocations they experienced. Yet I also follow him in exploring the tension between that response and others that attempted to defend or re-create ostensibly pre-colonial subject positions. Hegemony allows us to think both those options interactively, whereas other analytical options isolate and abstract them from each other.

At a more basic level still, however, hegemony challenges the idea that colonial power somehow took a 'pure' form independent from these relations of cultural transformation. Only through the formation of a colonial interculture could relations of indirect rule and tributary extraction emerge: to the extent that colonial 'power' existed, it was in that nexus. As we have seen, both subaltern and post-colonial forms of discourse analysis consistently reify power through Saussurean notions of binary linguistic value. The problem here is not the mutual constitution of the social and the linguistic that discourse analysis proposes but its inadequate structuralist understanding of language. Pragmatism provides a much better alternative by emphasizing the interaction between articulating and articulated elements as the crucial feature of signification (Voloshinov 1973). Relations between intrusive and colonized perspectives are always complex. Unidirectional understandings of articulation reduce subaltern subject positions and cultural formations to a passive medium for the realization of elite projects. Anything worth colonizing must also have something to offer. The subaltern are exploitable only because of their capacity for self-directed activity, which becomes a site of relatively autonomous cultural articulation even as it is exploited (Gramsci 1971: 8–9). This submerged recognition of subaltern agency and culture is manifest in colonial transculturation's complex bidirectional movements and recombinations. These alterations routinely exceed the post-colonial litany of ironic repetition, derailment, and mimicry, all of which concede too much centrality to the colonizer. Something far more fundamental happens when an external hegemonizing force enters previously independent forms. It wants something from them and will be changed by inhabiting them. They reflect and refract it and give its messages new iconic embodiments and indexical implementations. A hegemonic agenda never survives these consequences of its own success unmodified, and may not even recognize its extended realizations. As Andean people accepted Christianity and later the nation state as hegemonic frameworks, they systematically inflected them with their own orientations in ways that eluded elite control. A conscious strategy of resistance could not have produced more subversive results. Above all, hegemonic projects make themselves dependent on what they colonize, and so necessarily develop a certain vulnerability in the exercise of power. When overextended, their intrusions may even become self-extinguishing, as in the many pre-modern cases of conquerors becoming culturally assimilated by those they conquered.

Again, Latin American cultural theory shows a much more nuanced appreciation than its Indian counterpart of this assimilation from below (cf. Taylor 2005: 969–74). Cannibalism, as the Brazilian *antropófago* modernist Oswald de Andrade provocatively proposed in 1928, captures it perfectly. Europeans may have thought of themselves as conquering and colonizing subjects, but they were also devoured and digested objects. Colonialism notwithstanding, point of view continues to matter: what looks like invasion from one perspective may appear as consumption from another. Which view we adopt is above all a strategic matter, since both address the same configuration of facts. To Andrade's

'Tupi or not Tupi, that is the question,' Castro-Klarén (2000: 309–12) responds that this rhetorical appropriation of cannibalism has little to do with its Amazonian referent. Andrade may have intended the cannibal trope to define something more utopian, robust, and aggressively subaltern than transculturation, but it was assimilated as an unusually whimsical or eccentric version of 1920s primitivist nation building. Within these limits, however, it still denies conventional Eurocentric conceptions of power their accustomed foundational status, in marked contrast with post-colonial criticism and subaltern studies. By emphasizing that the breaching of boundaries labelled 'conquest' has alternative interpretations, the *antropófago* conceit reveals that there was nothing definitive about this event, and that its ultimate significance has still to be digested. Internalization of an external entity is the beginning, not the end, of this process, which is more likely to feature guerrilla war and hegemonic struggle than the outright triumph of either party. The cannibal image highlights the voracious agency of the ostensibly subordinated but encompassing (the Indian phraseology is deliberate) elements in hegemonic relationships. It illuminates hegemony's submerged reciprocal dimension, in which colonized entities gain their particular influence and revenge. This dynamic is sufficiently universal that no serious theory of hegemony can afford to ignore it. When properly integrated, it will mark the end of reductive, power-obsessed discussions of colonialism and open the way for a more serious discussion of colonial cultures.

2 Viracochas: Ancestors, Deities, and Apostles

Few historical events have been as heavily mythologized as the 1532–35 Spanish conquest of Peru (cf. Restall 2003). Conventional historiography holds that a band of 168 men led by the illiterate Francisco Pizarro subjugated an empire whose population may have numbered over ten million. When recounting their improbable triumph, many conquistadores gave divine favour a decisive role.[1] Subsequent histories (notably Prescott 1847 I: 413) have described the conquest with little analysis, as if the Spaniards' sheer audacity and military prowess spoke for themselves. Ostensibly the Spaniards' heroic individuality, buttressed by racial and technological superiority, allowed them to prevail when so outnumbered. Only recently has Peruvian nationalist historiography provided a more realistic view: a war of succession among the Inca elite, combined with provincial resentment of their Inca overlords, allowed the Spaniards to find Andean allies through whom they eventually won power. This chapter's first goal is to explore the tension between conquest and alliance in how Spaniards gained ascendancy in the Andes.

Its second goal is to explore the inter-cultural mythologies of alliance, which present a greater interpretive challenge than the unilateral triumphalism of conquest. Soon after encountering them, Andean people began to call Spaniards *viracochas*, after important ancestral deities in their own tradition. Exactly what this name meant when applied to the Spaniards is debatable. I will argue that it identified them as the founders of a decentralized pre-Inca political order, one that their Andean allies hoped to restore. As Spaniards learned more about Andean ancestral figures named Viracocha, many became convinced that the name designated the Christian God, or a wandering apostle of

Christ who reached the New World and conducted a primitive evangelization there. In this peculiar way, both Andean people and Spaniards
used the Viracocha notion to include the other in their own traditions.
Each party had its own motives for advancing this inter-cultural mythology, and its own changing interpretations of what it meant, but they
created it interactively, both as a means and a byproduct of their political alliances. To understand the complexities of the process, we must
first establish the ambiguous context of conquest/alliance in which it
occurred, and then turn to the role that these notions played in it. Let us
begin with a summary of the relevant events.

Brief Chronology of the Spanish Invasion

After two preliminary voyages from Panama in 1524 and 1527, Pizarro
began what was to become his voyage of conquest at the end of 1530.
During several stopovers en route, the Spaniards skirmished with the
natives they encountered, often over their demands for women and
gold. They reported devastation from plagues and internecine conflict
on arrival at the northern limit of Inca domination. Only when they
stopped to build the town of San Miguel did they learn of a war of
succession among the Incas. Two or three years earlier, the sovereign
Huayna Capac had died in a smallpox epidemic caused by Pizarro's
initial arrival on the Peruvian coast in 1527. Now his sons Huascar and
Atahuallpa fought over the succession. Atahuallpa was winning, and
camped in the mountains above Pizarro's coastal base. Instead of de-
ploying troops against the small band of intruders, he sent them a
stuffed duck, presumably to signify their fate. On September 24, 1532,
Pizarro set off with his men to find Atahuallpa, robbing Inca storehouses for provisions and torturing the natives to discover the Inca's
whereabouts, while sending word to Atahuallpa that the Spaniards
came in peace and wished to be his brothers. Messengers from Atahuallpa returned with golden goblets of corn beer, invited them to come
directly to Cajamarca, but also asked who the Spaniards were and what
they wanted. During their ascent, the Spaniards encountered towns that
Atahuallpa had destroyed for supporting Huascar in the war of succession.[2]

When they arrived in Cajamarca, the Spaniards found Atahuallpa
and an army of forty to fifty thousand men. Pretending to be calm, they
sent a party under Pizarro's brother Hernando to meet Atahuallpa,
whom they found bathing at a hot spring outside town. Hernando

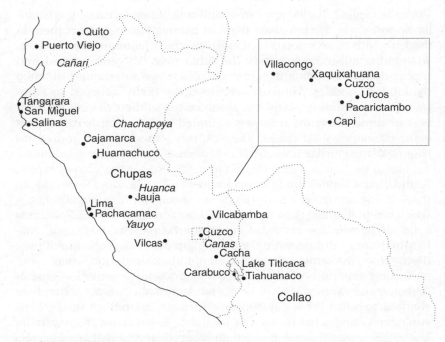

Figure 2.1 Geography of the 'Conquest'

Pizarro lengthily described their purpose, and was upset when Atahua-llpa responded only through an intermediary. With a smile, Atahuallpa conveyed that he was fasting, and would come to talk the following day. He added that his officials in San Miguel saw the Spaniards as poor warriors, and chastised them for raiding his storehouses and mistreating his authorities. The Inca nonetheless offered them drink, after which Pizarro ordered Hernando de Soto to stage a riding exhibition for the Inca and his army, to display their prowess and utility against any enemies the Inca might have. The display visibly frightened some Inca soldiers, and as many as three hundred were subsequently executed for their cowardice. The Spaniards spent that night in Cajamarca, feverishly planning. Next morning, on November 16, 1532, they held mass and awaited the Inca's visit. When the Inca arrived in a litter bedecked with featherwork, gold, and silver, with a contingent of five to seven thousand lightly armed soldiers, only Friar Valverde and an interpreter met him. The Inca asked where the rest of the Spaniards were.

Valverde replied that he appeared without soldiers because Christianity opposes war. He informed them of his mission to instruct them in the true faith as recounted in the Bible, which he offered to the Inca. Atahuallpa allegedly knocked the Bible from Valverde's hand and repeated that the Spaniards had raided his storehouses and mistreated his local authorities. Valverde recovered the Bible, returned to Francisco Pizarro's hiding place, and absolved the soldiers of guilt for what was to come. Then the trumpets sounded and Spaniards rushed out yelling, 'Santiago! At them!' They captured the Inca and routed his troops, losing one black slave in the process. Pizarro held the Inca in the Temple of the Sun and interviewed him. Shocked at this turn of events, Atahuallpa admitted that his plan was to sacrifice some Spaniards to the Sun, castrate the rest to be personal servants for him and the chosen women, and to breed their horses. Later, he agreed to pay the Spaniards a lavish ransom for his freedom. While he remained hostage, Atahuallpa's army did not attack the Spaniards to protect the life of their divine ruler, the self-proclaimed 'lord of foundation' (*ticsicapac*).[3]

Around the time of Atahuallpa's own kidnapping, his generals defeated and captured Huascar in a battle outside Cuzco, leaving both rivals as captives. This development further destabilized the political conjuncture and what was left of Inca state institutions. Many provincial rulers (*curacas*) came to pay their respects to Atahuallpa and assess his captors. Most were non-commital, but Cañari, Chachapoya, Huanca, Lucana, and Yauyo leaders openly pursued alliances with the Spaniards following Atahuallpa's capture, largely because of their suffering at the hands of his army. They gave Pizarro intelligence and military support that proved indispensable to the conquest. Atahuallpa's ransom was slow to arrive, so on January 5, 1533, several Spaniards under Hernando Pizarro set off to loot the shrine of Pachacamac at Atahuallpa's behest. Atahuallpa's forces also took three Spaniards in litters to Cuzco. En route they met the mistreated captive Huascar, who desperately offered the Spaniards a larger ransom than Atahuallpa's. Word of this encounter reached Cajamarca, where Pizarro told Atahuallpa to deliver Huascar to the Spaniards, who would judge their dispute. Fearing that the Spaniards would favour Huascar, Atahuallpa secretly ordered his brother's execution. The Spaniards continued south in their litters to Cuzco, where they received servants and sumptuous lodgings. They pillaged the Temple of the Sun for many days, collecting its artifacts of precious metal and tearing the gold and silver siding from its walls. In this enterprise they had no native help, however, and Xérez reports that their handlers did not allow them to see the rest of the city. Meanwhile, on its return from Pachacamac, Hernando Pizarro's party entered the central Peruvian highlands in search of Chalcochima, one of Atahuallpa's generals. The Huancas received them well, since their arrival halted Chalcochima's scorched-earth reprisals for supporting Huascar. This reception further consolidated the Huanca-Spanish alliance. Hernando Pizarro eventually found Chalcochima and persuaded him to return to Cajamarca with the Spaniards, arriving on May 25, 1533. As Atahuallpa's ransom was being completed and melted down, rumours circulated among the Indians that his army had massed and was marching on Cajamarca to kill the Spaniards. Although false, these rumours worked: after much debate, Pizarro had Atahuallpa executed for treason instead of releasing him.[4]

After consulting both factions, Pizarro installed another of Huayna Capac's sons, Tupac Huallpa, as Atahuallpa's successor in a ceremony that formally proclaimed him and all the attending *curacas* vassals to the Spanish Crown. In September 1533, a month after killing Atahuallpa, the Spaniards marched south with this puppet ruler and their indigenous allies, defeating an Inca army near Jauja, where they stopped over, built a church, and founded a provisional capital. Here, the new sovereign Tupac Huallpa suddenly died, allegedly poisoned by Chalcochima, who resented his open collaboration with the Spaniards. On the journey south from Jauja, Hernando de Soto's advance guard had several skirmishes with Atahuallpa's army, and took the town of Vilcas in a surprise raid. Hoping to take Cuzco single-handedly, Soto rashly pushed ahead across the Apurimac River without waiting for support, into an ambush at Villacongo, where he suffered heavy losses until reinforcements arrived. Sancho (1534) and Trujillo (1571) state that Almagro's cavalry saved him, but Titu Cusi (1570) claimed that it was actually Incas loyal to Huascar. Immediately afterwards, Spaniards and the Huascar faction, including their leader, Manco Inca, met for several days in Xaquixahuana, where they sealed an alliance by publicly burning Chalcochima. They then pushed on to Cuzco, defeating Atahuallpa's army in the process, arriving on November 15, 1533, amid great celebration. The Spaniards 'appointed' Manco Inca as the new sovereign, and through an interpreter on Christmas day of 1533, Pizarro's secretary, Sancho, read Manco the *requerimiento* that he become a vassal of the Spanish Crown, which Manco accepted. Spaniards raised the royal standard twice and sounded trumpets as Manco embraced Pizarro and offered him a golden goblet of corn beer.[5]

These unlikely allies defeated Atahuallpa's army in the battles of Capi (November 1533) and Maraycalla (May 1534), after which Estete (nd) provides a remarkable eyewitness account of an event that brings their relationship into a different light. Manco's subjects began a lengthy celebration by worshipping at the Temple of the Sun. The following morning, each royal kin group, in order of precedence went to their estate to bring their ancestral mummies, seated on stools in litters, to Cuzco. As they approached the plaza, the mummies' entourages sang songs of thanks to the Sun 'that their enemies had been expelled and the Christians had become their lords; this was the substance of their songs although I do not believe it was that of their intentions, but they wanted us to know that they were happier with the conversation of the Spanish than with the subjugation and oppression of the enemy.' On arrival in the plaza, they paraded by Manco and his mummified father, Huayna Capac, side by side in their respective litters, before each occupying his own specific pavilion in the plaza, where attendants used whisks to keep the flies off the mummies, as if they were alive. Each mummy had a reliquary or ark containing its teeth, nail and hair clippings, and any other separated body parts. Once established in the plaza, the royal kin groups began to drink for the next thirty days, and the plaza's drains ran full with urine. During this period, they sang of their respective founding ancestors' conquests, and the high priest of the Sun instructed Manco to emulate their exploits (Estete nd.: 317–19, cf. Sancho 1534: 333–4). These acts were almost certainly an investiture of Manco as Inca sovereign, and his juxtaposition with his father's mummy in the plaza dramatized the notion of succession. The exhortations to further conquest show that despite the *requerimiento*, Manco's subjects expected him to be an independent sovereign. Yet the songs of thanks apparently acknowledged the Spaniards in some capacity, even if it was not as lords. We will return to this scene below, but for now it establishes two crucial points for the first time in the historical record: first, that ancestor worship and Inca political sovereignty were tightly fused, and second, that the Spaniards entered into this Andean nexus in a way that is not yet clear.

While the defeat and dismantling of Atahuallpa's army remained a shared priority, Manco and the Spaniards needed no shared understanding of their relationship. With their common adversary defeated, however, this solidarity without consensus began to fray as the Spaniards increasingly acted like conquerors. They continued to sack Cuzco, melting down ancestral statues of Inca queens in the plaza and dividing the spoils. Pizarro established a Spanish town council and assigned *encomiendas* (allotments of Indian labour) to his men, gestures that Manco correctly interpreted as erosions of his sovereignty. Meanwhile, news arrived that Alvarado, who was supposed to bring reinforcements to Cuzco from Spain, had set off to conquer Quito instead. Tensions with the Pizarros arose when the Crown granted Almagro control of the realm's southern half, including Cuzco, and abated only when he set off to conquer Chile in July of 1535. As the Pizarros treated him with increasing disrespect, Manco plotted against them secretly. He dissimulated submissiveness, hoping to make them feel secure enough to disperse and be easier to defeat in an uprising. A servant of Manco's informed the Spaniards of this plan, so they placed the Inca under house arrest in mid-August of 1535. In February of 1536, however, they released him to search for a golden ancestral statue, and he escaped to join his military commanders. During 1536–37 his army laid siege to Cuzco and then Lima for extended periods. Cuzco nearly fell during the initial attack, but the Spaniards and their two thousand Cañari, Chachapoya, and Huanca allies held on. Simultaneously, Manco also attacked Huanca territory, where he took and destroyed their principal deity, Huarihuillca, throwing its remains into a river. However, the Huancas later defeated him in battle, which unnerved him greatly. Four prominent Inca aristocrats then decided to aid the Spaniards and their allies in Cuzco by sending them food during the eighth month of the siege. Slowly Manco's soldiers drifted back to their homes as the planting season approached. When Almagro and Manco's brother Paullo Inca returned to Cuzco from Chile, Manco sought an alliance with them against the Pizarros, but they fought instead, before retreating with more than seventy thousand soldiers into the jungle stronghold of Vilcabamba. From there, he continued to attack Spaniards on the Andes' eastern slopes until his assassination in 1545.[6]

When he entered Cuzco on April 17, 1537, Almagro met resistance only from Gonzalo and Hernando Pizarro, whom he jailed for usurping the town's government. After installing Paullo as Inca sovereign, he marched on Lima to challenge Francisco Pizarro. Meanwhile, Gonzalo and Hernando Pizarro escaped and also went to Lima, where many other Spaniards had joined Francisco Pizarro. They drove Almagro back in several encounters, captured him in the Battle of Salinas on April 26, 1538, and executed him shortly afterwards. Almagro's followers dispersed. Some took refuge in Vilcabamba with Manco Inca in a tactical alliance for both parties. Paullo Inca shifted his allegiance to the

Pizarros and helped them quell a rebellion in Collao during 1538–39. He then joined them in the fight against his old rival Manco in the jungle, where he saved them from a particularly serious ambush. Nonetheless, the Pizarros never recognized Paullo as Inca, not only to spite Almagro but presumably to show that they were the Incas' conquerors, not allies.

Almagro's followers reconvened and assassinated Francisco Pizarro in Lima on July 26, 1541, after which Almagro the younger proclaimed himself governor of Peru. Charles V sent Vaca de Castro to suppress this rebellion. After narrowly losing the Battle of Chupas on September 16, 1542, Almagro the younger briefly revived an alliance with Manco, but was captured and killed in Cuzco before they could act together. To end Peru's civil wars and anarchy, Charles V installed a viceregal system on November 20, 1542, and proclaimed the New Laws, which curtailed the *encomenderos'* powers. These grants of native labour were the principal spoil of conquest, and every new power bloc redistributed them. When Blasco Núñez Vela arrived as viceroy to proclaim the New Laws, the Pizarros were outraged that the Crown had repaid their aid to Vaca de Castro by curtailing their rights as *encomenderos*, and rebelled under Gonzalo Pizarro's leadership. Rallying other *encomenderos* to their cause, they killed Núñez Vela. In 1547 the Crown sent a stronger force under Pedro de la Gasca, who defeated them, executed Gonzalo Pizarro, and redistributed *encomiendas*, which postponed debates over their reform until the 1560s, since the colonial elite would not remain loyal without them. Although minor rebellions continued into the 1550s and similar conspiracies into the 1560s, Gonzalo Pizarro's defeat was the last great event of the civil war period.

Conquest or Alliance?

During this tumultuous politico-military history, *curacas* had many opportunities to side with various Incas who wished to retain or regain control over their old imperial territory. Some *curacas* remained loyal to their old masters, but many supported the Spaniards. Probably a greater number still abstained from the conflict as best they could, not wishing to incur either party's enmity. Espinoza (1971) and Guillén (1974, 1984, 1994) have combed the archives for testimony that reveals Andean people's neglected role in these events, and have used it to contest, augment, and correct conquest historiography. They (and Vega 1978) argue that more than any other factor, *curacas'* allegiances determined the outcome of the conquest. All these authors anachronistically lament the lack of Andean national solidarity in an era when it could not have existed, but they are surely correct in blaming it on *curacas* and their interest in enhanced local autonomy. Espinoza further suggests that conquest narratives prevailed not because they gave the best historical interpretation but because they supplied the key ideological premise for dividing the spoils of Spanish ascendancy through the *encomienda* (1971: 14). Thus he independently anticipates the power/ knowledge emphasis in discourse analysis but sensibly employs it as a critical aid, not a challenge, to realist historiography. This work remains indispensable even for its critics (Sempat Assadourian 1994: ch. 4), and deserves a more serious engagement than it has received.

Let us begin with Espinoza's key point regarding the *encomienda*, which presupposed conquest and had no other rationale. Established during the Christian reconquest of Spain, this essentially feudal institution recognized that the Crown was too weak to win territory and so offered regional warlords honour and economic privileges in return for military fealty and nominal jurisdiction (Spalding 1984: 110–11). The Spanish Crown also depended on entrepreneurial soldiers to establish its sovereignty in the New World and so transplanted the *encomienda* there, but it acquired new characteristics in the process. Pope Alexander VI's bull of 1493 made Spanish dominion over its new colonies conditional on the natives' evangelization (Levillier 1919: 7–22). Since the Spanish Crown delegated that responsibility to its *encomenderos*, they became its 'trustees' specifically regarding religious conversion. This responsibility was explicit in the first *encomiendas* that Francisco Pizarro granted: he paired particular conquistadores with provincial Andean rulers (*curacas*) and assigned their subjects' labour to the conquistador, who was to convert them in return (Pizarro 1926). By making *curacas* mediate this relationship and allowing their jurisdictions to define those of the *encomienda*, however, the system institutionalized elite inter-ethnic alliance, as indigenous commentators soon recognized (Urteaga 1920: 36). Spalding (1984: 108) and Stern (1982: ch. 2) show that *encomenderos* largely relied on their *curaca* counterparts to extract their subjects' labour. *Curacas* quickly became important economic players in their own right. Contemporary commentators were only too aware of this reality, and constantly complained that the *curacas* were the main beneficiaries of the Inca state's collapse, taking its lands, sumptuary privileges, and haughty bearing for their own.[7] Even if Polo (as the *ecomenderos*' advocate) overestimated *curacas*' power, their autonomy and status clearly increased during the early colonial period. Thus, in reality the *encomienda* turned out to be a vehicle of elite inter-ethnic collaboration, even as it promoted an ideology of conquest. Behind the unilateral pronouncements of this new colonial order lay a far more complex reality in which Andean people, their authorities, institutions, forms of sociability, and understanding still mattered.

To continue Espinoza's argument, this mercenary framework made military exploits the basis of subsequent entitlements, which in turn gave erstwhile conquistadores an interest in emphasizing the heroism of their deeds. The recounting of history, then, became an important vehicle for the adjudication of individual *encomenderos'* claims and for their standing as a social class. Highlighting native collaboration during the conquest could only damage individual and collective interests within this group. These considerations explain much about the nature of the historical record, particularly the 'primitive accounts' of the conquest, which all but erase native participation in the Incas' overthrow, and correspondingly emphasize the role of divine favour in accounting for Spanish triumph against such long odds. Thus, the victors told the story of the conquest through the grid of their own ideologies, institutions, and reward structures (cf. Restall 2003: 12–8).

Of course this same Spanish grid also produced the indigenous testimony that Espinoza and Guillén emphasize. Alternative narratives of inter-ethnic alliance were arguably just as partial and self-serving as those of conquest but merely advanced a different set of interests: those of Andean rulers who wished to maximize their privileges under the Spanish regime. We will explore these motives and their cultural expression shortly. Yet the broader outlines of the history just recounted lend them credibility. During the two decades of civil war following the conquest, *encomenderos* were too busy fighting to undertake the administrative functions of a local ruling class, even if they managed to appropriate like one. From 1555 onward, the Crown prohibited them from living on their *encomiendas* to keep their seigneurial aspirations in check. By this process of elimination, we must conclude that *curacas* were the only historical actors able to govern their jurisdictions into the 1550s and so ratify the alliance/indirect rule analysis of this situation, which Spanish complaints of *curacas'* haughtiness and tyranny over their subjects only confirm.

Let us provisionally conclude this brief discussion of conquest and alliance as interpretations of the Spanish invasion by turning to the first historian to discuss these questions, Pedro de Cieza de León. Writing in the invasion's aftermath but without a conquistador's personal stake in its portrayal, Cieza explains Spanish ascendancy primarily through the devastation and animosity that the war between Huascar and Atahuallpa caused (1553: 271, 295). He specifies that the Huancas, Yauyos, and Cañaris collaborated with the Spaniards politically and militarily out of hatred for Atahuallpa, and identifies these groups as part of the Huascar faction (1553: 8, 222–4, 270–1, 296–8, 302–3). Thus, Cieza inaugurates the inter-ethnic alliance interpretation of the conquest and derives it from pre-existing factional politics. Yet he also contextualizes such alliances in the horrific state of 'permanent war' in the Andes between 1530 and 1550 (Sempat Assadourian 1994: ch. 1), which makes his extended reflections on these events particularly valuable in assessing the relative merits of conquest and alliance as explanations.

Cieza does not overstate inter-ethnic alliance despite being the first historian to acknowledge it. He notes that many coastal people tried to repel the Spaniards and only allied with them after suffering defeat (1553: 233, 237, 272–3). When other coastal peoples favourably received the Spaniards later, it was against this coercive backdrop (1553: 250–2, 261, 264–9). Cieza portrays Andean people as aware that the Spaniards did not intend to share power with them but to replace the Incas through conquest (1553: 264–5, 267, 274). He notes that Pizarro tried to maintain a facade of alliance with indigenous rulers but insists that force and resentment nonetheless predominated in relations with them (1553: 261, 266–9). For Cieza, cavalry and sabres were a decisive military advantage that allowed Spaniards to prevail repeatedly in battles when outnumbered by as much as one thousand to one (1553: 275, 299, 301). Cieza stresses the fear that Andean people developed for horses but dismisses the notion that they viewed the animals as immortal or supernatural, while recording Spanish attempts to propagate this idea (1553: 260, 275, 295, 299, 304). He also notes that Andean people devised effective strategies against horses, such as the use of *bolas* and covered stake-lined pits (1553: 275–6, 300, 304 cf. P. Pizarro 1572: 136). These might have worked better had not disaffected ex-servants of the Incas constantly revealed them to the Spaniards and if morale in Atahuallpa's army had not been so low after his spectacular capture (1553: 295, 300, 344–7). Guilmartin's military analysis of the conquest (1991) ratifies all these points.

In short, Cieza convincingly argues that the conquest was a complex mixture of coercion and consent. Spanish cavalry and sabres might not have literally subdued entire Andean armies, but the spectacle of car-

Figure 2.2 Quotidian Spanish Violence

nage they regularly created decisively altered the terms of military encounter. Such violence had an intimidating efficiency that surpassed its immediate enactment (cf. Restall 2003: 24–5). It captured the initiative and reframed perceptions. Without it, we cannot explain why Andean people would deign to ally with a tiny group of Spaniards. This was its crucial persuasive effect. An important conversion occurred here: such violence was no longer purely instrumental but symbolically redefined Andean people's sense of the possible and the advisable. As Guaman Poma's drawings poignantly show, well after their initial invasion Spaniards continued to deploy it strategically to ensure Andean servility and assert racial superiority (see figure 2.2). By punctuating everyday life, conquistador violence set the basic terms of a hegemony whose primary feature was inter-ethnic alliance. From most Andean perspectives, emphasizing this harmonious understanding of the emerging colonial order was preferable, if only to gain some respite from its violent counterpart. Spaniards also had missionary reasons to elaborate the notion of alliance. Let us now explore the pidginized post-conquest mythologies by which both parties advanced this agenda.

Spaniards as Viracochas

During these events, Andean people began to call Spaniards *viracochas*. Literally, *viracocha* means 'lake of grease' or, as contemporary etymologies had it, 'grease or foam of the sea.'[8] Before the Spanish invasion, Viracocha was the title of primordial ancestors who created the existing social and material order in the Andes (Betanzos 1551: 13, Guaman Poma 1615: 49). Soon afterwards, however, the term found a distinct additional meaning. Various Spaniards (particularly missionaries) appropriated Viracocha as the indigenous Andean word for the Christian God. Exactly what it meant for Spaniards to receive this designation was actively debated at the time (Polo 1561: 154). Inevitably the very process of semantic colonization prevented clarity.

Modern historians continue to diverge sharply in their explanations of the Viracocha attribution. On the one hand, Juan José Vega argues that the conquest occurred because many provincial peoples and the Huascar faction saw the Spaniards as 'untouchable gods' and rallied to their side to win an improbable victory against Atahuallpa and Inca imperialism (1978: 12). On the other hand, Pease (1995: ch. 5), Mróz (1991: 94), Harris (1995: 13–4), and Estenssoro (2003: 102) treat the identification of Spaniards with Viracocha as a colonial myth, one that the Spaniards themselves propagated. In their view, no such native belief existed to promote the conquest. It was only afterwards that Spaniards became Viracochas in a triumphal self-apotheosis. This racist mystification of their own ascendancy converted what had been a process of alliance building into a retrospective native recognition of Spaniards' inherent superiority.

This divergence of opinion approximates (less polemically) that of the Sahlins-Obeyesekere debate over Captain Cook's 'divine' status. At stake is not just who first identified Spaniards with Viracocha and why, but whether any unilateral understanding of this identification is ultimately viable (cf. Haefeli 2007: 409–10). I will argue that neither position is defensible as stated, and will treat the Viracocha identification inter-culturally. Both positions focus on Viracocha's colonized secondary meaning of crypto-Christian deity and neglect its primary ancestral meaning. I will restore Viracocha's polysemy, including the tensions and interactions between these meanings. Such an analysis must identify how both groups contributed to this emerging mythology from their established cultural repertoires. It must also explore how interaction widened, realigned, and interconnected those repertoires so that they were no longer entirely separate. Exactly when and under what circumstances the Spaniards were first identified as Viracochas is uncertain. Exploring the question requires a critical approach to the sources that quickly transforms into the related but ultimately more interesting matter of looking at Viracocha as a composite, additive, and historical construction intimately related to the inter-cultural foundation of a colonial order.

A naive reading of the chronicles could date the Viracocha attribution to the Spaniards' first arrival on the northern coast in 1527, at the end of Huayna Capac's reign. Vega, for instance, argues that the Spaniards' mere disembarkation initiated speculation about their status as deities, that this question immobilized Atahuallpa on their return in 1531, and led the Huascar faction to view them as divine emissaries (1978: 14, 19, 21–2). Selected sources support these contentions, but if Andean people really saw the Spaniards as divine, they would have behaved differently. For example, the coastal people who periodically skirmished with the Spaniards would have accepted them unconditionally from the outset. Atahuallpa would not have harangued the Spaniards for looting and torture, nor would he have underestimated them so fatally in Cajamarca. These discrepancies undermine Vega's account. More plausibly, Guillén argues that Andean people initially dismissed the Spaniards as 'bearded ones,' 'thieves,' 'workshy,' and 'sons of the sea' (*capacochas*, a term that really denoted human sacrifices): only after they captured Atahuallpa, and through him, the Incas' aura of divine invincibility, did Andean people see them as *viracochas* (1974: 139–41, 154). Significantly, however, the word Viracocha does not appear in the 'primitive' Spanish accounts of the conquest, which suggests that even after Atahuallpa's capture, it did not figure importantly in their experience. Yet these accounts do report Pachacamac or the Sun (*inti*) as indigenous names for God (Sancho 1534: 309, Anonymous 1539: 581). Clearly the Christian interpolation of Andean religion was already under way at this early stage, but had not yet settled on Viracocha as its vehicle of choice. On these grounds, the Viracocha attribution appears to be a retrospective, post-conquest phenomenon. By paying close attention to when the Viracocha attribution appears in the historical record, who deployed it, and for what purposes, I will adopt a more critical perspective than these authors, but still allow that it might have played a role in the conquest that Spaniards did not recognize at the time.

Given this debate's complexities, I owe the reader a clear statement of my own position from the outset. Figure 2.3 presents my analysis of

	Quipucamayocs 1542*	Betanzos 1551	Cieza 1553	Santo Tomás 1560	Agustinos 1561	Titu Cusi 1570	Sarmiento 1572	Molina 1574	Cabello Valboa 1586	Acosta 1590	Huarochiri Ms. 1608†	Pachacuti Yamqui 1613	Guaman Poma 1615	Cajatambo 1656–63‡
Andean Substratum														
Ancestral cohort		X	X	X			X	X		X	X	X	X	
Journey and emergence		X	X				X	X		X	X			X
Colonization of territory		X	X	X			X	X		X	X			X
Subsistence arts										X			X	X
Subsequent conquest		X	X	X			X	X		X			X	X
Petrification		X						X		X				X
Moiety organization			X	X						X			X	X
Initial Andean Deployment														
Spaniards as Andean ancestors		X		X								X	X	
Viracocha as Spaniard	X	X	X			X	X		X	X	X	X		
Provincial peoples		X	X			X	X							
Huascar faction	X		X			X								
Atahuallpa faction		X					X							
Missionary Appropriation														
Viracocha as "God"		X				X	X	?	X	X			X	
Biblical creation scenario		X	X				X	X	X					
Viracocha as apostle		?		X			?			X		X	X	
Viracocha as Christian					X									
Further Andean Deployment														
No resistance to Spaniards	X	X		X						X		X		
Inca exculpatory version	X	X		X								X		
Spanish providential version										X		X		

*Urteaga 1920
†Salomon and Urioste 1991
‡Duviols 1986

Figure 2.3 Viracocha Analytics by Source

the Viracocha phenomenon as an additive project that went through at least four phases of construction. Vertically to the left is the sequence in which I think these layers of meaning accumulated, whereas horizontally to the right are relevant sources in chronological order. Since the main discussion below follows the sources chronologically, I preface it by briefly outlining my vertical reconstruction of the additive phases by which I think the phenomenon itself developed. Viracocha's Quechua derivation and its place in an ostensibly Andean genre of ancestral colonization narratives justify the assumption that the term not only existed but had a specific discursive function before the Spanish invasion (cf. Durston 2007: 66). This hypothesized Andean substratum is an inference from colonial sources, however, in which it is always subsumed by subsequent projects and deployments. It therefore appears primarily as a remainder that those subsequent uses cannot explain, one whose pre-existing logic is rarely more than residually present. The next layer of the Viracocha phenomenon was, I suggest, its application to Spaniards during the conquest. While this point is controversial, I accept that on balance, the evidence suggests that the Viracocha notion was in play in that context. A further layer of the Viracocha phenomenon is its missionary appropriation as the Andean name for the monotheistic creator God of the Judaeo-Christian tradition or, alternatively, for a wandering apostle. This layer is overt in most texts, where it significantly subsumes, edits, and reorganizes what might be construed as evidence for the previous levels of meaning. Finally, there is an indigenous appropriation of the missionary appropriation, in which various Andean political authorities claimed that they did not resist the invading Spaniards because they saw them as bearers of the religious truth. The Viracocha phenomenon enters the historical record already layered to this last degree.

   As far as I know, the earliest written source to use the term *Viracocha* dates to 1542, when Vaca de Castro's officials interviewed the *quipucamayocs* (record keepers) of Cuzco on Inca royal succession. They mention that when Huayna Capac heard of the Spaniards' arrival on the coast, he remarked that they would bring great turmoil and changes to the land. A year later, as he was dying of the smallpox epidemic they brought, Huayna Capac told his son Atahuallpa not to be jealous of Huascar (for inheriting high office), as he was leaving him only strife now that these new people had entered the land, who were reportedly nothing less than superhuman Viracochas (Urteaga 1920: 19, 22–3). Thus, Huayna Capac's identification of Spaniards as Viracochas implied that they would author a *pachacuti*, a cataclysmic overturning and inversion of the existing order.[9]

   Critical discussion of the Quipucamayocs' account must begin with its retrospective quality. First, it reads the conflict between Atahuallpa and Huascar back in time: were they really fighting for the succession while their father was still alive? Although it purports to describe events that occurred in the 1520s, the account clearly incorporates subsequent concerns. Christian pieties crop up repeatedly during accounts of the pagan past, further separating the text from the moment it describes. Above all, Huayna Capac's prophecy suggests foreknowledge of Spanish victory before they had even entered the Andes, and hence, a native fatalism that preordained and greatly aided the conquest. Can we accept this resignation as a contemporary stance, or was it a retrospective construction through which certain sectors of the Inca elite repositioned themselves around what became a Spanish victory? Obviously such fatalism is not consistent with the actions of Atahuallpa in Cajamarca, his generals after his capture, or Manco Inca's rebellion, and to that extent is dubious. After Manco left for the jungle and the Incas' loss of power became evident, that is, with the benefit of hindsight in 1542, the Quipucamayocs' story tells us what Huayna Capac should have said shortly before his death. The suggestion, however improbable, that the Incas had in effect conceded power, helped the Inca elite who remained in Cuzco to salvage what was left of their privileges under Spanish colonialism. Told from their subject position, the Quipucamayocs' account would mitigate the damage that Inca resistance did to their prospects under the new regime. It thus inaugurates what was to become an Andean tradition of denying that a conquest had occurred, since the Spaniards were received without resistance, and even in friendship (see figure 2.4).

Spaniards interpreted the fatalist prophecies attributed to Huayna Capac in their own way, as a providential intimation of Christianity's arrival. We have already seen that many Spaniards believed that the conquest would not have happened against such long odds without divine backing, and understood colonialism itself as a missionary enterprise. For those disposed towards Las Casas' position that Inca religion was a providential preparation for the true faith, Huayna Capac's prophecies would have been particularly believable. Thus, self-interested Inca elites and missionary imperialists, both seeking to position themselves advantageously in the emerging order, could each agree for their own reasons that the Incas foresaw their own collapse, and so did not resist. Whereas the former made this claim to reduce their losses under the new regime, the latter did so to prove its inevitability. The result was a pidginized consensus that continued to house conflicting interests. Despite its inter-cultural and even dialogical form, this apparent consensus necessarily took place through colonized Andean vehicles. As with the Viracocha attribution itself, it is hard to believe that Spaniards invented these fatalistic prophecies from scratch just after the

Figure 2.4 Alliance and the Denial of Conquest

invasion, when their knowledge of the Incas was still rudimentary. Once apprised of them, however, Spaniards quickly adapted them to their own providential theology, which required the true God to permit and even work through Andean peoples' idolatries. Thus, Spaniards could believe that Huayna Capac's prophecies were true without betraying their own faith. To the extent that the identification of Spaniards as Viracochas was part of this retrospective fatalism, it too would derive from the self-interested repositioning of the early colonial Inca elite.

The Quipucamayocs' document emerged in just such a process. Its central purpose was to claim that of all the surviving Incas, only the descendants of Paullo could claim legitimacy. Paullo becomes the true Inca sovereign in relation to his rebel brother Manco not only by imputed Andean criteria (Urteaga 1920: 23–6, 32–3, 47–8) but also by his exemplary conduct as a colonial subject: after saving a party of Spaniards led by Gonzalo Pizarro from Manco, Paullo returned to Cuzco and asked for baptism. The document specifies that he was the first Inca to do so and that he led many others into faith (Urteaga 1920: 45–6). Thereafter, he behaved as a model colonial lord, constructing the church of San Cristóbal near his house in Cuzco, receiving an *encomienda*, and leaving pious bequests on his death in 1551 (Urteaga 1920: 46–7). In summary, the document mentions native criteria of legitimacy but subordinates them to those of the colonial period, in which Christianity was paramount. Both Vega (1974: 15–8) and Duviols (1979: 584–7) show that this version of Inca history was produced to bolster the claims of Paullo's descendant Melchor Carlos Inca to special privileges and compensation between 1603 and 1608.

These circumstances raise obvious questions about the document's date. The document stakes its own authority on the Quipucamayocs' testimony of 1542, but does not distinguish that 'original' text or stratum from subsequent additions.[10] On various linguistic and heuristic grounds, Vega (1974: 11–15) and Duviols (1979: 588–9) argue that such an original stratum existed, even if its Quipucamayoc authors were largely reduced to a manipulable source of information and legitimacy for the later account. Neither compares the Quipucamayocs' document to the extensive documentation regarding the claims of Melchor Carlos Inca and his son Juan Carlos Inca, which includes Vaca de Castro's confirmation of the *encomienda* granted to their grandfather and great-grandfather Paullo Inca.[11] Thus, Vaca de Castro recognized Paullo Inca and, in so doing, collected the Quipucamayocs' testimony, which we can suppose to have been a document in its own right. For our purposes, it is particularly important to ask whether the Viracocha attribution is part of that original document or a later addition. Nothing in the text definitively proves either possibility.

If the Quipucamayocs did treat Spaniards as Viracochas, it would establish an important point: Spaniards did not initiate such claims in the 1550s as Pease (1995: 145–6, 150) and Mróz (1991: 92–4) claim. Rather, Andean people did so in the 1540s. By implication, then, the Viracocha attribution would not have originated, as Pease (1995: 151) supposes, in an act of colonial ventriloquism by which Spaniards secured their identification with this Andean 'deity' to proclaim their own divine invincibility. Instead Andean people would have authored it to collaborate with the Spaniards. Such a scenario fits with the elementary fact that *viracocha* is not a Spanish but an Andean term. The improbable alternative that Pease et al. propose requires that Spaniards persuaded Andean people to see them as Viracochas at a time when their knowledge of the Andean religions and languages was at best rudimentary. Undaunted, they are supposed to have claimed (and received recognition in) a position of great ontological significance within Andean culture. This claim's plausibility further evaporates when we ask what self-apotheosis as Viracochas would mean to the Spaniards who supposedly indulged in it. Why would they wish to identify with Andean ancestors, whom they came to view as devils? Self-apotheosis as the Christian God was even more problematic: such a supreme heresy would align the Spaniards with Lucifer. Far from 'legitimating colonialism' as Pease and Mróz suggest, it would provoke a visit from the Inquisition, which sentenced heretics to death for much less. Self-apotheosis would confirm one of Spaniards' worst colonial fears: that they themselves had succumbed to the natives' idolatries. Thus, Spaniards did not directly proclaim their own apotheosis but only attributed it to the natives and then disavowed it (Hamlin 1994: 432, 444).

Once missionaries appropriated Viracocha, Spaniards could indeed represent themselves as his 'sons' or 'emissaries' to state their Christian filiation. According to Santo Tomás (1560: 369), the term Viracocha itself quickly came to mean 'Christian,' but not necessarily in the term's ethnic sense, by which Spaniards systematically differentiated themselves from Andean people (Estenssoro 2003: 101). Such an understanding neatly sidestepped the problematic implications that too close an identification with their monotheistic 'God' would have had for Spaniards. For Andean people, however, the identification of a people and its deity was fully admissible, so they continued to call Spaniards Viracochas and left them to manage their translations of the term as best they could. Again, Spanish hubris makes no sense as the origin of this identification. The 'primitive chronicles' do not show the Spaniards feeling personally empowered as deities during the conquest, but as utterly dependent on external divine favour for their miraculous deliverance. Even accounts of the civil wars, which might impugn rebels against the Crown by having them boast that there was no God or king in the Indies but them, refrain from doing so. Instead they depict rebels chivalrously commending themselves to divine justice before battle (e.g., Anonymous 1539: 594–5). Any early-modern Spaniard knew that to make such incendiary claims in direct speech would be blasphemy and treason, speech acts that were inherently beyond the pale. Thus, only in colonial corruption discourses and post-colonial mythologies could Spaniards conceivably indulge in such self-apotheosis.

The next source to discuss Spaniards' possible status as Viracochas was Betanzos. His account is systematic and begins by establishing the place of Viracocha in Andean tradition. Contiti Viracocha first emerged from Lake Titicaca to create the earth and the sky, and an original humanity whom he left in darkness. These people offended Contiti Viracocha, who descended into Lake Titicaca, emerged a second time, and brought some new people with him to Tiahuanaco. There, Contiti Viracocha turned the humans he first created into stone by making the sun and setting it on its course: then he made the moon and the stars. Next he made various new peoples out of stone in Tiahuanaco, each with their rulers, women, and children. He gave them names and costumes and told them that they were to journey underground and emerge in specific territories. These Viracochas set off towards the sunrise for their various provinces. On arrival at the particular caves, rivers, springs, and mountains that were their points of emergence, they called out others who were to follow them. Contiti Viracocha then sent two assistants who had stayed with him at Tiahuanaco to call out other peoples similarly in Condesuyo and Andesuyo. He himself headed north towards Cuzco, also bringing people out. Those whom he called out in Canas tried to attack him, but when he summoned a firestorm, they surrendered and build a sumptuous shrine (*huaca*) for him near Urcos. He continued to make new peoples as he continued towards Cuzco, where he made the Alcabicça. He then ordered that the Incas should emerge after he left. So he continued until he arrived in Puerto Viejo, and reunited with the two assistants he had sent out to Condesuyo and Andesuyo. The three set off walking upon the sea, and disappeared.

Subsequent chroniclers of the Incas such as Cieza (1553), Sarmiento (1572) and Molina (1574), recorded similar versions of this Viracocha creation narrative. They describe how the Incas' ancestors emerged from the ground in Pacarictambo and journeyed to Cuzco, transforming the landscape and subduing its aboriginal inhabitants with prodigious feats of strength as they went. Despite their concluding focus on Inca origins, the narratives clearly state that the founding ancestors of other Andean polities also underwent a similar process of remote generation, subterranean travel, and emergence in a specific locality. These groups had similar narratives that formed an Andean genre in which Viracochas were primordial ancestors. Betanzos imposes some biblical features on this narrative, as did his successors. Starting with Cieza in 1553, several accounts rearrange Andean ancestral narratives to depict Viracocha as the *hacedor* or divine maker, and some even add the specifically biblical details that he created humanity out of clay, or 'in his image.'[12] Other less colonized Andean ancestral narratives (see chapter 5) strongly suggest that this genre featured no single moment of creation and no single creator along Judaeo-Christian lines. As an indigenous ancestral entity, Viracocha was not the name of a singular creator god, but a plural category of primordial beings who established local orders throughout the Andes. By singularizing Viracocha and treating him as the Andean creator, however, chroniclers and missionaries colonized Andean ancestral narratives and made them into precursors and vehicles of their own monotheism.[13]

When Betanzos committed this Andean narrative genre to writing, he did not merely record but actively transculturated it. Despite its etymology, Betanzos insisted not only that Viracocha means 'God' in the (Judaeo-Christian) sense of creator, but that when the Spaniards arrived and received this name, Andean people took them for gods (1551: 78). This statement looks like the first authentic example of Spanish self-apotheosis, and superficially confirms Pease's colonial hubris scenario. As we examine how Betanzos develops and dramatizes the claim below, however, it turns out to serve very different ends. Betanzos married Atahuallpa's sister and primary wife, doña Angelina Yupanqui: his position in colonial society, including his credibility as a mediator and translator, owed everything to his connection to her kin. Thus, his account consistently portrays Atahuallpa in a favourable light, as someone reluctant to fight the Spaniards out of a belief that they were gods. This same exculpatory strategy characterized the Quipucamayocs' account, in which Betanzos served as translator (Urteaga 1920: 5). Evidently his Inca informants and affines put words in Betanzos' mouth as adeptly as he did in theirs, particularly over the Viracocha attribution.

Betanzos resumes his discussion of Spaniards as Viracochas after they arrived on the coast and established the town of San Miguel. Three messengers carried the news to Atahuallpa, minutely describing details of the Spaniards' appearance, dress, and horses. When Atahuallpa asked what these people called themselves, the messengers did not know but added that they called them Viracochas, meaning gods, a designation that Atahuallpa asked them to explain. They replied that in olden times after Contiti Viracocha had created people, he departed over the sea, but when the Spaniards appeared, they thought he had returned (1551: 253). During a second interview, the messengers described their horses and swords in greater detail. Atahuallpa asked if they ate human flesh and, overcome by fear, considered hiding in the high jungle of Chachapoyas until his advisers convinced him that they should first send an envoy to determine the Spaniards' status as gods or humans, and what their intentions were. Should they be annihilators of people (*runaquiçacha*),[14] the envoy was to flee from them, but if they were benevolent Viracochas (*viracocha cuna allichac*), he should welcome and invite them to meet Atahuallpa. Through this plan, Atahuallpa regained confidence in himself and the idea that the Spaniards were indeed beneficent Viracochas (1551: 254–5). Thus, he sent a messenger south to Cuzco, who announced to the marvel and rejoicing of his audience of army captains that Viracochas had arrived on the coast, those who had created humanity (1551: 261–2). He also sent an envoy named Ciquinchara to meet and observe the Spaniards, probably the same person the Spaniards described encountering during their ascent to Cajamarca.

Ciquinchara evaluated the Spaniards as ordinary men who ate drank, mended clothes, and consorted with women, not as returning Viracochas, since they levelled no mountains and created no springs or rivers as Contiti Viracocha had done but brought water with them in dry areas. Recounting how they took young women, gold, silver, and clothing for themselves wherever they went, and how they chained, mistreated, and forced Indians into their service, Ciquinchara portrayed them as lawless brigands (*quitas pumaranga*). Astounded and saddened, Atahuallpa asked why people took them for gods, and why Ciquinchara called them Viracochas. He replied that he did not but called them devils (*supai cuna*) instead. When Atahuallpa asked who identified the Spaniards as Viracochas, Ciquinchara replied, 'the beastly coastal people' who inferred their divinity from how their horses made the ground shake, the flash of their swords, and the thunder of their muskets. Ciquinchara admitted fearing them also until he realized their muskets' ineffectiveness. When asked what to do about the Spaniards, Ciquinchara proposed burning them in their sleep. Atahuallpa preferred to evaluate them and instructed him to return with golden goblets to attract them to Cajamarca (1551: 263–5). This Ciquinchara did, prostrating himself before Pizarro and addressing him as the Inca's father while beseeching him to come (1551: 267).

Once the Spaniards arrived in Cajamarca and staged their cavalry display before the Inca's army, Atahuallpa asked Ciquinchara if the Spaniards were Viracochas after all, and whether to obey them. He replied that the Inca's men could overwhelm and kill them, that their horses should not awe them, and that those who had long observed them had many indications that they were not gods. The envoy then confessed that he had initially thought Pizarro to be Viracocha Pachayachachic and had ordered the coastal peoples to obey the Spaniards. When they asked him elementary questions about the highlands, however, he realized that Pizarro could not be Viracocha. Later, Ciquinchara discussed the Spaniards with the interpreter, who explained that they were not Viracochas but mortal, as were their horses. Atahuallpa then dismissed Ciquinchara and said to his captains that he still believed they were Viracochas who should be obeyed. The captains suggested waiting and seeing, and meeting with them the following day to learn their intentions (Betanzos 1551: 272–4). This was, of course, the day of Atahuallpa's capture. During his encounter with Atahuallpa, Valverde allegedly claimed to be a son of the Sun sent to tell Atahuallpa not to resist but to obey Pizarro, who was also a son of the Sun. Valverde added that the Bible he handed Atahuallpa depicted all this. Atahuallpa then opened the Bible and agreed that it spoke this message, but stated that he was also a son of the Sun, and threw the Bible down (1551: 277). Thus, even in Atahuallpa's supposed moment of defiance, Betanzos portrays him as merely proclaiming his equality to the Spaniards while accepting their evangelical message. For Betanzos, only those who fought against the Spaniards, such as Atahuallpa's general Quizquiz, definitively denied their status as gods (1551: 252).

We must suspect Betanzos' carefully constructed account of these debates over the Spaniards' possible status as deities, particularly his credulous portrayal of Atahuallpa. No first-hand Spanish account of the march to Cajamarca reports Ciquinchara prostrating himself before Pizarro or calling him Atahuallpa's father. Eyewitness accounts of Atahuallpa's pre-capture demeanour describe a self-assured ruler alternately ignoring and lecturing a band of invaders, not a deferential mortal appearing before gods. In short, contemporary Spanish descriptions of Atahuallpa's conduct challenge Betanzos' depiction. Aware of this historiographic problem, Betanzos attempts to reconcile Atahuallpa's purported belief that the Spaniards were Viracochas with reports of his arrogance towards them by depicting Atahuallpa as drunk and harassed by reports of Spanish misdeeds during his fateful encounter with Valverde (1551: 275–7). This unfortunate exception aside, Betanzos would have us believe that Atahuallpa saw the Spaniards as returning gods. Thus, Ciquinchara takes the blame for Atahaullpa's actions as the one who planted 'great evils' in the sovereign's mind, and as a 'traitor' (1551: 263, 272). Betanzos' marital alliance is the clear motive for this improbable exculpation of Atahuallpa. His version of Inca history faithfully served his affines' interests by rehabilitating Atahuallpa and portraying him as someone who had never intended to resist the Spaniards, unlike Ciquinchara and other 'bad' members of the Inca elite. Again, the Viracocha attribution is incompatible with Inca attitudes before the conquest but makes sense as a strategy to reposition themselves afterwards.

Other retrospective emendations, such as Ciquinchara's conjecture that the Spaniards were devils (*supai cuna*) are clearly present in his account. The term *supay* has a complex colonial history. Before evangelization, it apparently referred to a soul that would leave ordinary mortals during affliction or on death, travelling to the site of the afterlife (*upaymarca*). Early missionaries inferred that this place must be hell, and that as master of this place, *supay* must be none other than the Devil (Taylor 1980, Estenssoro 2003: 103–10). This colonial meaning is already present in Betanzos' account, which makes Ciquichara choose whether the Spaniards are good or evil supernatural figures. Andean pantheons lacked such ethical polarization, which underlines that Betanzos told this 'first contact' story after the fact in already colonized terms. As the Spanish author of these purportedly Inca ruminations, Betanzos is its most obvious source, but we cannot rule out his Andean affines, who systematically used his history to make amends with the Spaniards.

The next chronicler to discuss Viracocha is Cieza de León, who interrupts his exposition of Viracocha origin narratives to discuss how the Spaniards received this title, and thus links the two even more directly than Betanzos. He writes that the Huascar faction initially saw the three Spaniards sent to Cuzco to collect Atahuallpa's ransom as sons of Viracocha, but their behaviour soon revealed that they were worse than *supais* (1553: 152, 280). Cieza reiterates this analysis in greater detail while describing the conquest, noting that en route to Cuzco, the natives worshipped these Spaniards, believing that a deity inhabited them. On arrival, the defeated Huascar faction received them with great celebrations, and covertly hoped that the Spaniards would avenge them against Atahuallpa. They gave the newcomers fine lodgings, assigned them chosen women from the Temple of the Sun, and revered them with a gesture (*mocha*) reserved for divine rulers and deities (Cieza 1553: 283). Yet the Spaniards soon discredited themselves as deities by taking the priestesses as concubines, which outraged their erstwhile backers, who now saw them as worse than devils (Cieza 1553: 284).[15] Cieza pioneered a position that others would later develop:[16] that the Spaniards initially seemed like Viracochas because they intervened almost miraculously in the Inca war of succession, capturing Atahuallpa and delivering Cuzco from his generals' wrath when all was lost. During their defence of Cuzco, the Huascar faction offered sacrifices to Viracocha, and were rewarded with the news of the Spaniards' arrival and capture of their adversary.

Cieza's explanation of the Viracocha attribution is essentially political: Huascar's supporters saw the Spaniards as deities while they remained a remote and miraculous force that seemed to work in their interest. Once they arrived and revealed themselves as rapists and pillagers, however, the Huascar faction rued having ever equated them with Viracocha. This interpretation explains the Spaniards' previously nebulous role in the songs of praise during Manco's investiture, as related by Estete above. In thanking the Sun for the Spaniards' help in restoring them to power, the Huascar faction may well have identified them as Viracochas. This additional premise certainly makes Estete's account more intelligible, and it is compatible with the evidence of most other chronicles. While Cieza dates the Huascar faction's disillusion with the Spaniards to an earlier moment than Estete describes, his explanation survives this discrepancy. Their initial credulity was a hope born of desperation under Atahuallpa's occupying army, one that quickly dissipated with the realities of Spanish occupation. The shift from apotheosis to disillusionment is the basic structure of European rationalist accounts of 'first contact,' which cannot abide an unmodified apotheosis (Haefeli 2007: 407–9). Thus, Cieza denied that Andean people identified Spaniards as Viracochas simply because their maritime point of entry into the Andes coincided with the route of Viracocha's departure (1553: 152). They were not slaves to a mythical script like Sahlins' Hawaiians (or Carrasco's Mexicans). Rather, Cieza stresses 'pragmatic rationality' (in Obeyeskere's terms) over magico-religious gullibility in explaining Andean responses to the Spaniards.[17]

Yet the 'Inca history' that Cieza and other chroniclers were busy reconstructing had a mythical precedent for the Huascar faction's desperate situation when they identified the Spaniards as Viracochas. Many accounts describe a Chanca offensive against Cuzco before the Incas' imperial expansion. As the Chanca army approached, the Inca Viracocha fled Cuzco with his favourite son, Urco, an inveterate drunkard and womanizer. A previously marginalized but virtuous son, Yupanqui, stepped into the breach to defend the city. Before entering battle, Yupanqui purportedly consulted the ancestral deity Viracocha. As Yupanqui's forces fought the Chanca attack to a stalemate in a bloody battle, the *pururaucas*, a legion of stone monoliths in the hills around Cuzco, transformed into warriors who then turned on the Chancas and routed them. After this spectacular triumph, Yupanqui's troops pursued the Chancas and took their homeland. When Yupanqui returned to Cuzco, he allowed his father to tread on the enemy's captured weapons, a sovereign's prerogative that Viracocha tried to deflect to his favoured elder son, Urco. The assembled multitude intervened and demanded that Yupanqui be the one to tread on the Chancas' weapons. This act marked Yupanqui's investiture as sovereign, after which he sponsored lavish sacrifices, rebuilt the Temple of the Sun, and promoted the cult of Viracocha within the Inca pantheon. Yupanqui went on to enjoy a long and fabulously successful reign that firmly established Inca imperial ascendancy in the Andes. In the process, he was renamed Pachacuti ('earthquake' or 'epochal cataclysm') to recognize his fundamental reordering of the Andean world.[18]

By identifying the Spaniards as Viracochas, the Huascar faction arguably invoked several dimensions of this prior episode. Most obviously, they equated the Spaniards with the *pururaucas* of Yupanqui's day in saving Cuzco from attack and adjudicating a struggle between brothers over succession to high office. More important still, both the Spaniards and the *pururaucas* derived from Viracocha, the former explicitly and the latter as his agents against the Chancas. The *pururaucas'* normally petrified form links them with primordial episodes of ancestral creation like those Viracocha initiated from Lake Titicaca. Their very name suggests primordiality: *purur* denotes 'nomadic,' the condition of earlier ages of humanity in Andean thought (Guaman Poma 1615: 447, Pachacuti Yamqui 1613: 187), and *auca* denotes 'warrior' or 'opponent' in the dualist structure of a moiety system. Andean moieties typically differentiated an 'upper' group of intrusive colonists dominant in the present from a 'lower' group of conquered aboriginals dominant in the past (Gose 1996a), so the *pururaucas* clearly fall in the latter category. By reviving them to intervene in the sectoral struggles of a subsequent epoch, Viracocha (as primordial ancestral deity) showed that earlier forces remained latent in later moments, and could still decisively shape them. It is particularly tempting to treat the *pururaucas* as the ancestral deities of the aboriginal peoples of the Cuzco area, whom the Incas subordinated.[19] Thus, both Yupanqui and Huascar claimed the backing of forces from earlier epochs in struggles with enemies in their own day. Cieza must have been aware of this parallelism, but as the only major chronicler to omit the *pururaucas* from his account of the Chancas' defeat, he suppressed it. I suggest that he did so to preserve his pragmatico-rationalist account of how the Spaniards became *viracochas*.

Surprisingly, however, Cieza's own narrative repeatedly contradicts his explanation of the Viracocha attribution. First, he has one coastal group already treating the Spaniards as deities during the 1527 voyage (1553: 252). Second, he attributes this same belief to the part of Atahuallpa's army that defended Quito against a party of Spaniards and Cañaris (1553: 300). In both cases, he claims that Andean people deified Spaniards because they did so much while being so few, without elaborating on the claim or reconciling it with his earlier explanation. Third and most serious is that the three Spaniards sent to raise Atahuallpa's ransom travelled in litters and received reverence during their journey to and arrival in Cuzco. Again, it was the Atahuallpa (not the Huascar) faction that extended these markers of divine kingship to the Spaniards. Perhaps such treatment acknowledged only that the Spaniards were the Inca's high-ranking emissaries, but more probably reflected the known fact that they were his captors. Finally, early in Manco Inca's rebellion, after the facade of alliance had crumbled and they had killed Martín de Moquer, one of the three Spaniards who arrived by litter to sack Cuzco, Manco's supporters still called the Spaniards Viracochas (1553: 348). Contrary to Cieza's argument, even the Huascar faction's complete disillusion with the Spaniards did not deprive them of the title. Despite himself, then, Cieza provides some provocative evidence that various Andean factions saw the Spaniards as Viracochas during the conquest.

As a God-fearing Spaniard, he employed rationalist arguments and an air of scholarly detachment to minimize this phenomenon, but its trances nonetheless resurface in his own account to contradict him.

On Cieza's evidence, Andean peoples' apotheosis of Spaniards was not entirely retrospective. Testimony collected (in 1573) from indigenous witnesses who lived through the conquest also suggests it was a part of those events. These witnesses report ontological befuddlement and a significant measure of terror as initial Andean responses to the Spanish presence. Some thought at the time that horses ate gold and silver, perhaps from seeing bridles in horses' mouths. Spaniards exploited this notion to demand more gold and silver as fodder for their horses, and Andean people began to suspect that Spaniards themselves ate these metals. Some even saw Spaniards and their horses as a single being, whose tail (as sword) could cut men in half or whose fiery breath (as musket) might kill them at a distance (Guillén 1974: 41, 79, 80–1, 101, 115). More tellingly, these accounts describe the Spaniards as 'sons of the sea' (*capacochas*),[20] who emerged from the Pacific and conquered very much as in an Andean ancestral narrative: 'Then the ships in which came the Marqués don Francisco Pizarro and the rest of the Spaniards entered Payta and it was said throughout these kingdoms that some bearded people had come by sea in some houses and that they had come out on land and settled a town in Tangarara, and shortly afterwards another piece of news arrived in the province of Yauyos, where this witness is a native and resides, of how those men who had come out of the sea had arrived at the inn and valley of Caxamarca and that there they had destroyed and captured Atahuallpa Inca, and at this all the natives of these kingdoms in general marvelled at how, being so few those men whom the sea had thrown out, they had done so much in catching and destroying such a great lord as was said Atahuallpa' (Guillén 1974: 78–9). These accounts do not call Spaniards *viracochas*, but still place them within the same ancestral frame, in which the sea, Cieza notwithstanding, was an ultimate source of origin, like Lake Titicaca. Evidently Andean people recalled the Spanish invasion using the ancestral narrative genre, in which horses, swords, and muskets instantiated the Spaniards' superhuman power as ancestral beings.

Spaniards' strategic displays of force during the conquest explain why so many Andean groups saw them as ancestors. Colonization and conquest established ancestral status within Andean culture. Only through these activities could ancestors create new political orders and patrimonies for their descendants. Narratives of colonization and displacement routinely described the concerted, extra-human acts of force by which ancestors took charge of localities and left their physical imprint on them. When the Spaniards decimated Andean armies with cavalry and sabres, they did not just intimidate or seize the initiative they needed to establish alliances and predominate within them. Their actions were culturally intelligible, and announced the coming of a different order. That order was not a new one, however. By calling the Spaniards Viracochas, Andean people equated them with the authors of the pre-Inca regime of decentralized regional polities created in the origin myth recounted above. As powerful denizens of a suppressed primordial era, Viracochas were dangerous. Their appearance marked an epochal cataclysm (*pachacuti*) that would reverse the relation between dominant and subordinate orders, which Andean moieties embodied.

Cieza further undermines his derivation of the Viracocha attribution from Inca elite interests by noting that two provincial Andean peoples also represented their ancestors as Spaniards. Natives thought that bearded white people like the Spaniards, who had come from afar and settled in the area long before the Incas, built the ruins of Viñaque near Huamanga (1553: 113). Similarly, after describing the ruins of Tiahuanaco, Cieza mentions that the natives believed that the people who emerged from the Island of Titicaca were white, bearded, and like those of Viñaque (1553: 125, 128–9). The sites in question were highly significant during the Middle Horizon (AD 400–800): Viñaque was probably the Huari empire's maximal origin point and politico-ritual centre, as was Titicaca under Tiahuanaco. The ancestors who founded these sites were primordial in very much the same way as Viracochas were. Cieza describes the bearded ancestors of Titicaca in a separate section of his chronicle from the one that discusses Viracocha. Yet the two were probably the same, since Cieza's version of the Viracocha origin myth in Titicaca describes him as a 'white man of large body' (1553: 150–1).[21] When Andean people portrayed their ancestors as white and bearded, they reiterated the same connection that they made when they identified Spaniards as Viracochas. Coming from an observer as sober and critical as Cieza, this information is particularly valuable. It suggests that Andean people reconceptualized their ancestors as Spaniards whether or not they used the word *viracocha* to do so. Thus, evidence independent of this extensively colonized and therefore problematic title confirms that Andean people identified Spaniards as ancestors. The attribution ran deeper than a name.

What did representing Spaniards as primordial ancestors mean in

these provincial contexts? The answer must be that as primordial ancestors, not subsequent conquerors, the Spaniards' role was to restore the
Andes to its 'original' order, before Inca imperialism transformed it.
Recall that in Betanzos' narrative, Viracocha and his assistants created
various Andean peoples and assigned them their respective territories,
calling their ancestors from the earth in those places. In effect, the
Viracocha myth authorized a decentralized world of regional polities. It
was exactly to this sort of world that Andean *curacas* wished to return,
particularly those who allied with the Spaniards during the conquest.
As the leading agents of this transformation, Spaniards qualified as
Viracochas. Their small numbers and bravado thus became the stuff of
Andean and not just Spanish legend, although each version served a
significantly different political project.

From a provincial Andean perspective, the Viracocha attribution was
an ideal charter for post-invasion indirect rule. It gave the Spaniards
an extraordinary ancestral role, but assigned them to restore Andean
regional political autonomy, then leave (cf. Vega 1978: 11; Espinoza
1971: 48). Provincial peoples could ally with them to overthrow the
Incas but still insist that the Spaniards were an earlier order of humanity proper to the 'lower' moiety position, whereas provincial Andean
people were to be the Incas' successors in the 'upper' position. Eventually, Spaniards departed from the script when they did not disappear
over the sea to the north again after putting the Andean world back in
order. Rather, they lingered, and ultimately re-established an imperial
state of the sort that provincial Andean rulers rejected. When this
became clear (as we will see in the next chapter), an important reckon-
ing took place. During the civil war period and to the end of the 1550s,
however, the Viracocha scenario was still credible. Fittingly, it became
established, came to Spaniards' attention, and entered the historical
record during those years.

If correct, this analysis implies that provincial peoples (particularly
curacas) had reasons to identify Spaniards as Viracochas that were distinct from those of Inca elites seeking reconciliation with Spanish colonialism. Thus, Betanzos has Ciquinchara denounce the Viracocha attribution as a cowardly illusion of provincial peoples. Their involvement complicates but solidifies the Andean basis of this phenomenon
and squares with what we know about the political dynamics of the
conquest. Once we allow that provincial peoples participated in (and
probably inaugurated) this identification, we no longer need explain
how Spaniards convinced them of it, and so avoid Pease's dilemma. We

can also identify his mistaken assumption that when some Incas denied that the Spaniards were returning *viracochas*, they were arguing with the Spaniards themselves. Rather, we can see that the dispute was primarily with their provincial ex-subjects, who had the most to gain by propagating this view. The most important cleavage in this situation was not that between Andean people (as a unified bloc) and Spaniards, since the conquest could never have happened if this were so. Modern nationalist sensibilities may find it inconceivable, but the principal antagonisms were among Andean people themselves. The most important point, however, is that provincial versions of the Viracocha attribution denied the Spanish invasion the status of a conquest. Andean people, not the Spaniards, were to be the Incas' political heirs. We will return to this understanding below in Guaman Poma's remarkable treatise.

The next chronicler to deploy the Viracocha attribution extensively was Titu Cusi Yupanqui, son of Manco Inca, who composed a historical account during his negotiated surrender and conversion in 1570. Even more clearly than the Quipucamayocs' document, this one aimed to ease its author's passage into colonial society. Its stated objective was to solicit sinecures from the Spanish Crown, and it ended by granting power of attorney to Lope Garcia de Castro, outgoing governor of Peru, to pursue Titu Cusi's interests in Spain (1570: 4, 110–12). Thus, Titu Cusi tailored his account of the Spanish conquest and Inca resistance to those ends. He begins with Huayna Capac picking Manco Inca, not Huascar, as his successor (1570: 7–8). No other source makes this dubious claim, which conveniently established Manco's heirs, principally Titu Cusi himself, as the sole legitimate Inca descent line. With this matter summarily resolved, Titu Cusi begins an elaborate defence of Manco's conduct, in which the Viracocha attribution plays a prominent role. Briefly, coastal Indians reported to Manco that the Spaniards were Viracochas (1570: 8, 13–4, 77) and his initial encounters with them confirmed that interpretation (1570: 18, 26–7). Once they had triumphed over their joint enemy, however, the Devil caused his Spanish guests to lust after gold and one of Manco's wives, so they twice imprisoned him to extort the objects of their greed (1570: 29–31). Such atrocious ingratitude led Manco to question whether they were Viracocha's emissaries after all, and to suggest that they were worse than devils (*supaicuna*). Titu Cusi reproduces these musings in a series of theatrical monologues and dialogues that drive home the poignance of his betrayed trust in the Spaniards (1570: 30–2, 37–8, 45–6, 52–3, 61, 80). Manco becomes a paragon of crypto-Christian charity in contrast to the corrupt Spaniards, but Titu

Cusi lets him realize that God ordained their triumph (1570: 67, 69, 72). A saintly figure, Manco was forced to become the adversary of those he so generously accepted, repeatedly proving their moral superior, above all in his cowardly assassination by the band of Almagristas he sheltered. Titu Cusi did not deny that Manco led a nearly successful uprising against the Spaniards, but he tried to ennoble and redeem his father's conduct by inflecting it with Christian tragedy. Central to this dynamic was Manco's initial acceptance of the Spaniards as Viracochas, which, like Huayna Capac's prophecy in the Quipucamayocs' account, amounts to a claim of voluntary surrender. Only when the Spaniards stripped his capitulation of any dignity did he rebel, and even then against his will. With this largely believable tale, Titu Cusi negotiated for his return to the colonial world as an *encomendero*.

Against this broad backdrop, several interesting details emerge. First, Titu Cusi depicts Manco's disillusionment with the Spaniards through the Viracochas-turned-to-devils phrasing that Betanzos used for Atahuallpa and Cieza used for the Huascar faction. Thus, three different chroniclers who were not likely to have read each other's work used exactly the same language to describe the disillusionment of three different Inca sovereigns with the Spaniards. We have already seen that this formula derives initially from the Christian colonization of the Andean terms *viracocha* and *supay*. These passages all use such newly colonized terms to contest the Spaniards' self-presentation as the emissaries of God. They suggest an Andean critique, but one within a language that is only formally indigenous, and already registers significant ideological transformation. Titu Cusi's account makes these points particularly clearly. He describes how the coastal Tallanas told his father of the Spaniards' arrival, and how they resembled Viracochas, whose name derived from their old name for the creator of all things, Tecsi Viracochan (1570: 8).

Although he remained in the jungle and beyond the colonial frontier when he gave this account, Titu Cusi had clearly already assimilated the early missionary equation of Viracocha and the Christian monotheistic creator God, which he deploys deftly in this and subsequent passages (1570: 38–9, 47, 87). During their encounter at the baths in Cajamarca, he has Pizarro's captains tell Atahuallpa that Viracocha had sent them to teach his people so that they might know Viracocha better (1570: 11). Given Titu Cusi's previous equation of Viracocha and the Christian God, this passage can only mean that the Spaniards announced the goal of religious conversion. This notion gathers force as

Spaniards repeatedly portray themselves Viracocha's emissaries (1570: 13, 17, 20, 30, 32, 37, 45, 49–50, 72, 77, 80). Again, this amounted to a mere declaration of missionary intent, which the Spaniards surely would have made. The only debatable point here is whether the Spaniards would have used Viracocha to refer to the Christian God at that early stage of their invasion. Titu Cusi's narrative suggests that they did and, by extension, that Spaniards or their translators invented the Viracocha attribution.

Provocative as this suggestion is, recall that Titu Cusi describes the events of 1532 in the highly colonized language of 1570. We cannot know if the Spaniards' interpreters translated the Christian God as Viracocha from the outset. Still, Titu Cusi's account usefully dramatizes this possibility. If interpreters did use Viracocha to designate the Christian God in 1532, then in declaring Spaniards' missionary purpose they would have initiated their masters' association with this Andean deity. Whether this alone sufficiently explains the Viracocha attribution's consolidation is, of course, another matter. As argued above, that went far deeper than a name, and drew deeply on both Andean aspirations and Spanish conduct. Here the Viracocha attribution's salience derived entirely from established Andean ancestral scripts, on which any nascent Christian providential appropriation was dependent. There can, in short, be no question of a self-realizing missionary discourse, particularly at this early stage. A semantic mutation was entirely possible, however, and even likely.

While ostensibly speaking his own language, Titu Cusi (like Betanzos' and Cieza's elite Inca informants) used this key colonized term to engage with Spanish understandings and make claims on them. He did so with skill and self-awareness, rigorously stage-managing even minor details. For example, he consistently uses Viracochan to refer to the idea of a supreme creator God in the providential Christian sense until he decides to accept conversion (1570: 98), even accusing his Huanca adversaries of taking their provincial deity for Viracochan (1570: 87) just as Spanish priests accused Andean people of idolatry. Once he accepts conversion (1570: 98), however, Dios definitively replaces Viracochan in his vocabulary. Thus, he maximizes both the providential reading of the Andean religious past and the opportunity to display himself as a sincere convert who could differentiate one religious tradition from another. Mimicry and Machiavellianism intertwine indistinguishably in this narrative. Titu Cusi's own hardline followers took his conversion and negotiations seriously enough that they poisoned him to death shortly after he dictated this account. Yet his Spanish detractors viewed his attempts to secure an *encomienda* as a ruse to postpone their attacks on his jungle realm. Whatever the case, Titu Cusi adeptly engaged the Spaniards in their own terms, and nowhere did he show this better than in his virtuoso deployment of the Viracocha attribution. Still, his opaque intentions and sorry fate show the stubborn presence outside this narrative of a rebellious Andean agenda, whose reality we cannot endlessly bracket or ignore.

Let us now turn to Sarmiento and Molina, the other chroniclers whom Pease (1995: 146) accuses of fostering the identification of Spaniards with Viracocha. In fact, they do no such thing. Molina (1574) records a version of the Viracocha creation narrative, but does not discuss how it might have influenced Andean perceptions of Spaniards. Sarmiento writes that as Viracocha was about to take his leave over the sea, he told people that he would send messengers to help and instruct them in the future, but impostors would also come claiming to be Viracocha(s). Taguacapa, one of his disobedient assistants, did exactly this, but people eventually dismissed him as a fraud (1572: 109–110). When Pizarro landed on the coast in 1532, local *curacas* sent word that Viracocha 'which means their god' had arrived, bringing with him many *viracochas* (1572: 271). Atahuallpa rejoiced to hear that Viracocha had returned during his reign, as years earlier during Pizarro's second voyage of discovery he had heard similar news, and reversed his journey to Cuzco to meet them (1572: 271–2). Once they arrived in Cajamarca, however, he saw that the Spaniards were not gods as previously reported and was ready to attack them (1572: 273). Sarmiento thus allows that coastal people and Atahuallpa momentarily took the Spaniards for *viracochas*, but that this was a mistake within their own tradition, from which Atahuallpa recovered in time to resist the Spaniards militarily and so become culpable. The contrast with Betanzos on this last point is precise, as one would expect from Toledo's official historian. Polo sceptically noted that while the Huascar faction may have hoped that the Spaniards were *viracochas*, the Atahuallpa faction simply called them 'bearded ones' (*zungazapa*) (1561: 154, cf. Trujillo 1571: 202, Titu Cusi 1570: 48, 62, 77). In summary, none of these early chroniclers affirmed that Spaniards were returning *viracochas*, and most doubted that Andean people held such an idea. Even Betanzos, who improbably attributed this view to Atahuallpa, did so not out of Spanish chauvinism but for the sake of his Inca in-laws. We must conclude that the earliest propagators of the Viracocha attribution were Andean, either the Spaniards' translators or their collaborators, but not the invaders themselves.

It is not until Acosta that a Spanish author actually uses the Viracocha attribution for anything resembling the purposes Pease proposes. He begins by recycling Cieza: the Huascar faction beseeched Viracocha to deliver them from Atahuallpa's tyrannies, saw the Spaniards as the answer to their prayers, and so called them Viracochas. Acosta then comments that the Huascar faction was essentially correct, since God did send the Spaniards to deliver them. To make salvation available to them, He ensured that the natives were divided by the war of succession and regarded the Spaniards highly (1590: 425). This passage presupposes the providentialist view that Viracocha was the Andean intuition of the one true God, and explains the Viracocha attribution as an outgrowth of the emissary relation between Spaniards and that God in the Peruvian context. Acosta differs from Titu Cusi here only in that he has Andean people spontaneously recognize this relationship. He overlooks that Spaniards also proclaimed it, and so gave Viracocha a specifically Christian inflection. By endorsing the notion that Viracocha sent the Spaniards, Acosta merely restated Spanish colonialism's basic ideological premise: that it was primarily a missionary enterprise. So eminent a theologian would never heretically proclaim Spaniards to be invincible gods in their own right, but could allow that Andean perceptions of them as such were providential. Acosta thus recruited the Viracocha attribution to a divine plan that included colonial rule, but in the tamest possible manner and as a late and insignificant afterthought to the theology of conquest.

Thus, Spaniards used and promoted their association with Viracocha once they noticed it but did not invent it unilaterally out of sheer colonial hubris, as Pease suggests. They were clearly puzzled by their identification with this figure. Andean people were the Viracocha attribution's primary authors but did not control it, as their attempts to reposition themselves under colonial rule show. Rather, its multiple meanings derived from the ill-defined and open-ended Spanish-Andean alliances that overthrew the Incas. Neither fully indigenous nor fully Spanish, the Viracocha attribution arose in an early colonial conjuncture that forced innovation on both parties.

Viracocha as Apostle

Thus far, we have seen that Spaniards understood Viracocha as a mono-theistic 'creator God' comparable to their own, whose existence the natives deduced through 'natural reason,' despite their isolation from the true faith. According to this view, of which Las Casas was the primary theorist, Viracocha was simply the Andean name for the Christian God, one that missionaries could borrow to get on with their work. An alternative Christian appropriation made *viracochas* into saints (Jiménez de la Espada 1965: 245). Many Spaniards transposed Andean understandings of Viracocha as a remote ancestor figure into a wandering apostle who arrived in the New World, either Saint Thomas or Saint Bartholomew. They took literally the idea that Christ's apostles had dispersed to preach the gospel to all of humanity, and traditions that gave Bartholomew and Thomas the most easterly assignments, those closest to the New World. By extending their mission into the Americas they modified Church tradition to maintain the spirit of its teachings, namely that the apostles made the true faith available to all. Speculation about an apostolic presence in the New World began as early as 1493 (MacCormack 1991: 312, Bouysse-Cassagne 1997: 159–60) is implicit in certain 'primitive chronicles' of the conquest (Estete nd.: 281, Trujillo 1571: 197), and was commonplace by Betanzos and Cieza's time. Betanzos described Viracocha as a priest figure carrying a breviary and held that Andean mummy worshippers understood the resurrection of the flesh, which someone must have taught them in the past (1551: 14, 101). Cieza also discussed the possibility that Viracocha was a wandering apostle but concluded that Christianity arrived in the New World only with the Spaniards (1553: 151). Thus, the hypothesized pre-Columbian evangelization synthesized scriptural imperative, church tradition, and new geographical knowledge. Perceived similarities between Catholicism and indigenous religions thus derived from a failed earlier attempt to establish the church, whose true teachings degenerated into Andean idolatries.

Since even informed commentators such as Bouysse-Cassagne (1997: 160, 185) sometimes lump this theory with Las Casas' providentialism, a clarification is in order. Las Casas held that New World indigenous religions partially anticipated the true faith of Catholicism, and so were an important preparation for it. He explained this convergence by the independent application of human rationality and virtue to civic affairs, however, not the direct historical contact of a pre-Columbian evangelization (Pagden 1982, MacCormack 1991: ch. 5). Las Casas certainly knew of that thesis and discussed the evidence marshalled for it openly in his monumental *Apologética Historia Sumaria* (1561 VII: 882–3, VIII: 1574). Yet he did not endorse it and could not have done so without undercutting his entire argument. For Las Casas, New World civilizations deserved respect because they had made great intellectual and moral progress without access to the revealed faith. The *Apologética Historia Sumaria* ends by distinguishing barbarians who are merely ignorant of the true faith from those who have deliberately rejected it, and allows that war against the latter is just (1561 VIII: chs. 264–7). Clearly he would have had to renounce his defence of the Indians if they were previously evangelized but rejected the true faith. Despite his apparent open-mindedness about a pre-Columbian evangelization, then, Las Casas did not and could not advocate this view.

At stake was the Indians' official status as neophytes in the faith. If New World indigenous religions anticipated Catholicism but lacked the revealed truth, then they deserved the respect and leniency that Las Casas advocated. However, if they were an idolatrous reaction to or degeneration of the true faith, as the pre-Columbian evangelization thesis usually implied (contra Marzal 1985: 106–7), then Spaniards could treat these religions as incorrigible, like Judaism and Islam. This would potentially make Indians subject to the Inquisition, as powerful figures such as Viceroy Toledo were later to advocate. As Toledo's official historian, Sarmiento predictably accepted the interpretation of Viracocha as a white Catholic priest (1572: 108). Although his attack on the legitimacy of Inca institutions did not explicitly feature the notion that they had known Christianity and rejected it, Sarmiento cannot have deployed this insinuation unknowingly or without strategic purpose.

An Augustinian account of 1561 from Huamachuco had already used the pre-Columbian evangelization thesis for these 'Toledan' ends, however, well before the viceroy's arrival in Peru. It describes their discovery and attempted destruction of various local and regional deities, their shrines, material representations, cults, and traditions. The account therefore documents an early attempt to 'extirpate idolatry,' one that aimed to be exemplary as it appeared before the Council of the Indies. As a member of that council, Toledo may have read and absorbed its perspective before going to Peru, since it anticipates his subsequent actions.

The Augustinians began their inquiry much as had the providentialists, by asking the Indians of Huamachuco who was the creator of all things. The Indians replied that it was Ataguju, a sky deity (Agustinos 1561: 10). Ataguju sent a protégé named Huamansuri to live as a field labourer among the Guachemines, Huamachuco's original inhabitants. One day when the opportunity arose, he mated with one of their women, named Cataguan, for which they summarily killed him. Cataguan died shortly after laying two eggs, from which hatched the brothers Catequil and Piguerao. Catequil revived his mother's dead body, and she armed her sons with slings, with which they exterminated her people, the aboriginal Guachemines. Catequil reported his deeds to Ataguju, who bade him return to the peak of Guacat and dig open a hole, from which a new humanity emerged to populate the land and worship Catequil as their tutelary ancestor (Agustinos 1561: 17–8). As a remote ancestor, Ataguju resembles Viracocha. Their respective origin narratives share the themes of subterranean emergence, colonization, and ethnic displacement, as do later narratives we will discuss in chapter 5. Questions of genre did not interest the Augustinians, however.

At the Huamachuco origin narrative's conclusion, the Augustinians' commentary takes a surprising turn that I will not attempt to paraphrase:

> Thus your Lordship will see how undoubtedly in that land many years before there was memory of Christians, and the holy gospel was preached by the Indians, and it is well known that in Collao a stone statue was found in a famous place whose name I do not remember [Cacha], like an apostle with his tonsure and sandals of the sort worn here, and the Indians say that Viracocha wanted to make them Christians and they threw him out of the land; secondly the Indians say that because they killed the Guachemines and threw them out, now the Christians are their enemies and do them so much wrong and steal from them and take their women and estates; and because of this they are our [the Spaniards'] enemies, and because the Guachemines killed Huamansuri the Devil dislikes the Christians and is afraid of them and didn't want to receive any of the Christians' law, and there is no reason to doubt that the hate they have had for us [the Spaniards] is great. (Agustinos 1561: 18–19)

To understand this passage, we must identify its bizarre central premise: that the Guachemines of this origin myth were the Christian protagonists of the pre-Columbian evangelization hypothesis. This premise was clearly parasitic on an indigenous substratum of the narrative, however, not an omnipotent discourse that obliterated it. The Augustinians retained a recognizably Andean account of ancestral conquest and ethnic displacement,[22] onto which they grafted the notion of a pre-Columbian evangelization. Implicit in the host Andean genre is the notion that conquerors and conquered coexist in a moiety structure, in which the conquered retain a subterranean capacity to reemerge as dominant. Like the provincial articulations of Viracocha's return, this narrative recounts just such an epochal reversal (*pachacuti*) in which the conquered defeat their conquerors and restore a latent earlier order. Here, however, the Spaniards and provincial Andean people were no longer allies against the Incas but antagonists on opposite sides of the moiety divide. By reading this Andean construct through the interpretive grid of a pre-Columbian evangelization, the Augustinians converted the autochthonous Guachemines into the original Christians of Peru, whom followers of the Devil (in the guise of Ataguju) expelled. These, in turn, were the ancestors of the Indians whom the Augustinians found in Huamachuco, and the authors of their idolatries.

Let us linger on this view's rigorously anti-Lascasian implications. Native idolatries no longer represented an earnest striving towards knowledge of the one true God but a satanically inspired rejection of the revealed faith. Thus, any similarities between idolatry and Christianity derived from Satan's desire to be worshipped as God (Agustinos 1561: 10, 24, 26, 36), not the providential exercise of 'natural reason.' In the Augustinian account, the Devil actively and explicitly propagates the native idolatries they encountered (Agustinos 1561: 8, 13–17, 19, 22, 26–8, 30–1, 33, 37–9). Given these idolatries' fundamentally evil nature, extirpation becomes the only possible Christian response. These apostolic evangelists' martyrdom proved conclusively the futility of Las Casas' belief in converting the natives without force, by kindness and persuasion alone. Political and military control of the land were essential. Idolatry triumphed in Huamachuco because the Indians, as the Devil's followers, killed and dispossessed the Guachemines, its original Christian inhabitants. The natives explicitly recognized the Spanish conquest as a turning of the tables, in which Christians reclaimed their control over women and the land, and asserted the pre-eminence of their faith. If the natives did believe this, it suggests that they had already consolidated a view of Spaniards as primordial ancestors belonging to a separate and antagonistic moiety. By mapping the pre-Columbian evangelization onto local Andean traditions of conquest and ethnic displacement, the Augustinians presented Christians as the Andes' aboriginal inhabitants and Indians as invading interlopers. In effect, the Indians were the aggressors and the Christians were the victims. Since the Spanish conquest reversed this original act of illegitimate force, it was entirely justified, even in the eyes of Indians themselves.

The Augustinian account is an important reminder that not all elements in the early colonial Church accepted providentialism's missionary compromises and political accommodations. Much like the Jesuits who followed them, the Augustinians were latecomers to Peru who did not participate in the forging of those compromises or reap their benefits. Arguably their interests lay in criticizing the status quo, which they clearly did in this instance (Agustinos 1561: 9), and proposing an extirpating alternative through which they could consolidate parishes and influence. By attacking idolatry, they returned to a zero-sum view of the relation between religious traditions, one that shared much more with conquistador representation of Indians as Moors than it did with providentialism's inclusiveness and lack of firm boundaries. However, this and subsequent attempts to extirpate idolatry also learned from providentialism how to engage with the details of Andean religions, instead of simply imposing a Moorish script upon them. The Augustinian account adopts a largely ethnographic tone, recounting native beliefs and practices 'in their own terms' for long stretches, punctuated only by the demonic identification of Andean deities. This strategy reasserts boundaries between Andean and Catholic traditions far more subtly, naturalistically, and believably than its (literally) orientalizing predecessor. Extirpatory realism therefore became an important tool for colonial projects and interests that were incompatible with indirect rule and needed to contest the providential ideology that typically accompanied it. Once it emerged, providentialism no longer monopolized or even prevailed in the interpretation of indigenous religion.

The Augustinians did not continue their extirpating experiment in Huamachuco. Perhaps its protagonists were a minority within their own order, which would explain an alternative evangelical project in the region at the time (see Estenssoro 2003: 157), but broader conditions still inhibited such an enterprise. New outbreaks of civil war still seemed possible, and the colonial state was too weak to challenge indirect rule. While these conditions held, any concerted extirpation of idolatry was a destabilizing attack on the native institutions that made Andean society governable. Since many Spaniards shared the Augustinians' views on native idolatries, it is remarkable that they found so little institutional expression. Providentialism predominated not because of Las Casas' powerful moral conviction and persuasive efforts, but because it realistically expressed the balance of power on the ground. Those who denied the worthiness of native institutions still had no choice but to work through them. Thus, providentialist theories enjoyed a structural advantage over other alternatives, even if the Augustinian account better represented Spanish religious sensibilities.

The pre-Hispanic apostle hypothesis usually implied the degenerate or demonic character of Andean religions, but in Cabello Valboa's exceptionally charitable hands, it also ratified them as partly Catholic. Cabello Valboa believed that Viracocha's statue in Cacha represented a wandering apostle who tried to correct local people's vices. They would have killed him had not heavenly fire annihilated them (1586: 237). He also cited stories from the Marrañon, Quito, Brazil and the Yucatán that suggested similar encounters (1586: 237–8). Thus, he concluded, Saint Thomas's disciples must have evangelized the New World, as it was near the kingdom of Narsinga where he preached. Either they returned to their own land where people fully accepted the true faith or they were martyred (1586: 238–9, 242–3). Cabello Valboa entertained this chilling possibility and the view that the New World had become Satan's refuge after Christianity's rise in the Mediterranean (1586: 217–18, 236), but he still acknowledged that Andean people retained some good customs from their 'original' evangelization, such as fathers conserving their daughters' virginity by dedicating them to the idols, and charity to widows and the poor (1586: 259).

Despite endorsing the apostolic evangelization, Cabello Valboa also deployed providentialist arguments. Since he did not join Las Casas in linking providentialism to a defence of Indian sovereignty, Cabello Valboa did not necessarily contradict himself in so doing. Inca religion sometimes converged with Christianity, so that 'in the very errors of the progenitors their successors find a way to be right' (1586: 256). This statement almost endorses Lucifer's teachings as preparation for the true faith's arrival. More commonly, however, Cabello Valboa's providentialism took a Lascasian form. For example, he describes how Inca Yupanqui convened a theological congress in Cuzco's Temple of the Sun, which all the empire's priests attended to standardize and rationalize the land's great diversity of beliefs and cults. After long debate, they agreed that the Sun belonged at the head of the pantheon, since it regulated the seasonal and diurnal cycles. Lightning, the Earth (*Pacha Mama*), and then the stars should follow it in rank. As these conclusions emerged, Inca Yupanqui asked if there were not some power greater than the Sun, to which the assembled priests responded negatively. Inca Yupanqui then chastised them for their ignorance, arguing that if the Sun were the supreme creator it would not constantly be in movement like a mere labourer. Behind it must therefore lie a superior power, namely Ticci Viracocha Pachacamac, ostensibly the name Andean people gave to their emerging understanding of God as a universal, all-powerful, and celestial creator, prime mover and cause of causes (1586:

297, 307–10). Duviols shows that this was a standard Augustinian argument against idolatry, transplanted into an Inca's mouth as evidence of providential rationality (1977: 54–5). Andean people would not have engaged in such arguments, which do little more than presuppose the commitment to monotheism they were supposed to establish. But for Spaniards who emphatically did have that commitment, the argument was edifying, and portrayed Christianity as the telos of human reason. Thus, Cabello Valboa felt no need to distinguish providential arguments from those based on a pre-Columbian evangelization: both were about the progressive realization of grace in the world, and so were compatible.

For Cabello Valboa, Viracocha was a title of great excellence, one that derived from the Andean names of God, but applied to the Andean apostle, a wise Inca councillor, a powerful Inca ruler and finally to the Spaniards themselves. He considered it a great honour that the natives had extended this term to the Spaniards, and struggled to make its meaning clear to his compatriots (1586: 237, 283, 296–7). Cabello Valboa wove these various instantiations of Viracocha together in a utopian synthesis that linked the Andean past with various impulses towards Christianity and allowed the Inca state's best rulers and councillors to participate in the true faith's historical realization. Yet he also gave the Spaniards an exalted place. Although he does not say so explicitly, Spaniards' arrival and their designation by God's name suggests the completion of the evangelical project that the apostle initiated. Thus, Cabello Valboa used the Viracocha notion to dignify both parties to the colonial encounter, itself the culmination of a vast interlocking world history. His vision exceeded that of Las Casas in its generosity and inclusiveness. By giving Andean people a historical relation to Christianity and remaking their primordial ancestors into apostles, Cabello Valboa opened a historical space of recognition that was more concrete than a shared 'natural reason.' Beyond this abstract affinity, it posited a partnership realized over time: exactly the collaborationist *curacas'* project. In a society that officially denied its grounding in indirect rule, such a vision dared to celebrate the myriad forms of inter-ethnic coexistence already achieved.

Antagonistic articulations of the apostolic evangelization also continued. A Jesuit letter of 1599 (Polia 1999: 228–32) notes that the Indians of Omasuyo around Lake Titicaca believed that long ago, a bearded Saint Thomas and his twelve disciples visited their ancestors. They came via Paraguay, where they escaped from the hostile Indians of Brazil. On arrival in the town of Carabuco, the saint made a large wooden cross and placed it upright in the plaza. This act drove away a 'devil' that regularly appeared in human form to the local *curaca*. When its priests found that devil just outside town, it said it would no longer appear there because it resented them for worshipping the cross and sheltering those strangers. The priests replied that they did not worship the cross or listen to the strangers' doctrine or sustain them with food, but that they lived on what they collected by going from house to house. So the devil replied that they should tell their *curaca* to fell the cross and convene a day of drinking, which the devil would attend. The *curaca* tried to trick the disciples who guarded the cross into abandoning it so that he could fell and burn it. When they would not leave it, he had them killed. The demonic celebration then began, as people collected firewood and built a great blaze around the felled cross. On the following morning, however, the cross appeared intact, as before. At this, the devil fled again, ordering the people to destroy it with their adzes. No matter how hard they chopped, they could not dint it, so the devil ordered them to bury it. For many years it lay uncorrupted in the ground.

Meanwhile, the devil ordered the Indians to kill the saint. They found and took him to a steep slope where they bound him by three large rocks that formed the shape of a cross. Before killing him, they began a bout of drinking, during which the saint slipped his bonds, entered a reed bed in Lake Titicaca and disappeared across the lake using his mantle as a boat. This concords, the letter noted, with a fable the Indians tell about a holy figure named Tuncapa, whose crucifixion the devil ordered on those same three rocks. According to the letter, the bishop's investigations found clear signs of miracles in this place, most notably that in a land plagued by electrical storms, lightning never struck there. The cross eventually resurfaced when, during a bout of drinking, the *curacas* of the upper and lower moieties began to quarrel, the former charging the latter's ancestors with killing those Spaniards (the apostolic missionaries) and the latter charging the former's ancestors with being the witches who buried the cross. The parish priest overheard the accusations and began inquiries that reconstructed this story and led him to the cross. He took it from the ground and worshipped it, placed it in the church, and removed its two bronze nails as relics. However, an old Indian told him that according to tradition it had three bronze nails, so he went back and found the third, which he took to the bishop in the cathedral of Chuquisaca, miraculously curing a waiter of a terrible stomach ache along the way.

This Jesuit letter contrasts sharply with Cabello Valboa in its ideological use of the pre-Columbian evangelization. Even more graphically than the Augustinian report, the Jesuit letter establishes Andean culpability for the martyrdom and disappearance of these apostolic missionaries and anticipates the central role the Jesuits were shortly to play in the first extirpation of idolatry campaign (1609–21). The Cross of Carabuco narrative did more than just imply that Andean religious error was chosen and wilful, however. It cannot have failed to resonate allegorically with parish priests, working alone and undoubtedly feeling vulnerable among their Indian flock. They too might suffer the same fate. Yet the tale also held out the possibility of miracles, whose absence troubled the missionary effort and its primary theorist, the Jesuit José de Acosta (1576: 313–29). Like all recountings of the past, this one surreptitiously acquired relevance in its own present, here by heightening the evangelical stakes, both negative and positive.

3 Diseases and Separatism

Like Spaniards, Andean elites were ambivalent and internally divided over the post-conquest regime of indirect rule. The Vilcabamba rebels preferred war to accommodation with the Spaniards. Their stance was sometimes defensive, sometimes offensive, and sometimes (as with Titu Cusi) a negotiating position. By choosing confrontation, however, they differentiated themselves from those who acquiesced to the colonial order. Provincial *curacas* bent on maximizing their power as intermediary rulers had been the most enthusiastic collaborationists. Their gains were frequently significant but fell short of the real autonomy that many sought. As the chaos of conquest and civil war receded, they increasingly realized that Spaniards did not regard them as full partners in an alliance and that their intermediary status was a real limitation. By the early 1560s, both their ambitions and their misgivings crystallized during debates over the perpetual hereditary transmission of *encomiendas*, which many tried to block with a desperate, broadly organized but ultimately unsuccessful counterproposal that they pay tribute directly to the Crown as native lords (Spalding 1984: 149–56, Abercrombie 2002). Its failure quickly transformed into two interrelated initiatives this chapter will explore: a renewed politico-military alliance between highland *curacas* and Inca rebels in Vilcabamba, and a separatist ancestral revival movement called the Taqui Oncoy (Singing Sickness) or Ayra,[1] whose activist phase lasted from approximately 1564 to 1571.

A revisionist history that loosely parallels post-colonial criticism has recently questioned the reality of both these developments. Varón (1990) dismisses the evidence for an insurrectionary coalition between the Andean highlands and the Vilcabamba Incas, and Ramos (1992: 149, 155, 162), Urbano (1990: 268–9, 1997: 212) and Estenssoro (2003: 128–134) treat the Taqui Oncoy as a mirage of 'colonial discourse.' Since Varón and Ramos are unaware of important documents that bear on (and largely refute) their arguments, it is tempting to ignore them. Yet they have been influential enough that such an approach would be unwise. Rather than burden the text with polemics against them, however, I marshal the evidence they ignore and confine my criticisms to endnotes. The result vindicates the classic studies of Millones (1964), Wachtel (1971) and Stern (1982: ch. 3) but adds new sources and arguments to them. By placing the Taqui Oncoy's ancestral revivalism in the longer run of Andean ancestral politics, I hope to contextualize it properly and partly normalize it. Yet I also hope to highlight its true specificity as a separatist backlash against Christian colonization of the ancestral and related collaborationist strategies. The Taqui Oncoy reimposed boundaries between Catholicism and Andean ancestor worship that providentialism had blurred, and in this it resembled contemporaneous Counter-Reformation initiatives, as the revisionists rightly note. The question is whether it also had an independent reality as an attempt to re-establish Andean sovereignty separate from Spanish colonialism. I argue that it was such an attempt, one that failed but still had important (if ambiguous) long-term politico-religious consequences.

The Taqui Oncoy, 1564–65

On August 11, 1564, a parish priest named Guerrero wrote to the vicar of Parinacochas, Luis de Olvera, describing Indian idolatries in Vilcashuaman. People in Huancaraylla, Huamanquiquia, and Sacsamarca believed that when the star Choque Chinchay and the constellation Oncoy appeared, a cosmic reversal (*pachaticramunca, pacha cutimunca*) would occur and resurrect all the localized ancestral deities (*huacas*) and 'idols' destroyed since Pizarro's arrival. These *huacas* formed two groups, one comprising all those from the old Inca imperial divisions of Collasuyo and Antisuyo, under Titicaca's leadership, and the other of those from Chinchaysuyo and Condesuyo, under Pachacamac (see figure 3.1). The *huacas* took oracular possession of Indians, vowed to exterminate the Spaniards with sicknesses, and defeat their God. They also criticized Indians for adopting Christian names, saying that if they wanted their health and prosperity back, and to avoid dying of diseases the way the Spaniards would, they should renounce Christianity and refuse to enter churches or worship crosses. Pizarro killed Atahuallpa and took the land, they said, because God had defeated the *huacas*, but

Figure 3.1 Geography of the Taqui Oncoy

now they had revived to fight and would win, creating a new epoch (Yaranga 1978: 167–8).

Guerrero noted that these Indians painted their faces with *paria* and *llacsa* and assembled on Mount Tinca, which they addressed as 'father *guamani*' (an ancestral title). There some shook and went into oracular trance, during which they received worship, libations, offerings, and sacrifices for the *huaca* that possessed them. At night, the Indians did *taqui ongo* (singing sickness) ceremonies and sang in a circular group. They also preached against the Christian God, his religion, and the Spaniards. The sect's preachers went about in threes, two men and a woman. People called the men '*catun colla cocha*' and '*camac pacha*' which identified them with Titicaca and Pachacamac respectively, the movement's two principal *huacas*. They called the woman '*guamani tinca*' (ancestor tinca) or '*guamani carguaras*[o]' (ancestor carguaraso), which equated her with the local and regional mountain *huacas*. Oracular possession underwrote these identifications. Guerrero observed that Huancaraylla's four main *curacas* and their twelve wives had retreated to their 'main *guamanis* and *pacarinas*' leaving deputies to run their respective *ayllus*, all of which rebelliously participated in this 'idolatry' (Yaranga 1978: 168).

In reporting these developments to Olvera, Guerrero did not follow normal procedure, since his own parish lay outside Olvera's jurisdiction. However, by 1562 Olvera was an established extirpator of idolatries in the area (Guibovich 1991: 220), so Guerrero must have thought he would take such a report seriously. Whether or not this letter was the reason, Olvera investigated and confirmed that such a movement was afoot in the province of Parinacochas during 1564. He denounced it to the High Court (Real Audiencia) and archbishop of Lima, the bishop of Charcas, and the administrator of the bishopric of Cuzco, among others (Millones 1990: 178, Molina 1574: 132). Olvera's warnings represented these idolatries as different and more dangerous than those he had previously pursued, ones that required immediate action from the highest authorities, who apparently ignored him until weapons entered the picture.

By late 1564 or early 1565, Spaniards began to suspect that Indians were preparing for armed rebellion. In a letter of March 6, 1565, Governor Castro described how *encomenderos* of the Jauja Valley had discovered a cache of three thousand pikes. It stung him that this should occur in the territory of the Huancas, who had previously been such staunch Spanish allies (Levillier 1921–6 III: 59–60). Further investigations suggested that the suspected uprising extended from Jauja to Huánuco, Huamanga, and Cañete, and one report added that it would be coordinated with strikes from the Inca rebels in Vilcabamba. Inca involvement was only too believable since they had become more bellicose in recent years. After Manco's successor, Sayre Topa, left Vilcabamba to take an *encomienda* in 1557, only to die by poisoning in 1559 (Murúa 1613: 266–8), his successor, Titu Cusi,[2] stepped up raids and guerrilla activities against the Spaniards. Castro continued to receive reports and discerned plans for a concerted uprising from Charcas to Quito. He then warned the realm's various *cabildos* (town councils): one surviving example is his letter of March 21, 1565, to the Cabildo del Cuzco (Lohman Villena 1941: 6–7). In a letter of April 30, Castro reported to the

Council of the Indies that further investigations were pending. He also mentioned writing to Titu Cusi in Vilcabamba, admonishing him to convert, lay down arms, and leave the jungle (Levillier 1921–6 III: 80–2). On September 23, 1565, he wrote to the Council of the Indies that a local *encomendero* had confirmed the Jauja uprising's links to Vilcabamba (Levillier 1921–6 III: 99).

Among the surviving warnings about this uprising is Gaspar de Sotelo's letter of March 24, 1565, which describes a conspiracy of Titu Cusi and the Indians of Huamanga, Huánuco and Chachapoyas to attack Cuzco after the harvest. He observed that natives in the intervening territory of Aymaraes had accumulated arms, presumably to join this planned rebellion (Lohmann Villena 1941: 5–6). Unlike similar contemporary reports, however, Sotelo announced a religious dimension to the conspiracy, noting the arrival of 'those of Parinacochas because the Cacique of Villagran who is named don Juan Chancabilca sent a son of his whom I know dressed in scarlet like a Spaniard to this land [Jauja] to preach the sect. They captured him in Huánuco and he said everything that I write. Through him, I learned about this wickedness because what was said in this city about the resurrection of Pachacamac began in Parinacochas, and they made great sacrifices and offered much livestock to the Devil of Pachacamac' (Lohman Villena 1941: 3, Mogrovejo 1987: 18). Sotelo's references to Pachacamac's resurrection and the 'sect' with an epicentre in Parinacochas clearly reiterate Guerrero's earlier report, and directly link what would become known as the Taqui Oncoy to the planned insurrection of 1565.[3] Seemingly, extensive logistical preparations for an uprising were in place, and the Taqui Oncoy was their ideological counterpart.

Vilcabamba

Sotelo's letter had greater impact than Guerrero's and Olvera's earlier reports. He was a relative of Viceroy Núñez Vela, a veteran of the 1547 campaign against Gonzalo Pizarro, and an *encomendero* (Murúa 1613: 287), so his word was influential. Since his *encomienda* bordered on the jungle and had lost Indians to Vilcabamba,[4] an Inca offensive was his main concern. Predictably, both he and his fellow colonists also focused on the military threat as the most immediate danger, and relegated the uprising's religious dimension to the background. When the Cabildo del Cuzco considered Sotelo's letter on April 16, it sent him to Titu Cusi in Vilcabamba to announce that they had discovered his plans and threaten him with war (Lohmann Villena 1941: 8–9). They did not even discuss extirpating the idolatries that accompanied the apprehended insurrection. Thus, Guillén's claim (1994: 137–9) that the Taqui Oncoy's extirpation began in 1565 is questionable. Only the insurrection's military dimension mattered to the Spaniards at this stage. It was not until 1569 that its religious component resurfaced as a matter of concern. Although both were aspects of a single Inca initiative, the military preparations commanded immediate attention in a way that their religious counterpart did not. Thus, Sotelo's letter was the only source that mentions the Taqui Oncoy, whereas several describe localized preparations for armed rebellion.

For example, Matienzo recounts how in early 1565 word reached Cuzco that the Inca had planned with *curacas* throughout the highlands and the indomitable Chiriguanaes and Diaguitas to rebel and kill the Spaniards (1567: 295). Seizing the initiative, Matienzo wrote to Governor Castro, offering to negotiate Titu Cusi's surrender in return for amnesty. When Castro accepted, Matienzo sent Diego Rodríguez de Figueroa as an envoy to Titu Cusi with presents and two letters proposing terms of peace. Sotelo had preceded him, however, and disarmed the first rebel messengers sent to meet him, which angered Titu Cusi. Rodríguez de Figueroa waited over a month inside rebel territory to gain a tense audience with the Inca. Titu Cusi told him that he wanted to kill the Spaniards and let the jungle Indians cannibalize them, and that he could command all the highland Indians to rebel. As the Inca spoke, various nobles threatened Rodríguez de Figueroa with arms (Pietschman 1910: 98). Nonetheless, Titu Cusi's official response to Matienzo in a letter of May 30, 1565, was to accept enthusiastically Matienzo's proposals for negotiation. Even if the Inca wished to unleash the planned rebellion, he must have realized that its discovery greatly diminished the chances of success, and decided to buy time by negotiating. In his letter to Matienzo, Titu Cusi accepted the coming of missionaries, complained about Sotelo, and agreed to negotiate, provided that he not be slandered, as Cuenca, the outgoing *corregidor* (chief magistrate) of Cuzco, had done, calling him a 'drunken dog assaulter' (Matienzo 1567: 296–8). Matienzo was in Cuzco to inspect Cuenca's accounts, a notorious opportunity for indictment in the colonial administrative system, so Titu Cusi probably saw him as a potential ally and negotiated with him to ward off attack.

As Matienzo prepared to negotiate personally with Titu Casi, prominent citizens of Cuzco tried to dissuade him, noting that Sotelo had just received provisions from Governor Castro to attack Vilcabamba, and that he was risking his life to enter the Inca stronghold (Matienzo 1567: 298–9). To diffuse this situation, Castro had to cancel Sotelo's authorization to attack (Nowack 2004: 149–50), which allowed Matienzo to enter Vilcabamba, and met with Titu Cusi at Chuquichaca bridge on June 18, 1565. The Inca launched into a long account of his exile and the tribulations that he and his father had suffered at Spanish hands. He then gave Matienzo a written version of this account and a document outlining his conditions for surrender, in which he agreed to accept Christianity and cancel the insurrection he had planned with highland *curacas* (Matienzo 1567: 302). Not only did Titu Cusi acknowledge this conspiracy, but he also thanked Matienzo for intervening to prevent the torture of Indians and *curacas* suspected of complicity in it, and to dissuade the Spaniards from making war against him. For his part, Matienzo marvelled at how much the Inca knew about the disposition of different Spanish factions towards him (1567: 303). They eventually negotiated a peace agreement that entailed the entry of missionaries and a *corregidor* into Vilcabamba, and amnesty for the Inca, his secretary, and military captains. Titu Cusi would have an *encomienda* in Vilcabamba that included all the Indians who had joined him from elsewhere in the realm. He was also to retain the towns and fields he had established there. His son was to marry doña Beatriz Sayre Topa, daughter of Sayre Topa, Titu Cusi's older brother and predecessor as sovereign, who had left Vilcabamba in 1557. Their heirs were to enjoy in perpetuity her *encomienda* in the Yucay Valley, and legal recognition as Incas. Titu Cusi's younger brother Tupac Amaru was to have an annual pension of 1000 pesos. To assume these rights, both the Inca and his son were to reside in Cuzco and receive lands and houses there. Initially only one would leave Vilcabamba, however, and Cuzco's cabildo was not to attack them when they did (Matienzo 1567: 304–7).

These negotiations did not end reports of conspiracies in the highlands, however. On December 5, 1565, a textile factory (*obraje*) owner from Jauja wrote Castro describing plans for an armed uprising from Chile to Quito on the Thursday of Holy Week 1566, when Spaniards would be in penitential processions throughout the realm, and Indians would set upon them. A native carpenter reported a cache of thirty thousand pikes and battleaxes, ten thousand bows and arrows, and other weapons in the Jauja Valley alone, and that every jurisdiction had similar accumulations of weaponry (Odriozola 1872: 3–9). Unlike the year before, however, this appears to have been an isolated report, and

Castro did not mention it to the Council of the Indies. Meanwhile, on August 24, 1566, both parties signed the Treaty of Acobamba, which formalized the accord between Matienzo and Titu Cusi. Ratifications continued until July 9, 1567, when Diego Rodríguez de Figueroa became absentee *corregidor* of Vilcabamba. The Augustinian missionary Marcos García arrived in mid-1568, and a year later Diego de Ortiz, another Augustinian, joined him. Titu Cusi officially converted to Christianity but remained the high priest of the Sun, and apparently did not regard these affiliations as contradictory. Some of his subjects also converted, but many more refused baptism, rejecting Christianity as did *taquiongos* (followers of the Taqui Oncoy movement) in the colonized highlands.

Titu Cusi patronized Inca and Catholic cults, and freely practised both. The Augustinians lectured him on the impropriety of his continuing polygyny, festive drinking, and idolatry. Their relations with the sovereign were hardly cordial, but he stopped short of expelling them. On the native priests' insistence, the Inca kept the missionaries away from the town of Vilcabamba (Calancha 1638: 70–1). In one dramatic exception to this policy, however, Titu Cusi summoned them there at the end of January 1570 to dictate his account to García, but still isolated them from the town's religious spectacles (Murúa 1613: 269–70). This was an interesting decision. By dictating his narrative of persecution and conversion in the context that most fully displayed his ongoing political and ritual autonomy, the Inca conveyed that he chose collaboration with the Spaniards but still had other options. The missionaries may have taken this point, but drew their own conclusions. On their release from Vilcabamba, they returned to one of their parishes and exhorted the natives there to destroy the oracular shrine of Paranti. This enraged Titu Cusi's generals, who would have killed the missionaries if the Inca and other Christian elements in Vilcabamba had not intervened (Calancha 1638: 71–3, Murúa 1613: 270). Thus, the relationship between Christianity and Andean religion was as confrontational in Inca-controlled territory as it was in the colony. Despite Titu Cusi's evident pluralist commitments, the broader colonial context made religious affiliation into a flashpoint.

There is tantalizing evidence that Titu Cusi's religious open-mindedness alienated his more militant generals and subjects, causing conflict within Vilcabamba itself. Both Molina (1574: 129, 132) and Cristóbal de Albornoz (Duviols 1984: 215–7) state that the wandering preachers who promoted the Taqui Oncoy in the highlands came from Vilcabamba, and told adepts that their duty was to restore Inca rule. According to Albornoz, they particularly extolled the valour of Tupac Amaru, Titu Cusi's successor (Duviols 1984: 215–6). These reports are significant. Tupac Amaru was notoriously less willing to compromise with the Spaniards than Titu Cusi (Guillén 1994: 148). If the movement's preachers specifically backed him while his brother was still alive, then the Taqui Oncoy articulated not only a hard line against Spanish colonialism but also fraternal tensions within the Vilcabamba resistance. Once the Spaniards discovered plans for a coordinated uprising in 1565 and Titu Cusi began negotiations that included conversion, the Taqui Oncoy must have become more significant in Vilcabamba's internal politics. By cleaving hard to the separatist message, it supported the abandoned militant faction who wanted to stay the insurrectionary course. Tupac Amaru's acolytes who wandered the highlands preaching the Taqui Oncoy from 1565 onwards showed Titu Cusi that in their own way they, too, could negotiate with the outside world.

Meanwhile, progress was slow in enacting the Treaty of Acobamba's remaining provisions, which required the Crown's approval. Securing a papal dispensation for the marriage of Titu Cusi's son and doña Beatriz Clara Coya also took years. Many Spaniards saw Titu Cusi's reluctance to leave Vilcabamba as a sign of bad faith, but he was still vulnerable to attack at their hands until the treaty's final ratification in Spain. Guillén suggests that the longer the missionaries remained in Vilcabamba and the more information about the Inca's very limited military capabilities they gleaned, the less anxious Spanish authorities became to grant what they had conceded when they thought he was stronger (1994: 143). Neither party could finalize the treaty in the years immediately following its negotiation, so the process lost momentum without dying.

This holding pattern broke with Titu Cusi's assassination, probably in April 1571 (Guillén 1994: 145–6). The sovereign took ill after worshipping his mummified father, with the attendant feasting and drinking. That night he haemorrhaged from the mouth and nose, and his tongue began to swell. The following day he died. His followers thought he was poisoned with *solimán* (probably the sap of an eponymous tree) and accused his *mestizo* secretary Martín Pando immediately. They also captured Diego Ortiz, tied him to a cross, and severely beat him. Since he preached the resurrection of the dead, they demanded that he revive the sovereign by saying a mass over his body. When this failed, they perforated his cheek and jaw, passed a rope through, and led him to the new sovereign, Tupac Amaru, who ordered his execution. Pando apparently joined in Ortiz' persecution and various idolatries, but even this did not prevent Tupac Amaru's most militant backers from killing him (Calancha 1638: 73–6, Murúa 1613: 272–6, 291–2, Titu Cusi 1570: 133–7). Thereafter, the new Inca closed Vilcabamba's borders and destroyed its churches. Unaware of these developments, Viceroy Toledo sent an emissary to Vilcabamba on July 20, 1571, to announce royal approval of the Treaty of Acobamba and papal dispensation for the marriage of Titu Cusi's son and doña Beatriz Clara Coya. The rebels denied him entry, and he returned to Cuzco with that news in October (Guillén 1994: 149). Toledo then wrote a threatening letter to Titu Cusi, whom he still thought to be the sovereign, and sent Atilano de Anaya to deliver it at the beginning of Lent in 1572. When Anaya's party crossed the Chuquichaca without authorization, Inca sentinels killed all but a few Indians and Anaya's slave (Murúa 1613: 282–3). News of these events outraged Toledo, who organized a force to invade Vilcabamba, appointing Gaspar de Sotelo second in command (Murúa 1613: 287). They took Vilcabamba in August of 1572, captured Tupac Amaru, and executed him in Cuzco on September 23, 1572 (Guillén 1994: 302–3). Thus ended the last vestige of Inca sovereignty in Vilcabamba.

Titu Cusi's assassination was probably an inside job for which the Spaniards were scapegoats. A hard-line faction in Vilcabamba opposed Titu Cusi's reconciliation strategy after the thwarted uprising of 1565. It included the military captains Curi Paucar, Colla Topa, and Paucar Unya, who figured in Ortiz' and Anaya's deaths: all wanted to fight to the end (Murúa 1613: 291–2). They were already promoting Tupac Amaru through the Taqui Oncoy. As the Treaty of Acobamba's implementation became imminent, their resolve to eliminate Titu Cusi must have hardened. Poisoning was a classic manoeuvre in the intrigue that surrounded Andean high political offices. The Spanish style in such matters was typically more direct. Moreover, Vilcabamba's Spaniards had no reason to want Titu Cusi's death. Ortiz needed his protection, and his missionary activities could only benefit from Vilcabamba's coming incorporation into the colony. He lacked not only a motive to kill Titu Cusi but also the opportunity, as he was not with the Inca at the time of his poisoning. Perhaps Martin Pando had the chance to poison Titu Cusi, but surely he realized that if the Tupac Amaru faction came to power, they would blame him for helping negotiations with the Spaniards. His position in Vilcabamba was secure only while Titu Cusi lived. When the Tupac Amaru faction blamed these persons for the Inca's death, they conveniently deflected attention from their own motives and made a pretext for purifying Vilcabamba of all collaborationist elements, which they already desired. Probably they were Titu Cusi's assassins, and a clash of strategic orientations led to this final act in the long and venerable tradition of Inca fratricide.

The Rediscovery of 1569

As these events in Vilcabamba show, the Taqui Oncoy's context changed rapidly. Initially it was the ideological vehicle of an insurrectionary coalition. Once the Spaniards detected that conspiracy, Titu Cusi abruptly demobilized and began negotiating with them, leaving the Taqui Oncoy as a rallying cry for Tupac Amaru's militants. As a set of anti-Spanish beliefs and ritual practices, the Taqui Oncoy appears to have changed little during the 1560s. Yet it ceased to articulate a widespread political movement when Titu Cusi defected from the military cause. It then devolved into a narrower sectarian ideology of Vilcabamba hard-liners and their dwindling highland followers. Thus, when Cristóbal de Albornoz rediscovered the movement in 1569 as a religious 'apostasy,' it no longer defined the same political project it had in 1564.

Writing in 1584, Albornoz implied that he went to Huamanga in 1569 specifically to deal with the Taqui Oncoy (Duviols 1984: 215), which was indeed to become the principal focus of his activities there into 1571. Thanks to Guibovich's careful work, we now know otherwise. In October 1568, the Cabildo Eclesiástico of Cuzco instructed Albornoz to leave Arequipa, where he had been conducting ecclesiastical inspections, for Huamanga, where it gave him a similar assignment with specific instructions to enforce the payment of tithes (Guibovich 1991: 209). This concords with Albornoz' own account of merits and services from 1570, which states that his first assignment in Huamanga was to review the accounts of the vicar and other ecclesiastical officials (Millones 1990: 63). By December 1568, Albornoz had assumed these duties (Millones 1990: 46). On January 27, 1569, Albornoz gave power of attorney to an associate in Cuzco who initiated a request for his promotion (Millones 1990: 45). That request did not mention the Taqui Oncoy. Even at this late date, then, the Taqui Oncoy had yet to gain his attention.

Only when Albornoz finished his investigation into tithes and began an ecclesiastical inspection of the countryside did his mandate change to include the Taqui Oncoy (Millones 1990: 129). The available documentation suggests at least two ways this change could have occurred. One is that the Cabildo Eclesiástico del Cuzco finally decided to act on the information Olvera and Sotelo had previously provided, and ordered Albornoz to investigate the Taqui Oncoy. Testimony that Albornoz received orders to capture the movement's main agitators and send them to Cuzco (Millones 1990: 94, 103, 109, 112, 118, 120–1, 123–4, 126, 130) is consistent with this possibility. Alternatively, Albornoz may have reported on the movement from Huamanga's hinterlands to the cabildo in Cuzco, which finally took it seriously and authorized him to act against it. The most detailed testimony suggests this scenario. While in Laramati, Albornoz met Pedro Barriga Corro, a parish priest who reported that when he discovered a *huaca*, a man named Juan Chono fled from him. They captured Chono, and shortly afterwards Albornoz got instructions from the Cabildo Eclesiástico of Cuzco to attack the Taqui Oncoy (Millones 1990: 147). Elsewhere, Molina mentions that a Juan Chocne was one of the movement's principal 'dogmatizers' and that when sent to Cuzco, he subsequently recanted his teachings (Millones 1990: 181, 225). If Chono and Chocne were the same person, as previous investigators have assumed, the most likely sequence of events was the following: Albornoz and Barriga Corro captured Chono, interrogated him, and reported to Cuzco once they realized the gravity of his activities. The Cabildo Eclesiástico told them to send Chono and others to Cuzco, where Molina further interrogated them and persuaded them to abjure their preachings publicly. This spotlighted the apostasy, so the Cabildo Eclesiástico instructed Albornoz to extirpate it, which he did for the rest of 1569, most of 1570, and part of 1571.

Although Cristóbal de Albornoz repeatedly claimed to have 'discovered' the Taqui Oncoy in 1569, Guerrero, Olvera, and Sotelo had already detected it four to five years earlier. The more spectacular news of Titu Cusi's planned uprising upstaged their reports, however. By 1569, the situation had changed. Negotiations with Titu Cusi had successfully concluded, and only their ratification in Spain seemed to delay a peaceful end to the Vilcabamba resistance. In this context, renewed reports of militantly anti-Spanish idolatries in the highlands could shock and unsettle optimistic assumptions. News of the Taqui Oncoy can only have encouraged those elements of Cuzco's Spanish elite who had favoured a military solution to the Vilcabamba problem in 1565 and rallied around Sotelo before Matienzo gained the upper hand. These were the same people who doubted that Titu Cusi meant to honour the Treaty of Acobamba, and accused him of deliberately delaying his exit from the jungle stronghold. For them, Albornoz' revelations were indeed a 'discovery' worth proclaiming, although those associated with Sotelo and Olvera obviously knew of the movement for some time. Their strategic advantage lay in emphasizing its novelty and highlighting its anti-Spanish content as breaches of good faith and the Treaty of Acobamba itself. This, I suggest, was the agenda that underlay the reception of Albornoz' report as a 'discovery' in Cuzco. Whether or not Albornoz had his own careerist motives for making this fraudulent claim, we must still explain why so many others supported him. Its utility for the pro-war faction in Cuzco provides such an explanation. Even Olvera and Molina, who politely refuted Albornoz' claim of 'discovery' (Millones 1990: 178, 226), had to acknowledge that he was the first to take effective action against it. By being the first to draw attention to the movement successfully and mobilize a broad cross-section of Spanish public opinion against it, Albornoz valorized his claim socially. Nonetheless, he did not portray the Taqui Oncoy as something that arose only as he came to Huamanga. On the contrary, his account of merits and services from 1570 states that it was already ten years old (Millones 1990: 61), and so allows for earlier reports. Perhaps more than Olvera and Sotelo before him, he knew that his discovery of the movement did not mark its beginning.

A factional struggle in Cuzco clearly existed between those Spaniards who supported a negotiated peace with Titu Cusi and those who advocated military action against him. Several of Albornoz' character witnesses fell into the latter camp. For example, Cristóbal Ximénez, who testified for Albornoz in 1577 and 1584 (Millones 1990: 190–3, 219–221), lost his parish in Xaquixaguana when Titu Cusi wrote to Castro complaining of public statements Ximénez made against him, which presumably threatened the peace process. Castro relayed those complaints to the Cabildo Eclesiástico del Cuzco, which then removed Ximénez, alleging that he had failed to pay the Indians in his parish when they worked for him (Lissón y Cháves 1943–47, II: 489). During the long delay between the Treaty of Acobamba's negotiation and its ratification, Olvera was alert for signs of Indian insurrection. In 1570, he describes disguising himself to monitor an Indian penitential procession during Holy Week for drunkenness and superstition. He was alarmed to discover that many went armed but overzealously detained another disguised figure who turned out to be the diocese judge (*provisor*), who complained against him (Lissón y Cháves 1943–47 II: 486–7). In resurrecting the spectre of an Easter rebellion from 1566, Olvera portrayed the Inca ruler's plans as unchanged. For those who shared Ximenez' and Olvera's scepticism about the Inca's true intentions, Albornoz' revelations were timely and worth publicizing. This was the structure of the conjuncture in which Albornoz made his second-hand but politically effective discovery.

Several documents describe the substance of Albornoz' discovery, including his reports of merits and services from 1570, 1577, and 1584 (Millones 1990), his general report on Indian idolatries from 1584 (Duviols 1984), and Cristóbal de Molina's account (1574). These sources add details absent from, but remarkably consistent with, Guerrero's and Sotelo's initial reports of 1564–65, as does Álvarez' later account from what is now Bolivia (1588). Such continuity in descriptions of the Taqui Oncoy justifies a synthetic presentation in the following section.[5]

The Taqui Oncoy, 1569–71

For a first approximation of the movement during these years, let us begin with Cristóbal de Molina's account, which Varón (1990: 335) thinks the most reliable and Ramos (1992: 162) sees as the official Church version of events. The movement advocated a return to native 'idolatries' and covered a large area including Chuquisaca, La Paz, Cuzco, Huamanga, Arequipa, and even Lima. Although it was unclear who lay behind it, the sorcerers who surrounded the rebel Inca in Vilcabamba were suspected. Molina also accused them of fomenting Indians' widespread belief that Spaniards had come to Peru to slaughter them for their fat, which the Spaniards used as the only known cure for a disease they had. The movement's main premise was that all *huacas* the Spaniards destroyed had revived and formed into two groups under Pachacamac and Titicaca to do battle with the Christian God, whom they had nearly defeated. Its adepts held that when Pizarro took Peru, the Christian God had defeated the *huacas*, but now the world was turning around. The *huacas* would defeat the Christian God and kill the Spaniards. The sea would rise up to drown them, destroying their cities and removing their last trace. The time of the Inca would then return. Just as the Christian God had created the Spaniards, their land, and all the things that it produced, so the *huacas* had created Andean people, their land, and its products. The movement's preachers spread across the highlands, announcing the *huacas*' resurrection. To reclaim their domains, the *huacas* had sown many fields with worms to plant in the hearts of the Spaniards, their livestock and horses, but also in the hearts of Indians who remained Christian. The *huacas* were angry with those who had accepted baptism, and would kill them if they did not renounce Christianity but promised health and prosperity to those who worshipped them and observed traditional abstinences. Since Indians no longer offered the *huacas* sacrifices and libations, they were dying of hunger and thirst: they abandoned their normal embodiment in stones, clouds, and springs and flew through the air to possess and speak through Indians. Some Indians swept and tidied their houses in case a *huaca* should decide to enter. Others shook and rolled on the ground or threw rocks as if possessed, making faces and later coming to rest, declaring that specific *huacas* had entered their bodies. Handlers took the possessed person by the arm to a room prepared with straw and cloth and gave sacrifices and other offerings to the *huaca* in question. Adepts requested any piece of *huacas* that Christians had destroyed and, covering their heads with a cloth, libated the fragment and invoked the *huaca* that had resided in it, lifting up the fragment and proclaiming, 'Here you see our deliverance and here you see what it does to you, and gives health and children and fields: put it back in its place, where it was in the time of the Incas.' Preachers told Indians to abandon Christianity, their Christian names and clothes, and criticized those *curacas* and other Indians who did not. These activities occurred during bouts of dancing and drinking that lasted several days and nights (Molina 1574: 129–31).

Additional sources develop various points in this account, starting with the Taqui Oncoy's basic practices. A particular dance defined the multi-day events in which the movement's more spectacular practices of sacrifice and oracular possession occurred. Albornoz states that the dance was called *taqui ongo* and set the context for receiving separatist preachers (Duviols 1984: 216). Thus, the dance was the part that gave the whole its name, and the matrix for other events. Dancers painted their faces red and assembled in houses or outdoors in special enclosures (Millones 1990: 191, Molina 1574: 131). Álvarez describes how adepts danced in groups, raising and lowering their legs and arms in a vigorous stationary march with clenched fists, moving their heads from side to side with each step and making a high-pitched sound: 'u, u, u, u.' They ate little or nothing beyond coca but drank heavily while dancing up to three or four days and nights. Some became delirious from fatigue, hunger, and drink, while the rigorous dancing led others to collapse on the floor in groups. Those who pushed themselves the furthest were the most respected, particularly those who became possessed or died in these exertions (Álvarez 1588: 124–7). Such assemblies became ordeals, so they could speak effectively to issues of affliction and purification.

Five days' abstinence from salt, chile, maize, and sex, in which adepts drank only de-alcoholized corn beer, were to precede the dancing sessions (Millones 1990: 93, 98, 130, Molina 1574: 130). Thus, the Taqui Oncoy's bodily practices resonated with its ideological emphasis on purification. However, these practices long predated the specifically anti-Spanish and anti-Catholic character of the Taqui Oncoy as a social movement. Guaman Poma (1615: 253, 280) and other sources mention *taqui oncoy* as a disease without linking it to this movement, suggesting that it had an independent and probably prior existence. Varón plausibly suggests that the Taqui Oncoy arose from seasonal cleansing rituals like the Inca *situa*, which aimed to expel sickness from the community (1990: 349–50, 371–7). The structure of Molina's chronicle, which discusses Inca calendrical rituals at length and concludes with a brief but pithy discussion of the Taqui Oncoy, arguably suggests such an interpretation. Yet the Taqui Oncoy was an extraordinary movement, one that broke with established seasonal rituals and offered something new, even if it selectively recycled some familiar practices. By using seasonal cleansing rituals to expel Christian artifacts, and linking them to the diseases that decimated Andean people, the Taqui Oncoy creatively addressed a novel situation: Andean people's conversion to Christianity and their consequent neglect of the *huacas*. Expelling the foreign and pestilential was not an end in itself but a necessary first step in reinstating ancestral deities. As Molina's description of people sweeping and tidying their houses in preparation for occupation by a *huaca* shows, such cleansing aimed to give these deities a new embodiment.

Oracular possession figured centrally in the Taqui Oncoy. Not all adepts became possessed, but as Álvarez notes, those who did were the most respected. Such possession gave dramatic immediacy to the movement's central premise that the *huacas* were famished, disembodied, and seeking renewed contact with their Andean descendants. Álvarez thought that food and sleep deprivation plus the dance's physical demands were enough to produce a trance state that participants lived as oracular possession. Albornoz noted that *taquiongos* might administer a hallucinogen called *maca* to sceptics, which would make them dance frenetically and bang their heads against the wall (Duviols 1984: 216). Molina reported that the possessed danced, shook, rolled in the dirt, threw rocks, made faces, walled themselves inside their houses and shouted, tore themselves apart, or jumped off cliffs or into rivers, offering themselves to the *huacas* in their death (1574: 131–2). Diego de Romaní mentioned seeing six or seven deranged young *taquiongos* wandering about (Millones 1990: 99), presumably outside the dance circle. Perhaps adepts also used *maca*, particularly those who acted as oracular mediums. In any case, dancing as ordeal, oracular possession, and drug use all converged on a single trajectory. Whether or not they embodied the *huacas* as mediums, *taquiongos* got out of their heads, and the multi-day, multi-night character of their assemblies ensured that they broke mundane routines.

Previous commentators on the Taqui Oncoy have largely ignored that *huaca* possession was an institutionalized part of Andean politico-religious life, and therefore have overemphasized the movement's novelty in this regard.[6] No Andean ancestral deity could establish itself as such without giving oracles. Instead of dying and becoming mute like ordinary mortals, ancestors distinguished themselves by continuing to dispense life after death, most palpably in their ability to speak through others. All levels of Andean society, from the Inca court to peasant hamlets, greatly valued the answers and advice they gave through living mediums. Oracular consultations commonly occurred in seasonal rituals, when the living brought ancestral mummies into their company, gave them sacrifices, libations and clothing, and in turn expected them to communicate. Rulers also consulted ancestors when necessary and often secretively for advice on affairs of state (Gose 1996b). The Taqui Oncoy fell within this established pattern, as is clear from Luis de Olvera's report 'that said *huacas* were no longer embodied in stones nor in trees nor in springs as in the time of the Inca, but entered the bodies of Indians and made them talk and thus they took to shaking, saying that they had the *huacas* in their bodies and they took many of them and painted their faces red and put them in enclosures and there the Indians went to worship them as whatever *huaca* and idol they said had entered their body and they sacrificed sheep, clothing, silver, maize and many other things' (Millones 1990: 178). This passage indicates one potentially significant difference between the Taqui Oncoy and regular ancestor worship. Normally, Andean people made offerings to 'idols' or mummies that represented the *huacas*, not to the mediums whom they momentarily possessed. That Taquionogos made offerings directly to the mediums shows that they saw them as the *huacas'* principal embodiments, a view consistent with the idea that hunger and thirst made the *huacas* abandon their previous forms. Thus, the Taqui Oncoy's heightened emphasis on oracular possession underlined its analysis of the *huacas'* trauma. *Taquiongos* also ridiculed Christianity because its wooden crosses did not speak (Millones 1990: 147), which invoked and further promoted oracular possession as the traditional standard by which deities were to prove themselves. Whether this intensified focus on possession entirely undermined the distinction between deity and medium or led to the constitution of permanently sacralized 'human *huacas*' (Cavero 2001: 65–6) is another matter. The dramatic possession behaviour that Molina recounts cannot have continued indefinitely, and was probably confined to the extended sessions of *taquiongo* dancing. It was an exceptional enactment of the *huacas*' agony that recalled normative relations in the breach.

Within the Andean oracular tradition, the Taqui Oncoy presents an interesting limit case with exceptional features that prove general rules. In a normally functioning Andean politico-religious regime, people initiated sacrificial offerings to the *huacas* and engaged them in oracular dialogue. Such institutionalized communication broke down as Andean people converted to Christianity and progressively neglected their offerings to the *huacas*. Out of hunger and thirst, the *huacas* left their normal embodiments and flew about in the air, sometimes possessing people but above all making them sick. In effect, the *huacas* reasserted relations with their descendants by entering their bodies and imposing on them (through epidemics) a suffering comparable to their own. Thus, the *huacas* showed their descendants that they shared an indissoluble bond and a common fate. Epidemics negatively confirmed the standard formula of Andean ancestor worship, by which descendants sacrificed to the ancestor for life and prosperity. A breakdown in their relationship disembodied the *huacas* and sickened their descendants. Oracular possession dramatically restored this relationship, although no longer in the manageable form of a smoothly functioning ancestor cult. *Taquiongo* dancing's agonistic character and the indiscriminate style of possession it promoted both suggest that institutional channels were broken. Possession came upon people as unpredictably as disease, yet promised a renewed and mutually beneficial relationship. Juan Chocne, one of the movement's leading preachers, claimed to carry one of these disembodied deities around in a basket. He said it was the power that gave the Indians food and life, and that if they did not worship it, it would turn them into guanacos, vicuñas, and other animals (Millones 1990: 181, 225). Other *taquiongos* repeated these threats and added that those who refused to worship the *huacas* would walk about with their heads on the ground and their feet in the air, or die senselessly by jumping off cliffs so the *huacas* could make a new world with new people (Millones 1990: 130).

In short, a profound crisis of faith marked the Taqui Oncoy. The movement took its urgency and apocalyptic tone from the perceived breakdown of the most fundamental relationship in Andean society, that between ancestors and descendants. This was primarily an internal matter and only secondarily about relations with Spaniards. Despite its ostensible rejection of things Catholic and Spanish, the Taqui Oncoy was no simple chauvinism. Doubt drove it far more than certainty. As Andean people perished in unprecedented numbers during epidemics that followed the Spanish invasion, how could they believe that they still enjoyed the backing and protection of their ancestors, who were supposed to ensure life, health, and prosperity? Many signs suggested that the *huacas* were indeed planning to make a new world with new people. We must bear this key point in mind when we consider the movement's separatist leanings.

An alternative Andean explanation of the *huacas'* disembodied state was their burning and destruction at Christian hands (Millones 1990: 191). This view clearly registers the impact of early extirpations of idolatry, and suggests that the Huamachuco case discussed in the previous chapter was far from isolated. *Taquiongos* retrieved, libated, and invoked fragments of destroyed *huacas*, identifying them as Andean peoples' sustainers (Molina 1574: 131), which shows that the movement was in no small measure a response to early extirpations of idolatry. When *taquiongos* said that Spaniards had defeated the *huacas* that were now reviving to fight the Christian God (Millones 1990: 191), they probably referred to the *huacas'* destruction by extirpating priests on the one hand and *taquiongos'* resurrection of them on the other. The *huacas'* revival required that descendants resume their worship, which is precisely what Molina's passage describes. This alternative explanation of the *huacas'* plight led in a different political direction than the emphasis on Andean peoples' own neglect, since it clearly identified Spanish priests as the culprits. From this perspective, the Taqui Oncoy responded to a crisis that was primarily external.

This second analysis resonates with several other aspects of *taquiongo* ideology. The most prominent is the notion that Pizarro entered the realm and subjugated the Indians because his God (temporarily) defeated the *huacas*, who were now counterattacking and nearing victory (Millones 1990: 178, 191, cf. Molina 1574: 130). Here, the burning of *huacas* became the Spanish conquest's central expression, just as the *huacas'* coming triumph lay in reasserting relations of intensified possession with their descendants. *Taquiongos'* professed religious separatism also fits with the view that Spaniards had caused the *huacas'* plight. When *taquiongos* denounced Christianity as false because the unbaptized could enter its churches with impunity and its crosses would not give oracles (Millones 1990: 147, 181), they insinuated that its deity was weak and unworthy of worship. By counselling Andean people to reject Spanish names, food, and clothing (Millones 1990: 178, 191), they hoped to further weaken the Christian God. Some held that the *huacas* would soon send diseases to kill the Spaniards, but that they also resented Indians who had converted, and demanded that they renounce Christianity and revert to the names, food, and clothing that the *huacas* furnished if they wished to recover health and prosperity (Millones 1990: 191). Such ideas neatly reversed the notion of ancestral crisis and countered that it was now Christians' turn to be sick. They also show that *taquiongos* saw worship as the performative basis of deities and their relative strength. By adopting or abandoning a deity's cult, consuming or rejecting the things it provided, people could augment or erode its power. Therefore *taquiongo* religious separatism directed worship and everyday practice back towards Andean ancestral deities to reconstitute their power.

We can now understand Molina's report that Indians feared Spaniards would slaughter and render them for their grease, which Spaniards used to treat an otherwise incurable skin disease. Since Spanish conquistadores actually did render dead Indians for their grease to use as a salve for wounds (Díaz 1575: 233), we cannot dismiss this fear as imaginary. Even if such practices stopped after the conquest, they made a profound and readily intelligible impression on Andean people who related to their deities through sacrifice. During the Taqui Oncoy, this fear of being preyed on and rendered was part of the larger concern that an alien regime was disrupting relations between Andean people and their deities. Just as the Spaniards attacked and destroyed the *huacas*, so they also attacked and destroyed Indian bodies, preserving the notion that ancestors and descendants ultimately shared the same fate. Thus, extirpation and slaughtering were linked in the same way as neglect of the *huacas* and disease. That a skin disease motivated Spaniards to slaughter and render Indians is a particularly interesting detail. It suggests that like Andean people, Spaniards had strained relations with their own deity and so suffered disease. The analogy strengthens when we recall that Andean people suffered primarily from measles and smallpox, which ravaged the skin. By preying on Andean people and absorbing their grease, Spaniards sought an exogenous solution to an endogenous problem with their deity. Alternatively, Spaniards' skin ailment might signify the beginning of the *huacas'* promised counter-attack through disease. Only by taking the grease of Andean people who were in proper sacrificial equilibrium with the *huacas* could Spaniards stave off the *huacas'* attack. Either way, *taquiongos'* analysis of disease incorporated Spaniards and their colonizing violence.

Despite these dramatic images, the Taqui Oncoy may not have been as separatist as Spanish testimony suggests. When Albornoz convened a meeting of many *curacas* to refute the movement's beliefs, two women who named themselves after Santa María and Santa María Magdalena (and other saints) stepped forward to ask his forgiveness (Millones 1990: 89, 99–100). This information is significant (and particularly reliable) because it contradicts the primary sources' rhetorical agenda of portraying *taquiongos* as unreconstructed pagans utterly hostile to Christianity. If the women participated in the Taqui Oncoy under these Christian identifications, the movement's reputed separatism requires qualification. These women were not 'dogmatizers'[7] and may even have been mediums who embodied Christian saints on the same oracular basis as others embodied the *huacas*. Clearly some negotiation with Christianity was still at work within the movement, even if the sources currently available do not tell us what form it took. Albornoz also notes that the preachers sent from Vilcabamba were Spanish-speaking (Duviols 1984: 215–6), and so did not just oppose the Spanish world but also incorporated it, perhaps more fully than most of their followers. An important Andean strategy for dealing with post-conquest religious plurality was to reconcile the cults of victors and vanquished. Andean people expected to incorporate the cults of intrusive outsiders into their own religious world and thus were open to Christianity (Stern 1982: 57). Without reading these documents as resolutely against the grain as some recent authors, we can still suspect that some such process was at work here.[8]

Additional evidence suggests this more accommodating scenario. According to Luis de Olvera and Cristóbal Ximénez, *taquiongos* believed that the Christian God was powerful for things Spanish, just as the *huacas* were powerful for things of their land, as the creators of its people and the things that maintained them (Millones 1990: 178, 191, cf. Molina 1574: 130). Although this affirmation is consistent with separatism and the recommended rejection of Spanish food, practices, and artifacts, it also allows a different reading in the light of the two Marías. It may equally have meant that worshipping the Christian God for things Spanish was appropriate, but doing so for things Andean that the *huacas* still controlled was not. Thus, adepts had every reason to revive the cult of the *huacas*, but not necessarily to reject every aspect of Christianity. Quite possibly the movement was internally divided on this score.

Thus, we must ask whether the Taqui Oncoy's ostensible cultural separatism might derive from the Spanish sources who reported on it. The extirpating strain of Spanish missionary activity strongly promoted a mutually exclusive understanding of the relation between Catholicism and Andean ancestral religions. Even the more widely shared project of 'conversion' meant codifying each tradition as a distinct entity to allow a complete transfer of allegiance from one to the other. By contrast, Andean conquerors and conquered each adopted the cults of the other and rewrote their histories to live together. Under the Incas, this process generated hierarchical pantheons and *pacarina* networks, as Albornoz himself argued (Duviols 1984: 197–8). Chapter 5 will show that localized conquests tempered such hierarchy with reciprocity between the cults of conquerors and conquered. The Taqui Oncoy's boundary strategies therefore seem more Christian than Andean, possibly an effect of describing the movement through Spanish dichotomies. To accept this view fully, however, we would have to dismiss too many reports of Andean people fleeing Spaniards, dismantling crosses, using hallucinogens, and confessing to the movement's precepts. If Albornoz' careerism and the rise of a hard line against idolatry within the Church discursively fabricated the Taqui Oncoy, as Urbano (1990: 268–9, 1997: 212) and Ramos (1992: 149, 155, 162) suggest, then it would have been a largely stereotypical simulation. Descriptions of the Taqui Oncoy were highly original, however. Although missionary discourse pervades these reports, it provides no precedent for their details, which therefore should count as reliable. If, as I believe, the Taqui Oncoy not only existed but was significantly separatist in its own right, we must see it as an ambivalent phenomenon, one that repudiated Christianity but also tried to redefine and incorporate it.

Andean peoples' growing awareness of the missionary conversion agenda might explain these complexities. Although they rejected Catholicism instead of their ancestral practices, they retained the missionaries' zero-sum understanding of the relation between Catholic and Andean traditions. Thus, the Taqui Oncoy's militant traditionalizing would be profoundly non-traditional, as is typical of revivalist movements. This explanation has the advantage of fully locating the movement's boundary strategies within the force field of missionary colonialism. By resisting the missionary project, participants in the

Taqui Oncoy would have inadvertently adopted its terms of reference. Still, Foucauldian arguments about the complicity of resistance with power fail to explain why the Taqui Oncoy accepted this missionary dichotomy of traditions when Andean people rejected it, both traditionally and over the long run of the colonial period. Generally, they expected conquerors and conquered to create a new politico-religious order by integrating traditions. This observation also disqualifies other potential explanations. For example, one might argue that the movement's separatism was a reaction to the Christian appropriation of Andean origin narratives explored in the last chapter. By reasserting boundaries between Andean and Catholic traditions, *taquiongos* would have contested the colonization of their ancestral narratives. Again, however, the problem is that Andean people generally viewed such colonizations of tradition positively, and as necessary to post-conquest coexistence. Exactly why *taquiongos* abandoned hybridizing accommodation for separatism remains an important but unanswered question.

The best answer may be that the Taqui Oncoy took place in a moment of true crisis, when time-honoured Andean strategies no longer worked. By 1564, Spaniards were clearly not going to accept the reciprocal worship of ancestral deities that normally resolved conquest situations in the Andean world. Although the full inquisitorial force of Spanish Catholicism had yet to be felt, the Taqui Oncoy nonetheless registered the destruction of many important *huacas*. Such blatant non-recognition thoroughly contravened the Andean rules of post-conquest etiquette. Trying a new strategy made sense, even if it ratified the boundaries their Christian adversaries drew. Yet *taquiongos* also responded to the situational logic of thwarted reciprocity with their own ancestral deities. Their fundamental question was why Andean people suffered from devastating epidemics after the Spanish invasion. Although they interpreted sickness as an ancestral punishment for adopting Christianity, we should not let their anti-Spanish militancy mask that this was a serious internal crisis. Ancestors behaved like enemies, killing their descendants in unprecedented numbers when they ought to have nurtured and sustained them. Negative reciprocity predominated not just on the boundaries of group life but at its very heart. This, I would argue, is what Andean people found truly unnerving. Not only had proven strategies for dealing with intrusive outsiders gone wrong, but so had relations with the ancestors, the internal pillar of Andean life and livelihood. Under these circumstances, it is hardly surprising that many people felt a need to change established strategies.

In this context we can best understand the Taqui Oncoy's prophesied return to 'the time of the Inca' (Molina 1574: 130). Various modern analysts discuss what this phrase possibly meant (Cavero 2001: 160). Most opt for figurative readings that make the Inca emblematic of an idealized indigenous order opposed to the Spanish present, and mute any concrete relation to the Inca state or the Vilcabamba resistance. This epochal approach largely coincided with a reading of the Taqui Oncoy as a 'millenarian movement' that anticipated a cataclysmic reorganization of the world. In Andean terms, this rupture would be a *pachacuti*, or turning of the earth, in which the moiety-like relation between manifest and latent orders would reverse. Data that sustain this interpretation include the idea that the *huacas* might make their descendants walk upside down, or wipe them out and create a new humanity. *Taquiongos* also stated that the turn (*mita*) of the Christian God was ending, which also suggests an epochal understanding (Millones 1990: 93). Beyond these details, however, the supporting evidence is thin, particularly for the more overstated versions of the epochal hypothesis (e.g., Zuidema 1965, Estenssoro 2003: 130). Without altogether dismissing figurative understandings of 'the time of the Inca,' we should at least consider the more literal alternatives that would resonate with the political connections to Vilcabamba shown above.

The idea that the reviving *huacas* had formed into two groups under the leadership of Pachacamac and Titicaca to fight the Christian God (Millones 1990: 64, 130, 178, 191) definitely suggests a revival of something resembling the Inca empire. These *huacas* represented the lowlands and highlands, respectively. Titicaca was the maximal *pacarina* (ancestral origin point) throughout the sierra, as was the Pacific Ocean (which Pachacamac overlooked) for coastal groups (Gose 1993). In short, Titicaca and Pachacamac defined pan-Andean networks. Their differentiation of east from west and high from low was motivated. High-low distinctions commonly articulated moieties at various levels of Andean socio-political organization, but always implied that an overarching unit comprised the two divisions (Gose 1996a). Under the Incas, the sun's diurnal cycle expressed the unity underlying the maximal duality of coast and highlands. The sun began its course by rising out of Titicaca, continued through the sky before setting in the Pacific, and moving underground back to Titicaca again (Gose 1993). Thus, we may suspect that the Taqui Oncoy's *huaca* networks defined something that closely resembled this Inca totality.

The geographical distribution of the lesser *huacas* that *taquiongos* invoked also suggests a project of imperial scope. The documents mention few by name but some, such as Chimborazo in Ecuador, were far from the movement's putative heartland in Huamanga. Important Inca *huacas* from Cuzco also participated, including Tambotoco, the Incas' local origin point, and Coricancha, the imperial temple of the Sun (Millones 1990: 93, Duviols 1984: 216). The latter was the Inca empire's religious centre: provincial oracular deities travelled there to prognosticate, answer the Inca's questions about affairs of state, and receive rewards during the *capacocha* festival. Albornoz stipulates that the *huacas* that participated in the Taqui Oncoy were the same ones that the Inca regularly invited to Cuzco for such consultations (Duviols 1984: 215–6). One way to look at the movement, then, is as a post-imperial form of the *capacocha*. Although they no longer had any political centre on which to converge, and Coricancha figured only as another participating *huaca*, its formerly pre-eminent position lingered in the Titicaca–Pachacamac axis. Had that axis prevailed, the sun would have resumed its synthesizing role and Coricancha its central position.

Evidence that the Taqui Oncoy projected a literal return to the Inca order is limited, but stronger than that which exists for the 'millenarian' reading discussed above. It suggests that the movement tried to regenerate Inca institutions indirectly through *huaca* networks of imperial scope rather than frontally or from the top down. Instead of expecting Inca institutions to re-emerge full blown, as in the millenarian hypothesis, the strategy was to rebuild them from *huaca* cults by emphasizing their systemic interrelations, culminating in Titicaca and Pachacamac. *Pacarina* narratives, in which ancestors journeyed from these remote centres to the localities they were to populate, provided that systemic framework. They linked localities in nesting hierarchies that grew broader with every step back towards these two original sources. By emphasizing such grassroots linkages, the Taqui Oncoy registered well the political realities of its moment, when the Inca state's remnants were no longer strong enough to assert themselves directly and required the support of a social movement. Such a reading implies that the Taqui Oncoy's reach as a political movement ought to match the reach of the *huaca* networks it invoked, an important and frequently mishandled issue that I will discuss in the following section. Even more directly, it implies that the Taqui Oncoy connected with the Inca resistance in Vilcabamba.

Beyond this indirect evidence, both Molina (1574: 129,132) and Albornoz (Duviols 1984: 215–7) explicitly link the Taqui Oncoy to Inca resistance in Vilcabamba and preparations for an armed uprising discovered in 1565. The wandering preachers whom Tupac Amaru sent from Vilcabamba to promote the Taqui Oncoy exhorted followers to restore Inca rule. They held that the provincial *huacas* were no longer annoyed with the Inca and maintained daily communication with him (Duviols 1984: 215–6). This statement implies that the *huacas* were until recently estranged from the Inca, and so presumably had allowed the Spanish conquest to occur. By agreeing to back him again, the *huacas* also held the key to Inca restoration. The Vilcabamba preachers probably articulated this message as the *huacas'* mediums. One witness describes how they received sacrificial offerings of livestock and clothing for the *huacas* as they entered each locality in Huamanga (Millones 1990: 93), suggesting a close identification with them. Albornoz notes that they also sought the names of the local *huacas* and their priests, drank with them, and often killed and replaced them with their protégés (Duviols 1984: 216–7). In Inca times, such purges of oracular mediums were common and asserted imperial control over provincial oracles (Gose 1996b). By usurping the role of local priests and weeding out those unreceptive to their agenda, the Vilcabamba preachers asserted a comparable centralizing influence. Clearly tensions between provincial *huacas* and the Inca elite persisted. In practice, the Taqui Oncoy's regeneration of an Inca order was not as spontaneous as it appeared, and arguably remained a form of political ventriloquism. Although it adopted the guise of a grassroots *huaca* coalition, the Taqui Oncoy was, by these accounts, a centrally planned initiative that remnants of the Inca state launched from Vilcabamba.

Aftermaths

Scholars customarily treat 1571 as the terminal date for the Taqui Oncoy. Molina testified that the Taqui Oncoy went into decline once its major preachers publically recanted in Cuzco (Millones 1990: 181, 225), and Albornoz finished his assignment as ecclesiastical inspector of Huamanga midway through 1571 (Guibovich 1991: 228).[9] However, Albornoz may have simply moved on to more rewarding posts following his work on the Taqui Oncoy, without necessarily eradicating it. In 1571 he became a canon of the cathedral of Cuzco. There he met and sufficiently impressed Viceroy Toledo to become one of his inspectors during the colony's *visita general* (Guibovich 1991: 212–3). Since Toledo assigned him to Parinacochas, Andahuaylas and Chinchaysuyo (Millones 1990: 182), he may well have continued to eradicate the Taqui Onqoy. Albornoz' own account of these years shows that he viewed the extirpation of idolatry as an integral part of settlement consolidation, the prime task of Toledo's *visita general* (Millones 1990: 209, 212, 220, 224, 231, 233, 235, 239, 244, 248, 250–1). Yet he does not specifically state that he continued to encounter manifestations of the Taqui Oncoy during his subsequent activities as an extirpator. The fact that Toledo sent Albornoz back to the Huamanga area as an inspector might suggest that he did not share Molina's confidence that the movement had ended.

The Taqui Oncoy's relationship to Vilcabamba would explain why the movement declined in the early 1570s. With Titu Cusi's assassination between April and June of 1571 and Tupac Amaru's capture and public execution during August and September 1572 (Guillén 1994: 145–6, 302–3), the Inca resistance collapsed. As a political movement, the Taqui Oncoy no longer made sense, at least in its original terms, which must have been the main reason for its decline. The effectiveness of Albornoz' extirpation is debatable: it was no counterinsurgency operation but was too repressive to win hearts and minds. For Molina, the capture and public recanting of the Taqui Oncoy's principal 'dogmatizers' initiated its decline. Exactly when this occurred is uncertain, but it was probably not before late 1569. Yet Albornoz continued to extirpate until mid-1571. If, as Molina suggests, the Taqui Oncoy began to wane with the capture of main preachers, Albornoz must have continued his work some way into its decline. Only after Titu Cusi's death did he cease to prosecute the Taqui Oncoy, however. Did this important event dictate the timing of Albornoz' reassignment? At the time, neither Albornoz nor his superiors knew of this death, since Toledo wrote to Titu Cusi in October 1571, thinking he was still alive (Guillén 1994: 302). Indian insurgents who had been in contact with the Inca might well have known, however, and curtailed their activities accordingly. Only indirectly, then, could the events in Vilcabamba have influenced the timing of Albornoz' reassignment.

Albornoz' inspections may have checked the Taqui Oncoy in Huamanga by 1571, but elsewhere it did not end so early. Rather, it lost momentum as a movement and went underground. Molina implies that in 1577 some of its preachers were still active, if less publicly (Millones 1990: 181, cf. Molina 1574: 132). Similarly, Álvarez describes it as something that only became less public but never disappeared because it went unpunished (1588: 126). That the movement lingered in Upper Peru until at least 1588 undermines Varón's attempt to delimit the Taqui

Oncoy as a discrete entity in space and time (1990: 340–1). Not only did it endure beyond the conjuncture of the 1560s, it also existed over a much wider area than the Huamanga heartland where Albornoz worked. Molina originally claimed that the movement extended to 'Chuquisaca, La Paz, Cuzco, Huamanga and even Lima and Arequipa' (1574: 129), and Albornoz held that agents from Vilcabamba preached the Taqui Oncoy 'through all the provinces of Peru' (Duviols 1984: 215), an opinion that Olvera, Ximénez, and Sierra also ratified (Millones 1990: 178, 191, 216). Álvarez' report corroborates these sources and undermines Varón's view that the movement was confined to Huamanga and adjacent provinces (1990: 331–2, 341, 388–9, 403). Similarly, Sotelo's letter of 1565 suggests that northern areas such as Jauja and Chachapoyas participated in the movement. Thus, the primary sources are internally consistent and much more reliable than revisionist commentators on the Taqui Oncoy's geographical extent, just as they are on the Vilcabamba connection.

Clearly the Taqui Oncoy's wide geographical purview and its origins in the mid-1560s further suggest its intimate links with Titu Cusi's planned rebellion. The Taqui Oncoy took form in this conjuncture, but it recombined pre-existing elements and outlived the moment of its articulation. It may have been a specific political response to novel conditions, but by marshalling many well-established Andean ideas about ancestral authority, it also continued a tradition. Furthermore, the movement gained some autonomy from Vilcabamba by persisting beyond its demise. If something called the Taqui Oncoy was widespread in the Andes from 1564 or earlier to at least 1588, perhaps it requires internal periodization and differentiation. We can usefully distinguish the Taqui Oncoy as a political movement from its underlying ideology, which with appropriate modifications both preceded and survived a phase of mobilization. To the extent that the Taqui Oncoy derived from the Inca resistance in Vilcabamba, it took a severe blow with Tupac Amaru's capture and execution in 1572, and effectively ended as an activist project then. These events more plausibly explain the movement's general decline than Albornoz' repressive activities, which only affected Huamanga. Yet many Taqui Oncoy beliefs and practices reverberated long after it was moribund as a political movement. Several localized outbursts recycled its ideology, and they are key to assessing the movement's legacy. By examining them, we no longer see the Taqui Oncoy as a bounded and internally consistent entity but as an array of initiatives, some of which continued to orient a more diffuse and emergent colonial indigenous culture and others of which did not.

On July 15, 1578, the Cabildo Eclesiástico of the cathedral of Lima met to consider a report 'as was notorious, that in the province of Conchucos a certain Indian sorcerer had rebelled, who had induced the Indians of said province to abandon the evangelical law and worship the *guacas* and he offered other insults which do disservice to our Lord.' They eventually sent Bartolomé Moreno Vellido, vicar of Huánuco, to inspect 'the idolatrous Indians who have rebelled.' By September 19, 1578, Moreno Vellido reported back that 'it is advisable to inspect the province of Guamachuco and the city of Chachapoyas and its environs and the town of Moyobamba since it has been many days since they were inspected and to determine if the sorceries and evils that said Indian sorcerers of Conchucos said and did took hold in said parts, in order to remedy them.' The Cabildo Eclesiástico unanimously agreed to extend Moreno Vellido's commission for up to five more months.[10] No report from these investigations survives. We cannot say what further comprised this suspected rebellion, rejection of Christianity, and reversion to *huaca* worship, or whether it extended to the areas Moreno Vellido suspected. The spectre of 'Indian sorcerers' leading an anti-Christian rebellion certainly recalls the Taqui Oncoy, but perhaps more as stereotype than historical continuity. Yet in 1565, Sotelo did report that the Conchucos had joined Titu Cusi's planned rebellion. While I doubt that the Taqui Oncoy persisted undetected in Conchucos through to 1578 or continued to advocate insurrection after Vilcabamba's demise, we cannot rule out either possibility.

Similar reports surfaced in Huánuco eleven years later. Ramos Gavilán (1621: 49–50) writes that the smallpox epidemic of 1589 led natives with only a rudimentary knowledge of Catholicism to seek a remedy in revived ceremonies and sacrifices to their idols. On investigation, the Augustinian clergy found many of these idols and presumably destroyed them during the intensive preaching against idolatry that followed. They were also pleased to report the presence of a Christian faction that sought relief from the plague and God's wrath in processions and masses. The Augustinians publicized their actions, which were well received in the High Court of Lima. Apparently the Taqui Oncoy had made native idolatries a matter of public concern. Minimal as these details are, their similarity with certain premises of the Taqui Oncoy is unmistakable. In both cases, disease was the fundamental motive for action and signalled a breakdown of relations with ancestors, whose remedy was to restore or intensify their cults and attendant sacrifices. The Huánuco data do not specify that the ancestors sent disease as a punishment for their descendants' Catholicism. Whether or not this additional element of *taquiongo* ideology was present, however, its basic message that epidemics expressed a loss of ancestral backing clearly applied. Those natives who turned to Christianity for relief probably shared this analysis with the ancestral revivalists but abandoned the ancestors instead. Both strategies registered the traditional order's breakdown.

In 1590, 'in the province of Aimará,' presumably somewhere around their base in Juli, Jesuit missionaries reported that natives had rejected the Christian God. They reasoned

> that the God of the Spaniards was not their God because they [the Spaniards] were not touched by the plague and that this punishment came to them [the natives] to make them understand that they were guilty of having left their own ancient God, which the Spaniards did not do, always worshipping the same God without ever leaving him, and that because of this they lived healthily and happily. From this, the Devil had them infer with certainty that their God and that of the Spaniards were not the same and that [by] returning to sacrifice to their own ancient God, leaving that of the Spaniards, they would try to placate him with offerings and similar things ... Others affirmed that the Inca, the old king of Peru, had told them that it was by his command and will that this sickness had come; and others said other falsehoods, so that the poor Indians felt obliged not only to return to offer to the idols all that their mages asked that they do, but that they were also persuaded that they should not have anything that the Spaniards used, that they should not hear mass except as a mere formality and that when the priest raised the host they should strike their chest with the left hand and not worship the cross. Thus persuaded that their cure consisted in this, they removed images, crosses, blessed candles, rosaries, and even hats, shoes and other things that they used in the manner of Spaniards from their houses. (Vargas-Hidalgo 1996: 112)

The report also mentions that the natives resumed animal sacrifices to their deities and killed an old Christian woman who happened to witness them.

This account clearly contains basic Taqui Oncoy beliefs, including religious separatism and disease as a sign of neglected ritual duty to ancestral deities. Although the missionaries do not identify these notions as part of the Taqui Oncoy, they do mention that the Inca, presumably Titu Cusi, claimed to send sicknesses to punish Andean people for allying with the Spaniards. I cannot regard this as a separate phenomenon since Álvarez describes the Taqui Oncoy by name in western Bolivia two years earlier (1588). This complex of ritual and ideology clearly did extend into Collasuyo. The forms it took and the degree to which it recalled the Vilcabamba resistance probably varied, particularly after the latter collapsed in 1572. That these separatists still remembered the Inca eighteen years later in 1590, however, suggests that Vilcabamba's cause was formative and remained fundamental for some. Thus, Varón was wrong to confine this complex to the Lucanas area and to dismiss the Vilcabamba connection. On both counts, new documentation clearly confirms Molina's original claims and shows that the sceptics overshot the mark.

In 1592, a Jesuit mission went to the province of Vilcashuamán, which they described as overrun with superstitions and idolatries. Moved by a sermon, a woman confessed to having consulted a sorcerer who claimed the Inca sent him to free Indians from death. When she asked him to cure her of a disease, he took her to a confluence of two rivers and washed away the sins that had been afflicting her. He then sacrificed fifty guinea pigs and a llama and instructed her to worship a tree to deliver her from death. Another woman also mentioned that the sorcerer had removed all the rosaries, holy images, and crosses that he could. The padres, on investigation, found the confluence and the venerated tree named Vilca on one riverbank and chopped it down. They learned that it was where the original paramount *curaca* of the entire province was born – in other words, that it was a *pacarina*. Those travelling out of province went there asking for health and protection. Further inquiry revealed that local preachers threatened all Indians who practised Christianity, or had crosses, rosaries, holy images, and Spanish clothes, with death by plagues from the *huaca* as punishment for their conversion. Thus, people discarded all the prohibited articles along roads and in gullies, and some turned their heads away from crosses as they passed or refused to enter churches. The parish priest's native assistants (*fiscales*) confirmed all this, and retrieved the discarded items from the roads and *punas* (alpine areas) as evidence (Polia 1999: 206–9).

That these repudiated objects were still ambient in 1592 shows that separatism was more than a recollection of the Taqui Oncoy from 1564 to 1571. Apparently the cult itself, or something very like it, continued until the time of the Jesuit mission. Mention of a preacher who claimed to be an Inca envoy twenty years after Tupac Amaru's execution in 1572 is puzzling. Vilcas lay in Huamanga close to the jungle in an area that the Vilcabamba rebels frequently raided. Either this preacher went through the area then and people continued to observe his teachings, or his visit was more recent, and his claim to represent the Inca was of a different and more 'millenarian' order than when Vilcabamba still held out. In either case, this report dramatically and independently confirms the Inca revivalism of the Taqui Oncoy and its aftermath. One can suspect sensationalism and self-aggrandizement in Albornoz' and Molina's earlier claims of a connection between the Taqui Oncoy and Vilcabamba, but this later report had nothing to gain by that. The rest of the document shows that Taqui Oncoy–related notions coexisted with more routine *huaca* worship. Gone was the hope of imminent transformation and attendant manoeuvring of the Taqui Oncoy as a social movement.

A similar outbreak occurred in Piti, Maras, and Haquira, towns in the province of Yanahuara (modern Cotabambas) during 1595–96 (see Ramos Gavilán 1621: 56–8, Calancha 1638: 712–20, Torres 1657: 63–5). An unnamed native preacher, lame in the hands and feet but very eloquent, claimed His Majesty had sent him to speak for the Christian God to the Indians. His message, however, was separatist: the Indians had greatly annoyed their (ancestral) God by disowning his cult and adopting the Spaniards' law. The measles and smallpox epidemics that had recently consumed most natives in that area were his punishment for their conversion to Christianity, which they were now to renounce. They were to return to their old rites and deities, which had given their forebears prosperity in contrast to the poverty and affliction they suffered under the Spaniards. One moonlit night, more than two thousand Indians assembled on a mountaintop where the lame prophet preached to them from an altar on a nearby crag. To prove his powers, he then caused snow to fall from a clear sky and remain on the ground for many days. He subsequently augmented his reputation as a weather worker by calming the winds or summoning dark clouds and torrential rains. Once, he announced that he would be absent to preach elsewhere, and that meanwhile they should burn the cross on that peak and erect an idol in its stead. If they did, he predicted that the crag from which he spoke would collapse on a particular day following his absence, which it apparently did, further enhancing his credibility. An Indian present reported these events to the ecclesiastical inspector who was in the province at the time. He investigated it carefully and tracked down the guilty, including the prophet, who nonetheless escaped from jail on the day of his sentencing. The local *corregidor* also investigated the matter using torture, which killed an old woman who followed this prophet. Calancha reports that other followers had already moved to the city of Huamanga in 1595, where they continued to agitate until Jesuits ended their activities in 1615.

Like the Taqui Oncoy, this movement had extra-local aspirations. That the prophet left to preach elsewhere and his followers moved to Huamanga in 1595 shows that Yanahuara was not isolated in adopting this religious orientation. The successful escape and disappearance of the lame preacher also suggest a larger network. Exactly what comprised this organization is impossible to tell from the scant documentation available. The recurring figure of the itinerant preacher-medium in these outbursts is suggestive. Calancha calls the lame prophet 'this noxious enchanter who had his chair and the university of his synagogue in the Yanahuaras' (1638: 712). While this projection of Judaism and academic organization was surely a figment of an inquisitorial imagination, these movements clearly had their own proselytizing apparatus. Preacher-mediums recruited and distributed apprentices once they crossed a certain threshold of success. We cannot know how durable the regional links they established were, but the Taqui Oncoy seems to have bequeathed this form of organizing, along with its ideology.

Again, epidemics of smallpox and measles triggered this movement, which sought a cure in the return to ancestral cults and an ostensible rejection of Christianity. Here, not only the ancestors authorized separatism but also the prophet speaking as a medium for the Christian God and the king of Spain. Invoking Christian authorities to reject Christianity seems contradictory, but we cannot dismiss it as chronicler error or providential interpretive licence. These authors rigorously differentiate Christianity from idolatry. For Calancha, the movement's adepts were Jews. Torres wrote that: 'naturally simple-minded and dreamy, they went agape, following their false prophet from one place to another, and pathetically, nearly all apostatized against our holy faith, returning to their old idolatries like a dog to vomit' (1657: 64). Both lengthily argued that this preacher's exploits were mere illusions, not true miracles. Since their own agenda admitted no blurring of boundaries, they had no ulterior motive to fabricate the preacher's claim to speak for the Christian God. We must therefore accept that like the Taqui Oncoy, this movement did not necessarily reject Christianity per se, only its substitution for their own ancestral devotions. Thus, this reported separatism becomes more subtle on closer examination, and involved oracular consultation of the Christian deity, who actually authorized Andean people to return to their ancestral deities.

Such complexities belie Espinoza's claim (1973) that this was a national movement. Like other sixteenth-century epidemic-inspired revivalist movements, the Yanahuara moblization sought reconciliation with the ancestors. That it invoked the Christian God's and the Spanish Crown's permission to do so shows that it did not abandon strategies of political accommodation through reciprocal worship, however. No simplified essentialism defined this movement. Superficially, its rejection of the foreign seems anti-colonial, but it linked to no insurgency, only a revitalization of the ancestral polity. Nationalism may also invoke heroic ancestors as a standard of collective authenticity for remaking an impure and degraded present, but it does not mummify them, treat them as if they were still living, or use their oracles to run affairs of state. Sovereignty in these movements did not reside in the people but in their ancestors and the petty divine kings who descended from them. The Taqui Oncoy forged a coalition of such figures to overcome their local limitations, but it was segmentary, not homogenizing in character. None of these movements tried to form a republic, and only the Taqui Oncoy had political aims that went beyond revitalizing the Andean component of colonial indirect rule.

The final case we will consider occurred in 1599. A Jesuit mission to Aymaraes, next to Yanahuara, found that a smallpox plague, which the natives called 'speckled sickness' (*moro oncoy*), had devastated the province. A Spanish-speaking Indian prophet arose in the province's principal town of Huaquirca. He urged people to gather at a mountain to worship and sacrifice to a *huaca* and idol called Picti[11] who resented their transfer of worship to the Christian God. Picti threatened to annihilate them with the plague he had sent if they did not restore his rites and sacrifices. This prophet also convinced the *curacas* to resume their offerings to the idol, including those of gold. On the appointed day, all the residents of four nearby towns, even the elderly, assembled and climbed the steep mountain. Some paid the idol traditional obeisance (*mocha*) by placing the left hand on the forehead, extending the right, and making sounds with their lips. Others prostrated themselves before the *huaca* on the mountaintop, offering hairs from their eyebrows. At the shrine, a flat place atop the mountain, the prophet received offerings of clothing, gold, and sacrificed livestock for the deity, sprinkling the idol with blood. Each *ayllu* sent delegations of shaven men wearing horns and woollen nets before the idol to dance, sing, and do their own particular rituals in the *huaca*'s honour. Next, these men offered the idol coloured and white maize to the sound of drums and flutes. Then a devoutly Christian Indian woman passed across the mountain on her way to church. The prophet interrupted the sacrifices to announce that they could not continue without killing her, so the assembled multitude stoned her to death. Fearing repercussions, one *curaca* slipped away and decided to inform. The priest, *corregidor*, and other Spaniards found the Indians still in their sacrifices, apprehended and punished the ringleaders, and sent for the Jesuits. On arrival, they preached against idolatry and persuaded the prophet to repent, which culminated in a series of dramatic public confessions during Corpus Christi. During their investigations, they also found that a high-ranking *curaca* assembled everyone in his jurisdiction to say that their Christian marriages were not legitimate. They had sinned greatly and annoyed the idols by not taking wives from them. The *curaca* then dissolved Christian marriages and let the idols assign men new wives. An ecclesiastical inspector punished him lightly for this. He also learned that this *curaca* persuaded his subjects to worship in his house the disease that the Devil (*Zupay*) sent to punish them. One room had a screened-off pit that gave demonic oracles and received gold offerings from all worshippers (Mateos 1944: 107–11, Polia 1999: 222–4).

The prophet of Aymaraes, like those of Yanahuara and the Taqui Oncoy, switched from militant audacity to meek submission once apprehended. Such surrender may express little more than realism in the face of power, but I suspect that the matter is more complex and interesting. Many *taquiongos*, *huaca* priests, and ordinary Andean people preferred suicide to life under the emerging colonial order (Curatola 1989): such true believers made a choice that these prophets refused. Moreover, some leading *taquiongos* actually denounced themselves when Albornoz refuted their beliefs, most notably Santa María and Santa María Magdalena. Once exiled to Cuzco, Juan Chocne and others agreed to confess publicly before other Indians that the Taqui Oncoy was a fraud, which helped to diffuse the movement at its height (Millones 1990: 181, 225). These actions surpassed what was strictly necessary to surrender as painlessly as possible, if that was the goal. We must therefore allow that these changes of heart could have been sincere. To explain such shifts from separatist militancy to humble acceptance of a previously reviled doctrine, we must remember that these movements agonized over whether Andean ancestors still supported their descendants. Andean people's continuing decimation by plagues left them in a very difficult position, not only medically but ideologically. They could try to reconcile with the ancestors by intensifying their cult and rejecting Catholicism as its competitor, or they could decide that the ancestors really had abandoned them and embrace Catholicism as a refuge against their wrath. The prophets' vacillations probably reflect both horns of this nasty dilemma. Once apprehended, they were confronted with ancestors' failure to protect them, and 'conversion' to Catholicism might have been more than a cynical tactic. That documents repeatedly describe the prophets as Spanish-speaking (*ladinos*) suggests that they had fluently internalized what they rejected in their separatist preachings. Their cultural repertoire therefore permitted such a return to Catholicism.

Collectively, these incidents confirm that the Taqui Oncoy's ideology outlived its existence as a movement, and its connection to the Inca resistance. The ideology still generated local prophets in the movement's aftermath, and so retained a link to its activist past, even as it faded back into the routine *huaca* worship from which it originally sprang. Well into the seventeenth century, idolatry trials continued to record separatist sentiments: that Spaniards came from one set of *pacarinas* and Andean people from another; that Andean people should worship their *huacas* since they, not the Christian God, gave them food; that Christianity was a joke since its images did not give oracles; that Spanish food and clothes were polluting; and that the *huacas* sent plagues to punish those who converted to Catholicism.[12] Such notions persisted without animating political movements. Their articulation typically came from *huaca* priests who experienced increasing Church surveillance and had a professional stake in maintaining a separate religious domain with claims to moral and material support. Most aspired to little more than a stalemate with Catholicism, while ordinary Andean people moved easily between these two 'religions' and seldom distinguished them completely. In short, this separatism was defensive. Its relation to the *huaca* priesthood's special interests became clearer over time and it lost its ability to mobilize. By the mid-seventeenth century, it had become a tired refrain, the native articulation of the same set of boundaries propounded in church every week, and just as impossible for ordinary Andean people to live.

This separatist ideology clearly failed in its own terms, but it had important consequences that are not so easily dismissed. By trying to maintain a separate practico-religious domain, Andean priests colluded with their Catholic counterparts over the bounding of traditions but opposed them in their positive valuation of the ancestral. Their continuing intervention was the counterweight that prevented Catholic 'conversion' agendas from succeeding as the outright replacement of one tradition by another. This was no small accomplishment. Without reverting to a fully romantic stance on resistance, we must acknowledge the paradoxical truth that it was only by holding the line that Andean ancestral culture could become as fully hybrid as it eventually did.

4 *Reducción* and the Struggle over Burial

During the 1560s, the colonial project underwent an important shift in Peru as Spaniards became increasingly dissatisfied with indirect rule (Lohmann Villena 1967, Stern 1982: ch. 3, Spalding 1984: ch. 5). Some proposed replacing Andean society's most fundamental institutions with Spanish forms of governance. The Taqui Oncoy occurred in this context, but also helped create it by showing the dangers of leaving indigenous power structures in place. This chapter explores Spanish attempts to remake Andean society and the discourses of reform, corruption, and idolatry that arose in that process. In 1565, Governor Castro created Indian magistrates (*corregidores de indios*) to protect the Crown's legal interests and its Indian subjects against *encomenderos*, priests, and *curacas* (Levillier 1921–6, 3: 116–30; Lohmann Villena 1957: 509–19). A second reformist initiative occurred during 1567, when the Second Council of Lima rethought the Church's local procedures and strategies, particularly regarding Indians' conversion. The most ambitious initiative, however, was *reducción*: consolidating dispersed Andean descent groups (*ayllus*) into church-based settlements. In 1567, Juan de Matienzo wrote his *Gobierno del Perú*, which became a blueprint for settlement consolidation when Francisco de Toledo became viceroy of Peru in 1569. Toledo served as Spanish envoy to the Council of Trent and on the Council of the Indies before his appointment as viceroy. He knew of Matienzo's proposals and the Second Council of Lima's new regulations. Both figured in a larger plan secretly elaborated for him before his departure. Among these 'instructions' was one to establish the Inquisition of Lima, and another to evaluate *corregidores'* effectiveness in checking the *encomendero's* abuses. The Counter-Reformation's first colonial repercussions thus intertwined with an assertion of absolutist control, allowing the Crown to claim reformist credentials and the high moral ground in what was otherwise a sordid struggle for power with its trustees and officials. In summary, a broad upsurge of reform swept through colonial Andean society starting in 1565, and culminated in the 'Toledo reforms' that we will now examine, particularly *reducción*.

Reducción: Settlement Consolidation as Holistic Civilizing Project

The defining feature of *reducción* as practised under Toledo was the consolidation of dispersed Indian settlements into church-based towns of four hundred inhabitants or more (Levillier 1921–26 III: 341). This policy's primary motive was ostensibly evangelical. Toledo argued that when a single priest was in charge of two thousand Indians scattered over a hundred leagues, religious instruction was bound to suffer (Levillier 1921–26 III: 492). He further resolved that priests should not minister to more than a thousand Indians scattered across the landscape: *reducción* would localize their flock in one town, perhaps with a few annexes no more than two leagues from the principal settlement (Levillier 1921–26 IV: 111–2). *Reducción* was also to introduce Indians to what Spaniards called *policia*: organized public life. By relocating and rebuilding Andean towns, advocates of *reducción* hoped to reconstruct their inhabitants similarly, and to replace indirect rule with Spanish fiscal, administrative, and religious organizations. Early-modern Spaniards, whose intellectual culture strongly linked ideas of urbanism, civilization, and religious propriety (Pagden 1982: 18, passim), readily saw an intimate connection between consolidated settlements and the true faith. The same concatenation of ideas existed in *reducción*'s semantic field during the sixteenth and seventeenth centuries: core meanings of ordering, rational persuasion, religious conversion, and political subjugation subsumed the particular emphasis on physical incorporation and consolidation. Today's readers struggle to realize how central rational, moral, and political ordering were to *reduccion*'s early-modern meaning, and just how peripheral physical diminution and consolidation were. Loss of size mattered only to the extent that it featured some such ordering. Often the word denoted only ordering, persuasion or subjugation, without any reference to physical consolidation or shrinkage.[1] Thus, translating *reducción* as 'settlement consolidation' is inadequate: its true referent was the ethico-political agenda that underwrote this physical operation. Neither was *reducción* primarily a worldly concern: viceroys often assigned it to the ecclesiastical as opposed to the secular branch of government (Levillier 1921–26 IV: 397). In sixteenth-century Peru, 'conversion' would often be a more accurate translation than 'settlement consolidation.'

Declarations and limited enactments of *reducción* began with Spanish colonialism in the Americas (Málaga Medina 1974). Although Carlos V ordained settlement consolidation throughout the Indies in 1549, the pace of implementation was desultory in Peru as elsewhere, and Cajamarca was the only region to comply then (Levillier 1921–26 III: 341). Fraser (1990) shows that Spanish colonial town planning derived its regularities less from royal decrees than from established cultural premises, presumably those encoded in the term *reducción* itself. Yet by the 1560s, the political will to enforce *reducción* emerged specifically in Peru due to the chronic lawlessness and rebellion that had afflicted the colony since its conquest. As ordering and political subjugation, *reducción* became the perfect centrepiece for the broader reformist agenda that emerged during this decade. By 1562, even some Indians who were to be its subjects called for *reducción* (Ortiz de Zúñiga 1562 I: 41, 52, 57, 63, 73, 79, 83, 87; II: 37, 49, 58). Only with Toledo's arrival in 1569, however, did *reducción*'s administrative and evangelical components fuse into a single, sustained, and centrally organized policy. Toledo issued instructions for the *reducción general* of the Peruvian countryside in 1569–70, and amended, refined, and repeated these ordinances during the following decade. The sheer volume of his writings on *reducción* allows only the most cursory summary here.

When Toledo took office, he ordered a general inspection (*visita general*) of the realm, which established both the *reducciones* and their tributary obligations (Toledo 1975; 1986: 43–60, Levillier 1921–26 IV: 383). The first tributary project was usually to build the church and municipal quarters around which the new settlement was to cohere (Toledo 1986: 246). Most *reducción* centres already had churches, which nonetheless underwent expansion or centralizing relocation to receive new inhabitants (Levillier 1921–26 III: 508). *Curacas* were to make Indians build churches and were subject to exile and loss of office if they failed to deliver within a specified period (Lissón y Cháves 1943–47 II: 619). Each *reducción* was to establish its own community coffer (*caja de comunidad*) to finance local improvements and tributary payments. By 1575, as an incentive for completion, Toledo remitted a half year's tributary obligations in places where *reducción* was still ongoing and ordered that the other half be deposited in the community coffers (1986: 47, 95). Eventually, however, Indians assumed their full tributary obligations to the

Crown. Indians' religious status as neophytes figured in most rational-
izations of tribute, most commonly by presenting it as what they owed
temporally in return for their spiritual salvation, but also as penance for
their idolatrous past, or preparation for their gradual entry into Catholic
civilization. Thus, serious debates arose over whether *encomenderos* who
had failed to evangelize Indians adequately should refund them the
tribute they paid, a question that Toledo answered affirmatively (Lissón
y Cháves 1943–47: 744–65, Levillier 1921–26 IV: 136). For some modern
commentators such as Málaga Medina (1974: 141, 157–8), these fiscal
concerns were paramount, and made *reducción*'s religious dimension
into a fig leaf covering an otherwise naked colonial exploitation. Unde-
niably, the cash and tributary labour collected in these new settlements
enriched the Crown and often its colonial officials. Far from negating
reducción as a religious project, however, such corruption only provoked
further denunciations and cries for reform – a dynamic that we will
explore at length below. Furthermore, as Abercrombie observes, *reducción* disciplined and reshaped Andean society in ways that exceeded
tribute collection and were so costly that extracting wealth cannot have
been their goal (1998: 246). Let us therefore take a closer look at what this
program comprised.

New towns were to be as far away as possible from pagan settlements and their shrines. Once construction of new settlements began,
Indians were to destroy their 'old towns,' not only to salvage building
materials but also to make *reducción* definitive and irreversible. A grid
pattern was to define the new towns. Onto the central plaza were to
face the church, community buildings, the town council, court, and jail.
Additional buildings for the priests were also stipulated. Indians were
to construct their houses within the grid plan's blocks with their doors
facing the street. The *curaca*'s house was to be wider than the others and
have meeting chambers for discussing public business, a large kitchen,
and separate dormitories for the *curaca* and his wife, their girls and
female servants, and their boys. Ordinary Indians were also to have
such segregated dormitories, sleep on raised platforms, and keep their
floors well swept. Public-health concerns prohibited fields and irrigation canals within town, and houses could have only a small kitchen
garden. Finally, the town council (*cabildo*) was to have a full set of officials and thus involve Indians in Spanish modes of self-government.
These officials were to regulate and Christianize civic life: no pagans or
convicted idolaters could serve, and Indian *fiscales* were to prosecute
them. *Curacas'* jurisdiction was theoretically limited to collecting trib-

ute and enforcing *reducción* (Toledo 1986: 34–6; 1989: 217–66; Lissón y Cháves 1943–47 II: 709–17). The goal was clearly not just to consolidate Indian settlements for administrative convenience. Above all, *reducciones* were to embody an entirely different and more elevated way of life, including Catholicism, urbanity, public order, rational governance, improved personal hygiene, and morals.

Abercrombie notes the emphasis on visibility in this new regime and argues that *reducción* inaugurated surveillance techniques that other colonial regimes adopted only in the nineteenth century (1998: 247–8). The temptation to invoke Foucault here is understandable but conflates regimes of power that he was at pains to separate, and risks mistaking the will to inspect and correct, which Toledo's writings amply express, for their realization, which was at best episodic. By the end of the 1570s, many Andean people already found *reducción* to be insufferable and escaped it by fleeing to remote areas, other indigenous communities, or the private service of individual Spaniards. At stake was not just the realization of surveillance but also its goals, which derived from the Inquisition and Counter-Reformation more than modern forms of governance. Toledo announced the policy of *reducción* in his 1569–70 instructions with the following preamble: 'the principal cause of the *visita general* is to give order and a way that the Indians have competent religious instruction and can be better versed in the things of our holy Catholic faith, and can have the sacraments administered to them with greater facility and comfort, and so that they can be maintained in justice and live politically like people of reason and like the rest of His Majesty's vassals, and for all this to be effected, it is desirable that the Indians who live dispersed and scattered be reduced to towns with layout and order' (1986: 33). Religious indoctrination is clearly the primary goal here, although Toledo links it to political order and consolidated settlements. Ostensibly, the general tour of inspection's main goal was to convert the Indians and learn their religious doctrines to refute them better (Toledo 1986: 14).

On September 8, 1571, Toledo issued the first of several additions to his instructions for inspectors. He reminded them that the *visita*'s main reason was *encomenderos*' failure to give the natives adequate religious instruction (Toledo 1986: 135). After identifying Indian 'idolatries' as a major obstacle to *reducción*'s successful realization, he added that 'the principal effect of the general inspection and of my personal inspection was to extirpate idolatries, sorcery, and dogmatizers so that the Evangelical teaching would fall well disposed upon ground where it could bear fruit' (Toledo 1986: 136). He further specified that the ecclesiastical judge ordinary must punish idolatrous Indians, and ensure that they receive intensified religious instruction: 'And should it occur that an infidel dogmatizer be found who disrupts the preaching of the gospel and manages to pervert the newly converted, in this case secular judges can proceed against such infidel dogmatizers, punishing them with death or other punishments that seem appropriate to them, since it is declared by congresses of theologians and jurists that His Majesty has convened in the Kingdoms of Spain that not only is this just cause for condemning such people to death, but even for waging war against a whole kingdom or province with all the death and damage to property that results' (Toledo 1986: 137). Through this ordinance, Toledo hoped to compensate for Indians' exemption from the Inquisition, a situation that he eventually tried to change (Levillier 1921–26 VI: 53–4). The same provisos reappeared verbatim in a communication promoting religious instruction that accompanied revised instructions for *reducción*, both issued on March 6, 1573. In the revised instructions, Toledo acknowledged that some officials enforced *reducción* reluctantly and that Indians resisted it to pursue drunken festivities, vices, and idolatries in their old towns (1986: 245–9). Thus, he appointed Cristóbal de Albornoz, the Taqui Oncoy's nemesis, to reduce and extirpate idolatry in Chinchaysuyo.[2] Clearly missionary goals figured centrally in *reducción*.

Reducción as a Mortuary Regime

Toledo took Andean mortuary idolatries very seriously as an impediment to *reducción*. His revised instructions of November 7, 1573, warned inspectors against *curacas* who wanted their own hamlets to become sites for consolidated settlements, adding that 'the principal point of which you will have to be aware when making said *reducciones* is that said Indians be removed from the places and sites of their idolatries and burials of their ancestors, out of respect for which, and on the pretext of piety, they have tricked and are tricking inspectors into not moving them from where they are, which is in great detriment to their souls and against that which His Majesty has decreed' (Toledo 1986: 281–2). To counteract this perceived ill, Toledo announced penalties for inspectors who let themselves be dissuaded from enforcing *reducción*, for *curacas* who tried to prevent or subvert it, and for priests who undermined it. This passage specifically blames Indians' attachment to their mortuary sites for their reticence to accept *reducción*. Predictably, Toledo followed this analysis with his ordinances of November 6, 1575, on the proper manner of death and burial. Indian mayors were to take Spanish-style testaments from dying Indians, setting aside property for their children, but also pious bequests and suffrages for their souls: Toledo even provided a standardized form for such testaments (1989: 229–31).

As he neared the end of his term as viceroy in 1580, Toledo again denounced Andean mortuary idolatries:

> these Indians had as a very celebrated religious observance among themselves the adoration of the dead from whom they directly descended, ignoring the first cause of their creation as they did in all their other opinions, and thus they had their tombs by the roads, distant and separated from the towns, and in other places inside of them, and in others in their very houses, for in this they had different customs, and to avoid this said damage, I order and command that each magistrate ensure that in his district all the tower tombs be knocked down, and that a large pit be dug into which all of the bones of those who died as pagans be mixed together, and that special care be taken henceforth to gather the intelligence necessary to discover whether any of the baptized are buried outside of the church, with the priest and the judge helping each other in such an important matter, and that they have great caution in the doors of the temples since they remove and take them [the baptized dead] from the sepulchres at night when they are authorities and important people for said effect, and they kill some women and Indian men saying that they will serve them in the other life. (1989: 413–14)

What Toledo uncharacteristically failed to specify here was the firm expectation that Christian Indians be buried in church floors. Since the First Council of Lima had already done so in 1551 (Vargas Ugarte 1951: 21), this was technically redundant, but this was a viceroy who had no aesthetic scruples about repeating orders. Probably Toledo took church burial for granted as an integral part of *reducción*, as indeed it was. Surprisingly, the Third Council of Lima (1583) also neglected the rationale for church burial, given the debate with Protestantism over indulgences that shaped its Counter-Reformation context. It was not until the early seventeenth century that Archbishop Lobo Guerrero justified church burial through the 'doctrine of the saints' (1613: 138). Following his hint, let us turn to the communion of the saints as church burial's theological basis, leaving for the next chapter the question of why so few authorities actually invoked it.

Peter Brown's classic study shows that the cult of the saints arose in late antiquity by bringing the dead, previously banished to the periphery, into churches at the heart of the city (1981: ch. 1). Saintly relics became physically and categorically associated with the altar, which radiated grace to the living but also to the dead interred in the church and awaiting resurrection. Over a millennium later and an ocean away, *reducción* upheld this same basic pattern. The Spanish mediation and its intervening history deserve some discussion, however.

Ironically, the medieval Spanish Church struggled with its laity to prohibit burial *ad sanctos*: eventually it allowed interments in church floors covered with flat memorial stones but tried to ban raised monuments (Guiance 1998: 60–1). As the concept of purgatory emerged during the twelfth century, however, dead Christian souls increasingly depended on the living's ministrations; hence, church burial's spiritual benefits grew. Suffrages, acts of penance through which the devout might shorten their stay in purgatory, proliferated. They included prayer and fasting but also pious donations and sponsoring masses. The revised doctrine of the communion of saints rationalized both suffrages and church burial (Guiance 1998: 64–77). Indulgences allowed the living to help those in purgatory, but the Eucharist was even more effective as the one sacrament that reached beyond the living (Eire 1995: 210). Those whose bodies lay near the altar benefited from the Eucharists performed there, and they hastened through purgatory. This benefit diminished as distance from the altar increased, so people eagerly sought the closest burial places: while the church could not sell them outright, pious bequests and posthumous mass sponsorships might secure them (see Eire 1995: 99–100). As a redemptive organization, the Church promoted the circulation of grace through heaven, earth, and purgatory. A Christian community extended beyond the living to include members in these other domains. This cosmological communication of grace through the altar explains why Church and Crown insisted on church burial in colonial Peru. Thus, *reducción* applied not only to the living but also to the dead, as a woman in one idolatry trial realized when she confessed to hiding the body of her husband 'so that they not reduce him to the church' (Duviols 1986: 18, 14).

More specifically Spanish reasons for emphasizing church burial also existed. In Spain, Jews and Muslims usually buried their dead outside town in graveyards, so burial in urban churches distinguished Christians. Consecrated Christian graveyards fell into disuse as the Reconquest of Spain progressed. By the sixteenth century, nearly all Christian burials were in churches (Eire 1995: 91). Mourning customs also differentiated Christians from Jews and Moors. Late-medieval Christians explicitly attenuated their attentions to the corpse and frowned on exaggerated displays of grief during interments, which betrayed a lack of faith in resurrection (Eire 1995: 85–6, 151–2, Guiance 1998: 44). Thus, church burial was just one way that Christians used death to make an ethnic statement, marking their particular affiliation within late-medieval Spain's religious plurality. Furthermore, by burying their dead in town centres when Jews and Moors buried theirs outside them, Christians claimed a certain pre-eminence within these multiethnic settlements. Their religious life became more fully invested in Spanish towns than did that of Jews and Moors. Undoubtedly this contributed to the strong identification of urbanity, civilization, and Christianity that had emerged by the sixteenth century in Spain, which the very meaning of *reducción* embodied.

As Jews and Moors converted to Catholicism during the fifteenth century, old Christians closely monitored their burial practices. The Council of Alcalá, convened in 1481, prohibited all differences in the burial practices of old and new Christians. Even after their conversion, some of Toledo's new Christians still buried their dead in unconsecrated ground outside the city, either because they had always buried their ancestors there or because old Christians denied them burial in urban churches. A previous archbishop of Toledo had ordered new Christians to bury their dead in the cemetery of San Bartolomé outside Toledo's city walls, both to legitimate and control this continuity with past practice. Since old Christians speculated that the newly converted were reverting to their old religion, the council overturned this compromise. It ordered new Christians to bury their dead in the city, and that any new marble mortuary stones outside its walls be dismantled and donated to local parish coffers. The goal was not to persecute the newly converted but to include them in the communion of the saints instead of treating them as descendants of Jews and Moors. Thus, in the name of Church unity, these same ordinances anathematized confraternities that rejected new Christians.[3] Similar universalist motives arguably informed Spaniards' insistence on church burial for Indians in the Andes.

Contemporary with such decreed inclusion, however, was a powerful countercurrent of exclusion. In 1483, only two years after their enactment, the Council of Alcalá's measures were repealed during the Inquisition's inaugural attack on new Christians.[4] By allowing a return to mortuary segregation, this annulment also reinforced a parochial view of the communion of saints that emerged during the *reconquista*: Spanish old Christians saw the Church Suffering and the Church Triumphant as their own carnal ancestors who transmitted the true faith to them while fighting the infidel. Questions of ancestry subtly displaced those of grace and redemption in a universalizing faith. This peculiarly Spanish version of the communion of the saints began to generate or converge with the proto-racist ideology of 'purity of blood' (*limpieza de sangre*), which racialized and made hereditary a person's religious disposition (see Sicroff 1960; Netanyahu 1995). Old Christians received the true faith's grace from their ancestors, and so were 'pure.' By contrast, new Christians received only religious error's 'stain' and 'infamy' from their ancestors. Despite the Inquisition's watchful eye and firm hand, exactly how many generations it would take to remove the stain was an open question. Even moderates expressed some racial pessimism about new Christians' true conversion.

Similar doubts played out in Peru, where (as we have already seen) even the optimists like José de Acosta saw religious error as a racialized malady whose only cure was communion. Yet such a cure presupposed *reducción*: only by rebuilding Indian life from the ground up, educating, and preventing (with force if necessary) the return to idolatry could the missionary arrest these hereditary inclinations and modify them over time. We will see below that Spaniards tried to break idolatry's intergenerational transmission by attacking the 'cult of the dead,' which many thought the most pernicious in the vast panorama of Andean idolatries, a true bête noire (Taylor 1980: 53). They commonly interpreted Andean oracular consultations of the dead as veiled communion with the Devil (MacCormack 1991: 85–94), the ultimate source of racializing disgrace. Establishing a proper circulation of grace between the living and the dead was key, so Indians had privileged access to church burial within their own parishes. Commoners received church-floor burial without having to make pious bequests, but their bodies might later be exhumed and relocated. Confraternity members could claim niches closer to the altar, but their remains might also be removed subsequently to make room for newly deceased members. *Curacas* typically claimed the best burial niches closest to the altar in Indian parish churches. They had the means to make substantial pious bequests that permanently secured these places for their descendants, each of whom was likely to request elaborate suffrages on death. The earliest such bequest that I know of dates to 1592. By the early seventeenth century, we can assume that they were common, even if the archival record consists only of those that occasioned disputes.[5]

Crisis and 'Corruption'

In 1572, Toledo claimed that most of the new settlements' churches were already built, and that *reducción* ran ahead of schedule (Levillier 1921–26 IV: 410). Yet soon doubters emerged: in 1572 the Jesuit Bartolomé Hernández wrote to the Council of the Indies that *reducción*'s ever-expanding instructions obscured and left unrealized the basic goal of public order. In his view, Castro's *corregidores* could accomplish these ends more cheaply than Toledo's inspectors (Lissón y Cháves 1943–47 II: 603). Resistance and misgivings surfaced in official correspondence from various notable figures, who complained that inexperienced officials executed the policy hastily, with unintended consequences and much hardship for Indians, including an increased tributary burden.[6] Predictably, the Dominican provincial, Alonso de la Cerda, was the most strident. In 1572, he wrote that the *visita general*'s true goal was to raise Indians' tributary obligation. Indians hear mass in open air or under sheds in many reduced towns, he continued, since Toledo was too cheap to finance proper churches, to the Crown's great shame, considering the quantities of silver extracted from the land (Lissón y Cháves 1943–47 II: 623–6). After Toledo left Peru in 1581, his successor, Viceroy Enríquez, wrote to the king regarding *reducción*: 'from many parts there are complaints from the Indians, and they could hardly be fewer given that the matter was so violently executed, pray to God that with time, it will be remedied' (Levillier 1921–26, IX: 50).

Through *reducción*, Toledo hoped to assert absolutist control over privileged colonists' seigneurial pretensions and further impose Spanish forms of governance, settlement, and worship on Andean society. He unequivocally criticized earlier forms of indirect rule, particularly the *encomenderos* who had benefited from them, and disparaged their compromises with Andean institutions and officials. Nonetheless, even he realized the limits to this critique. Much as he railed against Incas and *curacas* as illegitimate tyrants and hoped to undermine *curacas'* local authority with Spanish governance structures, he still saw that indirect rule was insurmountable: 'these natives cannot be governed except with the caciques as the instruments of execution both in temporal and spiritual matters nor is there anything that can be done for them, be it good or bad. It is necessary that these caciques be good because with their example the good rubs off and since one word from them does more to make them abandon their idols and evils than a hundred sermons from priests. Necessarily and by the same token, if these caciques are bad they bring the whole multitude behind them in the imitation of their lives, which are frequently so bad that they have to be seen to be believed' (Levillier 1921–36 V: 315). The most common resolution of these conflicting impulses, one to replace indigenous politico-religious structures and the other to use them, was to treat indirect rule and indigenous institutions as corruption. A definite discursive formula governed this operation. First, reformists portrayed indigenous authorities and institutions as tyrannic, idolatrous, or contravening natural law. Next, however, they had to explain Spanish collusion with indigenous depravity. Here greed and lust became the salient motives for Spaniards' deviation from their noble mission of converting and civilizing the natives. Indian perversity and Spanish greed could each activate the other, or simply exist symbiotically in various unholy alliances to be explored below. Much early-colonial Indian legislation was separatist because of this fear that each estate brought out the worst in the other. Thus, reformist discourse could assume a racist guise that blamed Indians for the colonies' fallen character, a Lascasian form, in which Spanish greed was the primary corrupting influence or, most commonly, mix and match elements of each. Let us examine this dynamic in relation to indirect rule's most basic expression: the tributary economy.

Toledo formalized Indian tributary obligation around two requirements. First was the *mita*, a direct revival of Inca practice: one-seventh of male Indians between the ages of eighteen and fifty in every jurisdiction did tributary labour for the colonial state at any given time. This obligation was to rotate periodically so that every Indian took the 'turn' that *mita* denoted. Toledo allocated this labour to road maintenance, service at inns and in Spanish towns, but above all to the Huancavelica and Potosí mines. The second requirement was the *tasa*, a monetary tax that *curacas* collected semi-annually (Toledo 1989: 239). Both exactions varied according to population levels recorded during Toledo's general inspection. Each *corregimiento* kept a *padrón*, or roster of its tributaries, who, as the tributary population continued to shrink, absorbed an increasing share of the labour and tax that their jurisdiction owed. At *curacas'* instigation, subsequent reinspections could adjust tributary obligations to actual population levels, but these were infrequent and politically fraught.

The tributary rosters were a major entrée for local 'corruption' in this system. Exactly how many Indians a jurisdiction contained was always debatable. Only *curacas* knew their people well enough to say, and they frequently hid many in remote areas far from the *reducciones*, where priests or *corregidores* could not find them. They usually demanded a monetary bribe plus personal service from those they sheltered, and collected *tasa* from them to meet external obligations. Thus, as under the Incas (Moore 1958, Murra 1980), *curacas* took some tribute they collected for the colonial state as 'intermediaries.' Legally, the Toledo reforms excluded them as beneficiaries. In practice, Spaniards lacked the Incas' adroitness in Andean tributary etiquette, and could get Indian labour only through *curacas*, whose bargaining power thereby increased. Often, however, priests and *corregidores* colluded with *curacas* in sheltering tributaries, and collected similar rewards from them to supplement their own increasingly inadequate salaries. The same reasons propelled them into illicit commerce (variously designated as *tratos y contratos*, *grangerías*, *trajines*, and *repartos*), particularly selling wine to Indians in their jurisdictions. Priests and even *corregidores* also took contributions of food called *camaricos* from the Indians in their jurisdictions, a practice Toledo tried to prohibit (1989: 35). Priests, *corregidores*, and *curacas* all competed over these illicit tributary extractions, and might occasionally denounce one another, but they also formed coalitions to reduce this risk. Guaman Poma gives us the definitive depiction of these inter-ethnic conspiracies to exploit Indians and defraud the Crown (see figure 4.1), a visual counterpart to absolutist corruption discourses.

When we turn to the tributary economy's actual functioning, its Andean logic is unmistakable. *Encomenderos*, priests, and *corregidores* all depended on *curacas* to deliver Indian labour. Worse still, from a reformist perspective, was that these Spanish officials themselves resorted to Andean practices to recruit Indian labour. For example, Dr. Cuenca, a judge (*oidor*) of the High Court of Lima, discovered on an inspection of 1567 that in some districts, *encomenderos* ordered priests to gather single men and women together and forcibly marry them to increase the tributary population (Lissón y Cháves 1943–47 II: 355–6). A few years later, Toledo made a similar discovery: 'Of the priests in these parishes I have found hardly any who do not truck, contract and pawn-broke, many gamblers and all with aptitude. Most go about here with their servant

Figure 4.1 Portraits of Corruption

girls who are of marriageable age since in some provinces they already subject them to labour drafts just as they do the Indian men, and they give them to Indian bachelors who serve in the cities of Cuenca, Jaen, Loxa and Zamora as the *corregidor* of those cities told me of more than three hundred of these servant girls who were distributed there whom I ordered separated from the bachelors' (Levillier 1921–26, III: 385). To understand this practice, we must recall that under the Incas, marriage was a rite of passage into tributary status (Murra 1980, Gose 2000). Although Toledo assigned Indians tributary obligations starting at the age of eighteen, this report shows that the Andean criterion of marriage remained in force (cf. Spalding 1984: 175). Here, priests brokered marriages as Inca governors and provincial *curacas* had previously done. So Spanish officials not only accepted Andean norms but operated them to their advantage.

Elsewhere, Toledo reported that *curacas* continued to oversee the operation of indigenous socio-economic and religious institutions: 'In the course of this inspection it has been understood that on the Pacific plains two or three leagues [away] there are Indians who publicly con-

serve their rites and ceremonies with public shrines and houses of re-
clusion for chosen women [*mamaconas*] and idolatrous priests with
large herding estates and Indian servants applied to their false religion
and their dead, who remain with the same service they had in life'
(Levillier 1921–26 IV: 97). Of particular interest is the reference to chosen women, whom political authorities secluded as girls and later allocated in marriage to confer tributary obligations on their husbands.
While still in seclusion, they also contributed to the tributary economy
by producing corn beer and distributing it to labourers during the
working day, according to the Andean logic of *mink'a*, by which providing food and drink establishes the role of proprietor (Gose 2000).
Apparently much of this complex also continued, even after the rigours
of *reducción*. Thus, Toledo forbade *curacas* to enclose single women on
the pretext of helping their communities, and mayor's deputies to collect girls of age nine or ten, to prevent these indigenous practices from
continuing under *reducción* (1989: 244, 252). He also tried to wrest control over the production and distribution of corn beer from *curacas* and
centralize it in the *reducciones* (1989: 264–6), apparently without success.

Ysidro Sánchez' unsolicited report of 1589 on *reducción* confirms and
develops this picture. Despite Toledo's decree that only principal *curacas* should retain office and tributary exemption after *reducción*, in practice, the old towns' political hierarchies usually persisted in new, multi-
ayllu settlements. Moreover, by sponsoring festive drinking, *curacas*
controlled the *reducciones'* town councils, including their functionaries,
whom Toledo expected to undermine *curacas'* traditional authority.
Curacas amassed maize-growing lands and young unmarried women
to produce corn beer, whose distribution also let them extract tributary
labour and sponsor idolatrous festivities. One witness describes how
curacas kept the young women hidden in an old town where they produced vast quantities of corn beer. There they lived with other Indians
serving their *curaca*, more than one thousand in total, away from Christianity and off the tributary roster. Another describes how *curacas* systematically misrepresented missing Indians to local priests as dead or
fugitives, when in fact they hid in nearby fields or gullies. Several mentioned that the *curacas* used the women as concubines, and forbade
their parents to give them in marriage. One specified that *curacas* took
sexual advantage of the women during their tributary duties in inns
and textile mills, and made ten to twelve unmarried women accompany them in their travels, but also many married women, all to carry
or make corn beer.[7] Witnesses thought that *curacas* seized community

resources and anything belonging to their commoners, to the point that the latter lost any incentive to work for themselves. They also alleged that *curacas* collected more tribute than the Crown required, then pocketed the difference, and illicitly collected tribute from the elderly, unmarried women, and widows, all of whom were supposed to be exempt. Since these abuses went unpunished, witnesses saw them as rampant: should a priest try to curb them, the *curaca* would have his house burnt down or litigate to remove him from office using false testimony. According to one witness, *corregidores* frequently conspired with *curacas* to let Indians absent themselves from religious instruction, by failing to burn their houses in the old towns, or by letting them live in huts by their fields, all so that they too could keep them off the tributary roster and personally use their labour.[8] Since Toledo himself described most of these practices in 1574 (Levillier 1921–26 V: 315–6), we must conclude that *reducción* did not erode *curacas'* power within their communities.

According to this testimony, *curacas'* position derived mainly from distributing corn beer, which articulated labour recruitment, religious festivities, and diplomatic socializing. As was the case under the Incas (see Gose 2000), corn beer's cultural centrality meant that political authorities had to control young women's labour and marriageability. By secluding them in old towns and using their corn beer to articulate basic social bonds, *curacas* reproduced some central aspects of the Incas' 'chosen women' complex. Unlike these early colonial *curacas*, however, the Incas gave such women in marriage: either to tributaries in brideservice, or to polygynous political authorities as tokens of alliance. This testimony suggests that *curacas* sexually monopolized then discarded such women as an expression of their power. Any recognizable brideservice system for male tributaries had disappeared. The Incas' careful guarding of unmarried women's sexuality and use of marriage as a rite of passage contrasts remarkably with this testimony, which describes the public defloration of virgins and random copulation between men and women of all ages in drunken festivities.[9] If believable, these reports suggest that such a brideservice regime survived only in its transgression. The report that *curacas* drew on married women's labour to make and transport corn beer is also incompatible with the earlier 'chosen women' complex. What remained, however, was corn beer's extraordinary ability to articulate religious and political solidarity and authoritative claims to labour. No *curaca* could rule without it, so all tried to control the women (married or unmarried) who produced it, whether or not that involved the sexual excesses these witnesses describe or imagine.

Witnesses' attitudes towards festive drinking and *curacas'* control of women were predictably contradictory. On the one hand, Spaniards expressed their disgust at such debauched practices and used them to portray *curacas* as abusive tyrants. On the other hand, and less obviously, Spaniards recognized that they needed *curacas* and their corrupting sociability to recruit Andean labour. Thus, even the featured colonial reform project of *reducción* retained the *curaca* as intermediary. Indirect rule continued largely as before, but now as a disavowed 'corruption' in which indigenous depravity and Spanish greed were the primary actors. With various permutations, combinations, and emphases, this discursive formula set the tone for the entire seventeenth century and beyond. It established a fundamental tension between reform and disillusionment at the heart of the colonial project, whose 'fallen' character further emerged with every failed attempt to elevate the Indians spiritually. Even in 1589, we already see how thoroughly attempts at reform were captive to the same premises they decried. Thus, the proposed solution to *curacas'* sexual abuse of unmarried women was to confine the latter to textile mills that priests controlled.[10] When seventeenth-century priests achieved this end, their Indian parishioners often denounced them for similar forms of sexual exploitation.[11] The structural features of colonial extraction became a series of moral 'betrayals' that endlessly shocked and appalled absolutist corruption discourses.

Indian idolatries were the other major factor that brought *reducción* into crisis, according to Sánchez' report. Several witnesses mention that when a death occurred in a Spanish priest's absence, Indians would bury the body with pagan rites in the fields or the *huacas* but claim they had interred it in the church. One further described how in these rites, living mourners did dances (*taquis*) with dead bodies. Another noted that Indians disinterred the bodies buried in the churches of old towns and took them to their *huacas*. Yet another recounted that around 1559, an important *curaca* died and was buried in the cathedral of Lima, but his survivors bribed a slave of the archbishop of Lima to let them disinter the body and take it back to their *huaca*.[12] The most detailed account of all concerned don Luis Missa, *curaca* of Atun Larachu, who wanted to confess before he died. Once the local priest heard, he began the eighteen-league journey from the other end of his parish, but arrived to find the *curaca* already dead and buried in the fields with pagan rites. With the priest still there, Indians approached the sepulchre to worship.

When the priest objected and demanded they return their *curaca*'s body to church, the Indians refused and threatened him when he persisted: since (as the priest observed) the nearest town with resident Spaniards was thirty leagues away, he had no choice but to accept.[13]

These witnesses proposed measures to counteract indigenous mortuary practices, which further underline that *reducción* was, among other things, a mortuary regime. Foremost was that parishes with several small and far-flung settlements be subdivided to avoid the problem of priestly absences and Indians dying without confession. One witness lamented that in remote Indian parishes, people generally took bodies to the grave wrapped in a blanket and tied to a pole for lack of a decent litter, and buried them without suffrage if the priest was absent, often face down or crooked in the graves, or with coca offerings and pagan ceremonies. The implication was that if these towns had better Catholic mortuary infrastructure, such disturbing reversions to idolatry would not occur. Most witnesses also agreed that if Indian towns had hospitals, fewer would die and those who did would also receive spiritual succour in the process. In effect, hospitals would better integrate Indians into the Catholic mortuary regime. As one astute witness noted, however, Indians already feared Spanish hospitals as places people went to die, so it was preferable to cure Indians in their homes, where they were more at ease.[14]

In summary, most of Sánchez' witnesses held that *reducción* was improperly executed. Many consolidated towns still had fewer than three hundred inhabitants so several combined to form a parish whose priest visited each sequentially, leaving the others to revert to drunkenness and idolatry in his absence. When *reducción* did form larger towns, Indians still circumvented it by building huts in their old towns, near their fields or in gullies, to be near their *huacas* and free from tribute.[15] Although still unusual, these observations were not isolated or novel: respondents to a royal questionnaire in 1586 anticipated them, adding that Spanish governors and *corregidores* often approved such subversions of *reducción* (Jiménez de la Espada 1965: 184–5, 227, 238–9, 344). Similarly, Sánchez' witnesses were not alone in seeing fugitives from *reducción* as a massive fact. Bartolomé Álvarez, an obscure priest in the parish of Aullagas, began his lengthy and bitter letter to Philip II as follows: 'the *corregidores* are obliged, and the governors, to reduce the towns and order them reduced, and to build churches, take care to find out if the people come diligently for religious instruction and mass, to make them come and help the priest, and punish the careless, lazy, and bad Indians in the works of Christianity, as the ordinances of don Francisco de Toledo require, [but] they do not comply. Rather, many of the towns have yet to be reduced, and many churches are yet to be built, and a large part of the Indians are fled to many places where they neither see a priest nor receive religious instruction' (1588: 11). These sources inaugurate a crisis genre of writings about *reducción* that was soon to emerge. In 1589, however, the Crown and the Council of the Indies did not yet accept that *reducción* was failing. Sánchez did not present his proposals to the Council of the Indies until 1603, by which point many others were voicing similar opinions. Perhaps this delay suggests that Sánchez did not judge the political climate favourable to his requests when he first assembled his evidence.

A shift began in 1592, when Viceroy Marqués de Cañete wrote the king about the *reducciones'* massive depopulation due to flight and the epidemics of 1589–90 (Cole 1985: 63). A year after taking office in 1596, Viceroy Luis de Velasco wrote the king that Indians had fled the *reducciones*, oppressed by the Potosí *mita*, their *corregidores*, priests, and *curacas*, leaving the highlands from Cuzco to Potosí all but depopulated. After conferring with authorities, he struck a 'general agreement' with the High Court of Lima in 1598 to repopulate the *reducciones*. *Curacas* and *corregidores* were each to list the missing Indians and those from other areas (*forasteros*) present in their jurisdictions. *Corregidores* were then to write to their counterparts in *forasteros'* natal towns to prepare fields and houses for their return. On the appointed day, they were to return the *forasteros* gently and simultaneously to their original towns. Where he anticipated difficulties, Velasco appointed 'reducing judges' to oversee the transfers. He also prohibited priests from charging *forasteros* in their parishes one peso annually, since this revenue normalized the undermining of *reducción*. Spaniards, *corregidores*, and *curacas* were to return the Indians working for them privately on the threat of stiff fines or removal from office. When settlers dependent on *forastero* labour learned of these measures, they protested vociferously and forced a compromise from Velasco, who updated to May 21, 1598, Toledo's previous decree that any Indians who had lived outside their natal communities for ten years or more in the service of Spaniards could remain.[16] Velaso's successor, the Conde de Monterrey, extended these measures to the Audiencia de La Plata and appointed commissars with full authority and a retinue of ministers to enforce them. Later sources claim that these measures successfully returned *forasteros* to their *reducciones* but did not keep them there.[17]

By 1600, incessant complaints led the king and the Council of the Indies to order Velasco to stop Indian flight from the *reducciones* by protecting them from greedy Spaniards.[18] With such discussion now commonplace at the highest administrative levels, *reducción*'s perceived failure became an entrée for enterprising but less powerful subjects. In 1604, the Dominican friar Miguel de Monsalve wrote a treatise to the king that reiterated these established lines of argument. He stressed that the Crown lost untold revenues in Peru because Indians fled the *reducciones* to escape abusive colonial officials and live in remote gullies, jungles, and alpine areas. Within eight years, he thought Indians would completely abandon Peru's *reducciones* to escape their enslavement to *corregidores*, which was worse than the Israelites' in Egypt and threatened the legitimate interests of both Church and state. Not only did Indian escapees deny Spaniards tribute, personal service, or any other temporal good, they also suffered spiritual neglect. Adults returned to 'their old rites and ceremonies in their eternal idolatry,' and they raised their children without baptism. Monsalve estimated that at least one hundred thousand Indians lived and died in this deplorable barbarity, and advised the king to revitalize *reducción* by eliminating corrupt *corregidores*. Thus, he could gain an additional revenue of one million pesos in gold, and better discharge his spiritual responsibilities.[19]

Monsalve was hardly the first priest to claim that the Crown's functionaries subverted its spiritual mission in the colonies with their material interests. Yet we cannot take this moral rhetoric at face value. Despite Monsalve's wish to advocate the Crown's spiritual interests against 'corrupt' *corregidores'* temporal interests, priests were a worldly presence in the *reducciones*. Their material demands were fully comparable to other colonists,' and they directly competed with them for Indian labour. They could not credibly criticize the colonial project as if they somehow lay outside it. Monsalve, who in 1608 received a royal disposition to exploit a mine for twenty years,[20] was no exception. By the seventeenth century, priests lost any advantage they may earlier have had in wielding charges of corruption and worldly interest against other Spaniards.

As early as 1610, Archbishop Lobo Guerrero of Lima wrote to the king that the clergy's economic demands also caused Indians to flee the *reducciones*.[21] During his tenure in office (1608–21), Indian parishioners steadily litigated against priests in his archbishopric, often for such economic abuses (Tineo Morón 1992: 16–28). Lobo Guerrero also presided over Lima's first centralized 'extirpation of idolatry' campaign, which he strictly linked to *reducción* (1613: 42): 'The Indians resent nothing as much as that they be reduced as Your Majesty has ordered so that they be given religious instruction because, as the unfortunates are in their idolatries in the same manner as they were when they were conquered, they flee from *reducción* to better persevere in them and they are so daring as to try to disrupt it through illicit means and false stories.'[22] Arriaga later confirmed this connection between idolatry and *reducción*'s subversion (1621: 202, 220), which Toledo's decrees already noted. In summary, Lobo Guerrero rearticulated a reformist discourse in which Indian idolatries conspired with priestly greed and negligence to threaten *reducción*. Both had to be curtailed to rescue this project of civilization (García Cabrera 1994: 29, 1996).

The viceroy Marqués de Montesclaros proposed even more stringent measures than his predecessors to enforce *reducción* in 1608 but failed to gain royal assent.[23] He must then have decided to work through Lobo Guerrero's initiative. In 1613, he instructed *corregidores* to return Indians and their property from the old towns to the *reducciones*. Indians were to demolish their houses in the old towns and re-use the materials to build new ones in the *reducción*; otherwise, *corregidores* would burn their old houses. If their fields were near the old towns, they could have a lean-to shelter to prepare meals and stay overnight to complete agricultural tasks, but they were to be in church on Sundays, religious holidays, and days for religious instruction (Lobo Guerrero 1613: 234–5). Montesclaros' edict concerned only Indians who reverted to their old towns, not those living in Spanish towns or on *haciendas*, who were more numerous and therefore of greater fiscal concern. Similarly, religious instruction, not tributary shortfall, was the rationale for returning them to their *reducciones*. These changes of emphasis both register the revived presence of the extirpation of idolatry in the *reducción* debate.

Apparently Montesclaros also authorized extirpators of idolatry to enforce *reducción*. Arriaga wrote that 'for his part, His Excellency [i.e., the viceroy] also helps, ordering that the [idolatry] inspector can burn and disperse all towns that have broken away from their *reducción* without government decree, so that they return to their *reducción*, and this has been done in many towns' (1621: 235). A case in point occurred during the inspection of Cochas in 1615, an old town three quarters of a league from the *reducción* of Margos. The extirpator found no traces of idolatry in Cochas, but rather an active confraternity and a chapel that the priest regularly visited to administer the sacraments. Still, he argued that this chapel was not 'secure' and that its image of the Virgin could be stored with greater 'decency' in the church of Margos. Next he added that the Indians contravened many ordinances by living in Cochas, where returning to their ancestral idolatries was a real danger. So he ordered the *curaca* to transfer the Virgin's image to Margos, to dismantle the chapel in Cochas, and to ensure that the Indians living there immediately return to Margos, or receive fifty lashes and a shaved head. The *curaca* replied with a petition requesting this order's nullification: unlike those Indians who fled to gullies and remote areas, he observed, those of Cochas built a chapel, obtained a fine image of the Virgin, and arranged to receive the holy sacraments instead of returning to their pagan rites.[24] In the following year of 1616, a similar attempt to enforce *reducción* occurred in San Francisco de Callaguaya in Huarochirí, although the Indians also had a chapel in their settlement and a decree from Archbishop Mogrovejo allowing them to reside there.[25] Apparently the extirpation of idolatry did revitalize *reducción*, and challenged such peripheral settlements.

Struggles over Burial

Modern secular views of *reducción* assume that the policy applied only to living people as labourers and politico-religious subjects, but it was also very much about the dead. Whether or not Andean people buried their dead in Christian churches was a major test of *reducción*'s success. Often they clandestinely disinterred their dead from church floors and took them to their pagan ancestors in mortuary caves. This practice circulated religious error, not Christian grace, between the living and the dead. Acosta knew of it (1590: 326), and it must have epitomized the hereditary transmission of idolatry that so worried him. It directly undid *reducción*'s good example and prevented a proper church from forming. This practice thus became a major flashpoint in both the first and third anti-idolatry campaigns but also caused alarm during periods of official quiescence.

Reports of clandestine disinterments predate *reducción*: the earliest I know of dates to 1541 (Lissón y Cháves 1943–47 I: 143). In 1551, the First Council of Lima acknowledged the practice when it set punishments for burying Christian Indians outside consecrated ground. First-time offenders were to get three days in jail and fifty lashes in public, with escalating penalties for subsequent offences. Priests were to burn publicly the bodies of any Christians who secretly requested burial outside church or cemetery. When burying Christian Indians, they were to check the face of the deceased to ensure that their kin had substituted no other body for it. To promote Christian mortuary rites, priests were not to charge Indians for burial. Pagans were to bury their dead in a designated area within view of the settlement. Any Christian Indians with pagan dead in their houses or in large sepulchres were to rebury them in the pagan burial ground, with only one day of mourning. The council also forbade offerings of clothing, food, or drink in Christian graves. Above all else, priests were to bury Christian *curacas* in a church or cemetery and prevent their wives and servants from accompanying them through suicide (Vargas Ugarte 1951: 21, 81–2). Collectively, these ordinances suggest growing familiarity with Andean funerary practices, and a will to monitor and regulate them. Reports reached the king in 1558 that clerics charged such exorbitant rates for burying Indians in monasteries 'that many are buried in the countryside to avoid paying' (Lissón y Cháves 1943–47 II: 91–2). In 1566, a parish priest reported Christian Indians' clandestine disinterment in Huaylas. An inspection of the northern Peruvian highlands in 1567 saw the practice as widespread (Lissón y Cháves 1943–47 II: 305, 354–5). Following his inspection of the Audiencia de Lima in 1567, Cuenca urged that 'parish priests should have the keys to the church and not let the sacristan have them, since it is the reason why they can steal from the church the bodies of Indians, particularly those of caciques and *curacas* to take them to their *guacas* and shrines' (Lissón y Cháves 1943–47 II: 354–5). Polo agreed that Indians commonly exhumed their dead in secret, taking them from churches and graveyards to pagan shrines (*huacas*), mountains and plains, old sepulchers, and houses, where their kin and associates gathered to give them food and drink, and to sing and dance for them (1571: 194). These reports formed an emerging pattern and laid the backdrop for Toledo's burial decrees discussed above. Let us now turn to the post-*reducción* aggravation of this conflict.

Aullagas, 1588: An Inquisitorial Quasi-Ethnography

We encountered Bartolomé Álvarez above as a Taqui Oncoy source and an early alarmist who blamed *corregidores*, *curacas*, and ecclesiastical inspectors for *reducción*'s failure because they undermined parish priests (1588: 14, 17–18, 42–4). Like Toledo, however, he thought that Indians were even more responsible, and wanted them to answer to the Inquisition for their idolatries and sins against the sacraments, which his letter exposed at length. He claimed that his Indian parishioners regularly took bodies, particularly those of local *curacas*, from any unguarded church or graveyard for burial in pagan tombs (1588: 114–15). When his vigilance prevented them from doing so, they took hair and nail clippings instead, tied them in a bundle of cloth with coca leaves, and brought them to the pagan tomb as the body's substitute during acts of ancestor worship (1588: 116). Álvarez reported that they would also reopen graves to give the body a mortuary mask and the articles it had used in life, including clothing, footwear, adornments, musical instruments, tools, and eating, drinking, and cooking utensils (1588: 114–5). Sometimes they would even try to slip these items in during Christian burial itself (1588: 263). Although he advocated forcibly suppressing traditional Andean funerary practices, Álvarez immediately added, 'I do not pretend to insinuate that the baptized ones are really Christians, and that therefore they ought to be buried in the churches and enjoy holy or blessed ground and the sacrifices of the Holy Church: from this I would have them as deprived as their grandparents who did not hear of the faith nor knew the name of God. I only wish to make it understood that it is necessary to put an obstacle in the way of this evil [of traditional burial]' (1588: 98). Álvarez notes that he refused Christian burial to some Indian bodies, and thereby induced confessions of idolatry from their living kin: his entrée was to ask whether the dead they presented for burial were baptised, which often they were not. Yet no baptismal records existed, and frequently Indians claimed baptism from priests who subsequently died or left the area. Proving their assertions wrong was almost impossible. Álvarez discovered in confession that certain persons were unbaptized. When asked publicly to bury them in the church, however, he reluctantly complied since he could not betray the privacy of confession, nor did he want his flock to complain to the ecclesiastical inspector (1588: 172–5). This quandary led Álvarez to channel his mounting dislike of Indians into an investigation of their 'beliefs' (*doctrina*) and 'rites' (*ritos*), particularly those regarding death and ancestors, which I will now summarize.

Before the Spaniards' arrival, some Indian tombs were stone towers on hills and plains, their height proportional to dignity and nobility of the dead they contained. Others were subterranean and had basins for offerings: their doorways faced east and hefty stone slabs covered them. Founding ancestors lay in lowest levels with offerings, and more recent *curacas* higher up, with clothes and insignia, where the cold air perfectly conserved them (Álvarez 1588: 92–3). When a *curaca* died, his concubines were enclosed in his tomb, given food and drink, then killed to serve the lord in the afterlife: Álvarez mentions a woman who fled to a priest to avoid this fate (1588: 94). With the arrival of Spaniards eager to loot the tombs for silver offerings, and priests anxious to destroy their holy objects, people built new hidden subterranean tombs for their ancestral mummies, arranging them in order of seniority before carefully covering and disguising the entrances with vegetation. In these tombs, according to Álvarez, fathers buried sons, sons buried fathers, and brothers buried brothers, as before, and often with Spanish priests' tacit consent (1588: 95). Like his nemesis Acosta, Álvarez saw such idolatries' inter-generational continuity as a racialized habit that the church had to break (1588: 83, 110). Children were the weak link: a five-year-old boy told Álvarez of a tomb containing the body of Auqui Penchuca, the local founding ancestor, and his venerated descendants, more than sixty in all, including some who were young and recently buried, with their bodies intact (1588: 108, 96). Thus, Álvarez took children to look for another hidden subterranean tomb in the old town, kept them there three days until he found it, and then whipped them to confess who the bodies were and what the *curacas* did there: some of these bodies were baptized (1588: 108–9). 'It is necessary to order the burning of all the dead that there are in the countryside and fields,' he concluded, thus suggesting that his parish contained many such mortuary sites (1588: 96).

People sacralized these tombs and the dead they contained, calling them *huaca*, a generic term that designated both deities' stone statues and their shrines (Álvarez 1588: 75, 103). The statues represented dead Incas or *curacas*, who might give oracles or generate the appearance of more closely related dead who would speak (Álvarez 1588: 75–6, 82). Thus, Álvarez opined that the dead and their deities were actually the same thing, since it was primarily through the dead that the Devil appeared to Indians (1588: 155–6). He notes that in contrast to the mundane Aymara word for 'cadaver,' *amaya*, a more specific term *çupay* designated the venerated ancestors who received sacrifices (1588: 103). Other, less venerated ancestors lacked deity status and seemingly did not belong to the *çupay* category (Álvarez 1588: 89). Like so many churchmen of his era, Álvarez firmly believed that *çupay* was none other than the Devil (see Taylor 1980). He struggled to reconcile this *ideé fixe* that made *çupay* univocally malevolent, with his parishioners' view that as founding ancestor and tutelary deity, it was also benevolent (1588: 103).

Although Álvarez' account of the ancestors is thoroughly demonizing, additional details of what we may suppose to be their Andean character nonetheless filter through. Local tradition held that their ancestors emerged from a high snow-capped mountain named Anco-caua (Anconcagua, in modern Chile): elsewhere, people called these ancestral origin points *pacarinas*. Ancestors like Auqui Penchuca travelled in cohorts, pausing at several such points as they dispersed across the landscape to the various localities they were to colonize (Duviols 1978). These founding ancestors were the most revered of all the mummies and statues contained in Andean tombs and shrines. People called them 'creators of men' and gave them such honorific titles as 'condor' (*mallku*), which also passed down from one *curaca* to the next (Álvarez 1588: 77, 79–80, 94). Thus, political authority drew intimately from notions of ancestorhood (see Millones 1978; 1979).

Having thus identified the Indians' deities, Álvarez turned to their worship: they sacrificed camelids to the dead at their tombs, and gave them offerings of toasted maize, cooked food, corn beer, feathers, gold, silver, and coins (1588: 90–1, 116). Apparently people made these offerings at specific points in the agricultural cycle. Just before sowing (i.e., September to November), each *ayllu* congregated at its principal shrine. Its members confessed one by one or collectively to their ministers, who exhorted them to tell all or the *huaca* would punish the group with sickness, drought, frost, or hail. The ministers then did coca leaf divinations to learn if they had confessed truly. They then expelled the sins, embodied in the coca leaves and fat that each confessor gave, on a mountain or in a gully. Next, a minister collected offerings, engaged the *huaca* in oracular communication, sacrificing a dog and four guinea pigs for the crops (Álvarez 1588: 100–2). He wrung the guinea pigs' necks, stripped their hides from their carcasses, stuffed them with straw, and hung them on poles atop four high mountains that delimited the fields. Amid the fields, he similarly sacrificed the dog. The hide sacrifices were to the *huacas*, whereas the animals' flesh and bones went to the earth (*pachamama*). As this was their principal celebration, excessive feasting followed. People danced and sang to flute and drum and served each other corn beer until, as Álvarez so delicately put it, they fell vomiting 'like filthy pigs' into their concubines' arms (1588: 103–5). After opining that the entire ceremony was about nothing more spiritual than getting enough to eat, and their false confessions merely about avoiding sickness, Álvarez returns to dispassionate ethnographic mode, noting regional variation in such observances. For fear of priestly detection, he continued, people did not always perform them publicly. Sometimes they occurred indoors or at night, or in remote areas with rigorous internal vigilance for Christian informers and sentinels posted to prevent outsiders from approaching unseen (1588: 105–6).

Álvarez then describes the Indians' penitential flagellations during the week of San Lázaro, immediately before Holy Week, at the rainy season's end. One night, the *curacas* assembled their *ayllu* and its animals around their tomb. They tearfully invoked Auqui Penchuca, their founding ancestor, asked health for themselves, their animals and crops, then offered camelid sacrifices (1588: 107–8). A celebration called *casi* followed Easter and groundbreaking for the following agricultural year, when the rains stopped: people honoured the *huacas* with a 'solemn binge of drinking,' after which they harvested (1588: 110–11). Following the harvest, around Corpus Christi, they celebrated *chai* with another 'solemn binge of drinking,' in which *curacas* and other *ayllu* notables assembled in a large round house to bless the children born that year. Mothers presented their children to the dignitaries, along with camelids or camelid fetuses to sacrifice for the children and coca to burn in prognostications of their future. According to Álvarez, this ceremony ended like all others, in drunkenness and fornication under the Devil's influence (1588: 111–12).

This account of *ayllu* ritual and local organization is schematic but establishes all the basic points that later accounts develop (Arriaga 1621, Duviols 1986). It portrays *ayllus* and *curacas*' political authority over them as based on ancestor worship, which in turn addressed the health and fertility of fields, flocks, and people. Álvarez shows how *ayllus* appointed priesthoods and had corporate holdings to generate offerings for the ancestors in sacrificial and oracular rituals. Only through burial practices could he have 'discovered' these dimensions of the *ayllu*. Both parish and *ayllu* constituted themselves through relations with the dead, so their paths were bound to cross here. How he perceived and acted on this basic cultural similarity was another matter.

Álvarez saw Andean practices as a religious system opposed to Catholicism, one that required understanding, refutation, and eradication. He describes his wavering commitment to this systematic inquiry into Indian idolatries, and how he abandoned it for some time in disgust with what he discovered, before persisting (1588: 107). Such antipathy raises questions about his report and others in the same genre. Without adopting a facile anti-realism (Ramos 1992, Urbano 1996) that reduces 'idolatry' to a discursive fabrication, and denies it any existence beyond the extirpator's preoccupations, we may nonetheless suspect that Álvarez projected his own commitments to codification and dogma onto the Andean ritual life he described. We may grant that *ayllus* existed and had the characteristics he identified, but still doubt that their founder, Auqui Penchuca, was, as Álvarez claimed, the prophet of a doctrinal system that actively resisted Christianity (1588: 108).

His own account clearly shows that many Indians wanted Church burial, even if they were not baptized or fully conversant with Church doctrine. We should not lose track of this important fact in Álvarez' endless affirmations that Indians mocked the Church and its sacraments, and were as idolatrous as when the Spaniards first arrived. Exactly why these supposedly incorrigible pagans wanted Álvarez' mortuary services is an open question. Perhaps they wished to maintain or reconstitute their ancestral community in the face of Álvarez' persecution, and were even willing to house it in the church provided that he did not destroy their ancestral bodies. Whatever the case, many of Álvarez' parishioners did not adopt his polarized and exclusionary understanding of 'conversion,' and therefore asked for church burial despite maintaining some of their own practices. Even as Álvarez pessimistically depicted two tightly contained religious systems at loggerheads, leakages of people and ideas between the two were already well under way. Although not necessarily in the same way as Álvarez, other parishioners did oppose one tradition to the other, when Christians informed against the clandestine rites of their 'pagan' neighbours, and the latter held that the Spaniards had their origin point and customs, and the Indians another. This situation's complexity and its politics are all too easily erased. At least three positions existed within this Andean community: one that accepted Christianity and understood it in exclusive terms, another that rejected it on similar grounds, and a third that partly accepted it but did not share its sense of boundaries or exclusivity. Undoubtedly diversity also existed within that latter camp, which deserves special attention not only because it refused the dichotomies of 'conversion,' but also because it eventually prevailed among Andean people. We see it emerging in Álvarez' text and in several documents that follow.

Mangas, 1604–05: Power Struggles within an Ayllu

In September of 1604, an ecclesiastical investigation into the removal of bodies from the church to ancestral mortuary caves occurred in San Francisco de Mangas. The accused were three brothers from an aristocratic Indian family: Carlos Callan, Domingo Nuna Callan, and Hernando Mallqui Callan (see figure 4.2). Approximately ten years before the investigation, their brother don Domingo Julca Ricapa (then the *curaca* of Mangas) had died, and the parish priest buried him in the church. Carlos Callan apparently inherited the office of *curaca* from his brother. Shortly afterwards, he dispatched the priest's indigenous assistant (*fiscal*), Diego Huaman Ricapa, on an administrative mission to the Chingos mines for two weeks. During this time, the body of don Domingo (the dead *curaca*) disappeared from the church and resurfaced in the 'old town' of Arapayo. When questioned in 1604, Carlos Callan and his brothers claimed that the culprits were Rodrigo Guacho and Domingo Tachi, dependants (*criados*) of the dead *curaca* and his father. He admitted that he and his brothers knew of their actions but were afraid to report them for fear of punishment. On his return to Mangas, the *fiscal*, Diego Huaman Ricapa, discovered that don Domingo's body was gone and informed the priest in Cajatambo. When he arrived at the church to investigate, the priest discovered three or four adobe bricks in place of don Domingo's body. He then summoned don Carlos and his brothers to demand that they return the body. So the Callan brothers went to Arapayo, carried the body back on their shoulders, and buried it for a second time with a mass. Huaman Ricapa claimed that Callan and his brothers then confessed to removing the body in the first place.

Eventually, Carlos Callan appointed another brother, Hernando Nuna Ricapa, as *fiscal*, so removing Diego Huaman Ricapa from that office. Shortly afterwards, the body of their brother don Domingo again disappeared from the church and turned up in Copahirca, a holy site (*huaca*) and mortuary cave of the Callan brothers' *ayllu*. By 1604, Hernando Nuna Ricapa had died, and Gironimo Tanjos replaced him as *fiscal*. When Tanjos received complaints against the Callan brothers, he made the official denunciation that started the investigation. The local vicar, Juan Pérez de Segura, acted as judge and went with two elected Indian officials to the cave. There they found don Domingo's body in a black cotton shroud, his face and feet smeared with blood from recent sacrifices, the body of his older brother, Juan de Espinoza Callan Poma, in a white shroud, with a wooden nose attached to his face, and offerings of feathers and coca, and the bodies of their father, don Francisco Llacxa Ricapa and mother, Juana Guarme Yaro. Although Carlos Callan denied knowing who put the bodies in the cave, his two surviving brothers both contradicted him, testifying that their brother Hernando Nuna Ricapa did it when he was *fiscal*. One of the Callan brothers testi-

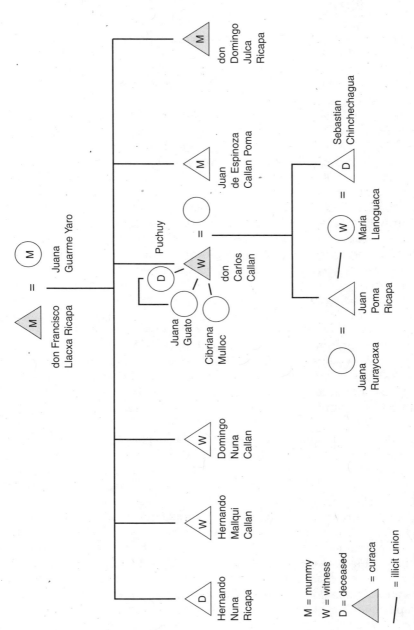

M = mummy
W = witness
D = deceased

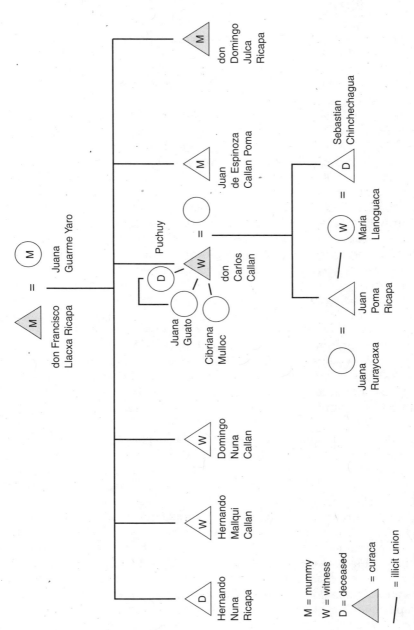 = curaca

——— = illicit union

Figure 4.2 The Callan Clan

fied that Nuna Ricapa was in charge of these bodies and offered them blood, corn beer, and feathers. This did not explain the fresh offerings made since Nuna Ricapa's death, however. The cave also contained the remains of Rodrigo Guacho and Domingo Tachi, who supposedly first removed don Domingo's body from the church, along with fifteen other unbaptized bodies. They brought the 'Christian bodies' back to the town's plaza and placed them in jail overnight to prevent their further removal and to guard them as evidence. Pérez de Segura instructed Carlos Callan and his brothers to rebury these bodies in the church, and threatened them with rigorous punishment should they commit similar offences in the future. Secular authorities received and disposed of the unbaptized bodies to prevent further idolatries.

Among this trial's many interesting features is the fact that denunciations within the native community drove it. Not only did some Andean people inform on others, but their collaboration ensured that interrogations were relatively sophisticated. For example, Diego Huaman Ricapa suggested that since Carlos Callan so readily identified the bodies in the plaza, he must have helped remove them from the church: the vicar incorporated this observation into his subsequent questioning of Callan. He also asked both Carlos Callan and Domingo Nuna Callan if don Domingo's last testament secretly asked for removal from the church and interment in a cave. Although both denied it, and affirmed that he was a Christian, the question suggests this practice was standard. Also at issue was whether don Domingo's body and the others deserved church reburial. These details confirm how important inside information from native informers was to this case. Unlike the Huarochirí situation in 1609 (to be discussed in chapter 5), where Ávila arguably 'discovered idolatry' to defend himself against his parishioners' litigation, Spanish–Indian conflict played only a secondary role here. The native witnesses against the Callan brothers knew that Spaniards would attack traditional burial practices, but informed for tactical reasons and probably did not oppose these practices in principle.

Some informers against the Callan brothers may have been members of that same family. For example, Carlos Callan's uncle, Martin Callan, started the rumours that led to the discovery of the bodies in Arapayoc. Based on his second surname, Diego Huaman Ricapa, the *fiscal* who denounced the first disinterment, may also have been related to the previous *curacas* Domingo Julca Ricapa and Francisco Llacxa (or Xulca) Ricapa. Since burial caves belonged to *ayllus*, the entire kin group might know of what went on in them, but why would some choose to inform?

Disputes over succession, which would pit the agnatic collateral relatives of dead rulers against each other, are an obvious motive here.
Doing mortuary ritual for one's predecessors was, in Andean terms, an
important way of consolidating one's hold on office;[26] therefore, it was
a flashpoint during succession. Thus, the Callan brothers persisted in
performing rites for the bodies of their dead brother and father, and
their opponents persisted in undermining them when they did.

Further charges of concubinage and incest against Carlos Callan and
his son followed in 1605.[27] These additional charges buttressed the earlier idolatry accusations against don Carlos, particularly since one of his
concubines was allegedly unbaptized. They suggest that his adversaries
wanted to discredit and remove him from office by whatever means
necessary. Clearly he had enemies among the other indigenous political
authorities of Mangas, and their factional conflict motivated this litigation. Similarly indiscriminate strategies of character assassination occur
in ecclesiastical litigation against indigenous leaders in the archdiocese
of Lima throughout the seventeenth century. Yet it was not until Francisco de Ávila's dramatic 'discovery' of idolatry in 1609 that this charge
became the weapon of choice in such disputes. In 1604–05, the Church
had yet to develop the 'extirpation of idolatry' as an institutional
response to such charges. In all subsequent idolatry cases, we cannot
easily disentangle local factional conflict from the Extirpation's institutional discourses, but here we see the former in a relatively pure and
independent form. Such local factional conflict was to appear repeatedly in later idolatry trials (see Griffiths 1996: ch. 4), and this case helps
us appreciate just how fundamental and primordial a dynamic it was.

Huachos and Yauyos, 1613–14: Circulating Cadavers

Disinterment of the dead from churches became a stock offence during
the first 'extirpation of idolatry' campaign (1609–22). Two Jesuit reports
on the 1613–14 mission to Huachos and Yauyos provide the earliest
detailed account of this practice from the first campaign (Romero 1918,
Polia 1996: 227–36). The first contains Pablo de Prado's report to the rec-
tor of Huamanga, which embeds descriptions of clandestine disinterment in another ethnographic sketch similar to Álvarez.' Prado first
mentions the cults of Pariacaca and Tambraico (another mountain near
Huancavelica), then notes that everyone in the area also worshipped a
huaca named Auquichanca and his son Cunaivillca. People came from
as far away as Cuzco to worship these deities four times a year: when a

constellation named *oncoy* first appeared in the sky, during Corpus Christi, Christmas, and Holy Week. Beyond these general celebrations, each town had its own principal *huaca* that was like a patron, and each *ayllu* and subdivision within it had its own particular *huaca*. By extension, each familial estate had its deities localized in stones and amulets known as *chancas*, *mayhuas*, *ingas*, and *pichiges*, which formed a patrimony transmitted by primogeniture. Fields and roads similarly had their deities. Many *ayllus* and estates had been extinguished or weakened, presumably by epidemics. Other groups tried to ennoble themselves by appropriating their *huacas*, while any surviving original owners tried to induce their return through acts of worship (Romero 1918: 183–4). Against this general backdrop, Prado turned to the cult of the dead.

He describes the worship of mummified 'pagan' rulers as generalized, and the offerings of clothes, gold, silver, incense, seashells, food, drink, and blood sacrifices they received. Prado also mentions commemoration of the recently dead once a year. Their kin removed them from their graves in the church, dressed them in new clothes, took them to valleys and cliffs, seated and honoured them with three days and nights of feasting, drinking, and dancing, then left them with offerings of food and drink (Romero 1918: 184). Apparently these rituals transferred the dead from the church to the burial caves, where they remained with their 'pagan' kin. Certain rivers, springs, and irrigation canals also received worship, as did lightning and the objects it struck. They knew lightning as Santiago, and the native ministers engaged it and other deities in oracular communication. These ministers also confessed their *ayllus* before the *huacas'* three annual celebrations and ordered them to provide the required offerings. Important *huacas* had up to twenty or thirty priests and servants, who were not baptized as children, remained in hiding as they grew up, and therefore did not appear in parish registers or have tributary duties. These *huacas* also had estates that included herds, clothing, precious metals, litters, and buildings that Prado described as churches and chapels. Their celebrations involved processions of the idols, dancing, music, and offerings of new clothes, fingernails and eyelashes, and the sacrifice of young children, camelids, and guinea pigs, followed by oracular communication. Sometimes the deities scolded Indians for their poor service, but at others they promised peace, rest, and abundant fields and flocks 'because the Indians aspired only to these things.' According to Prado, good relations with the deities required human sacrifice: the Devil would cease to appear to the Indians without it, and punish them with pestilence (Romero 1918: 184–6). Prado then listed the Devil's thirteen commandments to the Indians (Romero 1918: 187–9). Far more explicitly than Álvarez, he represented *huaca* worship as *doctrina*: a codified religious doctrine consisting of explicit commandments.

Next, Prado described the Jesuits' arrival in Huacra after lightning struck its church by the main altar and burned it down. Following this event, *huacas* told Indians that they sent Santiago to punish the Spaniards and prove the truth of their worship over Christianity. Suspecting that something inside the church must have greatly offended God, Prado and an extirpating judge entered. They found three *huacas* hidden in the church, and signs of blood sacrifice around the altar. The church floor was riddled with open empty graves and littered with the stone slabs that once covered them. Further investigation revealed that Indians had taken the bodies to mortuary caves in remote valleys and mountains, where Prado and his companion found them seated amid abundant offerings of food and sprinklings of sacrificial blood. They selected thirty bodies of *curacas* and other important figures, put them aside, and burned the rest on the spot. Then they took the thirty bodies to town, assembled its inhabitants in the plaza, paraded the mummies around on the backs of speckled lamas, and preached a rigorous sermon against mortuary idolatries. According to Prado, the assembled were so ashamed and repentant that they persuaded the *curaca* to light the fire that consumed all thirty mummies, including those of his parents and grandparents, as the event's finale (Romero 1918: 189–91). Prado noted that they conducted many similar investigations and *autos de fe* in other nearby towns, and burned more than four hundred mummies in all. In the process, they learned that the dying often asked their kin to remove them from the church after burial. Others asked to be carried straight to the burial caves 'to die there and gain indulgence' (Romero 1918: 191). This last phrase significantly projects Catholic notions of 'the good death' and salvation onto Andean 'idolatry.' In this context, however, even similarities between religious traditions could signify their absolute difference. Since Jesuit extirpators understood 'idolatry' as demonically inspired, any similarities to Catholicism became further evidence of Satan's will to usurp the worship due to God alone (see Duviols 1971: 29). Thus, the appropriation of Santiago as thunder and lightning deity, the presence of *huacas* in the church, and the use of its altar for sacrifices all become statements of religious separatism. Significant religious accommodation was clearly under way, but Prado would not allow himself to see it. For him, only the antagonistic force of idolatry could explain why the Almighty would smite a church and its altar, otherwise so central to His plan.

Checras, 1614: Baptizing the Ancestors

Another investigation in the Checras region of Chancay produced two documents that show such disinterments as widespread. The mission's Jesuits wrote the first, a general account of the area's first anti-idolatry inspection, also the first in the famous *visitador* Fernando de Avendaño's long career (Lissón y Cháves 1943–47 V: 225–6). They note the continuing worship of *huacas*, which they identified as high places that housed idols (Polia 1999: 366). A description of *ayllu* ritual follows, in which Indians confessed sins to their priests before engaging in extended celebrations involving music and drink. The Jesuits noted that the Devil greatly enjoyed seeing people thus separated from Christian doctrine, and persuaded them through their ministers that the Indians' salvation did not require Church disciplines and sacramental expiation of sins. They believe, the account continues, that people are not descended from Adam and Eve but some from the *huacas*, others from stones, and others from streams or springs: the account does not identify these sites as *pacarinas*, but that is clearly what they were. When the soul leaves the body, it goes neither to heaven nor hell but to the Upaymarca, which means 'shady land.' To arrive, it must cross a bridge of braided hair over a fast-flowing river. Black dogs, which they raise with great care, might also take them across. On arrival, they enjoy a very pleasurable afterlife. The Jesuits next note that Indians placed their dead in the *huacas*, dressed them in fine clothing, and periodically brought them food to gain their favour. As a culminating horror, they describe the clandestine disinterment of 254 bodies from the church floor and their removal to traditional burial caves (Polia 1999: 367–9).

The Jesuits then recount how Avendaño inspected the neighbouring district of Andajes, where he 'brought to light innumerable *huacas*' and 'removed cadavers from hidden deposits in the earth where they secretly received cult' (Polia 1999: 369). The most important was the body of Llibiac Cancharco, the first ruler and founder of all humanity in that province, whom his descendants worshipped for life, agricultural fertility, rain, and all foods. Although this mummy had its own shrine on a mountain peak, it also circulated from town to town in the region to receive offerings. Entering his shrine,[28] the extirpators found a curtained enclosure that the Incas provided, in which they found Llibiac

Cancharco's body (estimated to be two hundred years old) wrapped in six pieces of embroidered fine cloth (*cumbi*). It wore a diadem of coloured feathers, a golden half-moon-shaped decoration on its forehead, and fine chains around its neck. They sent this body and several others to Lima so the viceroy, archbishop, and people of society could marvel at them and deplore Indians' blindness. Then they carted the bodies back to Andajes 'so that they be delivered to the avenging flames' as their descendants watched (Polia 1999: 369–371).

Against this backdrop, let us now turn to Avendaño's report of February 1614, which describes this expedition in more detail.[29] Iwasaki (1984) published the document's first part: a collective confession of San Francisco de Musca's various 'dogmatizers,' which probably occurred within the three-day grace period stipulated in the 'edict against idolatry' read at the beginning of every inspection (Arriaga 1621: 273–5; Lobo Guerrero 1613: 39). It is a highly distilled quasi-ethnographic sketch freed from the evidential conventions of a trial, which outlines local pantheons, ritual, and cosmology. This sketch would not only prove Avendaño's knowledge of such matters but also that the natives had *doctrina*: a codified religion. We can infer the pragmatic motive for producing such a document from where it ultimately came to rest, in Avendaño's first c.v. and request for promotion. Among the 'errors' to which his informants confessed was having 'preached and taught in this town to all of its Indians that the souls of Indians cannot go to heaven, and that they had converted to Christianity for nothing, since the law of Christ was not necessary for the Indians to save themselves, and that the Spaniards have one law and the Indians another, and that the souls of Indians go to a place called Upaymarca where there is a bridge of hairs over which black dogs make the souls pass.'[30] Avendaño presents this fragment of Andean mortuary lore as evidence of religious separatism from below. The Jesuits make similar insinuations in their account of this *visita*, but let us see if the rest of the document actually confirms this separatist vision of the afterlife.

The document's second part records various people in San Francisco de Musca, San Pablo de Ayaranga, and Santo Domingo de Apachi whom Avendaño persuaded to produce the bodies of relatives they had taken from the church. Duviols published the proceedings in the first two of these three villages (1971: 355–6). In contrast to the first part of the document, which is interpretive in tone, the emphasis in the second part is essentially forensic. The rhetorical goal seems to have been to evoke the lurid factuality of native mortuary idolatries. Thus, various repentant ancestor worshippers 'exhibited' their dead relatives' bodies to Avendaño, who duly recorded their names and relationships. Again, no prosecutions accompany these 'exhibitions,' which suggests they occurred 'voluntarily' within the three-day grace period.

In San Francisco de Musca, Avendaño recorded a long list of bodies taken from the church of Santo Domingo de Apachi. Not only did the living kin 'exhibit' these bodies, but they also confessed to having taken them from the church 'to the *huacas* where they were worshiped, offering them sacrifices.' Although these bodies were baptized and received Christian burial, Avendaño nonetheless had them burned in the plaza (Duviols 1971: 355). Since the First Council of Lima mandated such treatment for those who secretly requested interment outside churches, Avendaño must have assumed that they had. Another list of bodies and kin emerged from the neighbouring town of San Pablo de Ayaranga. The kin took these bodies from the church to the *huaca*, where they worshipped them, asking for life and health. Besides those bodies 'stolen' from the church, the Indian parishioners also produced pagan corpses 'for baptism.' This is the single most remarkable piece of evidence from the proceedings. Apparently they hoped to import their existing mortuary cult, including its 'pagan' mummies, into that of the church. Of course, Avendaño summarily burned these unbaptized bodies in the plaza, along with those 'stolen' from the church (Duviols 1971: 356).

For Avendaño, this request to baptize the pagan dead only confirmed that Indians remained obstinately ignorant of the true faith. He probably offered this datum, like the lists of exhibited cadavers, as raw evidence of religious error. Once we denaturalize the extirpators' sense of boundaries, however, the hope of baptizing pagan ancestors ceases to indicate Andean ignorance or naivety. Such baptism has existed within the Christian tradition, both in antiquity and more recently in Mormonism. The wish for it expresses an understanding, and not necessarily a superficial one, that this version of Catholicism was also centrally about the disposition, conservation, and redemption of the dead. If San Pablo de Ayaranga's parishioners did not fully grasp Catholic eschatology, it was not because their understandings of ancestors and the afterlife were irreconcilably foreign to Christianity. Andean people metaphorically represented their most sacred ancestral mummies as seeds (*malqui*), also the oldest Christian image for the resurrection of the body (Bynum 1995: 3). In a context of regular if imperfect doctrinal communication, San Pablo de Ayaranga's parishioners must have had reason to believe that Avendaño would grant their request, either (duplicitously) from Avendaño himself or in the conduct of other

Spanish priests. Otherwise, they would have hidden these bodies, as so many other Andean people did before and after them.

This incident completely undercuts the dichotomy between Indian and Christian afterlives that Avendaño had earlier attributed to the 'dogmatizers' from this area. It suggests that as in Aullagas, the parishioners' main goal was to keep the dead together, preferably in the church. If the natives really wanted the religious separatism that Avendaño was so busy enforcing, they would never have made this request for Catholic inclusion. Perhaps the disagreement was, as the account suggests, between 'dogmatizers' who had a professional stake in separatism, and the rest of the population who did not (Mills 1994a: ch. 6). Although Andean people sometimes accepted separatist ideas, the labour of differentiation fell primarily to churchmen like Avendaño at this early stage of the Extirpation. If San Pablo de Ayaranga's parishioners requested baptism for their ancestors, they cannot have regarded Catholic and ancestral mortuary cults as mutually exclusive.

Finally, in Santo Domingo de Apachi, Avendaño produced another list of kin and cadavers. He burned these bodies, like the rest. Perhaps the most significant thing about all these lists is their generational shallowness. People produced no more than one or two lineal ancestors, who were objects of restricted familial cults that nonetheless took place in the '*huaca*,' probably a place of interment shared by an entire *ayllu*. Missing in these accounts but present in others (Duviols 1986) are the *malquis* (founding ancestors) that all *ayllu* members worshipped. Elaborate genealogies of mummified *curacas* would have linked these founding ancestors to the shallow and much more ephemeral lineages of commoner mummies described in this document. As Doyle (1988: 95–7) shows, *malquis* were vitally important to the religious life of their communities, whereas commoner mummies mattered only if their immediate families remembered them, later falling into neglect and decay. Except for the mummies offered for baptism in San Pablo de Ayaranga, none of the bodies described in this document appear to have had *malqui* status. Probably after Avendaño's refusal to honour that request, nearby parishioners held something important in reserve, and risked only what they would soon forget in any event.

Syntheses of the First Campaign

In 1617, when Avendaño wrote the first synthesis of Andean religion in the archdiocese of Lima, he presented the removal of bodies from the church to remote caves as a general problem (Duviols 1986: 447). The statistically oriented '*Relación de los medios que se han puesto para la extirpación de la idolatría*' of 1619 reports this practice in twenty-nine of the seventy-five towns surveyed in the archdiocese of Lima (see Duviols 1967). Many more of these towns retained ancestral mummies from before the missionaries' arrival. Also in 1619, a Jesuit annual field report (*letra anua*) described the discovery, in one town alone, of 478 baptized Indian bodies distributed among many mortuary caves (Duviols 1986: 452). Thus, when it came time to codify Andean 'idolatry' definitively, Arriaga did not hesitate to identify the removal of bodies from the churches as 'the greatest abuse that there is in these matters' (1621: 216).

Arriaga was a Jesuit who participated extensively in the first campaign, working with Avendaño for a year and a half, and several months with Ávila (1621: 199). During these inspections, he drafted *The Extirpation of Idolatry in Peru*, a manual to aid future extirpation, and a compendium of knowledge about idolatries gained during the first campaign. Its premise was that by knowing the nature of Andean idolatries, future extirpators could better eradicate them. Thus, Arriaga strove for accuracy, and assures us that he relied heavily on Avendaño's notes, then gave his manuscript to the Jesuit Provincial Council and five extirpators for comment and revision before it was further vetted at higher levels (1621: 193–4). Since his work bore the imprimatur of the archbishop of Lima and other ecclesiastical authorities, it was more than just a distillation of experience for future colleagues' benefit: above all, it was the canonical formulation of Andean idolatry, the official Church version of what it was and how to fight it. This authoritative status gave Arriaga's text a different historical role from any of the other sources considered here, for it, more than any other, defined how Andean idolatries were to be perceived and understood.

Mortuary idolatries figured prominently in Arriaga's account. He noted that everywhere they could, Andean people took their dead kin's bodies from the churches to mortuary caves. This they did out of love (*cuyaspa*) for their deceased kin, who felt great sorrow at being confined to the church, and could repose more comfortably in the open air of mortuary caves known as *zamay*, meaning 'resting place' (1621: 199, 216). Arriaga described with disgust how, during 'exhibitions' like those of Checras in 1614, *ayllus* lined up in the plaza with their founding ancestors' dried bodies along with those they had 'stolen' from the church. Likening this intermingling of the living and the dead to a scene from the Judgment Day, he lamented Andean people's low regard for Church ceremonies and suffrages that their mortuary cults implied (1621: 199–200). Ironically, his own Company of Jesus had disinterred mummies from Lima's sand dunes to stage the resurrection of the flesh before Viceroy Velasco in 1599 (Cobo 1653: 272–3): if Arriaga's comment recalled that spectacle, it differed in its inability to valorize Andean people's comparable concern with the flesh. Finally, Arriaga related that, just before he arrived in a town, an aristocratic Indian and his wife opened two of their children's stone slab burial niches in the church and took their bodies back to their house. Here, the dead children received a change of clothing and great festivities including a procession through town, after which they invited the whole kin group to drink, and returned the children's bodies to the church. Arriaga and his associates made the locals disinter the bodies again, break up the burial niche, and bury them in the ground. He concluded that even when they accepted church burial, Indians could not be allowed to inter their dead in niches (1621: 216–17).

Like Álvarez before him, but this time with official backing, Arriaga reconstructed the system of beliefs and assumptions that produced these 'abuses' in quasi-ethnographic terms. A wake (*pacaricuc*) of five days and nights followed death, during which participants abstained from eating salt, chili, meat, and white maize. At night, non-kin played a game with little sticks called *pisca* ('five,' the wake's duration in days), and spread maize flour outside the house, which they inspected for tracks the following morning. On the wake's final day, they washed the deceased's clothes and closest relative in a spring or river. A feast with much drink followed, after which participants thoroughly swept the deceased's room and resumed the vigil for a final night. An *ayllu* minister sang of the deceased's deeds, and those present awaited the arrival of his or her soul to eat and drink with them. By the following morning, they said that the soul was in the *zamayhuaci*, or resting place of the dead (1621: 216). In the highlands, many believed that dead souls went to Ypamarca, land of the mute. To arrive, they crossed a body of water over a bridge of hair, or on the back of a black dog, which they specially raised and killed for the purpose in some areas. Others believed that the dead go to their *huacas*. In Huacho, a coastal town, they believed that the dead go to the island of Huano on the back of orcas, which they call *tumi*. Survivors believed that the dead experienced hunger and thirst during these journeys, and great sadness if earth weighed them down, so they disinterred and removed them to mortuary caves where they would rest better (1621: 220).

Far more than previous writers, Arriaga took a sociological approach to 'idolatry.' While he shared his predecessors' distress over Andean peoples' false beliefs, he saw their grounding in social institutions: towns and *ayllus* worshipped common idols, sacrificing to them and maintaining their cults through a hierarchy of ministers (1621: 199, 221). Each *ayllu* had a principal idol or *huaca*, an ancestral guardian in whose cult all members participated, although they also worshipped others at a familial or town (i.e., multi-*ayllu*) level. Relations of marriage and descent linked these *huacas* in segmentary hierarchies: lower-ranking *huacas* were wives or children of the higher ranking. Senior *huacas*, those that presided over towns or *ayllus*, were generally of stone. Next down in the hierarchy were mummified bodies stored in remote caves (1621: 201–3). Below them were amulets (*conopas*), stone monoliths in fields (*huancas*), and maize-cob figurines (*saramamas*), whose cult was generally familial in scope, and oriented towards the fertility of flocks and fields (1621: 204–5). A priestly hierarchy mirrored that of the deities they attended. As they were missionaries' direct competitors, Arriaga describes in detail their activities as mediums, diviners, sacrificers, preparers of offerings, confessors, and consultants (1621: 202–10). Finally, he mentions the corporate resources that *ayllus* dedicated to their *huacas* (1621: 210). Although understated, this discussion was necessarily invidious when poor Indian parishes struggled to generate the incomes that comparable European parishes took for granted.

Arriaga also described semi-annual festivities in which these *ayllu* ministers brought their respective *huacas* and mummies to flat areas called *cayanes* outside mortuary caves. Here they gave them sacrificial offerings and new clothing, to the sound of trumpets and drums, amid great festivity and mutuality among *ayllus* (1621: 200, 202). These festivities occurred around the harvest at Corpus Christi and at the onset of the rains around Christmas. Ministers initiated them by instructing the *curaca* and others to prepare corn beer, and went around collecting offerings. Before the festivities began, *ayllu* members confessed to their ministers, who asked if they worshipped the Spanish God sincerely to the neglect of the *huacas*, and checked their answers through divination before washing and dressing them in new clothes. Once the celebrations began, the ministers made offerings, elaborately invoking and praising the *huacas*, while onlookers did *mocha*, a reverential kissing or popping sound while inhaling. For five days and nights, people drank and sang to their *huacas* and mummies, calling them 'creators of humanity' (*runapcamac*) and asking them for health, food, and life (1621: 212–13).

During these celebrations, ministers instructed their *ayllus* in the founding ancestors' exploits and journeys, and went to the places where they emerged on the surface of the earth (*pacarinas*). Thus, they worshipped tall mountains and hills as metamorphized men, or treated them as the abode of *huaris*, gigantic primordial inhabitants who lend their force to agriculture and house building (Arriaga 1621: 201–2). They also called the places where the *huacas* were kept 'resting points' (*zamana*), a term that also denoted mortuary caves and the final resting place of the dead (1621: 202, 216). Arriaga does not explicate the relationship between these places and *pacarinas*, although subsequent inquiries were to prove them identical. He did, however, note that Andean people thought Spaniards to have come from one *pacarina* and blacks from another. Each *ayllu* or subdivision thereof had its own particular *pacarina*, which they called *camac* or creator. So strong was their attachment to these *pacarinas* that it often made them leave the *reducciones* and return to their old towns (1621: 219–20). Thus, idolatry's most basic form was that of an ancestor cult, in which the group worshipped its founders' images or bodies, petitioned them for the necessities of life, and made settlements around their cult sites.

A growth in knowledge undoubtedly occurred from Álvarez to Arriaga, but the will to understand idolatry as a system opposed to Christianity remained invariant and blinded extirpators to non-conforming evidence. Here, 'extirpatory realism,' the quasi-ethnographic genre these writers deployed, played an interesting dual role. On the one hand, it emphasized systemic interconnection and closure in portraying the *ayllu* as a separate sociocultural form opposed to the parish. By treating idolatry as a formal heresy comparable to Judaism or Islam and incarnate in social institutions allegedly antagonistic to Catholicism, extirpators maximized its racializing potential. On the other hand, extirpatory realism committed its practitioners to recording specific scenes and details that often revealed dialogue and so subverted the official view of two inherently opposed socio-religious systems locked in a death struggle. Despite Arriaga's pessimism about Andean people's regard for the Church and its suffrages, his own descriptions paint a far brighter picture. His report that *malquis* routinely figured in the 'exhibitions' of cadavers during the first campaign suggests that Andean people willingly submitted their most central objects of worship for destruction. Similarly, the clandestine removal and celebration of the Indian dignitary's children ended not with their installation in a mortuary cave but their return to the church. Andean mortuary cults were thus capitulating to and restructuring themselves around Christianity at the very moment when Arriaga portrayed them as monolithically opposed to it. The closest he could come to acknowledging this progress was to observe that one of the Indians' most common 'errors' was to believe that it was possible to practice Catholicism and their ancestral religion simultaneously (1621: 224, 227). From Arriaga's rigidly monotheistic perspective this was no progress at all, but for us it opens important ways to read the extirpators against the grain.

These idolatry trials jointly revealed much greater acceptance of Catholic mortuary practice than extirpators admitted. Interment in church floor niches allowed the 'stealing' of bodies that extirpators so abhorred, but it also required pious bequests to the church or participation in religious confraternities. Prado and Arriaga railed against these 'thefts' because they so thoroughly frustrated the practical distinction between Christian piety and idolatry that the colonial Church worked so hard to establish. Their rage was well founded. In 1619, the archbishopric of Lima had an average of 2.4 confraternities per parish, the most common of which was that of Souls (Ánimas) found in nearly 20 per cent of them (Marzal 1983: 407). Members had claims to niche burial, which further promoted the clandestine disinterments documented above. Yet archival sources on confraternities' mortuary activities are remarkably scant; I have found none that make this connection. To attack confraternities because Andean idolatries used them strategically would be to attack *reducción* itself. Thus, confraternities mediated between Catholic and Andean mortuary traditions without generating conflict and litigation. Under their institutional cover and below the radar of official surveillance, subterranean religious accommodation flourished.

5 Strategies of Coexistence

As *reducción* superimposed parishes on *ayllus*, these social forms not only competed for Andean peoples' allegiances but also aligned and unofficially reconciled with each other. Such realignment was the backbone of indirect rule: a massive social fact that absolutist corruption discourses endlessly denounced but could not change. This chapter further explores that coexistence, starting with its geography. *Reducción* not only promoted the quasi-ethnographic 'discovery' of idolatry but spatially transformed it by driving it to the periphery of newly formed parishes. We begin with this tension between recording and transforming and then explore how *ayllu* geographies recalled previous, pre-Inca episodes of colonization and intergroup accommodation. I argue that Andean people deployed these memories critically, using them as models for the accommodations they sought with Spaniards. Such assertions of Andean post-invasion etiquette are evident in early-seventeenth-century idolatry sources but also the writings of the Andean intellectuals Pachacuti Yamqui and Guaman Poma. Finally, this chapter traces the saga of crisis and corruption surrounding *reducción* into the 1630s, by which time it lost momentum as a reformist cause but generated renewed struggles over burial in the process.

Reducción as a Spatial Regime

Living and dead Indians' flight from *reducción*, and official attempts to prevent it, produced a concentric spatial aesthetic. At the consolidated settlement's core lay the church, and at the church's core lay the altar. These were the toeholds that religious grace and civic virtue had gained in the otherwise godforsaken Andean landscape. Reformists saw these centres as outwardly radiating sources of grace and order that might transform all they touched. Stoics saw them as locked in an essentially unresolvable struggle with idolatry and greed that took refuge on their periphery. Whether conceived transformatively or statically, *reducción* established an enduring core-periphery axis on which all its hopes and disillusions found a place.

The altar was the innermost and strongest source of grace in this arrangement. Here, priests performed the mass, establishing the One True Faith through its most central and potent rite. At the altar, Indians might also receive communion. While most priests considered them unworthy, those who gave it to them believed that its profound transformative powers would in time cure them of their congenital idolatry and make true Christians of them (Acosta 1576: 383–419). Either way, the altar was the site of a fundamental statement about Indians' Christianity. Moving out from the altar, the rest of the church had to be 'decent,' that is, enjoy proper ornamentation and good order. Ecclesiastical inspections routinely addressed the issue of 'decency,' particularly the host's storage and display, which reaffirmed the centrality of mass and communion around the altar. Yet the entire church had to project the faith's gravity and splendour in its architecture and decoration. As the *reducción*'s focal building, the church had to project a quality that set the tone for the entire settlement. If it lacked gravitas, it set a bad example and jeopardized the larger project of civilization it was meant to articulate. The civic order that Toledo envisioned for consolidated settlements emanated from the church, which ideally transfigured the rest of the town with grace and order.

Beyond the town, with its inward focus on church and altar, lay the periphery where agrarian activity, industry, and commerce occurred. Their peripheral location expressed these activities' fallen, worldly character. All were to some extent opposed to *reducción* because they lured Indians away from spiritual instruction and towards the pursuit of temporal gain in fields, *obrajes*, *haciendas*, mines, or on distant trading circuits. The mines epitomized this opposition in their great distance from the *reducciones*, the damage they did to them, and their infernal extraction of the raw material for money, Christianity's root of all evil. For at least one commentator, however, itinerant commerce was a comparable antagonist, for the same Christian reasons.[1] In these cases, an opposition between stasis and mobility interacted with the centre-periphery dynamic to produce the crisis of *reducción* discussed above. Once the *reducciones* took hold, colonial authorities forgot that they were the product of population movement, and used the indigenizing term *originario* to describe their residents. They viewed any further movement as threatening and disorderly, even when officially mandated and central to the colonial enterprise, as with the Huancavelica and Potosi *mitas*. Experience showed that once Indians left the supposedly civilizing influence of their *reducciones*, they did not easily return.

Compared with mining and itinerant commerce, agrarian production on the *reducciones*' immediate periphery was a much less threatening and degraded Indian activity. Yet even it was dangerous: Indians' fields often remained near their old towns, several leagues away from the *reducciones*. They might spend several months of the year there, so Archbishop Lobo Guerrero allowed them to build roofed shelters where visiting parish priests could say mass. They were to be destroyed after the harvest, however, and a cross put it their place, to encourage *reducción* (Lobo Guerrero 1613: 68–9). On the one hand, this procedure replicated the mandate for destroying idolatrous shrines (Lobo Guerrero 1613: 40) and so implicitly equated idolatry and agriculture. On the other hand, it was a rare attempt to project Christianity outward from the otherwise exclusively centripetal emphasis of *reducción*. In the century following Toledo, however, the main concern was Indians' reversion to their 'old towns.' These centres of debauchery, idolatrous instruction, and communication with the Devil directly negated *reducción*. Even Andean people adopted this view: in 1656, the *curaca* of Otuco, don Juan Chucho Liviac begged the extirpator Bernardo de Noboa to enforce *reducción* so that his people would not live 'in great offence to God our Lord, returning to our rites and ceremonies' (Duviols 1986: 101–2, 2003: 283–4). In 1664, Noboa paraphrased this request when he wrote: 'and where I discovered the greatest force of their idolatries and the most abominable abuses ... was in the old towns of their gentility which are hidden many leagues from their principal *reducciones* to which many divisions and *ayllus* of Indians have gone to live, cutting themselves off from their principal *reducciones* carried by the love of their idols, where they live as such pagans that they neither hear mass nor receive religious instruction and most die without the sacraments for being so far from one another and the principal *reducciones* in the alpine zone and among crags and outcrops and on such steep routes and cliffs that their priests cannot attend to them except with extremely great danger and toil' (Duviols 1986: 423–4). This passage exemplifies the *reducciónes*' opposition to old towns, but also diffuses the old towns' concentrated negative qualities into the landscape itself. An adversarial view of the landscape was almost inevitable for Spaniards steeped in *reducción*'s urbanizing cultural values. Priests who served in Indian parishes far from their compatriots' company felt it even more acutely. Throughout the seventeenth century, they couched complaints about idolatry in descriptions of difficult travel and communication in mountainous regions.[2] These descriptions conveyed not only the geographical facts but also framed them as an obstacle to serious pastoral work. Complaints about the rugged Andean terrain also included the social and cultural obstacles it supposedly presented to the Church's mission of civilization.

Reducción alone did not generate this negative view of the landscape. Satan, as an active adversary, was also at work. Many Spaniards believed that when the gospel came to the Old World, Satan fled to the Americas. He was the true author of the idolatries that now found their last refuge in the Andean landscape. This broader teleological vision of Christianity's march across the globe contributed powerfully to Spaniards' sense of being on the Enemy's terrain. After all, they lived in similarly nucleated settlements in Spain without demonizing the countryside. Their urbanizing culture rejected residence in the countryside but promoted it as a place of spiritual renewal. Seventeenth-century Iberian miraculous apparitions strongly gravitated towards parish peripheries (Christian 1981: 19–21). They proved that Spain was a Christian land. Some miraculous apparitions occurred in the Andes during the first century after Spanish invasion, most notably the Virgins of Copacabana and Cocharcas, but their paucity worried theologians like Acosta. They would have been the perfect supplement to *reducción* in rooting out idolatry, but simply did not occur as often as they had in the Old World. Christian reconsecration of the Andean landscape was mainly to occur later, and in tandem with new forms of 'idolatry,' as we will see in chapter 7. For at least the first century and a half of Spanish colonialism, the parish was the lone source of light to combat the Prince of Darkness on his chosen ground. Like thousands of tiny stars, the *reducciones* were all that perforated an otherwise solid wall of night.

Mountains, in particular, cast a long shadow over the *reducciones*, and embodied the surrounding landscape's opposition to them. Church-based settlements routinely lay in valleys or on plains encompassed by mountains: a further contrast of elevation was therefore available to those who articulated an antagonism of Christian town to idolatrous country. Thus, Christian nucleated lowland settlements made mountains into their idolatrous negative counterpart. Such dichotomizing led even the most knowledgeable extirpators to affirm that Andean people 'worshipped mountains.'[3] In the following section, I will show that their own findings consistently refuted this conclusion. The extirpator Estanislao Vega Bazán also felt obliged to dispute this notion in 1656: the Indians' offerings were to particular idols, he noted, not to the mountains on which they might be found (Duviols 1971: 387–8). Yet this belief also turned out to be more than mere error, since it accurately registered the transformative pressure that *reducción* was exerting on Andean *ayllus* and their sacred geographies. Thus, the parish's concentric moral universe both revealed and changed *ayllu* landscapes. Spanish misapprehensions became progressively more accurate as the broader reordering of which they were part ultimately did lead to 'mountain worship.' Yet this transformation was not widespread until two centuries after *reducción*, and its completion involved later developments that subsequent chapters will cover. For now, the point is to reconstruct *ayllu* landscapes at the beginning of their transformative encounter with *reducción*.

Ayllu Landscapes

Let us begin with Albornoz' geographical compendium of the Andes' most notable sacred sites. He often states that mountains were *huacas*, but then specifies that this status was limited to particular stones on them (Duviols 1984: 206–14). The first mountains to figure in his account are the snow-capped volcanoes of Arequipa and Southern Ayacucho, including Sarasara, Solimana, Coropuna, Ampato, and Putina, all of which were ancestral origin points: *pacarinas*. Albornoz stipulates that the Incas gave these mountain shrines attendants (*mitimaes*), fields, herds, gold, silver, and cloth, and rebuilt many of them (Duviols 1984: 198). This final observation is significant. Presumably the Incas did not rebuild the mountains themselves but statues or architectural sites on them, which probably represented the ancestors and their *pacarinas*. The one surviving parish-level record of Albornoz' extirpation lists scores of *pacarinas*, only one of which he identified with a mountain itself, although several others occurred on mountains (Millones 1990: 267). Albornoz burned the remaining *pacarinas*, suggesting that they consisted of wooden constructions or statuary (Millones 1990: 265–8, 274–8, passim). Thus, what initially looks like mountain worship gives way to the more specific complex of ancestors and *pacarinas*.

The *corregidor* of Collaguas in Arequipa confirmed that his subjects saw the volcano Collaguata as a *pacarina* in an account of 1586 that neatly supplements Albornoz.' This snow-capped volcano lay on the boundary between Collaguas and Veillille, and from its bowels many people sprang forth in the past, conquering Collaguas' aboriginal inhabitants and expelling them by force. The Collaguas worshipped Collaguata as their source, and the site of their most important shrine and *guaca*. Similarly, the neighbouring Cabanas issued from Mount Gualcagualca and drove out the original inhabitants of that territory (Jiménez de la Espada 1965: 327). Ancestral hordes were these accounts' protagonists. They sacralized mountains by emerging from them, but only this ancestral contact made them significant; otherwise, they were mere conduits.

Mountains also figure as *pacarinas* in Álvarez' account. Aullagas' *ayllus* traced their ancestral origins to Anconcagua, the Andes' tallest mountain in the Chilean cordillera (1588: 147–8). Before Spaniards arrived, each *ayllu* also placed a statue of its most revered ancestral deity (*huaca*) in a shrine-and-tomb complex atop a high mountain within its territory. They took their statues with them when moving to new lands, or in war (Álvarez 1588: 75, 103). Thus, the mobility of ancestor-worshipping groups required the mobility of ancestral forms, which were essentially independent of the landscape. After the Spanish invasion, Catholic priests found and destroyed most of the statues and shrines on lower mountains, so people dismantled bridges and other accesses to high mountain shrines. However, some said that they moved and buried the statues in lower, more accessible places, including town plazas and cemeteries, where people still worshipped them (Álvarez 1588: 74, 81, 87). These stone statues represented dead Incas or *curacas*, who might give oracles or generate the appearance of more closely related dead who would speak (Álvarez 1588: 75–6, 82). Evidently, keeping ancestral statues connected to living communities and their mortuary sites mattered more than keeping them atop mountains. Similarly, a document of 1591 from nearby mentions that adepts took 'idols' formerly housed on the mineral-bearing mountain of Porco and four surrounding peaks to the distant Caltama Valley, where pilgrims could safely offer them sacrifices (Platt et al. 2006: 184–5). Ancestral representations, not mountains, were clearly the objects of worship here.

These reports describe relations between ancestors and landscape established in pre-Hispanic times, although Álvarez mentions some colonial changes. How did *reducción* and its new Christian version of ancestor worship affect these 'traditional' Andean ancestor/landscape regimes? One answer emerges from a Jesuit account of Omate's spectacular eruption in 1600. It reports that Indians fled the city of Arequipa, fearing that it would be levelled, offered animal sacrifices to the volcano, and engaged in oracular communication with the Devil 'who told them of the storms that were to come, and how the volcano of Omate had wanted to join with that of Arequipa [then known as Putina, now as El Misti] to destroy the Spaniards, and how that of Arequipa responded that he could not turn on them because he was a Christian and was called San Francisco, so that Omate alone exerted himself to realize this end' (Mateos 1944: 220–1). This remarkable passage appears to depict mountains as deities at a relatively early colonial moment. However, if Omate remained an ancestral figure distinct from the landscape, as Albornoz' descriptions suggest, it could still cause the volcano to erupt as an expression of its power, without thereby merging with it.

Exactly what, beyond the name of San Francisco, made the volcano above the city of Arequipa a Christian? Perhaps extirpators destroyed its indigenous shrines and placed a cross on its summit, but such generic actions were elsewhere insufficient to Christianize mountains. On these particular mountainsides, however, people built Marian shrines during the late sixteenth century (Vargas Ugarte 1956 II: 144; Sallnow 1987: 69). These shrines were derivatives of the Virgin of Cocharcas, not miraculous apparitions in their own right. Still, they reconsecrated Arequipa's periphery in Christian terms immediately before Omate's eruption. Apparently Christian and Andean ancestral forces were competing to animate this landscape, and this view is fundamental to the native analysis Mateos paraphrases. Omate's eruption was a spectacular ancestral backlash against the urban nucleus of the intrusive faith. Bouysse-Cassagne sees it as a *pachacuti* or cataclysmic restructuring of the earth, in which a new animating deity displaces an old one (1988: 174–9). This suggests that Omate's eruption represented a failed offensive, one that dissipated his force and signified defeat. While this is a possible reading, the document itself reports no such verdict, however, only polarization and struggle.

The Huarochirí manuscript, written about 1607, describes a remarkably similar cataclysmic struggle from the pre-Hispanic past. Pariacaca, the story's highland protagonist, appeared as five eggs on Mount Condorcoto (Salomon and Urioste 1991: 54). These eggs hatched into five falcons who in turn became men, wandered about, learned of the local ruler, and resolved to vanquish him. Once, the narrative individually names these five men and identifies them as brothers. Pariacaca is one of these specific manifestations but also a covering term for all five (Salomon and Urioste 1991: 59–60, 68, 92–4). Pariacaca's first act was to annihilate a lowland village by rising up as yellow and red hail, and sending torrents of water and mud down the slope to wash it away. Then he turned to a neighbouring village and withheld its water supply to blackmail one of its women, the beautiful Chuquisuso, into having sex with him (Salomon and Urioste 1991: ch. 6). To establish his claim to animating humanity, however, Pariacaca had to displace the autochthonous fire deity, Huallallo Carhuincho, who originally occupied the locality known as Upper Pariacaca. Pariacaca appeared there as lightning and yellow and red rain coming from five different directions, but Huallallo Carhuincho countered as a huge fire billowing into the sky from the earth. One of Pariacaca's five selves knocked down a mountain to dam the rainwater they collectively sent, which formed Mullococha Lake, swamping Huallallo Carhuincho's shrine and forcing him to flee east towards the jungle. Another of Pariacaca's five manifestations turned into a mountain guarding Huallallo Carhuincho's route into the jungle, to prevent his return. His remaining aspects returned westward, driving Huallallo Carhuincho's wife, Mama Ñamca, into the sea, and one of them remained to prevent her return (Salomon and Urioste 1991: ch. 8). Having thus secured his territory, Pariacaca finally came to rest on a mountain bearing his name, where his principal shrine was established (Salomon and Urioste 1991: 60, 71, 94).

Jointly the cases of Omate and Pariacaca suggest that it was during struggles with rivals that ancestral deities became most identified with the landscape. At stake was control over the land and who was most able to animate it, so it is logical that the struggle became a test of telluric forces. Even in this moment of heightened identification with the land, however, these competing ancestors remained distinct from it. Their violent modifications of the landscape asserted power along subject-object lines, not as self-inflicted wounds. Pariacaca displaced Huallallo Carhuincho from the towering snow-capped mountain that was henceforth called Pariacaca and drove him out of the territory: such substitutions imply nonidentity. Once the struggle ended, naming the peak after Pariacaca established an association without collapsing all distinctions. The manuscript states merely that Pariacaca and his sons entered a crag, not that their bodies transformed into it (or the mountain), as happened in other ancestral narratives. Crags were often *paca-*

rinas (Polia 1999: 307, 324, 345), and since this one merely contained Pariacaca and his sons, we must assume that such was its status. Near this crag were a shrine and an 'idol,' both called Pariacaca: this idol, not the mountain, was the object of Pariacaca's cult.[4] In short, Pariacaca was no exception to the mummy-, idol-, and *pacarina*-based complex of ancestor worship found elsewhere in the Andes at this time. Pariacaca the ancestor lent his name and presence to his idol, shrine, and mountain in descending order of intensity but remained conceptually and practically distinct from all of them.

Seven of Pariacaca's sons participated in his conquests, led by the most valiant, Tutay Quiri (Salomon and Urioste 1991: 70–1, 82).[5] The narrative mentions that Tutay Quiri's sons founded descent groups in settlements they took over, but does not give this progenitor role to any of Pariacaca's other six sons. Perhaps they were not relevant as ancestors, since subsequent investigations discovered Tutay Quiri's mummy but none for his brothers (Polia 1999: 306). Alternatively, they may have become ancestors outside the few localities that the narrative discusses in detail. Whether the process began with Pariacaca himself, his sons, or those of Tutay Quiri, the conquerors dispersed over the territory, representing their differentiation and unity through patrilineal descent, in classic segmentary fashion (see figure 5.1).

A particularly detailed account of the new order comes from the Checa region. The ancestors of the original Yunga inhabitants reputedly originated from a wild quinua plant near Upper Yauyos and went on to establish six villages in the area. Subsequently, invaders fell out of the sky as blood, landing on the quinua fields in a place called Vichi Cancha, thus superimposing themselves on the original inhabitants and their crop (Salomon and Urioste 1991: 117–18). Led by Pariacaca's son Tutay Quiri, these invaders ostensibly expelled the quinua-born Yungas from their villages, founding their own *ayllus* in each around Tutay Quiri's sons. Nonetheless, Yunga groups named Huanri and Chauti remained in the area: the invaders accepted them because they worshipped Tutay Quiri (Salomon and Urioste 1991: 80, 119–20). Furthermore, the intrusive *ayllus* retained the names and the *huacas* of their Yunga predecessors in each village. At least three of those *huacas* were the founding ancestors of those original *ayllus* (Salomon and Urioste 1991: 117–19). The reality of conquest clearly involved compromise with the vanquished, not just their (relative) dispossession, but the narrative does not highlight this information, preferring instead to dwell on the dramatic details of supernatural attack and expulsion. By incor-

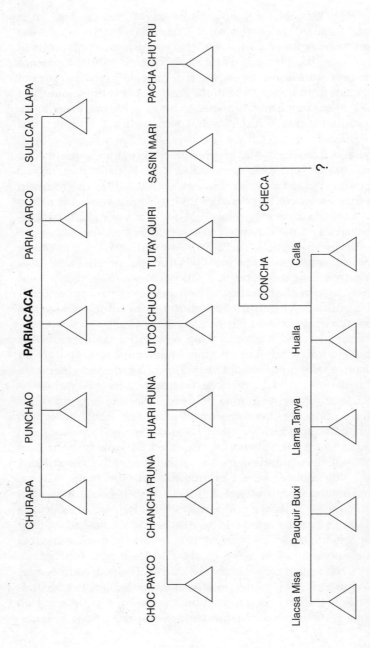

Figure 5.1 Pariacaca: His Subdivisions and Descendants

porating some original inhabitants and maintaining the cult of their deities, the victors claimed legitimacy and continuity from them and hoped to benefit from their agricultural tutelage. The Yunga population that remained in the area after conquest was large enough to sustain an alternating ritual structure: both groups jointly celebrated the conquerors' origin for two years and then the conquered's origins for another two years, before repeating the cycle (Salomon and Urioste 1991: 121n631). Both celebrations involved symbolic attacks on their respective ancestors (Salomon and Urioste 1991: 120–4). Such reciprocal aggression complicates their interpretation as commemorations of conquest or unilateral expressions of power, and suggests instead that memories of conflict now articulated ritual dualism. Clearly this conquest was not about ethnic cleansing: the vanquished shared their villages and patrimony with the victors, intermarried with them, and both worshipped each group's ancestors.

Other conquests may have involved the dispossession, expulsion, or annihilation that the narrative implies. For example, Pariacaca reportedly arrived as a poor man at a celebration in the village of Yaru Tini, where only one man would offer him corn beer and coca. Telling that man to hold on to a tree when he returned in five days, Pariacaca converted himself into a wind and levelled the town, blowing away all its inhabitants but the man, whom he turned into stone after promising him that intrusive newcomers would worship him (Salomon and Urioste 1991: 125–6). A similar episode followed in the town of Maca Calla, which Tutay Quiri later conquered (Salomon and Urioste 1991: 127–8). By converting an original inhabitant into a stone *huaca* in each case, the conquerors had the best of both worlds, claiming legitimacy, continuity, and tutelage from the Yungas through ritual, while appropriating their entire patrimony. Intrusive deities turn a territory's original inhabitants into stone elsewhere in the Huarochirí manuscript (Salomon and Urioste 1991: 59) and in other Andean narratives, which usually depict this fate as punishment for failing to heed the deity in question. Salmon and Urioste rightly argue that these stories mythically explain how conquering groups came to possess their predecessor's *huacas* (1991: 126n670). One might further suggest, however, that the petrification of the conquered rationalized their outright expulsion from a territory within an ideology that stressed ancestral continuity.

The Huarochirí manuscript nonetheless ends with an account of the conquest of Concha that hints at the accommodations encountered earlier. Five brothers and five sisters, all children of Tutay Quiri, emerged from the ground in Yauri Llancha. The brothers had stone helmets, the very sight of which was enough to kill some Yunga inhabitants and put the rest to flight. As the invading brothers established themselves in Concha, they found an abandoned Yunga boy named Yasali. The younger brothers wished to kill him, but the eldest dissuaded them. Then Yasali became his llama herder, married his sister, and eventually became a priest (*yañca*) in annual rituals like those of Checa. Since these rituals required the alternating sponsorship of conquering and conquered groups, we may assume that the latter continued to exist in numbers, despite the overt content of the narrative. The younger conquering brothers then dispersed to other parts of the territory, leaving the eldest, Llacsa Misa. He began to worship the *huaca* Collquiri at Lake Yansa, source of Concha's irrigation water. This *huaca* went looking for a wife and finally eloped with one from the neighbouring (Yunga) hamlet of Yampilla, for which he paid compensation by increasing their share of irrigation water. Meanwhile, Llacsa Misa's people complained of their decreased share, so Collquiri made a containing wall for the lake and set rules for water distribution that all followed thereafter (Salomon and Urioste 1991: ch. 31). As did Pariacaca above, this intrusive *huaca* paid in irrigation water for sexual access to indigenous women, a formula that initiates intergroup accommodation and the formation of a new social unit comprising both.

This recurring structure of accommodation is worth examining in detail. The opening 'exchange' of water for women suggests not only the categorical masculinity of the conquering group but their association with water, the medium by which Pariacaca attacked lowland villages and their deity. Pariacaca's battle with Huallallo Carhuincho is one of water against fire, cold and hot, high and low: terms opposed during their conflict but complementary thereafter. Specifically, the warm maize-growing lowlands need water from the cold highlands, just as highlanders need access to maize and so undertook the conquests described. As Salomon and Urioste note (1991: 139n775), all the irrigation myths depict *huacas* that control water as male and those that control maize-growing lands as female, so that sexual encounters inaugurate their productive relationship. Thus, they sexually code the agrarian complementarity of high and low that elsewhere figures so prominently in the resolution of conquest into social structure (Duviols 1973).

Besides giving wives to their conquerors in return for irrigation water, conquered lowlanders were to worship Pariacaca and claim descent from Chaupi Ñamca (Salomon and Urioste 1991: 71n228, 77n286). The narrative provides several versions of who Chaupi Ñamca was, each of which is significant. She first appears as the daughter of an indigenous Yunga ruler who became very sick. In exchange for a cure, she married Huatiacuri, a son of Pariacaca, before the latter annihilated her father (Salomon and Urioste 1991: 56, 77). Thus, Chaupi Ñamca was the first indigenous woman to marry an intrusive outsider, the one who established that pattern. Chaupi Ñamca's second role was mother of Pariacaca's children (Salomon and Urioste 1991: 72, 77). Here, she passes from being his daughter-in-law to his wife, hardly a surprise given Pariacaca's tendency to subsume his sons. In this situation, generational distinctions were secondary to that between wife-giving and wife-taking groups. Chaupi Ñamca's third and final role was as Pariacaca's sister (Salomon and Urioste 1991: 77, 84, 87). This perspective arises from her previous role as mother. Once her offspring began to regard her through the lens of descent, she became an apical ancestor comparable to Pariacaca because, like him, she was the maximal representative of one of the two groups, conquering and conquered, brought together in the post-conquest kinship system.[6] Her transformation from wife to sister expresses the fusing of conquering and conquered into a single new kin group, in which consanguinity tempered this ongoing gendered distinction. Implied is a shift from affinity to descent as the dominant kinship idiom, one that became manifest in the reciprocal worship of ancestral deities described for both Checa and Concha.

This detailed portrait of conqueror-aboriginal relations refers to pre-Inca times, but what did it mean to remember these events in 1607? The most basic answer is that Pariacaca's traditions mattered because they articulated ongoing local relations of kinship, agrarian complementarity, and political power in ways that the Inca interlude, for example, did not. After 1532, provincial Andean polities turned to their own pasts to claim sovereignty under indirect colonial rule. Such revitalization appears in the Taqui Oncoy, but was old news by the first anti-idolatry campaign, Burga (1988: 154–5) notwithstanding. Possibly a more compelling reason to recount past colonizations was to juxtapose them to, and so comment on, the Spanish colonial present. Other ancestral accounts explicitly realized this possibility, and so become parables of their colonial present. The Huarochirí manuscript discreetly avoids overt commentary, but its lengthy discussion of earlier colonial accommodations still had implicit relevance. By describing how conquest led to relations of political and territorial domination, but also marriage, kinship, and reciprocal ancestor worship, it presented an obvious alternative to Spaniards' refusal of marital and kinship obligations, or to recognize Andean ancestors. Inherent in these traditions are Andean norms for converting relations of conquest into those of coexistence. Their reiteration in a non-conforming Spanish colonial present could easily become a veiled critique.

Chinchaycocha

A similar narrative emerged from the town of Cauri, Huánuco, during 1615, when members of the town's two *ayllus* were charged with 'idolatrous' dancing. All testified that they danced at three sites (probably *pacarinas*) to honour Yanaraman, founder of the settlement named Guacras. They recounted his tradition as follows: one day a man named Atunchuca was hunting deer and vicuñas on Mount Raco on the plain of Bombon, when he found Yanaraman, a swaddled newborn child who fell from the sky. As this man had no children, he took this child home to raise. Within five days it grew up and took Atunchuca's many llamas to pasture. While on watch, however, Yanaraman turned into a puma and ate the animals. Atunchuca noticed his herd's decrease and asked Yanaraman to bring them back to the corral, which he did. Upset, Yanaraman then left, and would not heed the man's requests that he return. The llamas broke out of their corral and followed him to Mount Pumascatac, where he met his brothers Carua Pincollo and Carua Machacuay. When Atunchuca followed his animals to this spot, Yanaraman angrily told him to take his animals away. As he did so, Atunchuca and his animals turned to stone. The accused all added that they also knew Yanaraman as Libiac Cancharco, and that they also worship Atunchuca since he raised Yanaraman. The title Libiac Cancharco associates the intrusive ancestor Yanaraman with lightning, but as in Huarochirí, subordinated indigenes also figured as ancestors. Witnesses further noted that one moiety of Cauri danced in Llaspa, the other in Llibiac Binac Vilca, a half league from town. The latter was a mountain created when a man named Llibiac Binac Vilca fell out of the sky onto a plain, which inflated like a balloon until it became a mountain. This man had three children, Raria Paucar, Callupa, and Naspara, from whom all the townspeople descended. They worshipped Llibiac Binac Vilca and his sons as gods, believing the former returned to the sun in the sky. The accused offered these ancestors corn beer, coca, and dough (*sanco*) of white maize, and invoked them in these dances, call-

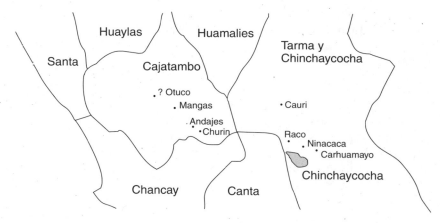

Figure 5.2 Ancestral Dispersions from Chinchaycocha

ing them saints of God because they came from the sky. Each had a shrine (*asiento*) on Mount Guancamarca, also known as Curman.[7]

This narrative addresses the arrival of intrusive lightning-worshipping groups in area both regionally and locally. The Yanaraman episode is of broad regional significance. People recognized Yanaraman as Libiac Cancharco, a maximal conquering ancestor all the way into Cajatambo and Checras.[8] We saw above that Avendaño found his mummified body in Andajes, where his journey of colonization ended (see figure 5.2). Llibiac Binac Vilca, however, was an ancestor of merely local significance. Each episode begins with an ancestor falling from the sky and ends with a group of three brothers possessing the land. This recursive structure suggests two waves of conceptually similar invasion, one of a maximal territory and the other of a locality. The two are related, though, since one of the accused in the trial describes Yanaraman's brother Carua Pincollo as her *pacarilla* (*pacarina*). Apparently this brother defined an overarching region that included Cauri, whereas the other two corresponded to distant sectors. Thus, we may suspect that Llibiac Binac Vilca was in some sense descended from Carua Pincollo, although a parallel but apparently separate episode recounts his origins.

Despite the largely commemorative nature of these traditions, they were not entirely backward-looking or focused on a pre-Columbian past. The claim that Llibiac Binac Vilca and his sons were saints of God because they came from the sky significantly engages with Christianity in the colonial present. Clearly people in Cauri took seriously the missionary idea of the saints and heaven and actively equated it with their own celestial ancestors. The indigenous priest Cristobal Ricra received greater punishment than others for advancing this idea, perhaps because it was so logical. Again we see an Andean attempt to fuse their form of ancestor worship with the Catholic cult of the saints, now outside the domain of mortuary ritual per se. Cauri had recently undergone a measles epidemic in which people threw crosses, holy images, and papal bulls out of their houses in the belief that those who owned them would die and those who did not would survive. Yet even more clearly than *taquiongos* who took similar actions, they were not religious separatists. Christian cosmology's equation of the sky with heaven and the underworld with hell meshed too well with Andean moiety distinctions to go unused. Ironically, it reinforced 'upper' groups' advantages over their 'lower' counterparts, and thus reinforced 'tradition.' Above all, however, this syncretized cosmology allowed Andean people to associate rain as the gift of life with divine grace, and therefore to reconcile the values of divine kingship with Christianity.

By portraying their lightning-worshipping ancestors as saints of God, Cauri's parishioners arguably joined those of Huachos and Yauyos, who probably appropriated Santiago to the same ends. Andean people had long connected Spanish use of gunpowder and shouts of 'Santiago!' with their own thunder and lightning deity named Illapa or Libiac. As early as 1527 during Pizarro's second reconnaissance voyage, a coastal *curaca* reportedly poured libations of corn beer down the barrel of a Spanish blunderbuss, saying, '[D]rink, drink, since they make such a loud noise with you, who is similar to celestial thunder' (Cieza 1553: 248). Santiago thus became a synonym for this deity, much to Spaniards' consternation (Silverblatt 1988). Spaniards wanted Santiago, as the Reconquista's patron, to signify Catholic militancy and purification, not syncretistic backsliding into idolatry or indigenous empowerment (as also occurred in Mexico, see Taylor 1996: 272–7). Yet Iberian Catholicism also associated Santiago with thunder and lightning, which ratified the Andean appropriation and gave it further significance. Since intrusive conquerors typically worshipped thunder and lightning deities (Duviols 1973), these understandings transposed easily onto Spanish ascendancy in the Andes. Ironically, then, the military technology that supposedly set Spaniards apart from Andean people to such advantage also made them intelligible within an established Andean cultural framework. Here, Spanish and Andean mythologies of conquest interacted in interesting and unpredictable ways. By appropriating and identifying with Santiago, Andean people made themselves into intrusive conquerors. By calling Spaniards *viracochas*, as we saw in chapter 2, they could portray Spaniards as conquered indigenes: legendary founders of towns and agriculture whose power went underground during the regional waves of conquest that preceded and constituted Inca imperialism (Duviols 1973). Thus, Andean identifications with the upper realm and their allocation of Spaniards to the interior realm subversively denied conquest. This was the primary statement Andean people made about their present in commemorating the past.

Other narratives from this area also describe ancestors falling from the sky onto mountains before moving on to the rich agricultural land of Andajes to the south and west (Iwasaki 1984: 86; Polia 1999: 345–54). This shared trajectory again suggests multiple waves of invasion by lightning-worshipping groups, a scenario that the rich data from Hacas confirm at the terminus of these ancestral journeys (Duviols 1986: ch. 5). The implicit focus of all these ancestral landfalls on the mountains around Lake Chinchaycocha is the lake itself. That so many ancestors fell from the sky here and dispersed to other areas confirms Chinchaycocha as a very high-ranking *pacarina*, one to which many central Andean polities traced their origins. Elsewhere (Gose 1993), I argue that maximal *pacarinas* were usually large bodies of water, and that the ancestors of those who claimed connection to them, usually pastoralists, ritually controlled the distribution of water. The case of Libiac Cancharco, whose mummy was believed to control the weather, certainly conforms to this pattern. Putative control over the vital agricultural resource of water further consolidated the dominance of intrusive lightning worshippers over conquered indigenous agriculturalists.

Of particular interest is a document of 1613 that describes how two ancestral brothers, Tumayricapa and Tumayhananpa, fell from the sky. The former landed on Mount Mamallqui Jirca, by Chinchaycocha's shores, and the latter on a crag named Ayracaca. From these *pacarinas*, their paths further diverged, and the narrative follows Tumayricapa's journey. He called together all the *huacas* where he landed before continuing to Bombon. There he turned himself into a child, whom a woman found and suckled. Within five days, he became a man and called together the snow-capped mountains Huacauencho and Arupa, each from separate but parallel cordilleras, and all the other *huacas* and mountains, to drive vicuñas into corrals on the plains of Uira Pampa by Bombon. Mount Quiru Machan, so tall that it reached to the heavens, scared the vicuñas away from the corrals. Tumayricapa ordered Quiru Machan (now as a *huaca*) to lower himself, and he agreed. As Quiru Machan was going down the slope of his associated mountain, Tumayricapa threw his bolas at a vicuña but hit Quiru Machan instead, cutting off his head to give the mountain its current form. Tumayricapa then descended to Chupachos in the Huánuco Valley and received its inhabitants as nephews, ceremonially cutting their hair. The Yanamates did not recognize or obey Tumayricapa, so one snowy day he went with his brother to raid their llamas, one as a puma and the other as a fox. The Yanamates found them by Mount Caytal, one as a puma the other in human form, eating maize and llama fat. The puma began to snort white hail from one nostril and red hail from another, and one of the Yanamates asked, 'My father, why did you take the llama?' Tumayricapa responded, 'Did you really call me father?' When they said they had, he told them to go to their town and bring him a llama at Mount Chuncrascayan so he could judge their sincerity by an entrail divination. They complied and the divination confirmed their pledge, so he received them as children (Polia 1999: 345–50).

This narrative reiterates the theme of lightning-related conquerors falling out of the sky as babies: indigenous people suckle or otherwise feed and raise them to maturity within five days. Then the foundlings prey on their hosts' animals until the hosts recognize them as deities. These displays of force and exploitative dependence mark their status as intrusive conquerors. By converting them into stone, like Atunchuca, the invaders assert their own supremacy and end their indigenous rivals' active careers, but also acknowledge their prior relation to the land and institutionalize their cults. Indigenes' role becomes essentially maternal: to nurture their conquerors' preternatural strength. Initially, however, the intrusive ancestors had to defeat the already-established local deities to stake their claims to animate descent groups and the land. As the struggle is partly territorial, the contending deities, particularly the aboriginal Quiru Machan, embody themselves in the land. Although this myth speaks of both *huacas* and mountains as agents, on closer examination we discover that Quiru Machan was not only a mountain but also a separable and presumably human form that descended the mountain's slopes and accidentally lost its head. Once decapitated, the mountain shared this fate by bearing a comparable wound. The identification of mountain and ancestor is evident, but their definitive fusion marks not only petrified apotheosis but defeat. Before decapitation, mountain and ancestor were not identical, although their relationship was intimate. I suspect that the narrative's distinction between *huacas* and mountains corresponds to that between intrusive and aboriginal ancestors, such that identification with the landscape signifies defeat.

By following Tumayricapa and Tumayhananpa through subsequent documents, we arrive at what is arguably the first case of Andean people practicing the 'mountain worship' that Spaniards attributed to them. An idolatry document from San Pedro de Ninacaca, 1617, records seventy-four-year-old Tomás Parinanco's worship of Tomayricapa and Tomayhananpa as his 'lords and gods' (*apoes y dioses*), to whom he confessed during semi-annual seasonal rituals. An extirpator punished him one year earlier for worshipping (probably as *pacarinas*) Mt. Raco and Lake Chinchaycocha, both of which figure in the document cited above. Now he wished to atone for worshipping two 'idols,' one of which represented a *curaca*'s spontaneously petrified body.[9] Since Arriaga (1621: 198) also mentions ancestor-oriented idolatries for Ninacaca, we may assume 'classic' *ayllu*-based ancestor worship as described above. A third document from the region reopens the issue of mountain worship, however.

In Carhuamayo during 1631, Felipe Nuna Vilca brought idolatry charges against Lorenzo Llacxa Guaroc, his father-in-law. Already a convicted idolater, Llacxa Guaroc was vulnerable to the accusation. Four years after Nuna Vilca married his daughter, Llacxa Guaroc allegedly called him to his house and told him that if he wanted to live well and long, he should sacrifice a fat llama, coca, corn beer, various coloured powders, and guinea pigs to a large spider in Llacxa Guaroc's care. First, however, Nuna Vilca was to confess his sins to Tomay Hananpa and Tomay Ricapa, deities that were either men or mountains, in the younger man's understanding. Nuna Vilca then denounced his wife, Ynes Guaroc, as complicit in her father's idolatries. He testified that once she brought him to the foot of Mount Mulluyanac at midnight, made a fire, and burned fat, coca, corn beer, and guinea pigs on 'many small plates of smooth stone, offering all of them to the mountain,' which she called 'her lord mountain and father-creator.'[10] The couple then washed away their sins in an irrigation canal that ran along the foot of the mountain and abstained from forbidden food and sex for twelve days. Nuna Vilca swore that he and his wife did this three times on their own, and twice in the company of Llacxa Guaroc, who 'had taught everyone to worship mountains from the time of their youth.' He concluded by noting that Llacxa Guaroc reminded him daily that the good life required adoration of mountains, and that were he to divulge these practices, he would die a bad death by lightning strike. Two witnesses who investigated Nuna Vilca's complaint later testified that they found traces of all the idolatries described. Both confirmed that Ynes Guaroc was an idolater: when they asked her if she thought herself to be a Catholic priest in presuming to pardon sins and perform mass, she responded that she could indeed perform mass in the offerings to the mountain. They further noted that they caught Llacxa Guaroc worshipping this mountain three years before, and that if the judge did not expel him from the parish he would ruin it by teaching others his idolatries.

This case is valuable for its depiction in the late 1620s of a mountain cult operating independently, it seems, of any ancestral cult focused on mummies, statues, or *paçarinas*. We must acknowledge the effect of previous extirpations: the principal culprit was a recidivist idolater, who may already have lost such ancestral relics and adopted mountain worship partly to avoid detection. He still confessed to Tomay Hananpa and Tomay Ricapa, but these regional ancestors were merging with mountains, at least in his accuser's view. Locally, Mount Mulluyanac may once have housed independent ancestral representations. Despite the occasional suggestion of 'idols,' however, none figure in the charges or investigations: Ynes Guaroc called the mountain 'lord mountain' and 'father-creator,' as if it were the locus of the life-creating and -sustaining powers that mummies and statues embodied elsewhere during this period. Were it not for this positive evidence, one could argue that this document provides an incomplete record of local religious practice that merely omits any reference to ancestors. Mulluyanac's titles suggest, however, that the mountain had actually taken over ancestral functions for these people.

Arguably this document merely continues the close identification between mountains and ancestors from the Tumayricapa narrative of 1613. In that document, such a merger signified defeat, whereas mobility across the land marked intrusive ancestors' victorious agency. Probably the extirpation of idolatry, with its destruction of independent ancestral forms, accentuated the landscape's absorption of defeated aboriginal deities, including those that may once have been triumphant intruders. Thus, the main culprits of both the 1617 and 1631 documents were recidivist idolaters who had probably lost previous objects of wcrship that the land replaced. Yet Catholicism's impact on these 'idol-atries' was not purely repressive. We have already seen that *reducción* selected and engaged with local mountains as the most salient feature of pre-existing *pacarina* landscapes. Here the engagement went further: like modern mountain spirits, Mount Mulluyanac received a 'mass' served on 'plates.' At this early date, Andean 'idolaters' asserted their claim to Catholic priesthood, blocked within the Church itself (Estens-soro 2003: 144), to reconsecrate a devastated and demonized landscape. Their outward ritual orientation contrasts markedly with *reducción*'s inward-looking emphasis, which was nonetheless the relevant refer-ence point. In short, we see here the first emergence of mountain wor-ship as a Christian idolatry.

Pachacuti Yamqui and Guaman Poma: Updating Myths of Coexistence

Let us now turn to two Andean intellectuals, Joan de Pachacuti Yamqui Salcamayhua and Felipe Guaman Poma de Ayala. These fervently Christian *curacas* wrote treatises on Andean history and society during the first anti-idolatry campaign. They rejected 'idolatry' but still sought to dignify the Andean past and reconcile it with Christianity. Thus, they followed Spaniards in using Viracocha and the wandering apostle as bridging figures, but their interventions were far from derivative. By appropriating these Spanish musings, themselves appropriations of Andean ancestral narratives, Pachacuti Yamqui and Guaman Poma did the labour of coordinating and integrating separate ancestral traditions that traditionally followed conquest in the Andes. In this crucial sense they were Andean intellectuals, despite writing in Spanish and ad-dressing Spanish debates. They did in writing much the same thing as Cauri's parishioners did in ritual when they identified their upper moiety with the saints and heaven. By juxtaposing their chronicles with such ritual accommodations, I will argue that they pursued a common project in different media.

Pachacuti Yamqui began his narrative by noting that his ancestors were the first *curacas* to convert to Christianity in Cajamarca and showed themselves to be enemies of idolatry thereafter (1613: 183). Thus, he suggests that his faction of the native ruling class was hungry for the religious truth, and needed only exposure to it to become firm in the faith. The rest of his chronicle explains this extraordinary predispo-sition's origins. Pachacuti Yamqui noted that like the rest of the world's nations, Peruvians descended from Adam and Eve (1613: 186) but then turned to the specifically Andean past, starting with the *purun pacha*, a primordial nomadic age. During this time, all the Andean nations came from above Potosí and formed three or four armies that set out (presumably in different directions) to possess unoccupied areas, where smaller contingents stayed behind as the main company went on. As time passed, however, land became scarce and wars over it common, so people built fortresses to protect themselves (1613: 187). On one night of this dark age, however, when Christ was crucified, the demonic *happiñuños* disappeared, crying out their defeat. Some years later, with these demons banished, an elderly, bearded, long-haired man arrived in the land, who taught the natives with great love, calling them sons and daughters. Although he travelled widely, doing miraculous cures, and spoke their languages better than the natives themselves, they ignored him, except to call him Tonapa, Tarapaca, or Uiracocham Pacha Yachachip Cachan, the servant or messenger of Viracocha (1613: 188). Pachacuti Yamqui suggests he must have been Saint Thomas, and states that the only *curaca* to take him in and understand his preaching was Apo Tambo, to whom the saint gave his staff, on which were inscribed the Ten Commandments and the Seven Precepts: only the names of God and Jesus Christ were missing. Tonapa–Saint Thomas preached tirelessly throughout Collasuyo, but in town after town people threw him out, so he slept in the country with only his long shirt and mantle and the book he carried (1613: 189). Sometimes he retaliated by depriving such towns of water, by melting mountains that housed idolatrous shrines into plains with his fiery embrace, or by turning those who would not listen to him into stone (1613: 190–1). Pachacuti Yamqui then recounts another version of the Cross of Carabuco, linking the natives' desire to kill Tonapa–Saint Thomas to his conversion of a local *curaca*'s daughter and attempt to baptize her (1613: 191–2). After his escape across the lake, he went on to the shrines of Titicaca and Tiwanaku, but the people there ignored him, so he turned them into stone before exiting to the sea via the Chaca Marca river (1613: 192–3).

So far, Pachacuti Yamqui ingeniously combines common generic features of Andean ancestral colonization narratives with those of Christian providentialism. The description of ancestral hordes setting out in different directions from a place above Titicaca (Tiwanaku) to populate the Andes is standard fare, as is the tension between conquest (here suggested by the formation of ancestral 'armies') and the settlement of unoccupied land. Possibly this tension got new meaning from Toledan polemics about Inca rule as illegitimate usurpation, but if so, Pachacuti Yamqui did not remove references to coercion as a result. Some origin narratives identify Tonapa as a rebellious assistant whom Viracocha eventually banished along the same route to the sea just described. His wandering, poverty, and rejection by settled villagers concord perfectly with the travails of other Andean deities such as Coniraya Viracocha in Huarochirí, as do his punitive, landscape-transforming retaliations against them and his infiltration of their groups via their women (here through baptism, not sexual appropriation). Although he does not portray a primordial monotheism grounded in Viracocha as creator God, Pachacuti Yamqui does posit human unity in a common descent from Adam and Eve. As a world-historical event, Christ's crucifixion had immediate repercussions in the Andes, driving away the demons. Pachacuti Yamqui's equation of Tonapa and Saint Thomas further integrates Andean tradition into Christian universal history, but he adds some very original wrinkles that are worthy of further exploration.

As the narrative continues, it turns out that Apo Tambo, the one *curaca* who listened to Tonapa's teachings, is none other than the father of the Ayar siblings who go on to found the Inca empire. On the birth of Manco Capac, his first son, the staff that Tonapa bequeathed turns into pure gold, as do two cups from which he drank (1613: 193–4). After the eight Ayar siblings' birth and their parents' death, Manco leads them to Cuzco, bearing these relics. En route, they defeat the *huacas* of Sañuc, Pinao Capac, and Tocay Capac (1613: 195–8). Once established in Cuzco, Manco architecturally enhanced the three windowed *pacarinas* of Tampo Ttoco, Maras Ttoco, and Sutic Ttoco and adorned two trees with golden roots and fruits to commemorate his parents. Pachacuti Yamqui remarks that in their idiocy, other Indians imitated Manco's actions without realizing their merely commemorative intent, thereby originating the idolatry of *pacarinas* (1613: 198–9). During the reign of Manco's son, Sinchi Roca, idolatries proliferated, but his successor, Lloque Yupanqui, did much to restore morality. The next Inca ruler, Mayta Capac, mocked idols, curtailed their public worship, and predicted the Holy Faith's coming (1613: 204–6). His successor was Capac Yupanqui, who delighted in exposing the *huacas* as frauds, and followed Tonapa's precedent in having his son, Inca Roca, 'anointed' (i.e., baptized) with water from Titicaca (1613: 211). Had missionaries come then, Pachacuti Yamqui observed, they would have fared very well. Unfortunately, Inca Roca was interested only in carnal pleasures, so idolatries flourished during his reign (1613: 213). The timid Viracocha

Inca succeeded him, and the Chancas attacked. Salvation came only when an angel appeared to his son Inca Yupanqui and told him to fetch the golden staff that Tonapa left his ancestors, which he used to command a host of stone monoliths (*purun aucas*) to life and rout the Chancas (1613: 217–9). Inca Yupanqui then conquered large territories and destroyed *huacas* in the process (1613: 223). Nonetheless, idolatry regained momentum in Huayna Capac's reign, and war between Huascar and Atahuallpa followed, leading to the Spanish conquest (1613: 248–50).

This part of Pachacuti Yamqui's narrative states that despite some backsliding into idolatry, the Incas were a powerful force for the establishment of the true faith in the Andes. Their father, Apo Tambo, was the only *curaca* to heed Tonapa–Saint Thomas during his Andean wanderings. The transformation of the apostle's wooden staff into gold sealed his compact with the Incas, and its reappearance at key moments later in Inca history helped them defeat idols and triumph. As Duviols notes, the Incas emerge as nothing less than the Andean 'chosen people' in this account (1993: 24). Yet their defeat also becomes intelligible because of their spiritual degeneration after Inca Yupanqui's reign. In short, the narrative concedes just enough to the Incas' Spanish critics to count as 'reasonable' while still maintaining that despite their weaknesses, the Incas were essentially an instrument of divine will. Pachacuti Yamqui implicitly acknowledges the necessity of outside missionary influence in this account, and explicitly regrets its absence during Capac Yupanqui's propitious reign. Thus, he gives external agency the primary role and makes local agency secondary. Again, this pattern is typical not only of most conversion narratives but also of Andean ancestral narratives, so we must not overestimate any dissonance here. Ultimately, the historical challenge was to synchronize the efforts of foreign and local agents of conversion. The period of indirect rule following the Spanish invasion finally realized this goal, but the original compact between the apostle and the *curaca* Apo Tambo prefigured it. Pachacuti Yamqui's treatise was a parable that reinforced and dignified this collaboration by writing its imagined history intelligibly and acceptably to all parties. Under different historical circumstances, he undertook the same reconciliation that occurred when *huari* and *llacuaz* groups coordinated their ancestral traditions and ritual lives to coexist locally. In this process, the conquered group surrendered certain claims to property, sovereignty and historical agency in return for recognition and inclusion as subordinate partners in the new order. Just such an order existed during the first four decades of Spanish colonialism, but began to slip away under the Toledo reforms and the extirpation of idolatry, which formed the context of Pachacuti Yamqui's writing. I suspect that he was trying to revive it by writing its historical charter.

Guaman Poma wrote the most comprehensive indigenous response to these various Spanish appropriations of Andean ancestral tradition. Like Cabello Valboa before him, he meticulously placed his version of the Andean past in Christian historical time. He begins by making the first inhabitants of the Andes, the Uari Uira Cocha Runa, into passengers on Noah's ark. No less astonishing, however, is his identification of these primordial Andean ancestors as Spaniards. Trading on the (by then) well-established designation of Spaniards as *viracochas*, Guaman Poma reasoned that because these original inhabitants of the Andes were also so designated, they must have been Spaniards (1615: 49). The claim is not merely that Andean people descended from Noah, belonged to the Judaeo-Christian tradition, and deserved full membership in it. Guaman Poma states that Andean people were nothing less than a lost tribe of Spaniards: an identical twin separated at birth, whose inherent virtues shone through in a different environment, where revelation was largely but not entirely absent. The rest of his primordial chronology systematically develops this position.

Utter simplicity marked the first Andean age of the Uari Uira Cocha Runa, who knew only agricultural labour but none of the domestic arts, as they wore leaves for clothing and took shelter in caves. They had no dealings with idols or *huacas* and were devout monotheists who called out to their God to reveal himself to them. Although they were barbarians, they lived virtuously and had a shadowy understanding of God, who ordered them to settle Peru as its rightful rulers. During one coordination of his account with un-Christianized versions of the Andean past, Guaman Poma calls these people *pacarimoc runa*, or 'primordial humanity' (1615: 49–52). The Uari Runa followed these original inhabitants, building houses, terraced fields, and irrigation canals, while still wearing skins and leaves. Despite this technical progress, Guaman Poma notes, they had no developed division of labour, property, or war. They continued their predecessors' monotheistic ways and prayed for revelation, learning of heaven and hell, and God's tripartite division (1615: 53–6). The third age belonged to the Purun Runa, who multiplied like the biblical grains of sand, perfected the art of clothing, the construction of houses, had kings, and bounded political units with public order and *ayllu* differentiation. They fought each other over territory and sometimes engaged in public drunkenness, but still maintained their monotheism and elevated morality (1615: 57–61). In the fourth age, Auca Pacha Runa made fortified settlements on hilltops to defend themselves from endemic conflict. Warriors took women, children, and estates from those they raided, yet charity continued to figure prominently in their groups' internal relations, and food production diversified. Political hierarchies emerged, but the great lords (*pacarimoc capac apo*) still traced their descent to the land's original inhabitants. Each *ayllu* developed its own dances and songs, but they were free from idolatry. Feminine virtue and modesty prevailed, a form of baptism emerged, and burial customs became very dignified. During this time, the wise men also knew of Spain's existence and its tribulations through reflection on their descent from Uira Cocha (1615: 63–78). Finally, the Incas began their conquests, ushering in a fifth age. Originally, they descended from Tocay Capac, who was as free of idolatry as all other Andean people. However, the licentious Mama Uaco, mother and wife of Manco Capac, introduced idolatry among the Incas, which they spread throughout the Andes with their conquests (1615: 80–1).

In Sinchi Roca's reign, Christ was born, and three wise men came to pay their reverence to him – Melchor, who was an Indian; Baltazar, a Spaniard; and Gaspar, a black. After the crucifixion, the Holy Spirit sent the apostles out to preach the gospel throughout the world. Saint Bartholomew went to the Indies and, during his travels through Collao, left the miraculous Cross of Carabuco. God's first miracle during Bartholomew's Andean ministry was in Cacha, where celestial fire saved the saint from the townspeople. From there, Bartholomew continued south to Collao and entered a cave to escape the cold. There he found an Indian priest whose idol was speaking to him. When the saint entered, however, the Devil ceased to speak through the idol. Later the Devil appeared in the priest's dreams, explaining that he could never speak in that cave again. The priest then hurried after the saint to tell him what had happened. Bartholomew instructed him to return to the cave and consult the idol again, which he did. The Devil then told him that the saint was more powerful and had defeated him. Again, the priest rushed after the saint and, reaching him, embraced him and kissed his hands and feet, asking his mercy. As a sign of this miracle, the saint left the Cross of Carabuco, which God intended and provided as the second miracle in Collao (1615: 91–4).

Although Guaman Poma and Pachacuti Yamqui disagreed sharply

over the Incas' historical role, their accounts are otherwise remarkably similar. Both portrayed Andean people as experienced in the true faith, and Guaman Poma occasionally argued that they should count as 'old Christians' in the peninsular sense (1615: 653). Their mytho-histories depict an evangelical partnership between Spaniards and Andean people, one that recalls not only the Huarochirí manuscript's complementary ancestor cults but also the post-invasion decades' inter-ethnic alliances. By welding the Andean past firmly to Christianity, Guaman Poma effected a reconciliation of myths that productively aligned traditions. This was a classic Andean strategy of coexistence between initially hostile groups, one that aimed to convert relations of conquest into those of complementarity. The etiquette of such relations presupposed the defeat and sometimes the expulsion of previous deities, but incorporated aboriginals without absolutely dispossessing them, once they accepted the new regime and its deities. In this spirit, Guaman Poma endlessly professed his Christian loyalties and opposition to 'idolatry.' He appropriated the providential tradition not ironically or tactically,[11] but to demand that Spaniards recognize Andean people as partners.

Above all, Guaman Poma objected to the idea that Spaniards had 'conquered' the Andes and its use to dispossess Indians. His most basic point was that Andean people did not resist Spaniards' entry into the land (1615: 386, 393, 395, 445). Rather, Huascar sent Guaman Poma's father, don Martín Guaman Malqui de Ayala, as his viceroy to Tumbéz. There he greeted Pizarro and Almagro in peace and voluntarily swore allegiance to Carlos V for the Inca empire's four quarters, announcing their intention to resume Christian worship (1615: 5–7, 47, 375–6, 550). The details of this story are clearly self-serving. Yet Guaman Poma's broader denial that Spaniards conquered the Andes and his insistence that sympathetic *curacas* helped them defeat the Incas and restore order after their civil wars are not deviations from historical accountability into poetic licence, as Adorno holds (1986: 53). Not only are these claims historically defensible, but they stem from Guaman Poma's Andean conviction that after a successful invasion, aboriginals have the right to dignified coexistence with intruders. Thus, *encomenderos'* claims to have earned their position through conquest were false (1615: 549–50). Spanish priests' claims to enjoy 'perpetuity' in their parishes, or to be 'proprietors' of them, were equally illegitimate (1615: 592, 657, 682). As the Crown's faithful subjects, Andeans could not legally be dispossessed. By denying conquest, Guaman Poma tried to steer relations with the Spaniards towards the complementary interaction of Andean moieties, as in the Huarochirí case. His concern with history, control of the land, and women (see below) all bear on this issue. Thus, he claims that Peru was a 'newer' and 'higher' land than Spain, and the word 'Indies' derived from the Spanish *en días* or 'in daylight' (1615: 368, see figure 5.3). In Andean moiety frameworks, this implied that Peru had 'upper' and Spain 'lower' status, much as did Andean identification with Santiago/Illapa and the labelling of Spaniards as *viracochas*. All these claims resolved intergroup relations into a partnership without conquest, in which Andean people implicitly held the upper hand, retaining their sovereignty, property, and women.

Yet Guaman Poma overtly advocated a separatism that fits poorly with moiety-like coexistence but perfectly with absolutist corruption discourses. He argued that *encomenderos, corregidores*, and priests united with *curacas* to exploit the Indians and usurp royal sovereignty (1615: 489–91, 504–6, 603, 712). Their abuses caused Indians to flee the *reducciones* to gullies where they adored *huacas* and avoided Christianity (1615: 446, 556, 565, 571–2, 578, 581, 602, 682). Worse still, these corrupt Spanish officials acted like Incas, travelling in litters, receiving *taquis* on their arrival in Indian towns, performing collective marriages, and allowing idolatries to flourish (1615: 554–5, 569, 571, 589–90, 601, 607, 624). Their culminating abuse was to monopolize single women, even married women and widows, as spinners, weavers, and concubines comparable to the Inca's chosen women. These women often rejected marriage with Indian men, gave birth to endless *mestizos*, and so sent the tributary population into further decline (1615: 446, 514, 518, 529, 556, 562–6, 568, 571, 573–5, 577, 580–1, 586–7, 590, 597–8, 606–7, 624, 644, 648, 662–3, 695). Guaman Poma was all in favour of Catholic interracial reconciliation, but when it came to sharing the land and women, everything changed. He strongly endorsed the Crown's policy of residentially segregating other colonial estates from Indians (1615: 533). Thus, he internalized and reproduced the Spanish reformism discussed above. Like so many colonial *curacas* who litigated over similar issues, Guaman Poma was fluent in absolutist corruption discourse.

Such use of Spanish rhetoric might well have been tactical, and did not necessarily nullify moiety strategies of intergroup accommodation. The concrete historical challenge was to prevent Spaniards from completely dispossessing and destroying Indian tributaries. Andean intellectuals expected to succeed only by adopting new cultural forms: the same compromise followed the pre-Inca conquests that their groups still commemorated. If they had to adopt Spaniards' separatist rhetoric to

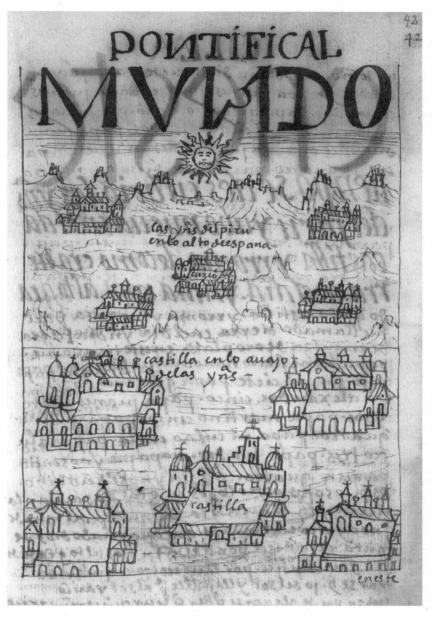

Figure 5.3 Peru as 'Upper' and Spain as 'Lower' Moieties

negotiate coexistence with them, then so be it. Such contradictions may equally have characterized the earlier conquests that Andean people remembered. The transition from invasion to reconciliation can never have been easy, and seems fragile even in its remembered forms. In the living, it probably required the same inconsistencies, silences, compromises and outright lies we see from Guaman Poma. If so, his very departure from Andean moiety accommodation strategies reveals something important about them: that they imposed a received cultural form on what was also a political negotiation of group boundaries and claims over land and women. A successful accommodation rendered this process progressively invisible, whereas it is blatant in Guaman Poma.

Reducción and the Second Anti-Idolatry Campaign

Despite their attempts to reform Andean people through *reducción* and the extirpation of idolatry, Spaniards also realized that they had to coexist with them. Like Pachacuti Yamqui and Guaman Poma, many of them wished to dignify this collaboration and not just dismiss it as corruption. With the deaths of Lobo Guerrero and Arriaga in 1622, an anti-extirpation faction took charge of the archbishopric of Lima, ending idolatry inspections. They launched a secret investigation into the extirpators' conduct during inspections and accused them of excessive material demands (García Cabrera 1994: chs. 1–3). For the first time, the prevailing discourse of corruption was used against (not just by) the Extirpation. Although the anti-extirpation faction left no extensive paper trail or elaborate treatises, they clearly took a brighter view of Indians' Christianity and saw idolatry as a matter of isolated survivals rather than a codified system. They considered the extirpators' negative emphasis to be counterproductive and their publicizing of Indian idolatries to be an affront to the Church's honour and achievements (Griffiths 1996: 54–60). While they enjoyed only middling short-term success, the Extirpation's opponents altered the terms of debate, and ultimately prevailed. This section traces the beginnings of that sea change, as the reformist project reached its limits and stalled during the 1620s and 1630s.

In 1620, the Marqués de Guadalcázar became viceroy of Peru. He avoided the Extirpation's controversies but championed *reducción*. His greatest concern was Indian population decline and the *reducciones'* dissipation, particularly as it affected the Potosí *mita*. Reports told him that most Indians living in Potosí's catchment area had hidden in remote areas, sometimes with their *curacas'* collusion. These Indians lived 'without religious instruction nor justice, and the tribute which they owe Your Majesty and the *encomenderos* ceases to be collected.' Since he and his predecessors had failed to enforce existing tributary obligations, Guadalcázar proposed lowering them. He noted that the Indian population had shrunk considerably since their obligations were last set, and that no sooner did they return from one stint of labour in the mines than the next came due: hardly Toledo's planned seven-year rotation. This increasingly onerous tribute, along with priests' and *corregidores'* local demands, led Indians to abandon the *reducciones*. Only thus, he lamented, could they reproduce and raise their families. Many *curacas*, realizing that they could never meet their tributary obligations, simply renounced their offices, and often nobody wanted to replace them. By reassessing each district's tributary obligation, enforcing previous decrees that *corregidores* return all *forasteros* to their towns of origin, and appointing an official in Potosí to ensure that all tributaries sent there actually returned home, Guadalcázar hoped to make the *reducciones* viable again. The mines would initially produce less metal, but the benefits of good administration would eventually prevail.[12]

The king and the Council of the Indies rejected Guadalcázar's proposal, largely because it entailed declining revenues. So Guadalcázar could only uphold Montesclaros' existing decree and instruct *corregidores* to return to their *reducciones* Indians living in 'the old towns or some gullies and solitary places, thus removing themselves from religious instruction and other Christian obligations, with the risk of committing idolatry.' On the king's orders, he reluctantly consulted parish priests about how best to combat this ill, and instructed them not to burn Indian towns or houses outside the *reducciones* without his expressed orders.[13] When Gonzalo de Campo became archbishop of Lima in 1625, Guadalcázar found an activist ally. They resolved to enforce *reducción*, and Campo ordered his clergy to comply with the viceroy's directives. Campo faced a debate over the reality of Indian idolatries, and undertook a pastoral visit of the entire archdiocese to see for himself. His entourage included Jesuits, secular clergy and Fernando de Avendaño, a veteran of the first extirpation campaign, who quickly convinced him that the archbishopric was rife with idolatry.[14] Campo blamed its persistence on negligent priests, particularly Mercedarians, who pursued business interests, not their spiritual vocation.[15] With unusual dramatic flair, he produced a perfect specimen of this stereotype: the friar Francisco de Ribera.

Campo had already decided to visit Ribera's parish of Bombom, since he had reports of idolatries and heresies there, and commissioned a neighbouring priest to investigate. Ribera impeded that investigation, so the archbishop intervened. His entourage planned to meet Ribera in San Juan, but took a wrong turn and arrived in San Augustín, where they saw an Indian named don Felipe leading public idolatry and witchcraft. They soon learned that Ribera told the assembled towns-people not to denounce don Felipe during the archbishop's inspection, or he would punish them. Campo also reported that Ribera approached the earlier idolatry inspection's Spanish notary and offered to pay the investigation's entire cost, and cede the idol's confiscated livestock, if the judge would simply punish the guilty without leaving any record to damage his reputation. Next morning, Ribera arrived, and the arch-bishop gave a sermon to the assembled Indians and their priest on the truth of the Catholic faith, the firmness of belief it requires, and the fal-sity of their idols. They then confessed their sins and tearfully asked for pardon. Campo absolvéd them, performed mass, and had them all recite the credo with him. Afterwards, so many came to testify about the town's idolatries that he and four notaries worked very late record-ing them. So he could do confirmations, Campo delegated the confes-sions to other priests in his entourage and left the idolatry investigation to Avendaño, who assembled an exhibit of idols and witchcraft objects that the archbishop took away in two chests. They discovered that the parish had pagan priests who heard confessions and offered public sac-rifices. Its idolatry was so notorious that priests from two neighbouring parishes did not allow their Indians to spend more than one night there for fear it would infect them. Not only had Ribera failed to report this problem, Campo decided, but he continued to impede investigations. Campo concluded that in the ninety years following the conquest, Indi-ans' instruction in the faith had been abysmal. Exceeding even Toledo in severity, he argued that both Indians and their priests needed to feel the terror of the Inquisition or they would continue to permit the idola-tries they should denounce.[16]

Campo's inspection of the archdiocese also addressed *reducción*. He noted that many of Toledo's functionaries did not execute the policy, and that ever since, the king had exhorted each subsequent viceroy over the matter. Although he instructed all parish priests to collaborate with their local *corregidores* in enforcing *reducción*, his tour of inspection revealed a complete lack of progress. Priests and *corregidores* never con-ferred over *reducción*, Campo realized, since they often lived more than a hundred leagues apart, and it would negatively affect their economic interests. Once he left any locality during his inspection, efforts to enforce the policy immediately stopped. Today in many parishes, he continued, the Indians live in the same settlements as they did under the Inca, although *reducción* was supposed to have removed them from their old shrines, and away from high peaks suitable in times of war, but not for receiving the faith. Campo wondered at the parishes' size and disorder: some were forty leagues long, and had up to twelve settlements, often interspersed with settlements belonging to other parishes. He made a map and census of the parishes during the inspection, presumably to rationalize them.[17]

Campo also forwarded the testimony of several priests and reputable Spaniards regarding *reducción* in the Huánuco region to refute allegations the king received from Hinostrosa, a sub-*corregidor* in Tarma.[18] Hinostrosa alleged that Campo overstepped his jurisdiction by personally ordering *reducciones* without consulting secular authorities, acted recklessly without due regard for Indian property or the sanctity of the churches in decommissioned towns, and that his entourage acted corruptly and extortionately. Witnesses defended Campo by arguing that idolatry and tacit rebellion increased on the margins of priestly surveillance, and became public in areas that priests and *corregidores* seldom reached. Friar Luis Lloscos added, after responding to the formal questionnaire, that even the Indians in the parish centres still did not understand the Holy Faith and continued their idolatries and superstitions, secretly maintaining their ministers of idolatry. Those living farther away practiced their idolatries publicly. Since Toledo's time, he continued, Indian populations had fallen by more than half, and there was now sufficient land in the parish centres to allow for *reducción*. If Indians failed to comply, it was to avoid masses and sermons maliciously. They wanted freedom to worship their idols, have concubines and incestuous unions, avoid justice and tributary obligations. When their own native mayors tried to correct these wrongs, they whipped them. Initially, he observed, parish annexes had lower populations than the centres, but over time the pattern reversed itself. Indian mortality was not the cause; rather, they left the centres for annexes to escape priestly surveillance and tribute. Campo's witnesses mention many specific towns where they enforced *reducción* immediately before or during his inspection.[19] We do not know how far these efforts extended, but it is remarkable that they generated litigation against someone so powerful.

As an activist who campaigned vigorously against the status quo in his jurisdiction, Campo predictably made enemies. His sudden death on December 19, 1626, by poisoning at the hands of a *curaca* he reprimanded in Recuay (Vargas Ugarte 1953–62 II: 336), must have come as a great relief to many. This event reminds us that Campo campaigned against entrenched interests, not mere figments of reformist discourse. We might dismiss Campo's musings on personal risk and unholy alliances in rural parishes as formulaic, but they proved correct. Furthermore, his assassination clearly deterred renewed attempts at reform. It abruptly halted the second extirpation campaign and the administrative will to enforce *reducción*. With his main ally dead, Guadalcázar could only complain to the king, who ordered him on March 15, 1628, to consult knowledgeable authorities, a classic stalling tactic. This request came at the end of Guadalcázar's term as viceroy, so its execution fell to his successor, the Conde de Chinchón. Although the latter immediately expressed doubt that he could resolve so controversial an issue as *reducción*, he duly requested position papers from prelates and government officials, who responded between 1631 and 1633.[20] The resulting corpus provides a fascinating picture of the politics of *reducción* during the seventeenth century, and merits far more historiographic attention than it has yet received or I can give it here.

Of particular interest for our purposes was the response of Hernando Arias Ugarte, who became archbishop of Lima on February 14, 1630 (Vargas Ugarte 1953–62 II: 337). His position was already emerging when he inspected the archdiocese and found that idolatry was a nonissue:

Although some people, perhaps moved by good intentions, say that there are many idolatries among the Indians, I have not found them, having proceeded with diligence and caution. In very few places I found some remains of the ancient, and some superstitions, and because of God's mercy I see that most Indians are well instructed in Christian doctrine and the things of our Catholic faith which, according to their capacity, they must know for their salvation. And this [knowledge] would be greater still if the Indians were reduced to their towns, as don Francisco de Toledo ordered, and if past viceroys (not the Conde de Chinchón) would not have so liberally given permission to the Indians to return to their old towns at the request of their badly-informed Protectors.[21]

Consistent with his rejection of the extirpation of idolatry, he did not use the *reducción* debate to articulate an evangelical crisis in his archbishopric. He simply observed that *reducción* was necessary 'for the conservation and increase of these provinces and for the Indians' Christianity.' He noted that the *reducciones'* depopulation was not uniform: the problem hardly existed in Quito but was serious in Lima and worse in Charcas. In these latter areas, towns that previously had one thousand Indians now had one hundred or even twenty. The solution, he argued, was to address the root causes of flight, namely *corregidores'* and *curacas'* exploitation and abuse of Indians in their *reducciones*. Striking a markedly different note from Guadalcázar, he argued that their officially required services, namely the payment of tribute and various *mitas*, were indispensable: only the unofficial services for corrupt local officials should end. In effect, he proposed little more than the usual moralization of local rule to reverse the *reducciones'* decline.[22]

Other position papers from secular officials stated more adamantly than Arias Ugarte the religious need to enforce *reducción*, and its contribution to the extirpation of idolatry.[23] Thus, the connection between these two issues forged under Arias Ugarte's predecessors survived, but only as an undercurrent, given his denial that significant native idolatries still existed. However unintentionally, this denial of an idolatry problem diminished the sense of urgency behind *reducción*, and encouraged a secular understanding of it that focused on the colonial state's tributary crisis. Participants agreed that Spaniards sheltered most *forasteros* as a private labour force, but so did *curacas*, particularly those in remote highland areas who so obsessed the extirpators of idolatry. They discussed previous policies' failure to return Indians to the *reducciones* and keep them there, blamed the usual suspects (corrupt *corregidores*, *curacas*, and parish priests), and proposed minor policy modifications, which mostly required collaboration from the same 'corrupt' figures they had just denounced. Despite the evident difficulties in enforcing *reducción*, some wished to intensify the program by further consolidating annexes and even whole parishes for efficient evangelization and administration.[24] No matter how badly the policy failed, the only imaginable solution was to persist and extend it. Participants in this debate openly expressed a sense of futility and immobility. When the king requested a recommendation, the Conde de Chinchón replied that any action would cause 'more than the usual sentiment' from colonists and proposed doing the utmost with existing legislation.[25] The High Court of Lima backed his position, opining that *reducción* would be hard to achieve and impossible to maintain since Indians hate their natal towns for the mistreatment they receive there, and because Span-

· iards will strive to retain *forasteros* in their employ. They concluded by
comparing the state of *reducción* in Peru to a mortal dagger wound: bad
as it might be to leave the dagger in, taking it out would only hasten
death.[26]

With the vanishing of any political will to pursue the extirpation of
idolatry and colonists' illegal Indian labour force, *reducción* went dormant as a reformist issue. For the next three decades, it virtually disappeared from administrative discourse, although reports of its demise
continued unabated. Yet scattered reports of continued settlement consolidation also occurred in 1634, 1651, and 1666.[27] Further research
would undoubtedly unearth more. As with the extirpation of idolatry,
local officials sporadically enforced *reducción* even when it was not a
policy priority.

More Struggles over Burial

As Indians fled the *reducciones* and various Spaniards sought to invade
them, Christian mortuary practice became another register for the
inter-ethnic negotiation of coexistence and separation. The previous
chapter explored how *reducción* sought to establish a communion of the
saints in Andean parishes. Irrespective of its success or failure, the very
fact that those attempts took place in Indian parishes, where Spaniards
could not live legally, made them ambiguous as expressions of Christian universalism. Instead of emphasizing the circulation of grace
within a single church spanning the realms of heaven, earth, and purgatory, it suggested various churches defined not only by residential
separation but above all by 'purity of blood,' in which some estates
shared grace with their ancestors and others idolatrous disgrace. This
section looks at how synodal instructions issued during the years from
1613 to 1638 handled such inter-ethnic questions, and how they played
out in various legal disputes.

Lobo Guerrero issued the first of these instructions in 1613. His stip-
ulations on burial begin with the treatment Spaniards and their religious specialists should receive, and disallow marked burials near the
cathedral of Lima's altar. He prohibited the burial of blacks, mulattos
and Indians anywhere in the cathedral, but allowed it in cemeteries
(1613: 135). The instructions reiterate previous policy that priests not
charge Indians in any way for burial, and give their bodies a proper
procession to the church (1613: 137). Unlike his predecessors, Lobo
Guerrero justified church burial theologically as an act of compassion

for those who die in the Lord, one that confers grace and many great benefits on them, according to the 'doctrine of the saints' (1613: 138). However, he immediately followed this observation with a list of those unfit for church burial, including the unfaithful, pagans, Jews, heretics, blasphemers, those who have not taken communion during the previous year, public sinners, and, finally, idolaters and ministers of the Devil (1613: 138–9). He also specified that if people moved a church from one place to another (another indication that settlement consolidation continued), they should re-inter its dead in the new building after another funerary procession (1613: 139).

As Lobo Guerrero's instructions show, Spaniards often understood the hierarchical distribution of grace in racializing terms: Indians and blacks categorically did not merit cathedral burials and so were marginal in the communion of the saints. An Indian confraternity in Lima tried but failed to subvert Lobo Guerrero's prohibition on cathedral burial,[28] which suggests that large multi-racial cities maintained this form of hierarchy. In Indian parishes, *curacas* and priests usually got the best niches, confraternity members the next best, whereas other Indian bodies were buried in peripheral areas. Occasionally, however, Spaniards who ran mines or *obrajes* (textile sweatshops) might reside in Indian parishes and complicate this standard mortuary hierarchy. For example, in 1614, García de Belaustegui and Frutos Martínez, Spaniards resident for twenty years in the Indian parish of Concepción de Mito, Jauja, made a pious bequest to secure burial niches for themselves and their descendants in its church. They each claimed half the niches along the wall running from the door of the main chapel to the altar of the Virgin, where they sat during mass. The goal seems to have been to ensure the physical proximity of each family's living and dead members during the mass, which again suggests, particularly given their intrusiveness in the parish, that they understood the communion of the saints in familial and racial, not universalistic, terms. Francisco de Ávila, then in the area as extirpator of idolatry, received authorization to adjudicate the matter. The local vicar supported the request, noting that since Mito was 'a town where there is no principal *curaca* or second person, and those that there are in it are tribute collectors [who] have their burials further up, there is no harm in giving them their burial niches and seats, because no niches in the area have been opened for Indians, although they have been buried in the places that said García de Belaustegui and Frutos Martínez request.' He listed their donations to the church over the last twenty years, and concluded that they justified their request.[29] Of particular interest here is the explicit articulation of what normally went without saying: that the best burial niches in their parish churches went to *curacas*, and that Indian commoners had no firm claim to their places of interment in the church floor, since they did not secure them through pious bequests. Nothing prevented the exhumation and relocation of their bodies in cases like this. Nonetheless, these Spaniards did not displace the local *curacas* from the best places 'further up,' that is, closer to the main altar. Since their presence in Indian parishes was technically illegal, this may have been the most ambitious claim they could press.

In the town of Huaraz, however, a full-blown inter-ethnic conflict arose over access to church burial niches. The saga began in 1635, when Santiago Dávila, son of a *curaca* and member of the Confraternity of the Holy Sacrament, asked that the parish priest assign him and his family a sepulchre in the church's main chapel. He listed his confraternity's many bequests to the church, noted that the archbishop had ruled that members should be interred in the main chapel, but that only Spaniards had that privilege to date, solely because they were Spaniards. In part because of his nobility, Dávila's request was granted.[30] The Confraternity of the Blessed Souls of Purgatory, founded in 1654 by the town's two indigenous governors, aired similar complaints. An article of the confraternity's constitution stipulated that it was to be for Indians only 'without Spaniards interfering in it or bothering us or trying to take it over, since we the natives founded it in our town, where we are moved out of charity and for the good of our ancestors' souls.'[31] In 1661, Huaraz' Spaniards obtained authorization to found their own Confraternity of the Blessed Souls of Purgatory, arguing that their Indian counterpart denied them membership and thus deprived Spanish souls of suffrages. By 1663, the two confraternities fought openly when the Spaniards sued for control over some buildings that one of their group left to the Indian confraternity. The Indians sued to retain those buildings, prevent the Spanish confraternity from using their chapel or competing with them to solicit alms, and to have it disbanded. They argued that the Spaniards had founded their confraternity out of envy and spite to undermine the Indian confraternity: the Spaniards were the separatists, they insinuated, since they claimed to have 'distinct souls' from the Indians. Regulations prohibited multiple confraternities for the same devotion in the same town, and since the Indian confraternity was senior, its Spanish counterpart was fraudulent and should be disbanded. Furthermore, their solicitor argued, Huaraz was an Indian parish that Spaniards were forbidden to inhabit by law. The church belonged to the Indians and their ancestors were buried in it, yet instead of helping them as new converts to the faith, the Spaniards intimidated and harassed them. Ultimately, the Indian confraternity won a judgment confirming its control of the buildings in dispute and equality with its Spanish counterpart.[32]

Meanwhile in 1662, Huaraz' *forastero* Indians joined in, claiming that the constitution of their Confraternity of the Holy Sacrament, plus their unremunerated labour in church construction, entitled members to sepulchre interment in the main chapel. The parish priest (and extirpator of idolatry) Joseph Lauriano Mena Godoy rallied Spanish residents (*vecinos*) and *originario* Indians to oppose the claim: they also had Confraternities of the Holy Sacrament and, like the *forasteros*, had worked in *minga* (for food and drink only) to build the church, but had to make pious bequests of twenty to thirty pesos for sepulchres. Since the church lacked other sources of income, and these were the most select interment places closest to the main altar, it simply could not afford to assign them to *forasteros* for one or two pesos, in their view. No *forasteros*, only those who made the appropriate donations such as *corregidores*, had occupied those sepulchres to date. Should lowly *forasteros* break that precedent and gain control of niches normally reserved for authorities, they argued, it would subvert the town's social hierarchy. As one witness put it, '[I]t would be to the distaste of Spaniards who do not want to be buried in that place to avoid mixing their bones with those of the Indians.' Finally, however, Archbishop Villagómez resolved that members of this *forastero* confraternity would pay four pesos for a sepulchre in the highest third of the church, three pesos for one in the middle third, and two in the bottom third.[33] Although a compromise, this ruling benefited *forasteros* disproportionately and clearly gave inclusion priority over hierarchy. It probably also reflected extensive burial simony charges levelled against Mena five years earlier.[34]

With this precedent in place, the Indian Confraternity of Our Lady of Copacabana got permission to inter its members in the main chapel of Huaraz' church without charge, stating that they had agreed with the parish priest that this would be the reward for their extraordinary contribution in labour to the church's construction. In 1664, the Spanish Confraternity of Our Lady of the Rosary argued that it had made the same agreement, and noted that several of their members had been interred according to it. Despite trying to ride the coat-tails of the Indian confraternities, Our Lady of the Rosary's *mayordomo* still sought distinction from them when he asked for an order to assign sepulchres to its members 'and a seat for my wife since it is not right that she sit with the Indian women.' Again, we see a familial and racial under-standing of the communion of saints at work. The documentation ends with a veiled endorsement of their request, but no verdict.[35] Competi-tion over burial niches continued to be fierce: in 1664, Mena unsuccess-fully tried to deprive the Spaniard Juan de Osorio of his family's sepulchre and seat in the church, as did León Garavito, his successor as parish priest, in 1673–4.[36]

This sustained conflict shows that Huaraz' Spaniards wanted to change the norms that usually applied to Indian parish churches. Instead of accepting curacas' implicit right to pre-eminence in their par-ishes, as they did in the Mito case above, here they frontally contested it. Much of this conflict arose over confraternities' mortuary entitle-ment stemming from the church's enlargement under a previous priest. This project and Huaraz' large Spanish population bespeaks the town's prosperity. Spaniards' dogged struggle to gain sepulchres and seats in the church was, among other things, an attempt to convert that pros-perity into honour and grace. Suffrages for the dead also conferred distinction on their living kin, who could sit with their illustrious ancestors during mass and apart from the unwashed Indian women. Several witnesses described the enlarged church's grandeur and called it 'a heroic work,' implicitly comparing it to a cathedral.[37] Huaraz' Spaniards arguably tried to impose the racial hierarchy that Lobo Guer-rero mandated for cathedrals onto what was legally still an Indian par-ish church. This scenario would explain precisely the details of Indian resistance in this case: that the parish was theirs, and Spaniards were interlopers pretending to racial superiority. Yet in 1664, the Indians of the nearby town of Carhuaz responded in exactly the same terms to local Spaniards' attempt to found a Confraternity of the Blessed Souls of Purgatory separate from its existing Indian counterpart.[38] Spaniards did not need the pretext of a quasi-cathedral to assert racial distinction from Indians in the mortuary realm. More significant, Indians' fighting response to Spaniards in these cases shows how committed they had become to Catholic interment. Clearly they wished to defend their stake in Christian burial, and their participation in it ran much deeper than the forced formal compliance that extirpators perceived.

Such Indian religious commitments strengthened the colonial Church's anti-extirpation faction, who, building on Lobo Guerrero's earlier instructions, strove to regulate (rather than question) the Christian burial of Indians. In 1629, Francisco de Verdugo the bishop of Huamanga, issued instructions for his bishopric. His discussion of testaments began with an order that priests not pressure their parishioners to request suffrages or leave pious bequests. The problem was particularly serious for Indians who 'as ignorant people, even though they have legitimate heirs, order in their testaments that all their assets be allocated to masses and pious works.' Thus, he prohibited priests from accepting more than one-fifth of the estate of those who died with legitimate descendants, and one-third of the estate of those who died with legitimate ascending kin. Priests were to respect the deceased's will regarding funeral arrangements and the number and nature of masses. Verdugo prohibited them from removing burials from choice locations in a church, charging exorbitant amounts for remaining places, or publicizing the amounts paid for each interment niche in the church. Nobody was to be buried under the main altar. Verdugo also vetoed free church burial, as it would impoverish the parish, but did not let priests demand advance payment for burials. He cautioned them, however, to be wary of any pagan dances or ceremonies when burying Indians or blacks, and told them to bury poor Spaniards gratis, as with Indians.[39]

These instructions suggest that Indians actually requested suffrages and made pious bequests in their wills. Although the *testamentos* and *capellanías* sections of the Archivo Arzobispal de Lima show only moderate levels of such activity, Verdugo must have had reason to worry about impoverished heirs. This issue reflects his systematic preoccupation with simony, which went well beyond Indians' welfare. Of particular note is the prohibition on removing burials from choice niches, one that stopped Huamanga's churches from becoming charnel houses like their Spanish counterparts. Verdugo had initially sympathized with the Extirpation, but turned against it after Lobo Guerrero's death in 1622. Thus, his caution regarding pagan ceremonies during Indian burials shows that such instructions were an alternative to the Extirpation precisely because they continued to take its concerns seriously.

A comparable source is Pérez Bocanegra's *Ritual y Formulario*, a confessionary and manual of correct ritual practice published in 1631. Its author was a parish priest from Andahuaylillas, Cuzco, whose questioning procedure for native confessions displays the influence of the first two extirpation campaigns. The lengthy section (pp. 567–80) on proper burial notes that burial inside the church signified reconciliation with the holy faith: burial outside the church or a consecrated cemetery implied non-reconciliation due to paganism, heresy, apostasy, excommunication, failure to take communion within the last year, or several other causes. Only as a temporary measure, however, were the faithful to be buried outside holy ground, and then with a cross over their head to signify that they died in Christ. Once buried 'forever' within the church, no body was to be removed except with the ecclesiastical judge ordinary's permission. Even within the church, there were important gradations in how various categories of people were to be buried. Parishioners were to be buried with their feet towards the altar but priests were with their heads towards the altar, closer to it and in better surroundings, apart from the laity.

Arias Ugarte's synodal instructions of 1636 said less about burial, but prescribed in greater detail how funerary processions from the deceased's home to the church should unfold (1636: 273–4). More important, it cautioned parish priests to prevent the illicit removal of bodies from the church to ancestral burial caves. Aware of the connection between mortuary ceremonies and succession to political office, Arias Ugarte warns that this practice is particularly likely for *curacas* (1636: 274). By recycling this bit of extirpatory wisdom after ceasing the Extirpation itself, this archbishop not only fended off any potential charges of negligence but showed his instructions to be a valid alternative to the Extirpation, one that could incorporate its insights without creating political turmoil or bringing the Church into disrepute.

A final source is the synod that Pedro de Villagómez convened in 1638 as bishop of Arequipa. Its doctrinal emphasis is noteworthy, but a long discussion of the communion of saints connects only to the question of indulgences, not church burial.[40] Of Indians, Villagómez noted 'Since the churches, cross, bells, and litter in Indian towns were made at the natives' cost and sweat, it is just that when they die, they be buried in their churches, and not in the cemeteries, and that they not be charged anything for the digging or choice of a grave site, nor for the lower cross, nor the tolling of bells, nor for the litter.'[41] For *indios forasteros*, cemetery burial was free, but those who wanted church burial had to donate to the church. Villagómez rigorously developed the idea that Indians had a right to burial in consecrated ground: he denounced Spanish landowners for burying Indians and blacks on their estates in chapels licensed for mass but not burial. When bringing the Indian dead from their houses, priests were to wear the surplice to ensure that schoolchildren and the choir accompanied them, and to conduct the body to church 'with the accustomed Christian order' for burial. Indians could have additional suffrages at fixed prices (deducted from the estate), but only on their expressed wishes. For those too poor to finance suffrages, Villagómez asked his clergy to provide a basic mass out of charity. He also reiterated the anti-simony proviso from the Second and Third Councils of Lima that priests could persuade but never force Indians into accepting additional burial-related suffrages. Priests should prevent Indians from placing food, drink, and clothing in the graves, or burying their dead outside the church in the sites of their forefathers. They should deny burial to anyone who left such an order in his or her will, and deliver the body to the secular arm of government. Nonetheless, they were not to disinter pagan Indians' bodies or disturb their graves, following a precept of Clemente III. Although this last instruction might have prevented decisive action against Andean ancestor cults, Villagómez was alone among these prelates in still allowing for the extirpation of idolatry in his instructions, an orientation that would surface in 1649 when he became the third 'extirpating archbishop' of Lima.[42] At this stage, however, Villagómez was careful to join Arias Ugarte's emphasis on standardizing ritual minutiae, and not to act ostentatiously on his extirpatory convictions.

Villagómez's strong defence of Indians' right to church burial without making monetary donations contrasts significantly with Verdugo's willingness to let priests charge for it. Like Lobo Guerrero before him, Villagómez combined a policy of free church burial with a theological emphasis on the communion of the saints and an evangelical promotion of the Extirpation. Despite their repressive reputation, extirpators arguably showed greater regard for Indians' spiritual salvation than their opponents by insisting on their right to burial *ad sanctos* and in engaging with them theologically. For example, during an idolatry trial of 1656, the extirpator Noboa exhorted his parishioners not to disinter the dead 'so that they may enjoy the suffrages of the church and that among them there could be many who might have been saved' (Duviols 1986: 16). By treating idolatry as a codified doctrine that required refutation, they showed it a certain (perhaps misguided) intellectual respect. Extirpators' surveillance and repression of Andean ritual practice expressed this greater engagement: they did not oppose orthopraxy to orthodoxy but heightened and interwove both. In their opponents' laxity, however, also lay an analysis and a strategy, not just dereliction of spiritual duty. The anti-extirpation prelates displayed the Counter-Reformation's distrust of theological discussion outside reliable ecclesiastical circles, and more specifically the colonial Church's realistic doubts about parish priests' ability to indoctrinate Indians successfully. On a more positive note, by emphasizing ritual detail and practical compliance, they maximized Indians' formal subsumption under Catholicism, hoping that fuller integration would follow. They contested the extirpators' view of idolatry as a tightly integrated system whose every practice signified false beliefs: instead, they allowed for survivals and superstitions without doctrinal meaning. By relaxing articulatory linkages, orthopraxy strategies allowed practices to become multivocal, fluid, and, most preciously of all, inchoate. Behind their prescriptive rigidity lay fertile and relatively depoliticized spaces for transition and negotiation.

These differences aside, all authorities worried that simony would curtail Indian participation in the Catholic mortuary complex, and thus discourage correct practice. Such concerns were long-standing. The first three Councils of Lima encouraged Andean people to bury their dead in churches by making basic interment free and limiting how much of their estates could go to pious works and contracted masses (Marzal 1983: 386–7). Arguably, the structural funding of parishes, not mere rapacity, generated priestly demands on Indian estates. In Spain, priests received much larger incomes from mortuary ritual than they did in Andean parishes, since more people participated and all had to pay in full. The shortfall led Spanish priests to cajole Andean parishioners into making such donations, or to outright simony, hence the repeated censure of these practices (Marzal 1983: 297). Such 'abuses' figured in the larger colonial corruption discourses discussed above. Eventually the Crown permanently reduced parish priests' salaries, so it permitted them to charge Indians for any postmortem masses according to a strict, centrally established schedule of fees (Marzal 1983: 424–5). The Church generically called these fees *derechos* (rights), a term that accurately captures the sense of ecclesiastical entitlement that surrounded mortuary ritual. They caused considerable friction within the Church, as parish priests had to remit one-quarter of them (the *cuarta funeral*) to their bishop, who regularly punished them for not doing so (Marzal 1983: 354), a point on which Álvarez' diatribe is particularly revealing (1588: 61–2).

While Spaniards also sued priests for excessive or illicit funerary charges,[43] the problem reached institutionalized proportions with Indians. At least forty Indian complaints against priests for mortuary simony exist in the Archivo Arzobispal de Lima,[44] but a systematic search would reveal many more. For brevity's sake, I mention only some typical charges: a case from 1641 alleged that a priest left his parish for four to six months at a time, allowing Indians to die without confession and their kin to bury them. When he returned, he purportedly charged twenty to thirty pesos for their burials, as if he had done them, flogging the next of kin and seizing their goods to realize his claims. When Indians died in the parish while he was present, he allegedly charged the same fees for burial, without saying a single mass for their benefit.[45] In 1643, Cochas' Indians complained that their priest refused to bury the dead and would let their bodies rot unless he received twenty to thirty pesos.[46] This was the most common price mentioned during the seventeenth century, but some documents cite prices as high as sixty, eighty and one hundred pesos.[47] In 1654, Indian parishioners complained against their priest for failing to perform the masses that Indians had contracted in wills, thus defrauding their souls in purgatory.[48] During 1665 in Hacas, a priest allegedly let an Indian die without confession (despite two requests) and left his body unburied for three days to punish the town's Indians for being litigatious (*capitulantes*).[49] In 1675, a priest allegedly often let his *fiscales* bury Indians, but charged fifteen to thirty pesos when he did so in person, saying that the money was not for his services but for the burial niche in the church floor.[50] A case from 1678 alleged that a priest was slow to confess dying Indians, and often left their burial to his sacristan or choir members. He was quick to charge for the Indian burials he did do, however, illicitly demanding twenty to thirty pesos, or confiscating their mules instead, without even performing a mass for the deceased.[51] Finally, Pararin's Indians claimed in 1692 that their priest forced them to pay for funerary masses, whether or not the deceased's will requested them.[52] The ecclesiastical courts sustained some, but not all, of these charges: my interest is less in whether they were true than in the orientations they expressed.

Did simony actually prevent Andean people from participating fully in Catholic mortuary ritual, as authorities feared? Some of these complaints were that corrupt priests forced participation in the Catholic mortuary complex, and others that they impeded it or defrauded Indian souls in purgatory. These widely diverging concerns are often present in the same case. Hardened idolaters and sincere Christians each resented simony, but for different reasons that are hard to disentangle since the strategic goal of complaints was to have priests reprimanded, not to express litigants' deepest convictions. The one thing they prove is that by the seventeenth century, Indians intimately knew

Catholic mortuary ritual and the obligations it entailed for their priests. Nonetheless, we must assume that these complaints were more than pretexts, and that their internal inconsistency reflected important differences of orientation within Indian communities themselves. Attacking priestly corruption may have been something that could unite Indians of different ideological persuasions. Thus, the solidarity-without-consensus dynamic that characterized orthopraxy as an evangelical strategy further replicated itself in Indian resistance. By cooperating in practical actions against a shared priestly antagonist, Andean Christians and idolaters could subordinate their own differences and reinforce their refusal to draw hard boundaries between these 'religions.'

In conclusion, priests escaped neither conflict with their Indian parishioners nor surveillance from their superiors during the slackening of reformist impulses during the 1620s and 1630s. An awareness of idolatries, particularly in the mortuary domain, persisted at the highest levels, but an activist extirpation was no longer the strategic response. Rather, Arias Ugarte adopted a more stoic approach that emphasized orthopraxy and minimized damage to the Church's reputation by avoiding debate. Distrusting the doctrinal acuity of both Indians and parish priests, he focused instead on maximizing participation in ritual and standardizing liturgical details. At once less confrontational and more elitist than its extirpating competitor, this formula was to prove powerful and arguably even better attuned to the Counter-Reformation context. Its effects on the ground are harder to gauge, in part because unlike its extirpating antagonist, it did not generate much documentation. Whether born of negligence, indifference, or benign neglect, this documentary hiatus ended only with attempts to revive the extirpation of idolatry in the 1640s, to which we now turn.

6 *Ayllus* in Transition

When Villagómez succeeded Arias Ugarte as archbishop of Lima in 1641, he came to the position as a known proponent of the Extirpation, an affiliation that must have figured in his selection. Although he appointed Felipe de Medina as general inspector of idolatry in 1641, he could not launch straight into a new anti-idolatry campaign with opponents entrenched in the Church and colonial government. First, he needed to create a pretext. Trading on the received wisdom from earlier codifications of idolatry, he began with two show trials of *curacas* for mummy worship, one that occurred during 1641–45 and the other in 1647. Both spectacularly failed to deliver convictions. Realizing how far the conjuncture had shifted, and wanting to upstage Ávila (1648), Villagómez responded by publishing Avendaño's sermons (1649) and his own pastoral letter of 1649, large portions of which reproduced Arriaga's manual verbatim. Only with these interventions in place did Villagómez finally initiate the third anti-idolatry campaign, which was to last until his death in 1671. This chapter discusses how the exhaustion of reformist discourse during the 1630s put this campaign on a less favourable footing than its predecessors. It also explores how idolatry itself was shifting away from its earlier codifications owing to a variety of colonial pressures.

Let us begin with the two failed prosecutions of the 1640s, both of which turned on the abuse of extirpatory knowledge as prejudicial stereotype, and so jeopardized its authority. The first case occurred during 1641–45, and concerned don Rodrigo Flores Caxamalqui, the hispanicized thirty-one-year-old indigenous governor of Ocros (see figure 6.1). In 1641, a rival *curaca*, don Cristóbal Yacopoma, denounced Flores Caxamalqui for concubinage, incest, and several idolatries, including the worship of Caxamalqui, his *ayllu*'s mummified founding ancestor, which he allegedly inherited from his father. The charge was particularly ironic since don Rodrigo faithfully executed his father's will when he died in 1633, leaving significant pious bequests, a chaplaincy, and requesting elaborate suffrages.[1] Nonetheless, various witnesses corroborated these allegations before the presiding judge, Felipe de Medina, who ordered the imprisonment of Flores Caxamalqui and his mother. Medina excavated Flores Caxamalqui's house and surrounding patio but failed to find the mummy. In 1642, the local *corregidor* found Flores Caxamalqui innocent, deprived Yacopoma of his office, and sentenced him to serve in a hospital for malicious prosecution. Medina persisted with the case in the ecclesiastical jurisdiction, however, and in 1644 ordered the confiscation of the *curaca*'s possessions, which included a copy of Lobo Guerrero's sinodal constitutions of 1613 and other Catholic tracts. Flores Caxamalqui's lawyer severely criticized Medina's conduct as judge, and eventually had him removed from the case, which resumed in Lima. When Yacopoma's original witnesses were re-interviewed in 1645, they said he bribed them to lie about Flores Caxamalqui's alleged idolatries to remove him from office. They also claimed that Medina pressured them to testify against Flores Caxamalqui and tortured him while in prison, asking him where he kept his money. One of Flores Caxamalqui's witnesses was Luis de Teruel, a veteran extirpator of idolatry, who vouched for his Christianity and noted that during the first campaign, Flores Caxamalqui's father had voluntarily exhibited their ancestral mummies to Avendaño, who burned them. In 1645, the presiding judge absolved Flores Caxamalqui of all charges, charged the trial's costs to Yacopoma, and upheld a diminished version of the earlier sentence against him. Medina received no punishment, however (García Cabrera 1994: 171–347). Despite the apparently local origins of this case in the rivalry between two *curacas*, it was clearly a trial balloon for what was to become the third extirpation campaign. During the proceedings against Flores Caxamalqui, Villagómez instructed Medina not to embark on further idolatry inspections (García Cabrera 1994: 211), presumably because he wanted a conviction to silence sceptical sectors of the clergy. Thus, Flores Caxamalqui's acquittal was a major disappointment since it strengthened the hand of those who held that idolatry allegations were a calumny not only against the integrity of the individuals involved but also of the Church in Peru. That Medina escaped prosecution for the allegations against him is particularly suspicious, and suggests that he had a certain immunity as the archbishop's protégé.

Another dramatic and complex case, also involving disinterred dead, dates to 1647. The accused was Tomás de Acosta, governor and *segunda persona* of Checras, and the accusers were his brothers, who wanted him removed from office. They charged Acosta with semi-annual worship of three crates of their grandparents' bones collectively named Apu Vequiche, and with incorporating their father's skull into this collection when he transported his body from the church of Tongos to that of Maray (see figure 6.1).[2] Far more clearly than in the Mangas 1604–05 case, control over the office of *curaca* was at stake in this factional struggle between agnatic kin. Acosta's brothers wanted to disinherit him with the charges of idolatry. Their testimony quickly proved false, however: an inspection of their father's burial niche revealed that his body still had its skull, while Apu Vequiche and another *huaca* were not in their alleged hiding places. To gain acquittal, however, Acosta had to break out of jail in Maray, where the local ecclesiastical inspector also imprisoned his wife and impounded their property. He fled to Lima and retained the services of the *procurador general de los naturales*, Alonso de Castro, who demolished the case against him and harshly criticized its procedural improprieties. Three months after his brothers initiated the case, Acosta was vindicated.[3]

In both cases, newly codified Spanish expert knowledge of idolatry created stereotypes that led to malicious prosecutions. The systematic and internally coherent nature of this knowledge did not necessarily make it credible or authoritative, particularly when it obviously served indigenous factional struggles or priestly extortion (Griffiths 1996: 182). On the contrary, this coherence could itself appear fabricated and deceitful when confronted with unruly pieces of evidence such as the presence of the skull of Acosta's father or the documented prior destruction of Flores Caxamalqui's ancestral mummy. Far from automatically promoting the efficient detection and conviction of idolaters, then, extirpatory knowledge could be self-defeating. Again, the power/ knowledge notion raises as many questions as it answers, including whether discursive articulations can secure their own realization. As Griffiths convincingly argues, the extirpation of idolatry failed to institutionalize itself over the long run (1996: 37–8), despite producing an initially reliable applied knowledge.

These cases revealed an important legacy from Ugarte's tenure as archbishop of Lima: a contingent of highly placed Spaniards who regarded the extirpation of idolatry as a failed evangelical strategy with its own corrupt tendencies. Their successful insistence on due process foreshadowed the stiff resistance that Villagómez would meet when he attempted to initiate the third extirpation campaign in 1649. The first case pitted Felipe de Medina, the first extirpator Villagómez appointed, against Luis de Teruel, a prominent Jesuit whose defence of Flores Caxamalqui presaged his order's initial refusal to participate in the third extirpation campaign. Apparently the battle lines were already drawn by 1644. The charge that extirpators practiced extortion against the Indians they inspected, so blatant in the allegations against Medina, resurfaced when Villagómez finally launched the third campaign. His attempts to make Indians finance the idolatry inspections with their depleted corporate resources met with determined and ultimately successful resistance from Francisco Valenzuela, the prosecuting protector for natives (*fiscal protector de naturales*).[4] Even as Villagómez was absorbing what was clearly to him a shocking defeat on this issue, new problems were brewing in 1654. Another opponent of the Extirpation emerged from within the imperial bureaucracy: Juan de Padilla, criminal judge (*alcalde del crimen*) of the High Court of Lima. Padilla decried Indians' persisting idolatries and their complete ignorance of the faith, but attributed them to parish priests' negligence and the Extirpation's failure as an evangelical strategy.[5] Coupled with Padilla's intervention were new denunciations from Valenzuela, which also identified priestly negligence as an important reason for idolatry's persistence (García Cabrera 1994: 58).

These letters caused a stir in the Council of the Indies just as *reducción* resurfaced as a political issue. Concerned with falling revenues, Philip IV ordered its renewed enforcement in 1650, but Viceroy Salvatierra staved off this impossible assignment until his appointment ended in 1655. His successor, the Conde de Alba, was equally reluctant to implement it (Cole 1985: 88–91, Wightman 1990: 29–30). In this context, Francisco de Ugarte (who had been a priest in Peru) sent a printed proposal from Spain to the viceroy of Peru in the late 1650s or early 1660s, proposing measures to end the *reducciones'* ongoing malfunction.[6] Ugarte started with *reducción*'s recognized importance, noting that many had previously tried and failed to address it. Since Spanish rule's legitimacy in the Indies depended on the true faith's propagation, the king, as vicar of God on earth, had to implement *reducción*, and yet never entirely succeeded, as Indians fled to remote areas where priests could not evangelize them. *Reducción* must also prevail, he continued, since those Indians who remain in the towns unfairly pay tribute for escapees. Ugarte denounced this tribute as unjust in the first place, a prohibited form of personal servitude, particularly work in the mines. His Majesty must address this situation, he continued, since the monarch's main obligation is to protect his subjects from violence and extortion, a responsibility that does not disappear because some claim the task is impossible. With *reducción* accomplished, however, all would be well since the Indians would be evangelized, the Crown and the *encomen-deros* enriched, and tyranny vanquished.[7] Ugarte then recycled the 1633 debate's procedural modifications. His treatise, along with a supporting letter from one Pedro de Loma, went before the king, who in 1662 referred them to Archbishop Villagómez for comment, which he provided at length in 1663.[8]

Villagómez commented that Loma and Ugarte were certainly well intentioned, and correct about *reducción*'s desirability, but naive about it prospects. He lengthily reviewed the policy's history, before turning to the specific proposals in Ugarte's treatise. Like the Conde de Chinchón before him, Villagómez concluded that short of lifting Indians' burden of tribute and personal service, and making their labour voluntary, as in Mexico, there was no way to stop their decline or reduce them to towns. Yet he saw Spanish dependence on Indian servitude as so ingrained in colonial Peru that its eradication was impossible. So he reluctantly recommended the status quo over Ugarte's reforms, arguing that change would only make things worse. Villagómez nonetheless agreed that *reducción* was vital to the Indians' religious instruction and to the extirpation of idolatry, which he staunchly supported. In principle, he backed further settlement consolidation to support parish priests. In practice, however, it was almost impossible since traditionally Indians did not move from their accustomed climates, but priests travelled to them instead. Although prelates disliked this arrangement, it persisted mainly because of Indians' attachments to their places of origin, one of the few reasons any of them ever return from the *mita*.[9] In summary, Villagómez viewed *reducción* as desirable but impossible, and implicitly portrayed dispersed Indian settlements and extirpators of idolatry to monitor them as necessary conditions of the tributary economy.

Villagómez' stoicism contrasts markedly with the unconditional reformism of Lobo Guerrero and Campo, the previous extirpating archbishops. Despite sharing similar anti-idolatry policies, their regimes' larger orientations differed. Whereas his predecessors still expected to moralize the Indians and clergy under their command, Villagómez accepted that the colonial enterprise was fallen, and required an equilibrium among its corrupted forces. His cautious and extensively prepared resumption of the extirpation of idolatry eight years after becoming archbishop acknowledged that he operated on different terrain from his predecessors. He knew that the reformist cause had foundered after the 1633 debates, but discovered to his surprise that its very character had changed, when Valenzuela and Padilla accused his own extirpators of corruption. Thus, the extirpation of idolatry, once a central plank in the reformist platform, became just another example of Spanish corruption and Indian oppression. Shorn of its connection to an aggressive campaign of reform and *reducción*, the extirpation of idolatry's meaning changed. It became a coping strategy, a way to manage a declining tributary economy without entirely compromising the colony's founding ideals. In one of Villagómez' few political successes in the Council of the Indies, his intervention appears to have quashed Ugarte's proposals.

The results of Villagómez' extirpation campaign also revealed important changes in Andean idolatries themselves. Some, such as those of Cajatambo, discussed below, conformed approximately to Arriaga's treatise. Yet they also clearly registered the colonial transformations we have reviewed: providential readings of the Andean past, *reducción* and the struggle over burial, and the growth of Andean Christianity. Most of the third campaign's trials depicted idolatries that deviated even more dramatically from Arriaga's formulae, as colonialism's multiple pressures, ranging from the tributary economy to the extirpation of idolatry, increasingly twisted *ayllus* out of their 'classic' form.

Cajatambo, 1656

Between 1556 and 1663 in the Cajatambo region (see figure 6.1), Bernardo de Noboa produced the Extirpation's single richest local corpus of idolatry documents (Duviols 1986). The first dates to March 1656. It arose when Juan Tocas, *fiscal mayor* of Ticllos, denounced Alonso Ricari, *camachico* of Otuco, for removing bodies from the church to mortuary caves, where they periodically received sacrifices (Duviols 1986: ch. 1). Noboa soon found that Ricari's activities extended into neighbouring areas, including the towns of Pariac and Pimachi, so three more inquests occurred from April to August in 1656 (Duviols 1986: chs. 2–4). The first was in Cajamarquilla, an annex of Ticllos, Noboa's parish, away from Otuco where the offences allegedly happened. Noboa's initial reliance on his own personnel and home base suggests a fear of native reprisal against his extirpating activities. He quickly became

F gure 6.1 Cajatambo, Chinchaycocha, and Chancay

bolder about occupying the districts he investigated, but the backlash he anticipated eventually materialized as Indians counter-charged him with torturing subjects to death during his investigation (García Cabrera 1996). Although he was acquitted, the charges slowed his investigations and ultimately led to his successful request for transfer to a coastal parish.

All the first document's witnesses concurred that the Indians of Otuco systematically removed their dead from the church. Noboa confirmed their accounts when he examined the church and found only a few bodies in their appointed graves, and signs that even they had recently returned from mortuary caves. Witnesses consistently de-scribed how Alonso Ricari exhorted the *camachicos* (lesser political au-thorities) of Otuco's various *ayllus* to remove bodies from the church. Testimony presented these people as an *ayllu*-based priesthood in charge of particular mortuary caves, deities' flocks and fields, and col-lecting offerings from *ayllu* members.[10] Sometimes the living disin-terred their dead kin because their spirits appeared in dreams, demanding that they be with their relatives in the burial caves, or com-plaining that they could not move, were rotting from being covered with soil, and stank (Duviols 1986: 62, 72). These disinterments took a regular pattern that only slightly modified traditional mortuary rituals.

During the few days that the dead remained buried in the church, their kin secretly made offerings of blood, corn beer, and maize on their graves. When they could, they removed the body to the deceased's house, where they gave it new clothes and arranged it in a flexed position. A five-day vigil followed during which kin and affines gave the sacrificial blood of llamas and guinea pigs, and burnt offerings of fat, corn, and coca to the deceased. Specialists also did entrail divinations to see if the deceased would take any living relatives into the afterlife. The mourners ate the sacrificed animals' meat, drank, and danced *cachua* to the beating of drums. At midnight, the principal female mourner (e.g., a dead man's widow) covered her head with the shroud from the body and left the house with other elderly women to go through town with the sacrificed llama's meat, hide, and a vessel of its blood, which they sprinkled with straw whisks on the streets, wailing and crying out to the deceased as they went, asking where he or she had gone. Mourners spread ashes around the house and inspected them the following morning for bird tracks, which they attributed to the returning soul. They interpreted any flies found in the house as souls of the deceased and told them that they no longer lived there and should go. Around noon after the vigil's final night, two principal mourners (spouses, parents, or children of the deceased) carried the body in a net on their backs to their *ayllu*'s mortuary cave. On arrival, each mourner gave the body more blood and burnt offerings. They intended these offerings to ease the deceased's passage to the afterlife across a bridge of hair (called Aychay Chaca or Guaroy Chaca) that separated it from the land of the living. Then mourners returned to town, where dancing and festivities continued through the fifth day after death, when they washed and stored the deceased's clothes.[11]

On 'anniversaries' (*cabos de año*) of the death, the deceased's kin took the body from the mortuary cave to a flat plaza nearby, gave it a change of clothes, sacrifices, burnt offerings, and festivities comparable to those on its removal from church, before returning it to the cave for another year. In Spanish Catholicism, the *cabo de año* referred to an anniversary mass for the soul of the deceased.[12] Doyle (1988: 226–8) believes that Andean custom featured similar anniversary commemorations of individual deaths. Yet she ignores one crucial piece of testimony (Duviols 1986: 25) that shows the term actually referred to collective forms of ancestor worship that inaugurated the sowing (*pocoymita*) and harvest (*caruamita*) seasons. Noboa eventually discovered that these semi-annual celebrations were called *vecochina* (Duviols 1986: 93), which I take to be the Quechua word glossed as *cabo de año*. A confession of sins to *ayllu* priests preceded these festivities, followed by bathing in a river and other purifications to remove sin. The celebrations proper involved five days of abstention from sex and prohibited categories of food, and so continued the emphasis on purification. They began when relatives took the bodies from the cave to a nearby ceremonial plaza (*cayan*), where they gave the body a new set of clothes from among those washed during the initial death rituals. Various sacrifices and offerings followed amid great feasting, drinking, and pouring of libations meant to ease the hunger and thirst of the recently dead during their passage to the afterlife. Living relatives then danced through the night, carrying the dead on their backs in the ceremonial plaza and at the mouth of the burial caves.[13] People called these rites *pacaricuc* or *pacaricuspa*, meaning 'vigil,' but also *pacarina* (Duviols 1986: 77–9, 81), which denoted the ancestral origin point to which the deceased journeyed during the year following death. Apparently they marked the soul's arrival to the abode of the afterlife (*upaymarca*). Witnesses located the *upaymarca* at varying distances from the locality along the same chain of *pacarinas* that the founding ancestors travelled. They also described mortuary caves as *pacarinas*. These data suggest that at death, a component of the person undertook the return journey to the point from which the ancestors had originated (Doyle 1988: 241, Gose 1993).

The *cabos de año* were not simply about the recently dead. People also celebrated the arrival of Otuco's founding ancestors, including the petrified forms of Raupoma, Choqueruntu, and Carua Xalia, from distant *pacarinas* such as Raco Cayan. *Camachicos* gave these ancestors sacrifices and new clothing and petitioned them for rainfall and to prevent untimely frosts or blight on the crops. All *ayllu* members offered them money.[14] Doyle argues that villages worshipped these highest-ranking and most inclusive ancestors first, then *ayllus* dispersed to worship their own particular founders (1988: 169). If so, *cabo de año* observances for the recently deceased probably followed, and integrated them into the low end of this ancestral hierarchy (cf. Doyle 1988: 232–3). The passage of the recently dead into this ancestral category, no matter how minor their rank within it, would explain the many formal similarities between individual death ritual and corporate ancestor worship that Doyle (1988: 240–3, 257) usefully notes. Thus, people celebrated the 'anniversaries' of individual deaths by merging their personal arrival in the afterlife with collective worship of the founding ancestors tied to the agricultural cycle. Presumably once mourners thought the deceased had arrived at the *upaymarca*, they continued to make the same offerings, no longer to complete the individual life cycle but as a manifestation of the ancestral category that the founders epitomized.

As Doyle (1988: 145) notes, the link between the ancestral and the agricultural was fundamental to the *vecochina*. To understand it properly, however, we must acknowledge that the *vecochina*'s seasonal time measured the transition to ancestorhood, not the precise 'anniversary' of an individual death, as Doyle proposes. Since people thought that ancestors controlled the weather, alternation between rainy and dry seasons was their primary temporal manifestation. Once ensconced in the *upaymarca*, itself usually conceived as a large body of water (Gose 1993), they joined an ancestral collectivity that also received seasonal worship. *Ayllu* rituals' seasonal regularity imposed a productive rhythm on the ancestors and harnessed their powers for agriculture. During these celebrations, *huari* and *llacuaz* segments of each *ayllu* reciprocally worshipped each other's deities, a feature that further confirms the *vecochina*'s collective and agrarian character. Since these groups personified agricultural and pastoral activities, respectively, this worship institutionalized the division of labour between them (Doyle 1988: 170–2), portraying the *ayllu* as an organic solidarity. Duviols (1973) represents that division of labour as complementary, but it was also hierarchical, since *llacuaz* pastoralists' thunder-and-lightning deity controlled rainfall, a crucial resource for *huari* agriculturalists. Thus, *llacuaces*' superior status as conquerors also extended into their position within the agrarian division of labour. Their origins in distant bodies of water such as Titicaca not only underwrote this association but confirmed their intrusive character, rigorously linking conquest to water control (Gose 1993).

Noboa's inquiries recovered a detailed ancestral tradition featuring conquest. According to the testimony of Andres Chaupis Yauri, star witness for the prosecution and himself a native *fiscal* (prosecutor), the region's original inhabitants were bearded giants called *huaris* who worshipped the sun as their father. They emerged from eight large caves on a mountain named Yarupaja, above the nearby town of Mangas, then dispersed to populate different parts of the region. Those who were to settle in Otuco passed through Yumay Purac, also above Mangas, then through Cusi, Llaclla, Canis, and Guamri, where two of those original ancestors' bodies were kept (Duviols 1986: 55). A second wave of ancestors called *llacuaces* later conquered the area, all of whom came from Titicaca via Raco Cayan and Picho Cayan (Duviols 1986: 59–61).

Their father was Apu Libia Cancharco, whom we encountered in chapters 4 and 5. Otuco's traditions held that he fell from the sky like a lightning bolt, and sent his many sons off on diverse journeys of conquest. Among the sons who took Otuco were Libiac Choquerunto and Libia Cargua Runtuy, who founded the Ayllu Chaupis Otuco; Libiac Nauim Tupia and Libiac Guacac Tupia, who founded the Ayllu Allauca; and Libiac Raupoma and Libiac Uchupoma, who founded the Ayllu Xulca. Their father, Libiac Cancharco, gave each a bit of soil, telling them to conquer similar lands so that they could have estates and their accustomed foods and drinks. When they arrived at Mangas, the *huaris* there did not wish to receive them, so they went on to Guancos, whose people treated them well for a year, before they moved on to Otuco. There they sent a boy and a llama down to ask for food of the Ayllus Guari Guachicho and Taruca Chicho. The *huaris'* response was to slaughter the boy and skin the llama alive. Seeing this, the *llacuaces* approached the Ayllu Chicho, and found them doing *guari libia*, a martial dance with drums and flutes. So they sent another Indian transformed into a chiuchi bird, singing its song, which the Ayllu Guari Guachicho distained. So the *llacuaces* raised a storm with hail the size of large eggs and appeared with slings of gold and silver, conquering and dispossessing those *ayllus*, killing all but a pair of brothers who surrendered. These conquerors founded three new *llacuaz ayllus* in Otuco, each of which had an elaborate subterranean sepulchre above the old town of Marca Putacum, where the *cabos de año* probably occurred (see Duviols 1986: 52–3).

Like the Huarochirí document, this account attributes conquest to the founding ancestors' supernatural exploits. The *llacuaces's* use of slings and hail emphasizes their categorical connection to the lightning god Libiac. That one of them transformed into the chiucho bird underlines their celestial orientation, as perhaps does the incorporation of *runtu* (egg) in the title of Chaupis Otuco's two founders (Duviols 1986: 52). Again, parallels with the Huarochirí document are striking. Yet the Otuco account is unusual in the Cajatambo corpus for describing how *llacuaces* subjugated *huaris*. Mostly the matter is left implicit, perhaps to downplay the element of conflict in *huari-llacuaz* relations or to convert it into the post-conquest complementarity that apparently prevailed among these groups. If so, this account is remarkable for its explicit, even exaggerated, violence. No *huari ayllus*, particularly not those (Guari Guachancho and Taruca Chancho) mentioned in this account, survived this *llacuaz* conquest. However, a close reading of the document shows that *huaris* remained in the Otuco area, despite this account. People retained *huari* mummies and worshipped them jointly with *llacuaz* ancestors: in local agricultural rituals, *llacuaces* invoked rain and *huaris* initiated maize consumption (Duviols 1986: 55, 60–1, 94, 120). Thus, *huaris* still existed in numbers, and reciprocal ancestor worship with *llacuaces* transformed their relations from conflict to interdependence. Probably the town's three *llacuaz ayllus* (Chaupis Otuco, Allauca, and Xulca) subsumed *huaris* and their ancestors as subdivisions (Duviols 1986: 52–3).

Like the Huarochirí narrative, the Otuco trial seemingly isolates this conquest-based local organization from the colonial present. The relations described took form in the indigenous past, with little obvious updating to include the Spanish. On closer inspection, however, these traditions were not quite as anachronistic and deprived of colonial relevance as they might seem. One witness described *llacuaz* conquerors as 'gentiles' whom the *huaris* 'reduced' to towns (Duviols 1986: 120), thus applying current colonial language to an earlier colonial situation. Chaupis Yauri mentions that the *huaris* were bearded giants and two other accounts specify that the god Huari appeared as 'a Spaniard, old and bearded, and distributed the fields and canals in all the towns and *ayllu* segments' (Duviols 1986: 11, 113). Although this is very much the traditional function of a *huari* ancestor, his appearance as a Spaniard is obviously a colonial innovation, and hardly a random one. The equation of Spaniards with remote aboriginal ancestors is, as we saw in chapter 2, precisely what Viracocha's early colonial pidginization promoted. The echoes of Guaman Poma's claim that Andean people were descended from Spaniards are also very clear. For the first time, then, we see clear evidence that theological discussions of a pre-Columbian evangelization ultimately worked their way down through the Andean intelligentsia and into peasant 'idolatries' themselves. The closing of this reflexive circle has many important implications. First, it shows that with only the slightest modification, one that might frequently escape detection, traditional ancestral narratives could indeed address the colonial situation. By equating the Spaniards with remote Andean ancestors that intrusive lightning-worshipping groups conquered, the latter could deny that Spaniards had conquered them, an opinion in which powerful *curacas* might still indulge. Such mapping of the moiety distinction of *huari-llacuaz* onto the ethnic distinction of Spanish-Indian also encouraged Andean people to identify with the celestial realm, which belonged not only to the thunder-and-lightning deity Libiac but also to the Christian God and saints. It therefore encouraged the widespread syncretism of Santiago and Libiac and the representation of *llacuaz* mummies as saints that we encountered in Cauri. Cajatambo's moiety logic could also place Spaniards in the 'upper' position: during a house rethatching, a mock battle occurred between one group dressed up as lowlanders (*yungas*) and another as Spaniards (Duviols 1986: 350). This scenario implicitly equated Spaniards with intrusive *llacuaz* conquerors, and figuratively subjected this later colonization to the cultural resolution of an earlier colonization. Thus, the Cajatambo idolatry material is not an untouched 'survival' of pre-Columbian traditions. Even though it may also faithfully reflect the indigenous past, it was very much a product of the mid-colonial moment to which it dates. This conclusion gains force when we return to the struggle over burial that motivated Noboa's inquiries.

Having confirmed the initial testimony that 'Christian bodies' were missing from church, Noboa resolved to recover them and even beseeched one of the accused to return the bodies so that they could enjoy suffrages of the Church, since many might already be saved (Duviols 1986: 16). Unlike Avendaño during the first campaign, his goal was not to burn them as pagans but to return them to the Christian fold. Each burial cave they visited belonged to an *ayllu*. Witnesses identified specific bodies as Christian by their clothes. Some still smelled or were worm riddled, indicating their recent interment. By contrast, green slime covered older pagan bodies.[15] Subsequent testimony confirmed that *ayllus* kept Christians and pagans in separate caves, but Noboa mentions a pagan cave that also contained many Christians. Several caves reputedly 'belonged' to living people, the *camachicos* of various *ayllus* or their subdivisions, who confessed to having taken bodies from the church to their respective caves at the behest of their *curaca*, don Alonso Ricari. He allegedly told them that he would kill anyone who failed to identify Christian bodies as pagans.[16] Presumably his goal was to prevent these bodies' return to the church. Noboa's investigations ultimately recovered 362 Christian bodies, which he stored in a house while awaiting instructions from the archbishop on how to dispose of them.

Following this first case, Noboa launched trials in the neighbouring towns of Pariac and Pimachi, both of which lasted from April to August of 1656 (see Duviols 1986: chs. 3–4). These trials also concerned the removal of bodies from churches, and reproduced essentially the same outline of local mortuary rituals as given above.[17] Nonetheless, some new details emerged. In Pariac and Pimachi, people disinterred the dead to avoid ancestral punishments that would jeopardize the health of the living and their fields (see Duviols 1986: 87, 90, 112). Throughout the region, *ayllus* placed the bodies of their baptized members in separate mortuary sites from those of their unbaptized members, although they maintained ongoing ritual responsibility for both.[18] Only rarely did Noboa find unbaptized and baptized dead together (e.g., Duviols 1986: 19–20, 213, 218, 271, 275–6, 288–9). Testimony often describes these 'new' mortuary caves for the baptized as belonging to the living heads of *ayllu* segments (Duviols 1986: 19–20). Andean 'idolaters' clearly recognized an important difference between baptized and unbaptized dead: no matter how 'traditional' their practices may appear, the impact of Christianity is unmistakable.

Beyond these generalities, each trial produced its own unique anecdotes. A witness from the original trial noted that previously, when the native leader Alonso Ricari heard that the extirpator Felipe de Medina was about to appear in Otuco, he ordered that *ayllus* take all the bodies in mortuary caves to the church, and that once Medina's *visita* was over, he ordered that they return them to the caves (Duviols 1986: 14). During a subsequent trial in Otuco, witnesses claimed that Ricari fraudulently passed off younger, less important mummies for those of descent group founders (*malquis*), to prevent the extirpators from destroying these important objects of devotion (Duviols 1986: 70–1, 80). This document also describes how a woman removed the body of her husband to a mortuary cave, had second thoughts, and brought it back to the church, where to her horror she found the body of another woman, also freshly brought from the mortuary caves, interred in his tomb (Duviols 1986: 50). Elsewhere, Noboa noted that Christian bodies recently returned to the church were easily identified by the seated posture and shroud they acquired in the mortuary caves.[19] People said that when Cajatambo had only one priest who said mass once a year in Lampas, they routinely took the dead from churches and worshipped them along with the pagan dead (Duviols 1986: 148). Noboa quickly took this circulation of bodies for granted, and these latter trials give increasingly routinized and attenuated descriptions of it, focusing instead on the finer details of mortuary ritual and the mythological exploits of particular mummies. Later trials from 1656–58 (Duviols 1986: chs. 5–7) barely mention the disinterment of bodies,[20] but they continue to probe systematically into funerary details and the broader panorama of local 'idolatries.' Possibly Noboa had already scared Andean people from disinterring their dead, but more likely the records of these trials reflect a learning and documentation process, in which he moved on to new topics after exhausting earlier ones. By 1658, Noboa reported having discovered and returned to their churches more than seven hundred bodies of Christian Indians, and to have burned the bodies of ten to twelve thousand pagans.[21]

Of particular interest to this analysis is the relatively systematic separation of Christian from pagan dead. Unfortunately the testimony does not directly explain this segregation, but it does suggest several possibilities. One is that separation was a strategy to prevent the discovery of *malquis*, mummies of *ayllu* founders central to collective ancestor worship. Otuco's *camachicos* knew that detection of their systematic removal of bodies from the church was probable. By returning bodies to the church before inspections, they could attenuate that risk, hence the circulation of bodies between church and burial caves. Since this circulation might itself be detected, and lead extirpators to 'pagan' bodies or even *malquis*, the wisest policy was to create a firewall by putting Christians and pagans in separate caves. Ricari's instruction that people should represent as pagans any Christian bodies discovered in burial caves fits with this strategy. By treating the recently deceased as if they were remoter and more important ancestors, he hoped to deflect attention from *malquis* and other senior ancestors housed elsewhere.

Significantly, however, Ricari himself violated this pattern by interring his son in a 'pagan' cave (Duviols 1986: 19). Apparently, *curacas* and lesser grandees were reluctant to break their descent line from the founding ancestors by storing their mummified kin in 'Christian' caves. By implication, Christian caves were for commoners, and their distinction from 'pagan' caves promoted the *ayllu*'s segmentation along class lines, a process already present in the traditional mortuary complex. Thus in Pimachi, the mortuary cave Sissim contained fifty-six *malquis* and was the pagan 'head' of an *ayllu* complex that included other Christian caves (Duviols 1986: 115–16, 130). 'Mixed' caves existed at the pinnacle of an otherwise segregated system to maintain descent lines from the *malquis* to living elites. *Curacas*' interment remained a moment of vulnerability for the older and more venerated ancestral community they entered. By interring commoners in separate Christian caves, however, *ayllus* dramatically lowered the odds of detection.

Another possibility is that some Andean people may have genuinely wished their kin to participate in both the Catholic and the 'traditional' Andean mortuary system. We have already seen that just such an agenda existed in the neighbouring province of Checras in 1614. If it also existed here, the circulation of bodies between church and mortuary caves would have been more than just a tactic to prevent discovery, but part of a deliberately bicultural strategy. Unlike the Checras case, this strategy did not attempt to bring *malquis* into the church but treated church and mortuary caves as poles between which the dead circulated. Differentiation was its basic premise, and Christianity, which defined the basic opposition of church to mortuary cave, further divided pagan from Christian caves. Pagan caves' occupants did not participate in this circulation because they did not participate in Christianity while alive. Segregation therefore expressed a new hybrid allegiance, one that involved the worship of 'God together with the idols and the mummies of their ancient dead' (Duviols 1986: 44). This circulation superficially resembles traditional alliance strategies of alternating worship between indigenous and intrusive ancestors. Yet its segregated premise contrasts notably with the openly complementary interaction between *huari-llacuaz* cults, and so reflects the Church's rejection of such coexistence strategies. In short, mortuary circulation represents hybridity not complementarity, since its structure conserved separatism.

We must also consider indigenous articulations of separatism. They characterized sixteenth-century epidemic cults and remained an important part of priestly ideology in Cajatambo. For some native ritual specialists and their followers, Christian affiliation was divisive: it caused a distancing from the founding ancestors, albeit a relative one, since Christians remained *ayllu* members. By storing their bodies in separate caves from those that housed the *malquis*, Otuco's *camachicos* expressed that distancing. Indigenous priests considered attending churches and eating Spanish food to be ritually polluting (Duviols 1986: 54, 61). Since Christian bodies had repeatedly done both, they may not have been permanently welcome around the founding ancestors. Doyle argues that the unity of mummified founding ancestor, origin point, burial cave, and mummified descendants was fundamental to this Andean mortuary tradition, such that the interment of ordinary persons should reproduce 'the archetypal act' of the *malqui* in returning to its *pacarina* on death (1988: ch. 3). If so, the interment of Christians in separate caves from the *malquis* implied rupture, and that they were destined for a different afterlife than their 'pagan' ancestors. This interpretation is not fully sustainable, however, since it cannot account for why people disinterred Christian bodies from the church to give them traditional rituals: some links clearly remained.

Once we break with Doyle's commitment to Eliade's theory of arche-
types and sacred time, however, the mortuary separation of Christian
and pagan can become relative. The Christian-pagan distinction makes
sense as a principle of *ayllu* segmentation, whereby people differentiated but also derived newer subdivisions from older unities. These
terms would be particularly relevant after *reducción* moved *ayllus* from
their old towns to new church-based settlements, where they still
existed as corporate groups, but no longer with the same claims to public legitimacy. Finding new burial caves was necessary when zealous
priests and extirpators monitored old towns for any sign of idolatry.
Most of Otuco's caves were in inaccessible mountainous locations, but
only one was more than half a league away, and it was a pagan cave
that contained some Christians in the old town of Guamri (Duviols
1986: 16–20). In Pimachi, all the caves were half a league or less from
town (Duviols 1986: 116). Such proximity strongly suggests that Christian mortuary caves arose around the new regime of church-based
towns. Their high mountain locations kept them sufficiently peripheral
to avoid detection, but they were also close enough to be convenient.
Apparently, then, Christian caves were a post-*reducción* revision of local
ancestral regimes and sacred geographies. Pagan caves still mattered,
and remained *pacarinas*, the termini of ancestral journeys as then conceived, but no longer corresponded to the settlements people lived in.
Christian burial caves were a dynamic response to that historical
change. Doyle (1988: 117) wonders whether they had *malquis*. Nothing
indicates that they did, but had Christian caves continued to house an
ancestral community over time, new founders might well have
emerged and with them, narratives of journeys ending in those caves.
Like all forms of social memory, ancestral traditions were retrospective:
they adapted to new conditions then ratified the result as established
practice. Although this process inevitably has a mythic component, it is
hardly as mystifying as Eliade's notion of 'sacred time,' a moment of
creation totally insulated from history. Just as the *huari-llacuaz* distinction registered the historical experience of the late intermediate period
before Inca expansion, so that between Christian and pagan registered
the impact of Spanish colonialism. Eventually, as we will see, Andean
culture would fully internalize that distinction, which here is only
emergent.

This differentiation of Christian from pagan burial caves probably
interacted with the idea that Christianity was beginning to animate the
landscape, which we encountered with Omate's eruption in the previ-

ous chapter. Thus, Noboa reported that 'when they thatch houses they pay reverence to the *malqui* idols named Pomachagua Tunsuvillac [and] Yngavillac because they have a tradition that these *malquis* were the first progenitors of the Ayllu Julca Tamborga [and] that they had their origin and were born from the large mountain, from the one right by the town of Mangas, which they call Apuhurco ["lord mountain"] San Cristobal' (Duviols 1986: 341–2). Here Mount San Cristóbal seems to participate in two landscape regimes simultaneously. On the one hand, it was the *pacarina* from which three ancestral brothers emerged, and the site of a cult to their mummies and statues, as were several other mountain *pacarinas* in the same locality (see Duviols 1986: 340–3). On the other, its name and location on Mangas' immediate periphery suggests that it was becoming Christianized, probably by the placement of a large cross (visible from town) on its peak, and perhaps by housing Christian burial caves. Instead of exploding, however, San Cristóbal seems to have reconciled these contending regimes by adopting the title 'lord mountain' (*apu hurco*). In this historical period, *apu* (lord) normally applied only to senior ancestors and *curacas* within a region. Later, mountains adopted this title as they absorbed ancestral functions that mummies and idols embodied, as they still do here. By taking on their lordly title, then, San Cristóbal was not so much replacing the mummified brothers as drawing them into Christianity. Reciprocally, San Cristóbal's sainthood became fully ancestral in the process.

Each of these scenarios evokes a different ideological position or set of circumstances that promoted the mortuary segregation of Christians and pagans in Otuco. By exploring a range of motives, I hope to have given this innovation a realistically multivalent explanation. Although the various motives diverged significantly, they were not mutually exclusive. Practical solidarity between native separatists and those seeking to participate in both Andean and Catholic mortuary regimes was possible not because they agreed but because both had to deal with extirpators. Their ideological differences remained, but their shared commitment to *ayllu*-based practices necessarily subordinated disagreement. For those who faced the Extirpation, no hard distinctions between strategy and tactics, volition and necessity, were possible. It is a moot question whether Andean priests were 'really' separatists or merely became so as a condition of carrying out their work. The same holds for those who participated in both systems. The horizon of the conceivable hovered closely over the horizon of the possible, and often, one suspects, the gap between them disappeared.

Behind the appearance of a traditional mortuary system holding out against Catholic orthopraxy lay a much more interesting, indeterminate, and interactive reality. The notary regularly used Catholic terms to translate indigenous practices: the *vecochina* became a *cabo de año*, *ayllu* ritual assistants became sacristans, and so on. Noboa even described pagan interment sites as 'chapels' (Duviols 1986: 249). Such ethnocentrism was reciprocal: separatist ministers of idolatry such as Hernando Hacas Poma described the Christian God and saints as *camaquenes*- that is, as ancestral animators like their own (Duviols 1986: 145, 180, 196, 207). Despite their authors' professed convictions to the contrary, such translations elided substantive differences between Catholicism and Andean ancestor worship. Beyond these superficial verbal coordinations lay more profound practical alignments. Since both 'religions' organized their festivities in an annual cycle, superimpositions were inevitable. All Saints' and Corpus Christi corresponded closely to the two yearly rounds of collective ancestor worship that defined the Andean seasons of *pocoymita* and *caruamita*.[22] This connection largely explains why they became the most important and generally observed colonial feasts. In an agrarian society, such overlapping celebrations regulated basic productive processes: their practical coordination profoundly legitimated the idea that no essential difference between the two religious formations existed. Ministers of idolatry still insisted that Cajatambo's parishioners ask the ancestors' permission to celebrate their towns' patron saints or even to go to church,[23] but apparently they never withheld it. Deities from both pantheons cooperated: to rid the town of sicknesses and crop blights, Otuco's elders insisted on prayers to the Christian God, along with the idols and mummies, saying that only thus would the rites be effective (Duviols 1986: 44). Moreover, indigenous deities could influence Spanish behaviour. Andean people made offerings to the sea, for good treatment from Spaniards, and to their own ancestors to win litigation in Spanish courts (Duviols 1986: 89, 228).

Even the corporate holdings of cults in the two traditions could merge. For example, the *curaca* Cristóbal Pomalibiac ordered his *ayllu* to sow their ancestor's field for the Catholic confraternity of souls, much to the 'dogmatizer' Hernando Hacas Poma's displeasure (Duviols 1986: 245–6). Elsewhere, a *camachico* made offerings to the ancestors that were ostensibly for this same confraternity (Duviols 1986: 370). None of this is surprising because Andean confraternities often corresponded to *ayllus* (Celestino and Meyers 1981: 125–31). Confraternities did not necessarily provide cover for ancestral cults, however. Rather, an Andean institution harboured a Catholic devotion in the first case: Andean and Catholic mortuary organizations used the same corporate holdings and had become functionally interchangeable for all but the most committed ideologues on both sides. The ownership of some fields was uncertain: did they belong to the 'idols,' the *curaca*, or the community (Duviols 1986: 25, 344)? Such confusion derived not only from describing Andean institutions with inappropriate Spanish categories (Gose 1993: 486–7), but also from real beneficiary fluidity. If this field's ownership transferred from mummies to confraternities seamlessly, not all the *ayllu*'s corporate manifestations fared as well: *camachicos* frequently solicited sacrificial animals from their *ayllus*, which suggests that they no longer held flocks. Furthermore, they often distributed maize to its women to make corn beer for festivities. Apparently they no longer had secluded 'chosen women' to do that task.[24]

'Idolatry' evolved in relation to Christianity. As *ayllus* moved to church-based towns, their mortuary regimes neither disappeared nor persisted unmodified, but changed to meet those new circumstances. Certainly increased surveillance and repression figured prominently. Witnesses describe Avendaño's previous acts of extirpation throughout the trials, and one even mentions that fellow extirpators Alonso Osorio and Francisco de Estrada Beltrán joined him during the first campaign (Duviols 1986: 89). We have already seen that Felipe de Medina inspected this area before Noboa during the third campaign. Extirpators had already burned many of the region's petrified ancestors and most important mummies. People still worshipped them, however, poignantly addressing them as 'flower of fire' and 'burned lord' in their prayers (Duviols 1986: 7). Sometimes they saved their ashes or replaced them with new stone monuments. The extirpators' notion of 'idolatry' is hard pressed to explain the reconstruction of these objects of ancestral worship. What persisted was increasingly not any 'original' set of ancestral relics or sacred geography but a sensibility that allowed their appropriate reconstruction under new (and less favourable) circumstances.

That sensibility derived, of course, from the *ayllu*'s ongoing existence as a relevant social form. Many researchers, I included (Gose 1993, 1996b, 2000), have used the Cajatambo corpus to reconstruct the pre-Columbian past because of the unparalleled window it provides on *ayllus* as functioning ritual units. For such reconstructions to be reliable, however, we must first understand these sources as products not only of their own colonial moment but also of an already complex colonial history. Indirect rule conserved but also transformed and eroded the *ayllu*. As long as Andean people accepted the *ayllu* as an institution that was still partly their own, the impulse towards corporate ancestor worship remained, but the specific forms it took shifted significantly. Extirpatory repression and the need for clandestinity explain only some of these transformations. Far more basic was the broader disconnection of Andean ancestral traditions from the colonial state and its political processes. We glimpse attempts to revive an older politics of inter-ethnic alliance through the equation of Spaniards with *huaris*, but the colonial state's refusal to engage in such dialogue tended to freeze and anachronize Andean ancestral traditions, robbing them of their once overt political functions. As their ability to articulate alliance atrophied, these traditions not only became more historical but also more indigenous, more local, and more agrarian (cf. Burga 1988: 194–5). Burga astutely notes that Noboa's Cajatambo campaign targeted *camachicos*, the lesser political authorities more closely involved in peasant life, and largely ignored the higher-ranking *curacas de huaranga* (lords of a thousand households) accused in earlier trials (1988: 91–2, 321–68). Apparently even indigenous governors were opting out of the idolatries that had long articulated their power. Behind the appearance of an intact *ayllu* system, a cultural and political breach was opening between indigenous lords and their underlings, one that was to become general and consequential. That such transformations are traceable, however, is the premise not only of 'ethnohistoric' reconstruction but of colonial history itself, and so makes these tasks logically and practically inseparable.

Santiago de Maray, 1677–1724

If Cajatambo's *ayllus* retained enough mummies to suggest 'traditional' ancestor worship, such appearances were harder to maintain in neighbouring areas where *ayllus* had experienced greater corporate erosion and lost more ancestral forms to the Extirpation. One response was a concerted ancestral revivalism closer in inspiration to Cajatambo's separatist preachers than to those who merged ancestor worship with Christianity. This revivalism's defining feature was the reinvention of extirpated ancestral forms, typically the substitution of stone monoliths for burned mummies. Let us explore it through two documents from Santiago de Maray in Checras, where at the beginning of the chapter we encountered Tomás de Acosta's alleged mortuary idolatries.

The first document dates to 1677: a Spaniard found sacrifices to a stone monolith near town, so the local priest, Juan de Esquivel y Aguila, detained and interrogated indigenous priests until they eventually confessed before a notary. He then extirpated all the shrines and idols mentioned in their confessions, and conferred with neighbouring parish priests, who reported similar activities. Esquivel sent the documentation he assembled to the archbishop of Lima with the following summary: 'from these reports and from what I have seen and experienced among these Indians, who seem so hispanicized and eager to attend religious instruction and the divine cult, I am persuaded that the entire archbishopric is corrupt and idolatrous, and that it greatly needs remedy, which will be that which your lordship would be pleased to order.'[25] The archbishop did not grant this thinly veiled request to resume the generalized extirpation of idolatry, suspended only six years earlier with Villagómez' death. However, he did authorize Esquivel to assemble a case against the idolaters he discovered, and forward it to Lima for judgment. A detailed picture of *ayllu*-based ancestor worship emerges from the meticulously assembled and corroborated testimony he eventually sent.

Four times a year in a place called Llaullacayan, all Maray's Indians gathered to offer sacrifices to the sun as their creator and ask for good agricultural conditions. They also made offerings to a crystal monolith named Guacra Yaru twice a year there, once at the rains' onset and again at the harvest. People said Guacra Yaru was a solar priest who turned into stone. He interceded with the sun and lightning and was the conduit of offerings to them. Guacra Yaru was also the town's protector: before he turned into stone, he summoned a valiant man named Rupaygirca, who brought his brother Punchaogirca and sister Chuchupuquio with him to guard the town. The two brothers then turned into stone monoliths and the sister into a spring, all near Llaullacayan. During a previous idolatry inspection, Bartolomé Jurado found, burned, and destroyed Rupaygirca's monolith, but the Indians successfully hid the rest. Chuchupuqio, the sister and spring, featured three oven-like stone tombs that contained the bodies of twins and breech births, and several mummified founding ancestors. The three stone tombs presumably corresponded to Maray's three *ayllus*. More *malquis* had once existed, but despite the Indians' attempts to conceal them in their houses, Jurado had found and burned many during his previous inspection. Only those they hid in a gully and subsequently retrieved still survived. All these deities were subordinate to Guacra Yaru and received the same semi-annual sacrifices.[26]

Although the entire town participated in these seasonal rituals in Llaullacayan, the site belonged to the senior of the town's three *ayllus*, Allauca. Before the rituals, only the members of Allauca confessed to Guacra Yaru's priests. The Ayllu Ychoca confessed to the priests of their founder, Utcupullam, another stone monolith. Afterwards, they went to part of its shrine named Uchautcuna, a cave or tunnel that perforated a cliff, through which the penitents passed, leaving their sins behind. Since only two of Ayllu Quimallanta's members testified during the trial, the document does not describe their activities and idols well. One admitted to worshipping Culcuyguanca, but since all of Maray worshipped this stone monolith, it could not have belonged exclusively to Quimallanta.[27] Perhaps this *ayllu*'s corporate cult evaded detection, but more probably they were dissolving as an autonomous ritual entity.

Caruayacolca, the most senior local ancestor reported during the trial, also figured in the traditions of nearby San Pedro de Hacas, where he belonged to a set of brothers from Chinchaycocha (Duviols 1986: 158, 210). Thus, Maray lay towards the westward terminus of *llacuaz* expansion into rich, maize-growing lands. Witnesses described Caruayacolca as both a mountain and a tall crag near its peak, which overlooked Maray. The crag's eastward face had nine moons, ten Indians and two rivers painted in red. At its feet lay a stone niche for sacrificial offerings and a chapel-like structure made of stone slabs, in which a carved stone figure lay. Many stone monoliths (*huancas*) surrounded and guarded this shrine. Some resembled condors, pumas, or frogs.[28] Remains of many offerings suggested that Caruayacolca's cult was active, yet Esquivel did not pursue it.

Another complex of deities that all *ayllus* worshipped semi-annually consisted of a spring named Curi Calla at the foot of Mount Guanpucani, and a one-footed ancestor named Llaullactullu. According to tradition, Llaullactullu opened a canal from the spring and led it to Maray. People worshipped these three entities – spring, mountain, and ancestor – as the source of water twice a year, once in October (when irrigation began), and again during canal cleaning in April. They made offerings to Mount Guacra Hirca, did a vigil (*pacacricuc*), and played a game called *pisca*.[29] As these last two observances figured in semi-annual *ayllu* mortuary rituals, we may suspect a link between death and irrigation ritual here, following a well-established Andean pattern (see Gose 1993).

The one-footed ancestor Llaullactullu gave his name to Llaullacayan, the paramount shrine where people kept the petrified bodies of

Maray's other founding ancestors. Similarly, Mount Guacra Hirca, which received offerings at the beginning of irrigation, probably took its name from Guacra Yaro, the town's founding ancestor, who turned into a crystal monolith. After opening the canal, Llaullactullu became a mummified *malqui*, but Avendaño had discovered and burned his body in 1614. By 1677, however, witnesses consistently described Llaullactullu as their *pacarina*.[30] This term suggests an identification with the landscape, one that his intimate relation with spring and mountain accentuates. Apparently people conflated the ancestor with his point of emergence on the landscape, and might even have thought he disappeared into it. Such metonymy occurs elsewhere in the idolatry corpus, and Doyle treats it as a normal part of Andean ancestor worship (1988: 94–5). However, the sequence of events in Maray suggests that the Extirpation could have caused the conflation. We must explore that possibility before accepting Doyle's interpretation.

Significant evidence elsewhere in this document suggests that the landscape was taking on functions that ancestral mummies previously embodied. The latter still existed, at least in Llaullacayan's shrine, but previous rounds of extirpation and defensive relocation had destroyed many important bodies. Other important shrines such as Caruayacolca's had no ancestral mummies but were replete with stone monoliths, which probably substituted for bodies lost to Avendaño and Jurado. Gonzalo Paico, one of the three *ayllu* priests accused of idolatry, mentioned that he made offerings to the mountains Caruayacolca and Guampucani before consulting his *malquis*, who then appeared to him as a man and a woman in dreams. He also added that mountains and rivers gave good advice about where to find lost objects because they had 'direct correspondence with the sea and roads and that they told each other about what went on and that the mountains he invoked would tell his *malquis* so that they could advise him.' Here the landscape actively interceded with the *malquis* who no longer occupied the locality. The document confirms that impression elsewhere when a witness said the sun transported the souls of the dead to where their *malquis* are, presumably their distant original *pacarinas*. Everything suggests that extirpated ancestors had somehow returned to the earth through their *pacarinas*, perhaps retracing their original subterranean journeys. To the extent that the ancestors were no longer present, the landscape assumed agency: previously the passive infrastructure of ancestor-focused narratives, it now acted in their stead. Thus, while making offerings to the sun for a patient, Paico intoned, 'Gullies, springs, mountains and earth: you have entered and afflicted the body of this sick person. Leave and return this sick person to health.' Similarly, when asked if she was an idolater, María Quillay answered affirmatively, confessing to worshipping the sea, the earth, and all springs.[31]

How far did the landscape's absorption of the ancestors extend? Griffiths (1996: 207–8) believes that mountain spirits existed in Maray by 1677 and went by the title *apu* ('lord'), a term that appears nowhere in the document. This amounts to a claim that the document features an ethnographic pattern of mountain worship, in which the landscape wholly absorbed ancestral functions previously embodied in mummies and statues. Although just such a process eventually occurred, it is at best incipient in this document. Some mountains do figure as agents, but many retained their traditional role as *pacarinas*, or sites for shrines and idols. The most important of these mountains, Caruayacolca, took its name from the sculpted crag that represented the petrified body of that founding ancestor. The mountain continued to house an entirely traditional ancestral form, whose presence precluded any development of the mountain as an autonomous, quasi-ancestral agent. Moreover, the proliferation of stone monoliths in the document suggests that when previous extirpators destroyed ancestral mummies, people probably remade them in this form (see Doyle 1988: 66). This strategy contrasted with that of letting the landscape swallow previously distinct ancestral forms in that it kept the latter present in the locality and therefore available for *ayllu*-based worship. Both strategies were present, but not equally. Those that conserved or reconstructed the ancestors in forms distinguished from the landscape predominated, as did the corporate forms of worship they articulated.

To conclude with this document, by mid-1679 those charged with idolatry had yet to be judged or sentenced. They openly proclaimed victory against Esquivel and that the worship of their gods was licit and true. Meanwhile, various Indians of Maray, Puñon, Canin, and Mayobamba, including many who held minor offices, launched a series of charges against Esquivel. These included simony (especially regarding burials), excessive demands for material support and personal service (most notably that he kept thirty young women to spin cotton, tend his chickens, and as concubines), and cruelly whipping the *alcaldes* (mayors) who served him and arbitrarily dismissing them from office. Many witnesses against Esquivel denied the charge of concubinage, however, a fact that he successfully exploited in his defence. He produced Indian witnesses who identified many principals in the case against him as previously charged idolaters who vengefully filed these complaints. The plaintiffs' attorney vigorously contested the counterattacks and reasserted the original charges. Nevertheless, the exaggerations and logical inconsistencies in their case, and above all the fact that it followed the original idolatry charges, were decisive. The judge absolved Esquivel and sentenced his accusers to two hundred lashes and four years' service in the galleys of Callao.[32] Esquivel's denunciations failed to inspire a new round of extirpation, however, or even to produce convictions: they only obliged him to defend himself against this counterattack. This again proves that idolatry denunciations did not automatically rally the institutional support they required to become 'discourse.' By this time, the ecclesiastical hierarchy in Lima increasingly viewed both idolatry charges and the counterchanges of priestly abuse that so frequently accompanied them as nuisances to be discouraged by denying satisfaction to both parties.

A second idolatry document from Maray dates to 1724. The year before, when taking a dying woman's confession, the town's interim priest Joseph de Beramendi discovered a shrine hidden inside a house in the old town opposite Mayobamba. The house contained three stone monoliths named Caninbilca, Togorbilca, and Angobilca, offerings of feathers, food, and drink, and it reeked of the blood sacrifices these stones regularly received. Beramendi's investigations revealed that María Tinya was their priestess. When he apprehended her, she described how these 'idols' gave oracles and how young women served them as wives after being deflowered before them by a male lieutenant described as a *'cholo robusto'* (robust semi-acculturated Indian). Following her confession, María Tinya fled, and was found dead four days later in a nearby town. Beramendi widened his investigations: several other idols and report of human sacrifice surfaced in the annex of Puñun. Meanwhile, complaints against Beramendi for economic abuses, most notably the seizure of cattle to pay for burial expenses, were launched in the name of the *curaca* Antonio Pomalibia and Maray's commoners. However, Pomalibia immediately denied his involvement, and identified a clique of Indians inculpated in the earlier idolatry charges as their true authors: he claimed that they had falsified his signature when presenting their complaints, which he also rebutted at length.[33] On 20 October 1724, Pedro de Celis arrived from Lima to investigate both charges and quickly substantiated Pomalibia's version of events. He completely vindicated Beramendi and intensified the idolatry inquest.

Celis questioned two Indian witnesses who described Beramendi's discoveries of idolatry in the district, and added that the sacrifices in Puñun were to two anthropomorphic stone statues that gave oracles. They also identified Pedro de la Cruz Quiñones, an eighty-year-old man from Pachangara, an annex of Churin just to the north in Cajatambo, as the priest who had officiated over the human sacrifice. Since Celis had already apprehended Quiñones and his grandson, he immediately took their confessions. Quiñones described acting as priest for two stone idols named Apulibiac and Apulibiac Cancharco in Pachangara, giving them many offerings, including human blood. He mentioned that participants in these rituals observed a prior five-day period of dietary and sexual abstinences, and then described his activities as an oracular medium. When asked about the human sacrifice in Puñun, Quiñones named the victim and described how assistants sliced his chest and thigh, collected the blood in a vessel, and offered it to Libiac Cancharco's statue, which they kept in a house. He said they offered sacrifices for a good agricultural year, so the priest would forget to charge those who had taken animals from a local confraternity's herds, so women would get good husbands, and so the priest would not return from his recent trip to Lima. Finally, he mentioned other idols in the region, and estimated that they had sacrificed at least fourteen people to them. Francisco Bartolomé, Quiñones' sixteen-year-old grandson and apprentice, then testified, saying that he accompanied the old man, who constantly travelled to places with *huacas*. When he corroborated his grandfather's account of the two idols in Pachangara and described the two idols in Puñun similarly, Celis became suspicious and gave him fifteen lashes, after which he said that one idol found in Puñun was Apu Quichunqui and people worshipped it atop a high mountain. A subsequent search failed to find the statues of Apulibiac and Apulibiac Cancharco where Quiñones had said they were in Pachangara, but Celis did discover and destroy Apu Quichunqui.[34]

On 7 December 1724, Quiñones appeared before an ecclesiastical magistrate in Lima, where he recanted nearly all his previous testimony and claimed innocence, adding 'that he knew very well that stones don't talk.' He still admitted to some priestly activities but denied the charges of human sacrifice. His grandson's testimony was also far less frank, although it still inculpated the old man in several idolatries. On 9 December 1724, the ecclesiastical prosecutor in Lima laid the first formal charges against them, summarizing Celis' evidence, describing

Andean shrines as 'synagogues' and their rituals as 'vain Jewish super-stitions.'[35] On 1 September 1725, he found them guilty and sentenced them to exile, flogging, and service in Lima's Convent of San Francisco.

The idolatries discovered in this document deviate from the canonical *ayllu*-based practices that Arriaga codified a century earlier. Traditional moiety systems and tributary units continued to exist in the area,[36] but these idolatries lacked any overt connection to them. Unlike the earlier document of 1677, the monoliths reported in 1724 are not obvious replacements for mummies in ancestor cults that otherwise persisted despite the Extirpation. The house-shrine containing three monoliths suggests some continuities with an *ayllu*-based regime, as it was in an old town, but lacked corporate worship. Similarly, Quiñones mentioned observing some prohibitions typical of seasonal *ayllu* rituals, yet he was clearly not an *ayllu* priest but a regional specialist who exhorted people to maintain or revive older cults falling into disuse. Such a figure most probably emerged in a context where local priesthoods and cults had lost their hold on the groups they once defined.

Precisely because he failed to find evidence of Apulibiac and Apulibiac Cancharco, Celis continued his investigations in Churin during April 1725. In Quiñones' home village of Pachangara, he eventually discovered their 'idols': a dark and a white stone respectively, each carved in the shape of a human head. The whole town worshipped the deities, making their particular requests and offerings through Quiñones and other priests, who sometimes moved the idols from place to place (García Cabrera 1994: 503, 515). For agricultural purposes, the town worshipped Tinllacocha, also known as Apuctinçicocha, a huge earthenware brewing vat that, when filled with corn beer and stirred, made noise and produced rainbows. When people consumed the corn beer collectively, it purportedly made them strong for work and lent fertility to the fields (García Cabrera 1994: 503). Another important deity in Pachangara was Apucmucac. Quiñones apparently appointed its oracular priest, Juan Ramos, whom the settlement's *camachicos* and *alcaldes* supported materially (García Cabrera 1994: 504). Celis continued his investigations in the neighbouring village of Nava. There he found a pair of stone monoliths named Apu Llaruguaina and Mama Guanca, whose shrine was a cave high on a mountain named Llaruguaina. These stones gave oracles to one remaining priest: the others died in the epidemic of 1722. People asked them for good harvests and other kinds of wealth, to make matches between men and women, and to ensure smooth relations with priests and *corregidores*. In turn, they received offerings of corn beer, maize dough (*sanco*), blood of guinea pigs, llamas, and other animals, coca, and shells (García Cabrera 1994: 491–2). People still celebrated canal cleaning and the harvest collectively. They also observed five-day wakes following deaths and periods of abstinence before worshipping the deities (García Cabrera 1994: 493–4). In Mallay's old town of Barrios, people worshipped another pair of monoliths, one of which was Apucguarmi. An oracular priest offered them sacrifices and relayed individual requests to them (García Cabrera 1994: 497–9). The town of Oyon had a small house with a shrine containing Apucancha: a painted round stone, 'in the form of a bronze,' that weighed eight pounds. It gave oracles through a priest and received sacrifices, which people asked it to pass on to the dead who were 'dying of hunger' (García Cabrera 1994: 500). In Churin, Quiñones left Antonio Capcha with a clay figure of a man named Liviac, telling him to give it offerings (García Cabrera 1994: 500–1). Palpas was the one settlement whose main ancestral deity was still a mummy: Apu Casapaico, whom people described as a 'governor.' Its shrine was a cave or small house that Celis called a 'synagogue' in the old town of Cotomarca. The deity gave oracles to its priests, who asked permission to plant crops, and for aid in legal cases with priests and *corregidores*, for which they made the usual offerings, including some to 'our elders who are in limbo' (García Cabrera 1994: 501–2).

This situation resembles that of Maray in 1677, where corporate worship continued, but substituted stone monoliths for extirpated ancestral bodies. Nonetheless, certain exceptions to this pattern suggest a more diversified and subtle strategy than just a dogged retention and recreation of ancestral forms. Even as people conserved ancestral deities in peripheral locations, they also tried to infiltrate church centres. Pachangara's church contained two much-adored images of seraphim, which people regarded as the offspring of Apu Libiac Cancharco and his wife, Apu Mucac, both of which were burned along with them. A dark stone idol in human form along with other statues were found in the church of Nava, and destroyed (García Cabrera 1994: 515). These data recall extirpators' worries about 'idols behind altars' but also suggest a more thorough integration of Catholic and Andean traditions than they could imagine. For instance, the seraphic children of Libiac Cancharco and his wife again show that people continued to rehabilitate these Andean lightning gods in Christian terms through their close positional association with heaven. Similarly, ancestral statues' presence in the church suggests ongoing attempts to reconcile ancestor worship and the cult of the saints. Over a century after the first anti-idolatry campaign in the archbishopric of Lima, and despite ongoing repression, Andean people had not allowed their own attitudes to harden: they apparently still refused to recognize the extirpators' dichotomy between their forms of ancestor worship and Christianity. None of the witnesses professed separatist beliefs or denied being Christian. When asked how, as a Christian, she could worship Apu Libiac Cancharco, the witness Juliana Juana simply replied that in Pachangara, everyone did (García Cabrera 1994: 505–6).

In November 1725, Celis' investigations turned to the district of Andajes, near Maray. As we saw in chapter 5, Avendaño discovered Libiac Cancharco's mummy there in 1614. Nothing suggests that Celis knew this or went there on that deity's trail: after all, he had just found and destroyed its statue in Pachangara. Rather, he pursued Antonio Tapaojo, an indigenous priest who fled Churin during Celis' inquest (García Cabrera 1994: 520–1). When he apprehended and interrogated Tapaojo and several priestesses, Celis learned of various stone monoliths, crags, and anthropomorphic statues in the vicinity, including Auquillay Libiac, Mama Raiguai, Juchapamaman, Marca Aparac, and Apo Misay Guanca (García Cabrera 1994: 521–8). People kept the latter in a mortuary chamber in an old town where it still presided over some ancestral bones (García Cabrera 1994: 527). The priestesses' testimony is very attenuated and does not describe *ayllu*-based worship. It does mention, however, that the deities had estates and young women for their service, and that people observed periods of abstinence before interacting with them (García Cabrera 1994: 526), all of which conforms to that pattern of worship. Other practices were not entirely traditional. Quiñones also animated and oversaw these local cults, which explains why Apu Libiac Cancharco no longer resided in Andajes but in Quiñones' hometown of Pachangara. While this important ancestor had always travelled throughout its jurisdiction, its principal shrine and resting place was in Andajes (Polia 1999: 369). This move suggests that the regional system Quiñones articulated was innovative, even if it recycled an established cast of deities. Apparently Quiñones revived Libiac Cancharco's cult in Pachangara, then reconnected it to remaining local cults in its former catchment area. I suspect that *ayllu*-based worship's decline enabled this reorganization, and that Libiac Cancharco would have stayed in Andajes had he enjoyed an active cult there. Thus, even in its decline, ancestor worship was remarkably flexible and could traditionalize the most recent of innovations.

The *Ayllu* Eroded

When the third anti-idolatry campaign of 1649–71 swept the archbish-opric of Lima, it revealed that functioning (if highly transformed and Christianized) *ayllus* like those of Cajatambo were already remarkably scarce, and to be found only there and in Canta. The next chapter will show that the cases just discussed were atypically conservative. The loss of vitality that Maray's *ayllus* experienced as ritual entities be-tween 1677 and 1725 occurred earlier almost everywhere else. Most areas had apparently abandoned their ancestor cults after the first anti-idolatry campaign of 1609–22, or simply failed to revive them after the extirpators' ravages. Those that succeeded, either by hiding mummies or substituting stone monoliths for them, did so only to the extent that *ayllus* still commanded their members' ritual loyalties. More than the Extirpation itself, such loyalty was the crucial test that *ayllu*-based ancestor worship faced, and largely failed to meet. To understand this failure, however, we must recall the larger pressures to which *ayllus* were subject.

The *ayllu*'s reduction to a purely fiscal entity under Spanish colonial-ism promoted its long-term decline as an ancestor worshipping group. Andean people were ambivalent about their *curacas*' role as point men in colonial tribute extraction and indirect rule. So were many *curacas* themselves: many resigned in the 1620s without leaving successors.[37] By 1659, authorities regularly resorted to torture in extracting revenue from *curacas*, one of whom even committed suicide rather than deliver his subjects to the Potosí *mita* (Cole 1985: 92). Those who remained in office became culturally more hispanicized, and often used their posi-tion to accumulate personal wealth at their subjects' expense. Under these circumstances, people became progressively less enthusiastic about rituals that celebrated *ayllu* solidarity and *curacas*' political authority. We will see below that these developments came to a head in the mid-eighteenth century. Several preceding shifts in fiscal policy fur-ther eroded the *ayllu*, preparing the ground for this final crisis of indi-rect colonial rule.

Seeing the *reducciones*' depopulated ruin and the impossibility of making fugitives return to them, Viceroy Palata decided in 1683 that all Indians resident in a locality, be they natives (*originarios*), migrants (*forasteros*), or Spaniards' personal servants (*yanaconas*), should have the same monetary and labour tribute obligations. He began tributary reas-sessment in that year, but it caused such an outcry that by 1685 the king suspended its implementation pending study of its impact. Eventually Palata's opponents fought him to a standstill, until his successor took office and quickly restored the status quo (Cole 1985 ch. 6, Wightman 1990: 31–5). Although unsuccessful, Palata's initiatives again revealed the declining number of Indians who lived in *ayllus* and the continuing desire to extract tribute from those who no longer did. After assuming the Spanish Crown in 1700, the Bourbons showed little interest in Hapsburg and Inca forms of indirect rule, mainly because of the dwindling tributary revenues it produced. As a supplement, they tolerated and in 1752 legalized the forced sale of goods (*reparto de mercancías*) to Indians, which had previously counted as 'corruption' in Hapsburg absolutist discourse (Spalding 1984: 188). Despite the occasional reversion to earlier concerns like the hiding of tributaries,[38] they largely lacked their predecessors' appetite for monitoring and reforming Andean society. Under Bourbon rule, the *ayllu* became increasingly irrelevant as a unit of tribute and indirect rule. Abandoned from below and neglected from above, the *ayllu* quietly continued its disintegration through the first three decades of the eighteenth century, only to undergo a noisier collapse thereafter.

7 The Rise of the Mountain Spirits

'Traditional' ancestor worship as sketched in the last three chapters eventually ended. Mummies, 'idols,' and important living *curacas* lost the ancestral titles (*apu*, *wamani*, and *mallku*) that they had shared to mountains, which developed anthropomorphic spirits in the process (see Gose 2006). These mountain spirits acquired nearly all the ancestral functions mummies and 'idols' once had, but also the sense of indigenous sovereignty that *curacas* embodied.[1] Thus, they did not emerge definitively until the late eighteenth century, when the Crown stripped *curacas* of their powers after the Tupac Amaru rebellion, a watershed this chapter will emphasize. Nonetheless, many changes preceded this moment of consolidation through the landscape. In previous chapters, we saw that from their inception, the moral geography of *reducción* and the extirpation of idolatry were already reorganizing Andean ancestor worship around mountains. Thus, we partially and haltingly glimpsed entities that resemble mountain spirits in earlier colonial moments. This chapter links those earlier developments to the culminating crisis of the eighteenth century. To the baseline pressures of *reducción* and the Extirpation it adds the slow erosion of indirect rule through *ayllus*, their reduction to units of tribute extraction, their declining relevance with the growth of *forasterismo*, and, most decisively of all, the collapse of internal solidarities between *curacas* and their subjects. This chapter argues through a series of regional case studies that these later developments ultimately completed the transformation of ancestor worship into mountain worship.

Previous historical discussions of mountain spirits recognize that they bear colonialism's imprint, and one proposes the shift from mummies to mountains that I will show here (Isbell 1997: 131). Others assume that mountains were always objects of indigenous worship, however. Reinhard (1983), for example, explicitly equates Inca sacrifices on mountains with contemporary mountain worship. Griffiths treats mountain spirits as entities that both pre-existed and survived the colonial Church's extirpation of idolatry campaigns (1996: 26, 270). Silverblatt also assumes that mountain spirits were present at the onset of Spanish colonialism (1988: 178, passim), then explores their syncretic interaction with the Devil and Santiago after Spanish conquest (1987: 182–3, 1988). Even Salomon appears to join them (1995: 323). These authors treat mountain spirits as primordial and so ignore their (derivative) relation to pre-existing ancestor cults. By treating mountain worship as an enduring historical thread, they neglect the shifting cultural and political contexts in which mountains changed their significance. However inadvertently, they project an ethnographic pattern onto the past and create a false sense of historical stability around it. While I disagree, I do acknowledge important historical continuities between mummy- and mountain-based regimes, and that various readings of the evidence are possible. Let me clarify what is at stake by articulating the full historical scope of my argument, even at the risk of redundancy.

The two previous chapters showed that colonial ancestor narratives largely differentiated ancestors from landscape. In journeys that were otherwise subterranean or celestial, ancestors emerged from the ground or fell from the sky on *pacarinas*. Contact with ancestors transformed and sacralized these places, allowing *ayllus* ritual access to distant sources of power. Ancestors forged those connections, however: they were active subjects and the land their malleable object. Origin narratives repeatedly depict the way ancestors shaped and reshaped the land with their acts of emergence, rivalries, and prodigious feats of strength.[2] Mountains were among the artifacts they created. In 1615, the people of Atabillos explained to Jesuit extirpators that their ancestors emerged from the bowels of the mountains (Polia 1999: 376–7). Similarly, a witness in Otuco's 1656 idolatry trial held that the oldest ancestors ascended from their original *pacarina* in the Pacific to the snow-capped mountain of Yarupajá, where they emerged from eight caves to populate the Cajatambo region (Duviols 1986: 55, cf. Arriaga 1621: 201–2). Mountains were not agents here but the product of the ancestors' subterranean burrowing and emergence.[3] Alternatively, celestial contact could create mountains, as we saw in Cauri when an ancestor fell from the sky onto a high plain, which swelled up like a globe and ultimately became a mountain.[4] In *ayllu*-based regimes, the landscape took the ancestors' imprint but remained distinct from and subordinate to them.

By contrast, contemporary mountain spirits directly personify the landscape. As don Mateo Garriaso told Arguedas (1956: 235), 'wama-niqa orqom:' the *wamani* is a mountain. This basic assumption is evident in an alternative title for mountain spirits: *tayta urqu* or 'father mountain.'[5] These deities also appear as humans, falcons, or condors, but even when they do, their association with the mountain (and the territory under its sway) continues to be primary, and influences their secondary manifestations. Thus, the Apu Utupara appears as an old man with a pronounced limp, since mining the flanks of that mountain injured his leg (Gose 1986: 303). Similarly, when a condor circled above a mountain pass during road construction, workers identified it as a local *wamani* objecting to the project (Salazar Soler 2002: 178). No matter what their appearance, these spirits personify the landscape above all else. Mountains are their classic and most common localizing feature, but such spirits may also inhabit lakes, plains, crags and other anomalous land forms, and even human houses.[6] In any locality, place spirits form a hierarchy, often based on the height of their respective abodes. Thus, the tallest snow-capped mountains are usually the most important, and subsume lower-ranking places in a regional segmentary hierarchy. People consider these spirits the true owners of particular territories and as custodians of the plants, animals, and minerals therein, offering them sacrificial tribute for their use (Earls 1969: 67). The next chapter will explore the ethnography of mountain spirits more fully, but these details suffice for now.

When mountain spirits took for themselves the titles that mummies, idols, and *curacas* previously held, they redefined the groups to which people owed their fundamental social allegiance. By emphasizing landscape and territory, mountain spirits made the co-residential community into such a group. In Mangas, for example, a ritual emphasis on marriage and territorial integration replaced the descent idiom that mummy worship had so strongly articulated in *ayllus* under *curacas'* direction (Robles Mendoza 1982: 21–31; Burga 1988: 10–20). The shift from descent to residence and affinity as dominant social principles changed people's understandings of the landscape. While *ayllu*-based mummy worship predominated, ancestors animated and modified the land through their emergences and violent struggles: they were subjects and it was an object. When *ayllus* collapsed as descent groups, the land absorbed ancestral functions previously embodied in mummies and idols, and mountain spirits arose to personify the new co-residential basis of group unity. Such changes responded to widespread demographic extinction and amalgamation of *ayllus* (Spalding 1984: 178) and the high percentage of *forasteros* in most Andean communities, Indians who fled their natal villages and lacked any *ayllu* affiliation where they resettled. To include themselves as full members, these people led the redefinition of local groups residentially and through marriage. Above all, this shift eliminated *curacas* and the indirect colonial rule over which they presided, and gave Andean communities the markedly more egalitarian character they have today. The ancestral authority that once backed *curacas'* rule now attaches to a very particular imagining of the republican state. This Andean shift from descent to territory as a dominant social principle did not conform exactly to coeval European shifts from hereditary monarchy to the 'modern,' territorially based nation state, but it interacted with them in interesting and unpredictable ways.

Many continuities spanned the transition from colonial to republican rule, including the basic format of localized divine kingship that both *ayllu* ancestor worship and contemporary mountain spirits exemplify. In this framework, the land's fertility is the measure of political legitimacy. As mountain spirits assumed the titles and functions that mummies and *curacas* previously had, they applied this fertility standard to republican regimes with fascinating results. Arguably, the recycling of the term *'ayllu'* expresses this continuity. With the demise of the ancestor-worshipping descent groups to which it once referred, it reattached to both the egocentric bilateral kindreds and the mountain-worshipping residential groups that were their legacy (Isbell 1978: 105–8; Allen 1988: 106–9). By subsuming these changes, the term *'ayllu'* shifted its meaning but continued to articulate core values of social solidarity and ritual responsibility that it had previously. Yet in the transition that concerns us here, these values acquired a notably more subaltern and egalitarian character.

The shift from mummies to mountains as objects of worship also involved continuities. Older *ayllu* regimes largely separated ancestors from landscape, but as we have seen, this distinction broke down when ancestral deities fought each other to animate a territory, pitting forces in telluric mode. When a victor emerged, he might turn his adversaries into stone, or himself become a crag or mountain. Petrified apotheosis could also follow the building of agricultural infrastructure or the founding of descent groups, besides conquest.[7] It figured intimately in the founding of descent groups and their patrimonies and represented a permanent accumulation and dispensation of life, not ordinary death. Thus, ancestors' petrified deification could fuse them to the landscape in ways that possibly prefigured contemporary mountain spirits. Arriaga, for example, states that people saw some mountains as ancestors' transformed bodies (1621: 201), and the Huarochirí manuscript describes such a fate for one of Pariacaca's sons (Salomon and Urioste 1991: 93). Other Spanish claims that Andean people 'worshipped mountains' may refer to such transformations but are too vague to be certain. Similarly, people sometimes conflated ancestors metonymically with the *pacarinas* from which they emerged.[8] *Pacarina* landscapes' permeability allowed them to contain the ancestors. Like Pariacaca, ancestors could end their activist careers by re-entering the earth from which they emerged. If an established *huaca* was no longer needed or content in a particular locality, it too might journey underground to another *pacarina*, emerge, and regulate a new locality (Salomon and Urioste 1991: ch. 20). Finally, several sources mention that Andean people buried their 'idols' to avoid detection,[9] but perhaps also because they wanted the earth to reclaim them. Thus, *pacarina* landscapes could incorporate the ancestors and anticipate a landscape defined by mountain spirits, despite the significant differences between the two regimes. Such associations were inherent to *pacarina* systems, and do not necessarily imply transition towards a new landscape of mountain spirits. Rather, they were part of an old regime that could articulate a new one.

Nonetheless, mountain spirits as we know them from modern ethnographies did not exist in *pacarina* landscapes. When a mountain was a *pacarina*, the relevant site was usually a specific shrine (*huaca*), not the entire mountain.[10] Many accounts specify that such shrines were on the peaks of mountains, and some state that this location was normative.[11] Often people built them around a particular feature like a cave or crag.[12] More precisely, *huaca* meant 'holy place or object' and so referred not just to shrines but also to the sacred relics they contained, including ancestral mummies stored in or around the shrine,[13] and stone or wooden statues.[14] Sculpted or unmodified crags on the mountainside also represented founding ancestors,[15] but might also be *pacarinas* that merely contained them (Polia 1999: 307, 324, 345). Thus, crags did not necessarily represent transformed ancestral bodies, nor were they the most common form in which *ayllus* conserved their ancestors. Usually mummies and statues were the ancestors' sole representations. Only as the extirpators of idolatry repeatedly destroyed these smaller and more

Figure 7.1 Location of Case Studies in Chapter 7

vulnerable ancestral forms did landscape features such as crags begin to enjoy any strategic advantage.

Let us now turn to several regions for which there is sufficient documentary evidence to assemble case studies in these transitions. By examining their temporality and geographical distribution, and the factors that apparently mattered in each case, we can better understand how mountain spirits arose from preceding *pacarina* landscapes.

Yauyos, 1607–60

A cluster of documents from Yauyos can initiate our discussion: one dates to 1607, another to 1621, and the remainder to 1660.[16] The earliest is the famous Huarochirí manuscript discussed above, the classic narrative of pre-Columbian invasion and accommodation featuring Pariacaca and his sons. During his conquest, Pariacaca assumed a highland position and used its corresponding arsenal of rain and hail to defeat the lowland fire deity Huallallo Carhuincho. In this phase, Pariacaca's identification with the landscape was so vivid that Salomon and Uri-oste compare him to a contemporary mountain spirit when he and his sons enter a crag (1991: 94n410). This impression appears to gain strength from the fact that the name Pariacaca applied to the mountain where that crag occurred, also a nearby shrine and idol.[17] On closer examination, however, the idol, not the mountain, emerges as the object of Pariacaca's cult. Furthermore, the Huarochirí manuscript states merely that Pariacaca and his sons entered a crag, not that their bodies underwent lithomorphosis, as happened in other ancestral narratives. Thus, they did not become consubstantial with the landscape, and we must assume that this crag was a *pacarina*. Conceptually and in practice, ancestor and landscape remained separate. Like other ancestral inva-sion narratives, however, this one could suppress these distinctions: the struggle to control and animate a territory obliged ancestors to test their power in a telluric mode, with catastrophic effects on the landscape. Once they resolved the issue of supremacy, however, ancestors ceased operating destructively. They came to rest, established descent groups, and became objects of institutionalized cults. Then the mummy-, idol-, and *pacarina*-based complex of ancestor worship prevailed. Pariacaca and his sons conformed exactly to this pattern and were not mountain spirits in the making.

A complementary document of 1621 comes from Guaquis, and records the idolatrous priest Cristóbal Curis Yananpa's trial. Blind and well into his sixties, Yananpa had eluded Ávila's earlier *visita* to Yauyos when his *curaca* hid him. Most witnesses described his curing activities. One, Magdalena Tunqui, confessed that she asked Yananpa to sacrifice to the idol Llanquecocha so her son might recover from illness and she might have more children. Yananpa not only agreed to officiate but pro-vided the sacrificial animals and even suggested that she sleep with him to conceive children. Yananpa's sister-in-law, Catalina Tunsu Yana, definitively revealed his priestly activities, however, stating that he had asked her a year earlier why she had not come to him about her llamas, which were dying in unusual numbers. When she observed that God would do as he wished with the llamas, Yananpa replied that she should give him corn beer, potatoes, and coca to offer to the mountain Rasu Yacolca. When she insisted that she did not want to, he retorted that it was not God but the idol Rasu Yacolca that mattered, and per-suaded her to join him in making offerings to the idol. Later, Yananpa returned to her herding estate with his daughter, who brought corn beer and a young llama to sacrifice to Marco, a *chanca*, or small stone idol, for the multiplication of Tunsu Yana's flocks. Yananpa admitted to these activities, and noted that he had inherited his priestly office from his parents and grandparents.[18]

Domingo Parian and his sister Ynes Cancho Molloc, whom Ávila punished during his *visita* to Yauyos, emerged as Yananpa's priestly assistants during the trial. They quickly returned to idolatry and, like Yananpa, exhorted those with infertile families, herds, and fields to sacrifice to Marco, or did so for them. Yananpa confessed that every month he sacrificed corn beer, coca, seashells (*mullu*), and maize dough (*sanco*) for the increase of his herds, for long life, and the return of his sight to Guaman Yaco, a snow-covered mountain next to the famous Pariacaca (Salomon and Urioste 1991: 93). Every six months he sacrificed a llama by cutting it open on the left side and extracting its beating heart, bathing the *chanca* called Marco in its blood to assuage its thirst. Witnesses alternately describe both major deities these priests attended as mountains (*cerros*) and idols (*ydolos*): one even describes the mountain Rasu Yacolca itself as an idol. Clearly they identified these deities significantly with mountains, but their priests interacted with them as idols. Parian and his sister kept Rasu Yacolca's idol and its herd of six alpacas and two guacays. Yananpa kept Guaman Yaco's idol and its herd of thirty alpacas on his herding estate and the *chanca* as a familial idol, using it to divine and cure.[19]

Nobody explicitly identified Rasu Yacolca and Guaman Yaco as *ayllu* progenitors. Yet the fact that they had their own estates and a priesthood with collective responsibilities suggests that *ayllu*-based corporate worship still prevailed in the area. Marco, however, was a *chanca* deity of more circumscribed, familial influence. During domestic prosperity rites, not only the *chanca* but one of the higher-order idols received offerings. A segmentary relationship between familial and *ayllu* idols prevailed, in which the group's deities still mediated domestic ends. Mills hypothesizes that *chancas* interceded with *ayllu* deities as did Catholic saints with God (1997: 76–7). Yet here, higher-order deities interceded with those of lesser standing. When the idol Nina Curi became annoyed with Domingo Parian and burned his entire body, Yananpa invoked Rasu Yacolca to learn that he should placate Nina Curi by sacrificing a young llama. We see this same subsumption of lesser units by greater ones in how *ayllu* priests did individual households' fertility rites in all the incidents this document mentions. As Mills notes, specialists usually held *chancas* for extended families or sub-lineages within *ayllus*, and sacrificed to them for their individual members' welfare (1997: 76, 80–1). The healing and herd-increase rituals documented here addressed individual and household needs but through *ayllu* deities and specialists.

In summary, this document supplements the Huarochirí manuscript by documenting the cults of Guaman Yaco and Rasu Yacolca, important ancestors closely associated with Pariacaca. Their cults pertained to the herders from Yauyos who reputedly invaded Huarochirí under Pariacaca's leadership (Salomon and Urioste 1991: 6–7). As described in 1621 near the first anti-idolatry campaign's end, these cults were *ayllu*-based and organized the landscape around *pacarinas*, not mountain spirits. They venerated idols, not the mountains or shrines that housed them. A document of 1660 states that the Guaquis-Guañec area had become a region of refuge for idolatrous Indians who fled *reducción*, so such worship probably continued there then.[20]

Elsewhere in Yauyos during 1660, *ayllu*-based ancestor worship coexisted with a tendency to deify mountains. A document from Tupe begins with Magdalena Sacha Carua admitting to offering *sanco* to Mount Suni Vilca and asking it for health. When he investigated the mountain in question, however, the inspector Sarmiento discovered a shrine containing paintings, offerings, 'idols,' and many mummies, which he duly burned. Despite this clear physical evidence of ancestral forms distinguished from the landscape, adepts addressed Suni Vilca in a prayer as 'my father-creator' ('*iaia camagniy*'), as if he were an ancestor.[21] Perhaps Suni Vilca was also one of the 'idols' in question, but the document does not state that, so we must allow that this mountain might have been a pre-eminent ancestral manifestation in local ritual. Whether this was a recent development is impossible to tell, but loss of ancestral statues and mummies cannot explain it, since they still existed in the shrine.

Another case of 1660 from Omas begins with Francisca Mayguay's denunciation for 'sorcery.' When she appeared before Sarmiento, Mayguay immediately confessed, but only to petitioning Santiago (as lightning deity) for rainfall, and Mount Cotoni for good potato and maize crops. Subsequently other witnesses linked Mayguay to Francisca Ianac, another alleged sorceress who reputedly killed people. Mayguay initially denied their association, but confessed to it under threat of torture. She then described joining Ianac in sacrifices to Mount Maguacacoto, asking for longer life, and to a shrine (*mochadero*) with a stone pillar named Suyurumi opposite Ianac's field in a deep valley that protected it from theft. When she took a delegation to Suyurumi, however,

Sarmiento did not believe that the site corresponded to the one her confession described. The rest of the document largely concerns Sarmiento's unsuccessful attempts to find this shrine. In the process, he went to another mountainside shrine named Quircay, which had several burials. He learned that Maguacacoto had been a shrine (*mochadero*) until Francisco de Ávila destroyed it and placed a cross on the mountain top.[22]

This document gives an impression of mountain worship on first reading, but also vents Sarmiento's suspicion that a more traditional 'idolatry' centred on stone figures and human bodies might lurk behind this facade. Mayguay's first two confessions both began with 'idolatries' committed on mountains, as if they were somehow less damaging than those in shrines, which she was more reluctant to admit. We cannot know if mountains had become the primary objects of ancestral devotion here, and it may not be the most interesting question. The document is more valuable for the reflexivity its Andean protagonists displayed, both the accused and those who collaborated with the *visitadores*, in portraying a sacred landscape already transformed under the Extirpation (Mills 1994b). Whatever these people 'really' believed (and surely variation and disagreement existed here), it responded to the experience of extirpation.

A third document, also from Omas, further develops this picture. Here, the principal accused was Pedro Villanga, a witness in the previous case against Francisca Mayguay, who emerges as a fellow idolater in this trial. Villanga confessed that about twenty years previously, a *curaca* had sent him as part of a party to make offerings on Mount Guacaguasi during an epidemic. By feeding the ancestors with three rounds of burnt offerings, blood sacrifice, and libations, they hoped to stop the disease. It continued unabated, however, killing the *curaca*, members of his immediate family, and many ritualists who made the offerings in question. He told how Juan Tomás, the party's leader, erected four stones on Guacaguasi to represent the ancestors, lit a fire amid them, gave them burnt offerings of food, poured libations into the fire and towards the mountain top and the plains below. He also acted as the ancestors' oracular medium, addressing them with such titles as 'powerful one' (*capac*). They also tried to stop the epidemic with sacrifices to a stone on Mount Guamantianga, splattering it with blood and serving it food. Villanga concluded that these efforts failed, since most of the participants died shortly afterwards, proving his ancestral religion's falsity (see Griffiths 1996: 209). Among the survivors, however, were

Francisca Mayguay and Juana Conva. The latter appeared before Sarmiento and, after denying that she was a sorceress, ultimately admitted participating in the sacrifices on Guamantianga. She contradicted Villanga, saying that the sacrifices were not for that mountain but the sea, which had ultimate powers of life and death in matters of disease, and also since local people were about to do labour tribute on the coast. On further questioning, Conva identified the Ayllu Llampa's shrine on Mount Maururu, which Ávila had destroyed and replaced with a cross, and the Ayllu Tamara's shrine, an old town on Mount Tapurcu that Francisca Mayguay and her ilk still frequented.[23]

This document describes a reconstructed ancestor cult oriented towards stone monoliths that people raised and equated with the ancestors. According to Villanga, the sacrifices went to Mount Guacaguasi as a proxy for (or conduit to) the ancestors, who presumably were not directly accessible before the erection of the four stone pillars. The epidemics seemingly posed the question of whether the ancestors were actually present in the locality, and able (or willing) to safeguard their descendants' health. This situation contrasts markedly with contemporaneous accounts from Cajatambo that describe people's physical interaction and oracular dialogue with powerful ancestral mummies in ritual. Witnesses mention no such bodies here, which suggests that extirpators had burned or otherwise destroyed them, diminishing them to something like ordinary mortals' *upani* souls: powerless entities that left their locality at death and migrated to distant maximal *pacarinas* (such as the Pacific) where they no longer influenced local events (Gose 1993: 498–500). As they did in Maray, people approached ancestors through mountains that were conduits to these distant sources, not ancestor substitutes in themselves. Thus, they still operated within a *pacarina* regime that treated the landscape as a conduit for ancestral journeys, not as an active agent. Yet previous extirpations had significantly modified this regime: those who wished to persist in their 'idolatries' had to reinvent them creatively. They could either replace destroyed ancestral forms (mummies) with new ones (stone monoliths), or accept that the ancestors no longer inhabited the immediate environment and approach them through mountain *pacarinas*. Both strategies are evident here.

A final document from Omas begins with allegations about an idol and the Ayllu Tamara's shrine named Tamaguasi. It then narrows to charges against an old couple for living together unmarried in the *puna* (alpine zone), and practicing idolatry and 'sorcery' there. Juan Chapa, the old man, readily admitted to offering maize, coca, and ear cuttings from his llamas to Mount Patacaca semi-annually, once on San Juan and again at Christmas, to increase his herds and the water and pastures they needed. He denied making blood sacrifices or contracting other ritualists to make offerings for him. These rites occurred in a corral on Mount Patacaca, also the site of a shrine with a small plaza where the Ayllus Guanpara and Tamara once did corporate rituals. He suggested that María Ticlla, his conjugal partner, knew much about those rituals, and taught him the domestic rituals just described. When called to testify, however, she presented him as the expert. To prove her point, she recalled recruiting another ritualist, Juana Tunque, to make similar offerings to another nearby mountain, Antanama Horcu, that had an ancient shrine so their struggling herd (of thirty-one head when Sarmiento impounded them) would multiply. She then described the burnt offerings of llama ear cuttings that Chapa made to the mountain during these rituals. As both were recidivist idolaters, Sarmiento did not care who was the more responsible and convicted both to public humiliation in Omas followed by time in Lima's Santa Cruz house of corrections.[24]

This final case contrasts instructively with that of Guaquis in 1621. Both documents describe domestic rites of increase for llamas, but under very different regimes. Whereas in the Guaquis document, *ayllu* priests conducted these rites for *ayllu* deities, by 1660 in Omas, households addressed the mountains directly, without the mediation of *ayllu* forms (cf. Spalding 1984: 262–3).[25] This domestic orientation makes the Omas rites comparable to *t'inkas* (libations) for today's mountain spirits, as do their bipolar seasonality (San Juan and Christmas), the cutting of animals' ears in them, and their goal of increasing herds, pastures, and water (Gose 1994: ch. 7). Although an *ayllu* shrine still existed on Mount Patacaca, these rituals did not use it but rather the owners' corral, as do modern rites. Evidently these fertility rituals had disengaged from *ayllu*-based idol worship, and were now a household concern addressed to mountains, which had taken over the relevant ancestral functions. A new ritual system was emerging amid an older one's ruins and memories.

Such an image does not properly summarize the composite picture these documents create, however. 'Traditional' *ayllu*-based worship that upheld a distinction between ancestors and landscape still existed in Yauyos during 1660, if less prominently. These cases show that ancestral mountains both coexisted with and displaced 'idol' and mummy cults during the seventeenth century. Modern ethnography encourages us to see displacement as the long-term historical trajectory, but it tells us nothing about when and how it happened. This seventeenth-century evidence does not deliver us to the threshold of the ethnographic record: at best, it gives us raw material for what later became mountain spirits. Nor does it show any clear, unidirectional pattern of historical change. Rather, these documents portray several experimental rein-vestments of the ancestral in stone monoliths and mountains, as the Extirpation destroyed ever more mummies. They record a time of flux when multiple impulses and strategies coexisted, and did not necessarily appear as contending options.

Canta, 1650–56

In 1650, the town of Pomacocha, Canta, produced two cases relevant to this discussion. As so often happened, a quarrel among Andean people caused the first trial. Pedro Curichagua accused Juana Ycha of witchcraft, illicit worship, and divination. Apparently she had threatened Churichagua's son, who was having an affair with her daughter. Within three days, proceedings against her began: the investigating priest, Antonio de Caceres, impounded her meagre belongings, captured her and brought her before him. In her confession, she described herself as a widow, and admitted to learning 'sorcery' from Catalina Suyo and Alonso Caxa Guaranga, starting about ten years previously. Caxa Guaranga promised to teach her how to cure the sick by privately consulting and feeding a quarter-sized silver 'idol' of a person seated on a mold-casting (piña, literally 'pineapple'), which represented Apoparato, the trial's featured 'demon.' Early in Ycha's apprenticeship, however, Caxa Guaranga died, leaving her and Catalina Suyo as this deity's only priests. Ycha and Suyo mention no collective rites for Apoparato: they approached the deity only for individual patrons (mingadores). The most frequent requests were from women who wished to make men enter or stay in conjugal relationships. Nearly as common were requests for the deity to cure sicknesses, intervene in difficult births, or find lost property. Other requests came from a man who wished to change tributary jurisdictions, another who wished to avoid prosecution, a coca vendor eager to make sales, a native tax collector seeking an Indian who owed him tribute, and a woman who wished to depose her unpopular son-in-law Francisco Pomacondor as curaca. According to Ycha, Apoparato generally granted these requests if appropriate offerings accompanied them. Ycha also made offerings to maintain her relations with Apoparato. Strikingly absent are any descriptions of collective, semi-annual *ayllu* observances for Apoparato, although people called him 'father or nurturer' ('*yaya o criador*') and requested favours that ancestral deities typically provided.[26] Possibly selective testimony concealed collective *ayllu* rituals here, but probably they no longer existed. The *curaca* Pomacondor's collaboration with the prosecution suggests he disliked such rituals, and his attitude can only have hardened when testimony revealed that idolaters schemed to remove him from office. Pomacondor's antipathy could well explain the absence of corporate support for Apoparato's cult and this *curaca*'s personal unpopularity within his *ayllu*. When indigenous political authorities and corporate structures no longer sponsored or cohered around *ayllu* rituals, only these more individual forms of worship sustained the deities.

Lack of a collective cult seems to have underwritten Apoparato's occasionally violent behaviour towards Ycha. He came to her periodically as a whirlwind that transformed into a dark Indian man in a black cape: he demanded food and corn beer and would rage and beat her if she did not serve them promptly. While Alonso Caxa Guaranga was still alive, Apoparato ate and talked quietly with him, and did not beat Ycha like this. During nocturnal visits, Apoparato sometimes took the form of Ycha's dead husband, and slept with her if her grandchildren were not present, ejaculating a cold yellow fluid. Leading up to the trial, other more recently deceased kin joined him, also to demand food and drink that she could scarcely provide. Ycha noted that Apoparato worked her fields when no men, Spaniards, or priests (whom he feared and avoided) were present, revealing his thin black legs and rooster-like feet. She then returned to the beatings he gave her and the destitution she experienced since becoming his priestess. Ycha dwelt on his stinginess, and refusal to give her any of the silver he sometimes brought in a sack, perhaps to elaborate his statue. She could not recruit others to serve Apoparato, and so remained trapped in this increasingly onerous office.[27]

Silverblatt (1987: 185, 1988: 184–5) invokes Andean people's material impoverishment and the breakdown of reciprocity with their ancestral deities under Spanish colonialism to explain Ycha's estranged relation to Apoparato. She argues that Andean people accepted their deities' demonization because their own relations with them became highly problematic. Griffiths (1996: 116–19, 126–7, 131) and Mills (1997: 228–

40) dispute this interpretation. They note that Apoparato still acted as a tutelary deity, and regard his demonization as an imposition of the investigating priest. I think both positions are largely correct, and the drama of this case derives precisely from Apoparato's traditional ancestral functions on the one hand and the collapse of his *ayllu*-based cult, with its corresponding resources and specialists, on the other. By treating Apoparato as a traditional ancestor whose cult was in decline, we can reconcile these interpretations. Only the most senior ancestors in a region held his prefixed title of *apu*, or lord (Doyle 1988: 52–4). The requests that Ycha referred to Apoparato are all typical of those that Andean people made of their ancestors. His appearance as Ycha's dead husband suggests that he still oversaw *ayllu* mortuary processes. The quasi-conjugal relationship Apoparato maintained with Ycha was also typical of that between other Andean deities and their chosen women that many idolatry documents and chronicles describe. Priestesses like Ycha were part of most Andean deities' traditional retinue. However, the rest of this entourage was missing, particularly after Alonso Caxa Guaranga's death. Ycha admitted that she had not mastered all the divinatory techniques he practised, which may partly explain Apoparato's more abusive stance towards her after his death. That nobody else would replace either Caxa Guaranga or Ycha suggests a cult in crisis. People still wanted these specialists' services but no longer supported them sufficiently to attract new recruits. The paramount question was how to provide for such a deity when there were no longer fields or flocks dedicated to its sacrificial maintenance. Ycha's increased ritual responsibility and material destitution speaks eloquently to this point. She and other followers may not have demonized him definitively, but their relationship certainly changed in a less harmonious direction. It was less a question of 'reciprocity' breaking down than of it shifting into a negative mode, in which the ancestor asserted an ongoing relationship punitively, when his living adepts failed to maintain his cult adequately. These circumstances destabilized the deity's behaviour, but also his physical form and geographical location, which are remarkably pliable in this document.

Apoparato existed as a silver idol, a whirlwind, and an Indian man, but also appeared through a pair of spiders and the coals of a fire. Various adepts worshipped him in their houses, Pomacocha's irrigation canal and two different mountains (Julcan and Cochayoc).[28] When asked if she hid any other illicit practices or worshipped any mountains, Ycha replied that she did not but once went to Mount Julcan to invoke and give Apoparato offerings on a straw surface. When asked if she and Catalina Suyo had a 'pact' (i.e., sex) with him there, she replied that they only fed him. One midnight while she was imprisoned in church during the trial, Apoparato appeared to her. Ycha said she was now in the hands of God, and he replied, 'I wish to return to where I am, above Cajapalca, to a high mountain that has a *cocha* or lake at its summit.' He had previously asked her to accompany him to this place, but she refused.[29]

When rebuffed by one of his last remaining mediums, Apoparato significantly announced his wish to 'return' to his mountain of origin, probably the *pacarina* from which he had first emerged. With an eerie awareness of his fate, he may have been announcing his imminent transformation into a mountain spirit there. That his name contains the prefixed title *apu*, by which mountain spirits in the Cuzco region are known today, tempts this presentist reading. In nearly all mid-colonial cases, *apu* refers to an idol (or a mummy) in a regime of *ayllus* and *pacarinas*, but here that regime's disintegration is so patent that we can no longer assume its salience. Even if Apoparato was merely returning to his *pacarina*, this may have been the mechanism by which a new landscape of mountain spirits swallowed a previously independent ancestral manifestation. While no such transformation occurred on Ycha's watch as priestess, this farewell clearly marked the end of an era and hinted pregnantly at the beginning of another.

A separate investigation of Ynes Carhuachumbi emerged from this inquiry, also in Canta during 1650. The document begins with reports of her curing activities, and comings and goings to a mountain called Apoquircay to feed a deity of that same name. Carhuachumbi initially denied everything to the investigating priest, but when threatened with torture, she confessed to offering black and white sheep to the mountain Quircay occasionally, initially as an assistant to her husband, and after his death, on her own. Like Juana Ycha, Carhuachumbi purportedly had sex twice with Apoquircay, who appeared and behaved as her dead husband, ejaculating a warm white fluid. She seems to have developed a more satisfactory relationship of mutual sustenance with him, however. As questioning turned to Apoquircay, Carhuachumbi described him as a white anthropomorphic standing stone (*guanca*) about the size of a boy, painted and girded in bronze, hidden in a walled-in cave with stone benches on the mountain. The investigation's next phase was a journey to the cave near the mountain top, where they found an idol that did not conform to Carhuachumbi's description. Her explanation was that someone must have moved it. When the investigation tried to locate this and other idols mentioned in previous testimony, it failed and the documentation ended.[30]

Apoquircay's description is much less detailed than Apoparato's, but his firm identification with a mountain of the same name initially makes him a more convincing precursor of contemporary mountain spirits. Yet, like Pariacaca, he turned out to be a statue associated with a cave. Also as with Pariacaca, we may suspect that the cave on Quircay was a *pacarina* because of its architecture, although no testimony names it as such. Witnesses said Apoquircay was 'from Chinchaycocha,' so they thought of him as a journeying ancestor.[31] Since Apoquircay's primary embodiment was still a statue, the eponymous mountain had not yet assimilated his ancestral functions: a distinction between ancestor and landscape still prevailed. That the investigation did not recover his statue further suggests that it may have been his privileged embodiment, one that people worked to save from the extirpators. The mountain had not subsumed or substituted itself for this independent ancestral form, so this is clearly a *pacarina* regime, not a contemporary one of mountain spirits.

A similar case surfaced in Huamantanga during 1656. Several idolatrous priests led by Hernando Carhuachin 'spontaneously' confessed their activities to Pedro Quijano Zeballos, the visiting idolatry inspector, and recounted that the deities they served beat them. Here, however, material privation cannot explain the deities' violence, since a corporate form of ancestor worship prevailed, in which the idols held estates of money, clothing, fields, and flocks (Mills 1997: 229). Carhuachin described an *ayllu*-based landscape focused on Guaracani, a mountainous crag containing several shrines and idols. Chief among them was a buried stone anthropomorphic idol, alternately called Guaracani and Chontabilca. Nearby was another shrine with a white stone statue of 'Mother Nurturer and Creator,' Chontabilca's wife. These deities were highly revered, and only their priests dared enter their shrines. On the other side of Mount Guaracani from these statues was the rock-covered entrance to an old shrine called Marca Aura, the *pacarina* of the Ayllus Chaupin and Yanac, also where they kept their mummies. This shrine contained a *huaca*, also named Marca Aura. Quipan's third *ayllu*, Julcachuri, had its *pacarina* on Mount Pomabamba, a league out of town. It housed two idols, one a stone statue called Yaropalpa surrounded by three monoliths, and the other an unsculpted stone the size of a person called Chimchaypalpa, in a thicket of thorns. The Ayllu

Julcachuri kept their mummies in a large cave at a place called Uru-acuto.[32] Despite their favourable material conditions and conformity to the classic pattern, these *ayllu* cults were in trouble.

Carhuachin recounted a sequence of visions that began while he looked for a horse on Mount Guaracani above the town of Quipan. On passing a painted cave called Macha, he saw a panting white dog in its entrance. Walking a few steps on, he turned to look again, but the dog was gone. Greatly afraid, Carhuachin began to vomit copiously, fainted, and fell to the ground, where he lay as if dead. From these signs, he inferred that the dog was the Devil. Three days later, while he was tending sheep on the same mountain, a mule presented itself in the distance, appearing and disappearing, until he returned to town in the evening. In his sleep, it returned, saying, 'Come with me, I want to take you to Lima.' Somehow they arrived in Lima, and the mule took him to the church of San Sebastian, prompting him to go inside. The church doors opened of their own accord for him, while the mule waited out-side. The same scene repeated itself in all the churches of Lima, until the mule left Carhuachin at a wooden bridge where, exhausted and drip-ping with sweat, he collapsed into a deep sleep. Two weeks later, while he was irrigating his cornfield at midday, the Devil appeared before him as an old Indian. Although Carhuachin had not imbibed, he sud-denly felt very drunk, and the Indian began to beat him on the back with a stick, without saying anything to him. He returned to his house bewildered and confused. A week later, while gathering firewood, the same Indian appeared before him, dark, with an ugly face, a thin long brown beard, and glowing red eyes, and began to beat him as before. This time he asked Carhuachin why he had neglected his rituals, gave him packages of coloured powders, and told him never to neglect the worship of *huacas* and the sun. These powders he used to cure a man made sick by a spring, but later they did not always work. The Devil continued to appear to him in various forms, sometimes with horns, sometimes as a lion, a condor, or a fox, but they never spoke to each other again. He continued to exhort the people of Huamantanga to con-tract him as a ritual specialist, but his relation with Guaracani was dete-riorating. The deity accused him of hiding his sins, called him to his shrine, and flogged him until he fainted. Carhuachin's wife described this incident differently, saying that four years previously on Holy Thursday, he undertook a penitential self-flagellation from Quipan to the shrine of Guaracani, where he passed out in a bloody heap in front of the idol.[33] Both the timing and the trajectory of this penance again suggest *reducción*-based Christianity's growing influence within 'idolatry's' peripheral realm.

María Ticlla Guacho, one of Carhuachin's associates, said that during the five years she served as a *huaca* priestess, the Devil appeared to her ten times, five as a dark lion, and five as a large brown fox, saying that he was to live with her always and that she would not return to the Christian God because she was his. These appearances happened around the idol Malmaimi, a stone monolith in Curcuycocha when she went to worship there. She always agreed with the deity that things would be as he declared, including that she would worship no other god but him. On three different occasions, Malmaimi gave her small black pieces of dung to eat, smelly, hard and bitter, saying that it would stop her from forgetting him and remembering the Christian God and allow her to divine the future. Twice he appeared before her very upset, denouncing her for believing in the Spaniards' God and praying as they did, flogging her over all her body with a leather whip, leaving her naked and half-dead. After the whipping, he gave her his hand to kiss and demanded that she kneel before him, which she did. He twice gave her coloured powders to use in sacrifices, which consoled her greatly as it satisfied him and allowed her to cure, increase wealth and crops, and move people to love or hate one another. Beyond these ten appearances, the Devil also came to her twice at midnight as a lion, copulating with her and ejaculating cold semen, asking her why she did not love and enjoy him, to which she responded, 'How can I love you if you are the Devil and a lion?' The first time she tried to resist him, and he beat her with a stick, breaking her arm and leaving her permanently injured.[34]

Several other witnesses gave less extensive testimony. The last, Leonor Rimay, described going, forty or fifty years previously, when she was still single, to an arroyo near town. There the Devil appeared to her as a black llama. When he asked what she was doing, she replied that she had come to drink 'his water' and hurried home, but the llama followed at a block's distance. Fright overcame her, and she was sick for many days, but soon married Christóbal Yauri. While he was alive, she never practiced 'witchcraft,' but after he had died, the Devil reappeared to her in a dream as a lion, telling her to worship Coriguanca, a white standing stone near her house. When she gave it offerings, the Devil again appeared to her, now as an old, heavily bearded padre, who showed her how to cure with guinea pigs and herbs, which she did thereafter. During that same appearance, he spat on her right arm and told her to lick it, saying that she would now know how to divine the future and find lost and stolen objects, which henceforth she did, never making a mistake. Twice more the Devil appeared to her as a lion around the idol Coriguanca while she offered sacrifices and invoked him as 'my lord and god' and 'the god of my ancestors.'[35] Evidently some local specialists still had viable relations with their ancestral deities, especially when the latter appeared as Spanish priests! For this witness at least, 'idolatry' seems fully reconciled with Christianity, despite the notary's diabolic overlays.

These accounts were massively self-incriminating, yet strikingly rich in detail and a vivid sense of experience. Seemingly these Andean priests denounced their cults to unburden themselves of such hallucinatory experiences. The world was somehow shifting under their feet, and a diffuse reality sense, a complex web of cultural judgments and orientations, was at stake. At another level, however, their testimony was calculating: some aimed to incriminate don Rodrigo de Guzmán Apo Rupaychagua, Huamantanga's indigenous governor and their erstwhile patron. Carhuachin alleged that Rupaychagua had contracted him thirteen years earlier to beg the Mamacocha (Pacific Ocean) and Sun to help him regain the indigenous governorship and come home from Lima safely. When Rupaychagua returned a year later with the case still pending, he accused Carhuachin of bungling the invocation. Nonetheless, he twice contracted Carhuachin to perform similar rituals in the following months. Ten to twelve years previously, don Rodrigo came to Carhuachin saying, 'Grandfather, I am in great trouble because the *corregidor* has sent constables [*alguaciles*] to capture me. Tell me what I should do.' Carhuachin advised him to descend through a valley to Pauaray, and from there to make for Lima, where he would not be found. Don Rodrigo asked that Carhuachin meet him in Pauaray, and make offerings for him there, which Carhuachin did, going to the old town of Pocaca, and weaving together some of don Rodrigo's hair with some blond hair from a Spaniard, and offering sacrifices to the ocean so that don Rodrigo would win his court case. Carhuachin further recounted that four years earlier, while he was at the idol Guaracani's estate, the grandmother of Rupaychagua's wife approached him with jerky and corn beer, asking if he had made the sacrifices requested of him. He replied that he had invoked the sea and sacrificed to it many times now, that he was tired of making offerings for Rupaychagua's success from his own resources without receiving any recompense, and that they should provide him with any further offering they wanted him to make to Guaracani.[36]

The intent was clearly to damage don Rodrigo, who appears as the trial's primary suspect in the *cabeza de proceso* (opening charges) even though only Carhuachin's testimony seriously inculpates him. Despite the apparent spontaneity of these confessions, they were a part of an orchestrated but veiled attack whose source can be gleaned from Ynes Ticray's testimony. She mentions that the trial grew out of a regular inspection of the area, announced in advance. On hearing this news, she fled the parish with her husband, returned, and was jailed in Huamantanga. When she was released, she went to don Rodrigo's house, where his wife said that they would ensure that she was tortured as one of don Cristóbal's 'witches.' As we will see below, don Cristóbal Mexía Rupaychagua was don Rodrigo's paternal cousin, lieutenant (*segunda persona*), and rival as indigenous governor. This testimony suggests that don Rodrigo initially tried to use the idolatry inspection against his cousin, who counterattacked with the idolatry charges that this case comprises. Somehow, don Cristóbal persuaded Carhuachin and associates to testify against don Rodrigo. As they were members of his retinue, their testimony was potentially very damaging. Yet those charges initially rebounded on his accusers without don Rodrigo even having to testify or defend himself. Their testimony dates to April and August of 1656, as do the sentences they received. On 6 October 1656, the trial records arrived in Lima, where they languished until late 1668. Then Juan Sarmiento de Vivero, who became idolatry inspector in the area shortly after 1656, revived the earlier charges to jail don Rodrigo. The document ends in February 1669, with don Rodrigo incarcerated for five months, asking that the charges against him be revealed, that Sarmiento be recused, and for permission to testify.[37] Thus, the attack against don Rodrigo failed, lay dormant for twelve years, and then found new life. Complementary documents from the intervening years help explain what happened by illuminating the struggles over Huamantanga's indigenous governorship manifest in this case.

In December 1658, Cristóbal de la Cerda, Sarmiento's prosecutor, charged don Rodrigo and his consort, María Carua, with concubinage. By May 1659, Nicolás Rodríguez, another of Sarmiento's prosecutors, raised the charges to concubinage and incest, since María Carua was don Cristóbal's ex-concubine. The enmity between the two men was over more than political office: allegedly they had a knife fight when don Cristóbal encountered don Rodrigo with María on a road out of town.[38] In June of 1659, Rodríguez charged don Rodrigo with violently resisting arrest and hiding María. He asked that don Rodrigo be imprisoned in Huamantanga, not Lima, to continue idolatry investigations against him, presumably those described above. Finally, he asked that don Rodrigo be prohibited from using the title *apo* (lord) since it implied a false hereditary claim to the governorship. Rodríguez claimed that don Rodrigo only called himself *apo* to Indian interlocutors and that the title had the whiff of idolatry about it.[39] These new charges were clearly meant to revive the original idolatry charges against don Rodrigo, which must have stalled. Apparently don Cristóbal, whose earlier liaison with María Carua went unprosecuted, not only recruited Quijano to his cause but also his successor, Sarmiento, who resumed don Rodrigo's pursuit. By denying don Rodrigo's hereditary claim to the governorship and insinuating that his use of the title *apo* smacked of idolatry, don Cristóbal's Spanish agents finally revealed their agenda. To disqualify don Rodrigo from office, they presented him as an interloper whose indigenous power base lay in sponsoring idolatry.

The saga resumes in 1664, with charges that don Cristóbal's father-in-law was an idolater and one of don Cristóbal's 'witches.'[40] Don Rodrigo was one of the witnesses and clearly sought payback for the charges of 1656 and 1658–59. However, the 1664 case's main protagonist was the wife of Juan Carua Capcha, who, along with his brother Miguel Menacho, led a third power block based in such offices as mayor and scribe in the parallel Spanish system of indigenous self-government.[41] These brothers also sought the governorship and attacked both don Rodrigo and don Cristóbal's father-in-law, who responded by publicly denouncing them as commoners with aristocratic pretensions.[42] Nonetheless, don Rodrigo happily joined these upstarts in denouncing don Cristóbal's father-in-law as a witch to discredit his main rival. Also in 1664, probably as fallout from this failed idolatry prosecution, Sarmiento's prosecutor de la Cerda charged Miguel Menacho with concubinage and deplored his litiginous propensities and those of his brother.[43] Yet sometime between 1669, when don Rodrigo was still governor but in jail, and 1673, Menacho won the indigenous governorship. By 1697 his daughter had married don Rodrigo's son, who became Menacho's lieutenant governor, so sealing an alliance between those two factions.[44] Again in 1678, Menacho was allegedly party to the kidnapping and flogging of Angelina Chumpi, to induce her to declare falsely that she was an idolatrous priestess in the employ of don Cristóbal Mexía's wife.[45] Although this scheme also failed, it suggests that Mexía remained a player in the struggle over the governorship, as in the 1656 document.

Against this background of endemic intrigue and cynical litigation, let us return to what motivated Carhuachin and associates to testify against don Rodrigo. We can rule out material privation, since the deities had their own estates and don Rodrigo also supported their cults.[46] Whatever their problems with don Rodrigo, and even if he arranged their beatings, these priests attributed them to the deities they served. Since the ancestors' authority and that of the *curaca* were intimately linked, these priests' disputes with don Rodrigo could understandably play out as inner conflicts over their supernatural allegiances. Griffiths convincingly argues that indigenous deities beat their priests because of their emergent Christian sympathies (1996: 130), that is, not out of starvation but betrayal. Despite being a known idolater from the first campaign, Carhuachin and his wife received the most lenient sentences of all as 'good confessors,' so they must have been convincingly repentant. Opaque as their motives may be to us now, their actions are consistent with a repudiation of 'idolatry.' The rapes and beatings they described express the bodily pain and disorientation of breaking with these deities, and the political order they articulated.

By turning on the ancestor cult they had hitherto served, these priests challenged not only don Rodrigo but the indigenous governorship itself. Apparently they were willing to destroy the collective rituals and world view they orchestrated, even their own livelihoods and professions, to attack this office. Theirs was a suicide mission that went well beyond personal antipathy for don Rodrigo. Carhuanchin even volunteered to guide Quijano to the *huacas* he mentioned and particularly encouraged him to destroy the shrine of Guaracani, the deity he served as oracular medium, as they would find an ancient treasure buried there.[47] By rejecting idolatry and exposing their *ayllu*-based observances, these priests struck hard at the Andean foundations of the authority don Rodrigo and other duplicitous *curacas* exercised. Their actions were radical and held no hope that a better *curaca* might succeed him. Instead, these priests tried to topple *ayllu* authority's ritual edifice once and for all. That such desperation could exist at the heart of a materially thriving ancestor cult shows that we must assess such institutions' viability in other terms. The rift between don Rodrigo and Carhuachin was essentially about political solidarity. By disparaging Carhuachin's priestly ability yet repeatedly asking him to do rituals for him, and then not paying for them, don Rodrigo eventually crossed the line. When he, don Cristóbal, Carua Capcha, and Menacho used idolatry charges against *ayllu* priests to attack each other but still wanted internal legitimation through those same rituals, their power struggle violated the commitment to mutuality that conditioned *curacas'* authority. Such cynicism from above could hardly inspire loyalty from below and put the *ayllu* on shaky moral ground. Yet unlike his fellow *curaca* Pomacondor in nearby Pomacocha six years earlier, don Rodrigo was not yet ready to abandon *ayllu* rituals outright, even if he treated them instrumentally. This attitude seems to have undermined and infuriated Carhuachin, who challenged don Rodrigo by denouncing the rituals himself. In both cases, however, the real question was these *curacas'* allegiance to their *ayllus*. Thus, these cases from Canta dramatically anticipate the eighteenth century's generalized crisis of ancestral authority, and show that the issue of *ayllus'* internal solidarity had already begun to simmer a century earlier.

Cuzco, 1596–1697

The Aymaraes–Cotabambas area, now part of the Peruvian Department of Apurímac but then part of Cuzco, is already familiar to us as the scene of the Moro Oncoy (1590) and Yanahuara (1596) movements that followed the Taqui Oncoy. Both featured separatist prophets who acted on mountains, and identified them as places of proper ancestral worship, as opposed to Christian towns in the valleys. Recall that the Yanahuara prophet convened people from the towns of Piti and Maras atop a mountain, where he exhorted them to destroy a cross and erect an idol in its place. Thus, no matter how important the opposition of mountain to valley town may have become, the 'idol' remained the focus of ancestral worship: as of 1596, mountains had yet to supplant idols in this regard. Arriaga (1621: 226–7) briefly characterizes Aymaraes, Cotabambas, and Condesuyos as 'an uncultivated jungle where it seems that the faith of Jesus Christ has never been preached.' Apparently the area escaped extirpation early in the seventeenth century, but could have experienced it under Bishop Ocón during the 1640s (see Villagómez 1649: 274).

This relative exemption from extirpation campaigns makes a case of 1697 from Haquira in Cotabambas particularly interesting (Gose 1995b). Neighbours denounced an *indio forastero* named Pasqual Haro for trying to increase his herds, ensure his work's success, and cure the sick through sacrifices of llamas, corn beer, coca, *sanco*, rock scrapings, and coloured powders. He prepared these offerings on various surfaces: gunnysacks, carrying cloths (*llicllas*), straw, and a stone 'altar,'

complete with a cross and images of the Virgin and San Juan, to intercede with the mountains who received the sacrifices. Several local
mountains figured in the trial, but Haro had particular affinity with one
named Asoca, whom he addressed as 'lord' (*apo*). He also invoked and
sacrificed to more distant and influential mountains like Salcantay and
Qoropuna. One witness described Haro as an oracular medium for several local mountains, and someone who helped and advised other
householders in making offerings to them. Besides curing the sick, he
kept toads, which he allegedly used in witchcraft. Once he diagnosed
a sickness as the result of a *huaca* entering a person's body, but the
reference is clearly to Mount Asoca. The document mentions no other
huacas, nor any ancestral mummies, monoliths or statuary, and is
remarkably modern in its ritual vocabulary and sensibility. Mountains
are the only deities the document records, and they clearly dominate
the local pantheon.

One hundred and one years after the Yanahuara movement, mountains were no longer merely sites of ancestral observations but their
primary object. In the intervening years, mummies and idols had
apparently disappeared as objects of veneration, and with them, *ayllu*-
based forms of worship. A 1689 parish survey of the bishopric of Cuzco
reported four *ayllus* for Haquira, with only seventy men of tribute-pay-
ing age but over eight hundred women. The Huancavelica *mita* was
killing many men and causing others to flee, as did the *corregidores* and
their forced purchases of goods. Haquira's *ayllus* had once grouped into
larger moieties that formed the parishes of San Pedro and San Martín
de Haquira, but the latter had become so depopulated that it ceased to
have any functional *ayllus*, and the priest of San Pedro called for their
amalgamation (Villanueva 1982: 35–7, 40–1). As *forasteros*, Haro and his
neighbours lacked any local *ayllu* affiliation. His innovative form of
worship reflected that fact: the saintly images and mountain spirits that
Haro and his followers venerated belonged to a more fluid religious
universe no longer organized around corporate descent groups. Outside an *ayllu* framework, they offered the same ritual services that *ayllu*
functionaries typically provided: witchcraft, curing, and sacrifice for
the fertility of flocks and fields. This suggests that Haquira's decimated
ayllus may have been on shaky ground as ritual units, and that Haro
was filling a void. As an unaffiliated practitioner, furthermore, Haro
threatened the local *curaca*, who ultimately denounced him to the parish priest and so initiated the investigation. Instead of reinforcing the
curaca's authority within the *ayllu* format, Haro's services attracted a

personal following of his own, one that the *curaca* quashed with these idolatry charges. Clearly this new form of worship both presupposed and promoted the *ayllu*'s breakdown as a ritual unit, to *curacas'* detriment above all.

This is the earliest clear transition from a mummy- and idol-based ancestral regime to one based on mountain spirits that we have seen so far. Extirpators were probably not responsible for this change, which had already occurred by the time they intervened. Rather, the main cause was the *ayllu*'s reduction to its tributary function and the consequent rise of *forasterismo*. To the extent that it became a purely tributary unit, the *ayllu* could no longer command ritual loyalties, and collapsed as ·a ritual entity. The individual and domestic concerns it once addressed remained, however. New forms of worship arose in their place, and reinvented notions of ancestorhood around mountains and saints. Later, and by different routes, the same transformation was to occur elsewhere. *Ayllu* collapse and residential mobility were nonetheless key processes by which new forms of worship could spread. As both colonialism and indigenous responses to it promoted migration, they not only undermined loyalty to *ayllus* but promoted interregional communication and new social bonds. This case gives the first solid glimpse of what that new synthesis would be.

Huamanga–Huancavelica, 1656–1811

The Huamanga–Huancavelica region also provides relevant information on the transition in question. No elaborate accounts of mummy worship in the region have yet surfaced, but Arriaga (1621: 225–6) summarizes a letter from Teruel that indicates it existed and was similar to such practices in other Andean regions. Apparently offerings to mummified dead continued there until at least 1709 (Millones 1984: 142). In short, mummies appear to have been the primary ancestral form in Huamanga, as elsewhere. Nonetheless, the term *guamani*, which was later to refer to mountain spirits, appears in several early colonial documents, most commonly to designate an administrative unit of the Inca state (Jiménez de la Espada 1965: 166, 181). Guaman Poma echoes this usage, but once deploys it as a subcategory of *huaca* (1615: 282). Albornoz mentions a *guamani guaca* as a perforation on a hillside (Duviols 1984: 207), probably a *pacarina*. In a document of 1564, *guamani* appears in a list of venerated entities alongside *huaca* and idol (Yaranga 1978: 168). Its terminological distinction from these other categories is a useful clue. That same document mentions a mountain named Gua-mani Tinca, and at least two Cerro Guamanis appear in early colonial documents.[48] None appears to have been the object of a cult or associated with anything like a contemporary mountain spirit, however. Moreover, since people called only some mountains *guamani*, the term clearly did not refer to mountains generically. Like its modern synonym *apu*, *guamani* probably referred to ancestral mummies at this stage, entities that could give mountains their names should they house them.

A case of 1656 from an unspecified town in Huamanga already portrays a different religious landscape: 'in this province of Vilcas where some great traces of idolatry were confirmed and discovered in a parish where an Indian pretended to be Santiago and told those of his town to absent themselves from it, because it was to be wiped out and destroyed, at which everyone abandoned it, as their priest informed me, and went to a mountain to offer sacrifice.'[49] Clearly the ongoing seventeenth-century struggles over *reducción* underwrite this outburst, but it also occurred in a late- or post-extirpation setting, with few or no mummies, 'idols,' or pre-Columbian settlements left to articulate an alternative. When these idolatrous traditional foci were lacking, the mountain emerged as the site and perhaps even the object of an activist devotion that aimed to destroy the valley town. Whatever this mountain's status may have been within a *pacarina*-based ancestral regime, its opposition to the valley town was clearly what mattered in this context. This mobilization confronted *reducción*'s morally dichotomized geography, which presented the town as a beacon of Christian righteousness and the surrounding landscape a repository of idolatrous evil. It clearly opposed the church-based settlement, but not through an unreconstructed idolatry. Rather, its leader proclaimed himself Santiago and operated from the mountain, asserting the Christian status of the despised periphery but also its power to destroy the centre. Certainly older moiety-like distinctions between highlands and valleys, *llacuaz* and *huari*, where also relevant here: the scenario recalls Pariacaca's destruction of valley towns with his highland arsenal of rain and hail. By subsuming these powers, Santiago could simultaneously threaten from the periphery and revindicate it as Christian. Elsewhere in the Andes, miraculous apparitions of Christ achieved this second end less militantly (Sallnow 1987: 89–90). In short, we are dealing with a transformed and evolving idolatry here, one that was coeval and intertwined with missionary Christianity, and contested its stigmatizing of the undomesticated landscape in terms that were partially Christian.

A final late case comes from Lircay and dates to 1811 (Pease 1974: 230–52). The document is an inquest into native idolatries, initiated by complaints from the subintendent and the local priest. On November 11, they alleged that an eighteen-year-old '*cholo*' named Pedro Alanya and his lame mother descended from their highland herding estate accompanied by more than fifty Indian and *mestizo* followers, playing drums and cornets, singing and dancing. They approached the sacristan and demanded that he let them into the church so Alanya could preach from the pulpit as (or in the name of) Santiago and perform the Eucharist for him. The sacristan sent word to a resident military captain asking him if he should comply: in response, the captain came with a militia to make arrests. Subsequent investigations revealed that Alanya's followers had accompanied him to Lake Canlalay where his assistants had sacrificed twelve guinea pigs and offered maize to the lake, circumambulating its shores. Then they filled their flasks with its waters and brought them to town, hoping that this act would make Santiago send rain and ensure a prosperous agricultural year. As the multitude descended towards town, they stopped at Tauricay, where Santiago addressed them through Alanya: 'Be here, all of the towns and wait for me, order the church to be opened, where you should wait for me with wine.' At this point, the captain apprehended them.

Starting before All Saints' (November 1), they had done similar acts by night at the lake and placed a cross on Mount Lachaqui. Instead of descending to the church, however, they went to a house in town, where they prepared a ritual table (*mesa*) with a cross at its head. There they offered coca, wine, flowers, and various raw and cooked grains to petition rainfall from Santiago, who spoke through Alanya as medium (*pongo*) in the darkened room, saying, 'My children, return to God. You must sow [a field] for my medium (*pongo*) and give him the fruits that you reap from it. Should you not do so, you will not be worthy of my grace. You must also pray for my old mediums. In the time of Vicente Alanya, they burned me so I went to Colcabamba. Now I return so that you can return to earlier times, and will no longer suffer from hunger' (Pease 1974: 238). According to another account, Santiago said, 'My children, the time has come to renew the past, since they burned me in the times of Alanya, the years were barren with frosts and hail. I have now returned to Colcabamba, are you all here?' (Pease 1974: 235). The assembled then knelt and recited the credo and the Lord's Prayer three times. They then left to 'irrigate' the town's plaza and council building (*cabildo*) with the lake's waters. Once they had returned to the house,

Alanya decreed that Santiago had consumed the offerings. They extinguished their candles to convoke a seance of mountain spirits (*guamanis*), several of whom arrived amid the sound of flapping wings, and asked for wine and other offerings before announcing (again through Alanya as medium) that they would return at dawn. One account of the night's proceedings had Santiago requesting the host and wine, but another specified that the offerings to Santiago were really for the mountain spirits. A third said the mountain spirits came to confer with the saint. Apparently these entities worked in concert and were not rigidly distinguished in Alanya's seances.

The authorities expressed horror at these acts, which they considered superstitious and idolatrous. They sentenced several participants to thirty lashes, and Alanya to an additional three months' labour in the mines. He broke his manacles and escaped, however. As Sala i Vila (1990) argues, we must place royal functionaries' exaggerated portrayal of this event as an uprising in the political context of the late colonial period, in which they would interpret any rural plebeian or Indian mobilization as seditious. Nonetheless, the specific concern was 'to extinguish the superstitions of these idolaters, both Indians and Spaniards, who have conspired in this execrable evil' (Pease 1974: 230). Despite its recourse to the Extirpation's language and judicial procedures, this case contrasts notably with its seventeenth-century predecessors. Catholicism is clearly integral to the offending practices, and only the prosecuting authorities attempt to distinguish the two as separate and incompatible traditions. Alanya was no separatist. If he competed with the Church at all, it was only over material support and authorization for his priestly activities. Whereas Santiago's earlier medium in Ayacucho wanted to destroy the valley town from a mountain top, Alanya wanted to preach in its church and irrigate its plaza. In his vision, the periphery of mountains and lakes did not oppose the town centre as idolatry to Christianity. Rather, the circulation of water, simultaneously understood as the gift of the mountain spirits and the grace of Santiago, connected them. The saint had assumed the ancestral function of ensuring agricultural fertility. When Vicente Alanya (Pedro's father?) was his medium, one of the saint's manifestations, presumably an image, was burned, so he abandoned the community, leaving it sterile. The younger Alanya hoped to bring the saint back and secure its beneficial presence with these observances. Far from proving the persistence of idolatry, this shows the extent to which Christianity had subsumed the ancestors' traditional role.

Arequipa, 1671–1813

Perhaps the most complete sequence of relevant documents comes from Arequipa.[50] It illustrates both the long-term changeover from mummies to mountains as objects of ancestral devotion and this process's internal vicissitudes. In chapter 5, we discussed Albornoz' early accounts of mountains as *pacarinas* and Omate's explosion in 1600 as a response to this landscape's Christinianization. Let us now turn to a 1671 case from the town of Chichas, with ninety-year-old Diego Vasuaio as the primary accused (Duviols 1966). Vasuaio was the priest and oracular medium of Sorimana (Solimana), a stone figure at a place called Canjirca at the foot of a snow-capped mountain also called Sorimana. He described Sorimana as having 'created the earth and everything else,' and admitted to invoking the idol for food and life, while washing its face with corn beer and making burnt offerings of fat so that it would talk. A one-hundred-year-old woman named Angelina Vancuipa frequently joined him in these ministrations and made clothes for the idol, which they renewed at specific times of year, including just after Corpus Christi. When threatened and flogged, Vasuaio revealed the idol's whereabouts, but a team of extirpators could not find it there. Ultimately Vancuipa's son turned it in. Vasuaio then disclosed another twenty idols in Angelina Vancuipa's possession, and helped find them. Another of the accused, Pedro Vanatuma, described making sacrifices to the idol Vampuvilca in an old town on Mount Urupampa. He also sacrificed to other deities, mostly on mountains, whom he described as *criadores* (creators, nurturers) of specific people, and helped others offer figurines to their *criadores* to increase their herds. A succession of witnesses presented similar testimony, until finally Angelina Vancuipa appeared before the inquiry. She confessed that a *curaca*, long since dead, designated her to make clothing and corn beer for Sorimana's idol, and that two other women sometimes accompanied her and Diego Vasuaio when making offerings to that deity, although one of those women kept another idol.

This document suggests that in 1671, *ayllu*-based ancestor worship still prevailed around Mount Solimana, which later became one of the more important mountain spirits in the southern Peruvian Andes (see Gose 1994: ch. 4). Sorimana's idol was clearly that deity's principal embodiment:[51] its seasonal changes of clothing recall the treatment ancestral mummies received in Cajatambo. Although not identified as such, the mountains in this document are *pacarinas*, not ancestor substitutes. In Sorimana's case, mountain and idol share the same name, but each had a separate name in the other cases mentioned. Thus, people distinguished deities from mountains, and when their names coincided, they named the mountain after the deity, not vice versa. No mummies figure in the document, but the idols described as *criadores* throughout the document were clearly ancestral in character, and their devotees treated as them as givers of life and wealth. Collective worship of these deities may have been in decline, but the idolaters who testified in this document did associate individuals with specific ancestral deities, which suggests *ayllu* affiliation. The fact that a *curaca* appointed Ange-lina Vancuipa to her servant-priestess role shows that a corporate, polit-ically orchestrated form of ancestor worship had been in place.

Another long document from the nearby town of Andagua dates to 1751–54.[52] The principal accused was Gregorio Taco, a prosperous Indian muleteer and political authority, who originally attracted atten-tion for refusing to obey or pay tribute to the local *corregidor*. He appears, however, to have allied with the local priest, the one Spaniard in Andagua who received payments from the Indians. Only when these fiscal matters came to a head did Carlos Tintaya, an interim *curaca* look-ing to dislodge Taco, charge him with idolatry. These charges quickly subsumed the unruliness that Taco's enemies presented as traditional in Andagua, where Indians had already killed a priest and violently confronted various judges and commissioners who tried to collect trib-ute. As it emerged that the idolatries attributed to Taco were general in Andagua, witnesses recycled calls from previous centuries: Indians liv-ing by their fields or pastures should comply with *reducción*, public order required fewer native political authorities in the area, starting with idolaters like Taco, and so on. Clearly offended by the charges against him, Taco maintained his innocence, noting his substantial par-ticipation in confraternity activities and sponsorship of important Church festivities. The documentation ends without a verdict, and Taco requesting liberty to pursue his defence.

The main charge against Taco was that he kept a shrine (*mochadero*) in a cave on a high volcano. There he allegedly sacrificed to mummified pagans (*gentiles*) in traditional clothing when he wished to find an aus-picious day to begin his wool-selling trips to La Paz and Potosí. The tes-timony and material evidence presented during the trial make it clear that many Indian 'families' (also 'lineages' or 'factions,' i.e., *ayllus*) in Andagua had similar shrines in caves on high volcanic mountains. Most contained mummies who dispensed fertility of fields and flocks, or commercial success in return for sacrifices. People treated these mummies as ancestors and the area's original rulers, to whom they owed reverence and sacrificial tribute. Several witnesses mentioned that the mummies had to give oracular approval if their descendants wished to marry, and that they consulted them on many other issues, particularly after Holy Week, when the muleteers began their journeys. One stated that they addressed the mummies as *camaq*, and the shrines' male and female statues as *capachica* and *cuyaqmama*, respectively, although the latter title also applied to several female mummies discovered, and few statues or ancestral monoliths actually surfaced. This witness said that all Andagua's Indian muleteers used a single shrine, also named Capachica, which contained many mummified pagan bodies and a stone *mesa* for their offerings. Others describe offerings prepared on straw, burnt and interred offerings, libations, and blood sacrifice. The document ends by recounting the discovery of many such shrines and the burning of their mummies.

That such an ancestor cult continued to exist at this late a date is remarkable. Even the most 'traditional' areas of Cajatambo and Checras had lost most or all of their mummies by 1725 and replaced them with stone monoliths. In Andagua, no such attrition seems to have occurred. We have seen that the Extirpation afflicted other areas of seventeenth-century Arequipa, but it apparently had little effect here. Perhaps this was because its inhabitants were willing to kill priests, or in Taco's case because they were willing to parlay their wealth into factional alliances with them. Whatever the case, both the *ayllus* of this area and their founding mummies survived into the middle of the eighteenth century. Of course Catholicism had influenced these practices. Ramon Sacasqui, one of Taco's henchmen, called one mummy a 'saint' named Santiago, and another Indian witness likened the cave shrines to chapels. Such characterizations show that even these most persistent of Andean idolaters continued to deny that their ancestor worship was fundamentally different from Catholicism. In addition, certain divinations required blowing powder into the air while reciting the Lord's Prayer. Participants secretly sealed the outcome of other divinations by kissing an image of Christ. This evidence hardly suggests a wholesale Catholic rethinking of Andean ritual, but it does temper the extirpators' habitual vision of irreconcilable differences. Unlike in Cajatambo a century earlier, Andagua's idolatrous priests of 1751 did not define Catholicism as separate from and inimical to their ancestral order, which suggests their relative strength.

An administrative survey of manners and customs from Andagua in 1813 (Millones 1975: 54–64) paints an entirely different picture. In the intervening years, the Tupac Amaru revolt occurred, the Crown installed the intendant administrative system, abolished colonial labour tribute, and Creole agitation was on the rise. Gone also, largely because of these developments, were the *curacas* whose jockeying for position figured so prominently in the Gregorio Taco document (Millones 1975: 62). Most significant of all, the document reports that 'neither do they observe ceremonies with cadavers; but on holidays, some do put meals out in their houses, believing that the dead will come to eat, of which error they are becoming disabused' (Millones 1975: 62). This passage clearly shows an end to the old mummy-focused ancestral regime. Elsewhere, the document specifies that mortuary ritual involved killing a black dog to accompany the deceased into the afterlife, and washing his or her clothes, which kin retained and treated as surrogates in rituals that took place on the *cabo de año*, probably the All Souls' Eve following the death (see Millones 1975: 60). All these details figure in this area's contemporary mortuary rituals, as the next chapter will show. Thus, between 1751 and 1813, the entire corporate structure of *ayllus*, native governors, and ancestral mummies collapsed, and the mortuary observances that once knitted them together atrophied to the modest pattern that twentieth-century ethnographers described.

In place of mummies, a new ancestral order based on mountain spirits emerged. The 1813 document states that Andagua's Indians 'believe that the land, mountains, mines, and foodstuffs have life like them, and rationality and ability to harm or favour them' (Millones 1975: 56). It then describes how people made offerings to mountains for successful journeys, their herds' well-being and increase, and when building new houses for their inhabitants' prosperity. This document is not an idolatry trial, so it does not give further details, but its observations are entirely consistent with the *t'inka* rituals of the ethnographic record. An idolatry document from Yura, Arequipa, dating to 1788,[53] describes similar rites as devotions to the mountains designed to increase herds, and explicitly names them *t'inkas*. The accused, Pascual Mamani, also mentioned that should he abandon these rites, his herds would diminish and he would die haemorrhaging from the mouth, mountain spirits' signature punishment (Gose 1986: 303). This document also describes dramatic oracular performances in which the mountain spoke through human mediums, much as ancestral mummies had done. In short, the Yura 1788 and Andagua 1813 documents bring us to the threshold of the ethnographic record, describing practices that exist in that area today.

Here, the contrast with the Andagua 1751 document is remarkable, particularly since that town lies at the foot of what has long been the ritually most important mountain in Arequipa: Qoropuna. People over most of the southern Peruvian Andes have long seen Qoropuna as the abode of the dead,[54] initially as a *pacarina* and later as a supremely high-ranking mountain spirit, whose exploits figure in oral traditions throughout this area today (see Roel Pineda 1965: 25–6, Gose 1986: 303). The thorough inquiry into Gregorio Taco's idolatries would surely have discovered such an important regional deity if it existed then, so I suspect it did not. Qoropuna had yet to transform, in the local imaginary, from *pacarina* to mountain spirit. Despite repeated reference to shrines on volcanic peaks, the 1751 document does not mention mountains as supernatural or ancestral agents, reserving this role exclusively for mummies. The documents of 1788 and 1813, on the other hand, describe mountains as the unique vehicles of ancestral devotion. It seems impossibly tidy to conclude that a definitive transformation between one ancestral complex and the other happened precisely between 1751 and 1788, especially since the Yura 1788 document suggests that people already considered the *t'inkas* a tradition from time immemorial, not a recent innovation. We have already seen that both regimes coexisted in other areas. Yet neither is there any gainsaying the evidence that a succession of ancestral regimes occurred in Andagua between 1751 and 1813. Crucially, the ethnographic record, which is far more extensive, systematic, and reliable than even the best extirpation documents, simply does not mention worship of mummified ancestors. However gradual and complex the changeover between ancestral regimes may have been, it undoubtedly happened, and Andagua gives us an intriguing regional glimpse of when and how.

Analysis

To explain the ancestral transformations just documented, let us consider, evaluate, and synthesize several relevant factors that have already emerged (see figure 7.2). The Extirpation itself clearly mattered, but just how much does it explain? By emptying burial caves, burning mummies, smashing *pacarina* statuary and architecture, uprooting trees, and toppling crags, the extirpators certainly tried to harass the old ancestral forms out of existence. Duviols (1971: 347–8) argues that the Extirpation particularly affected the mummified dead but drove most Andean cults underground and favoured the landscape as an object of devotion it could not easily detect or destroy. Let us treat this hypothesis as a first approximation and explanatory point of departure.

This explanation's merits are obvious. The Extirpation systematically suppressed older ancestral forms, and created an ideological and institutional environment that favoured change. Whether it can explain the nature of that change, however, is another matter. Repression does not specify why people displaced ancestral cults onto the landscape, or singled out mountains within that domain, when many other environmental features were equally available and indestructible. A more precise explanation would include the constitutive agenda of *reducción* that made mountains the negative counterpart of parish centres. It would also acknowledge the metonymic relation of ancestors and mountains in *ayllu* landscape regimes. Thus, emphasizing the Extirpation and its repression obscures the positive structuring effect of the two cultural orders at work here. Furthermore, when we pursue the idea that ancestral transformation directly correlated with extirpatory repression, a surprising result emerges. This notion suggests that mountain spirits would have arisen first in the archbishopric of Lima's repeatedly inspected areas, such as Huarochirí and Cajatambo. Instead, they appear first in Cuzco, Huamanga, and Arequipa, where the Extirpation was never as systematic as in Lima. This finding significantly diminishes religious repression's explanatory importance. It reveals the limitations of viewing the Extirpation as a historical sieve that mechanically removed idols until only the landscape was left to worship. Ironically, Duviols' hypothesis recalls the thinking of the extirpators themselves. It assumes that Andean people really were idolaters, misguided empiricists fixated on their objects of worship, whose sole creative innovation was to choose the landscape as a new object that the extirpators could not eradicate. As we have seen, however, when *ayllus* lost their mummies to the extirpators but otherwise remained functional, they simply fashioned new ancestral representations and carried on as before. Clearly it was the sensibility behind the objects, and not the objects themselves, that mattered.

To a limited extent, even the extirpators realized that 'idols' were only the tip of the iceberg. For example, Arriaga believed that whereas extirpators could physically destroy movable *huacas* (mummies and idols), they could combat Indians' idolatrous attachment to immovable ones (planets, *pacarinas*, and mountains) only with education in natural science (1621: 202). While he advocated suppressing all 'external' manifestations of idolatry, Arriaga also realized that extirpation could never be a matter of simply destroying idols. It had to engage effectively with Andean hearts and minds; otherwise, continuing ancestral attachments would only generate new idols, such as stone monoliths and mountains. Opponents of the Extirpation's repressive approach articulated essentially this point as the third extirpation campaign began in 1649, causing Archbishop Villagómez significant problems for several years. They favoured a more intensive evangelization with pastoral inspections from the archbishop to stop parish priests' various abuses. A less corrupt and more activist Christianity could defeat idolatry without the Extirpation. Their positive emphasis found many echoes in Andean people themselves.

Despite the parish clergy's tendency to treat mountains as the antithesis of church- and altar-based Christianity, the Extirpation itself inadvertently inverted *reducción*'s spatial message. As Mills (1994b: 104–12) rightly notes, the extirpators' routine placement of crosses in what had previously been idolatrous shrines was profoundly ambiguous. On the one hand, it directly expressed *reducción*'s concentric moral geography: the landscape surrounding church-based towns would engulf them in idolatry were it not for the extirpators' outward forays. On the other hand, extirpation gave those same places Christian resacralizion, and transferred ancestral powers to the cross (see González 1989: 38–42, Taylor 2005: 966–8). Any worship in these places was potentially, perhaps necessarily, double-edged. Over time, crosses' resacralization of parochial peripheries had as lasting and comprehensive an impact on the landscape as the Extirpation itself. When seen from valley towns below, the large crosses on surrounding mountain tops, often called *calvarios* to commemorate the crucifixion on Mount Calvary, became identified with the mountain spirits and promoted their Christianity. Parish rituals moved other crosses from the church out to the fields on the Exaltation of the Holy Cross (September 14) to start the sowing, and from the fields back to the church on the Finding of the True Cross (May 3) to open the harvest. This seasonal movement had several important effects. First, it allowed the peripheral landscape to participate positively in *reducción*'s altar- and church-based regime. Second, it equated crosses and crops, drawing Christianity into agrarian activities that once belonged exclusively to mummified and petrified ancestors. Third, it extended this agrarian significance to crosses on shrines and mountain tops, those traditional and emergent focuses of ancestral devotion. Finally, it linked all these developments to previous acts of extirpation, which special masses and processions commemorated during the Exaltation of the Holy Cross (Arriaga 1621: 255–6).

Andean people themselves consistently pushed Christianity outward from churches into the mountains. They incrementally transposed Christian notions of altar, mass, and sainthood onto reconstructed sacrificial rituals of ancestor worship on parish peripheries. We see this as early as 1631 in Chinchaycocha, a much more elaborate version in Cuzco by 1697, and a virtuoso performance in Lircay, 1811. As they clandestinely took their dead from church floors out to *ayllu* mortuary caves, the latter eventually became Christianized, as we saw in Cajatambo. When baptized bodies entered *pacarina*/mortuary caves, they began to Christianize the landscape through these strategic nodes. This directly explains how Christianity began to animate the land, creating such saintly mountains as San Francisco (Arequipa 1600) and Apuhurco San Cristóbal (Mangas 1662). These early examples foretell the thoroughly Christian character of modern mountain spirits, a subject the next chapter explores. What matters now is that the struggle over burial inadvertently rerouted the communion of the saints away from an exclusive focus on the church altar and extended it across the landscape. As bodies circulated between church and mountainous mortuary caves, they opened up new lines of communication through which Christianity could animate the land. New *pacarina*/mortuary caves arose around *reducción* centres, creating a new ancestral synthesis in which saints and mummies could at last reveal their fundamental commonalities.

A loss of will to enforce church burial further aided these developments. After Noboa's extirpation trials of the 1650s, no further moral panics over clandestine disinterment occurred. Subsequent debates about *reducción* focused narrowly on tribute, and generally omitted religious reform. *Curacas* may still have expected church burials, but commoners increasingly ended up in cemeteries. Reports from the 1740s (Thomson 2002: 123, Serulnikov 2003: 37) suggest that cemetery burial had become the norm in the Bolivian Andes. In 1784, Cochabamba's reformist town council denounced (as a custom dating to 'time immemorial') the disinterment of those buried in cemeteries over the past year. On the eve of San Andrés' festival (November 30), 'Indians' arrived at the graveyards with large quantities of corn beer and dug up the bodies (in various states of decomposition) of their recently deceased kin, adorned them with flowers, and took them to their houses for veneration, dancing while carrying them on their backs so that they might also enjoy the festivities. The next morning, kin placed the corpses in coffins, mantles, and carrying cloths, and gave them a procession over which various priests presided. They then interred the bodies in the church, paying the requisite contribution to the Cofradía de Ánimas, after which they believed the dead were predestined for salvation and able to intercede miraculously for them. Concerned that the corpses might transmit their corruption to the living via gaseous emissions or flies, enlightened witnesses condemned this practice in the name of public health, but also argued that the celebration's mass drunkenness, carnality, and idolatry posed a threat to public order (Gentile 1994: 92–103). Three years later, in 1787, Charles III prohibited church burial throughout the Indies, also for reasons of public health and piety (Voekel 2002: 1). Thereafter, cemetery burial was legally obligatory, although sometimes avoided in practice.

The Cochabamba document gives a radically unprecedented snapshot of popular mortuary customs. Gone is any residual concern to preserve the body as in previous mummification practices. On the contrary, this celebration positively revelled in the putrefaction of the flesh, much to its enlightened critics' disgust. Like secondary reburial worldwide, this practice coordinated the stripping of flesh from bones with the soul's fate and the mourners' bereavement period (Hertz 1960, Huntington and Metcalf 1979). Clearly, Andean people had abandoned the early-seventeenth-century horror that they and their ghosts felt at the body's decay in Christian tombs. Although they retained earlier practices like dancing with corpses on their backs, they no longer valued corporeal integrity. They still wanted church burial, no longer to preserve surreptitiously mummified bodies but to mark a salvation that correlated with the body's definitive corruption. Church burial followed cemetery burial in a larger process. It drew bodies in from the periphery and sacralized them. Arguably this process retained *reducción*'s earlier spatio-moral poles but linked them instead of flatly opposing them. Allowing the periphery to participate in the centre's sacredness complicated their relation much as did the placement of crosses and miraculous apparitions on mountains. Above all, the mingling of flesh and soil completed the land's Christianization in the most literal and materialistic manner. No longer were the two preserved in a state of relative distinction. Thus, as the land became ancestral, it also became Christian: these two processes were inseparable.

All these developments enabled, anticipated, or correlated with the rise of the mountain spirits, yet none adequately explains why mountains definitively and generally replaced mummies as objects of ancestral devotion only in the second half of the eighteenth century. Bourbon colonial officials inadvertently precipitated this breaking point by de-ratifying many hereditary *curacas* and appointing other Indians or *mestizos* in their place. Such parvenu *curacas* often lacked any ancestral connection to the *ayllus* from which they extracted revenue, and generally made no pretence of offering them paternalistic representation in return. Simultaneously, however, the Bourbon state gave tributaries greater autonomy through land redistribution (Spalding 1984: 206–7). Both measures deprived older rituals of ancestral solidarity and dependence of any lingering relevance. By the 1740s in many areas of what is now the Bolivian Andes, *ayllus* were accusing their *curacas* of the same abuses levelled at priests and *corregidores* in the seventeenth century. Allegations of tribute embezzlement were particularly common and effective, given the pressures that *curacas* faced to deliver revenues from their jurisdictions. Yet Indians' discontent was not primarily economic in nature, as they frequently offered the colonial state an increase in tribute in return for removing offending *curacas* and replacing them with locally approved commoner representatives who would protect community interests (Thomson 2002: ch. 3; Serulnikov 2003: 20, 30–1, 112–13, 119, 137–40). While the colonial state largely accepted this revived 'pact of reciprocity' with its tributaries, it did not thereby endorse the larger vision of moral economy in which it was (from an Andean perspective) embedded. It attacked 'corrupt' local officials for tributary embezzlement but also encouraged them by legalizing the forced sale of goods in 1751. A wholesale destabilization of colonial fiscal and governance relations resulted, out of which the great insurrection of 1780–81 arose. While this pan-Andean crisis asserted traditional paternalist values more than those of republican nationalism (but see Maticorena 1974), its emphatic rejection of Bourbon mercantilism still linked it negatively to those European developments.

Following the insurrection, the Crown banned rebel *curacas* from holding office, but the vast majority had been royalists. Those *curacas* who still collected tribute were officially relieved of that responsibility in 1784, but in practice many still did, so the office still attracted interest (Walker 1999: 62–3, 75–7). The Tupac Amaru rebellion definitively ended the institution of the hereditary *curaca* (O'Phelan 1997), however. With it went the venerable tradition of indirect colonial rule and the last vestiges of mummy- and idol-focused ancestor worship in the few areas where it still persisted. In most areas, such ancestral articulations of hereditary *curacas'* internal authority had long since collapsed along with Andean people's loyalty to their ethnic rulers. Thus, the decline of traditional ancestor worship was a leading indicator of the coming crisis in indirect rule. The rebellious sentiments Thomson and Serulnikov document for the 1740s were already dramatically present in Hernando Carhuachin's determination to attack his ungrateful *curaca* in 1656, even at the cost of destroying the ancestor cult over which he presided.

As this crisis of solidarity and political identification between colonial *curacas* and their *ayllus* unfolded, mountain spirits displaced mummies as objects of ancestral veneration. The shift decoupled the ancestral from hereditary political office and so deprived *curacas* of their primary internal legitimation. It signified that they no longer fulfilled the ancestral function of ensuring the descent group's well-being, the fundamental condition of rule in divine kingship. Thus, the repudiation of mummies had fundamental political significance. Instead of disappearing in this crisis, however, notions of the ancestral reformed around new vehicles. As Thomson argues, commoners did not reject ascriptive power as such, only its indifference to community needs (2002: 275). Mountain spirits rearticulated ancestral patronage in an idealized form no longer compromised by the *curacas'* long history of collaboration. They preserved this paramount cultural value by rejecting its previous institutional embodiment and figuratively placing it beyond society, in the mountains. We must not overstate this retreat from the social, however, since the mountain spirits also exemplified emerging social forms. Just as mummies embodied *ayllus'* descent principle, so mountain spirits embodied the geographically based community as the new social unit that emerged from the struggles over *reducción*. Our first glimpse of mountain spirits came from Cuzco in 1697, courtesy of Paqual Haro, an *indio forastero* in conflict with *ayllu* authorities because he articulated a new form of ancestor worship from a marginal subject position. Over the eighteenth century, however, community-based (as opposed to *ayllu*) political forms such as assemblies and delegated or rotating forms of authority replaced *curacas*: these levelling tendencies took an increasingly anti-colonial inflection and eventually led to the great insurrection of 1780–81 (Thomson 2002: 262–8, Serulnikov 2003: chs. 5–6). The rise of the mountain spirits accompanied these relatively democratic practices and formulated them around the landscape. Residence rather than descent became the basis of social inclusion.

These egalitarian developments spawned a non-liberal, nineteenth-century community-based nationalism in the Peruvian Andes. As Mallon (1983, 1995) and Thurner (1997) show, Andean people's sense of civic order derived from participation in communal institutions of self-government. Since whites and *mestizos* rejected such communal involvement, they frequently failed to qualify as 'Peruvian' in Andean people's eyes. Rotating staff-holding authorities (*varayoq*) became the backbone of communal government: they collected tribute, policed and dispensed justice locally, and reported to regional non-Indian political authorities, mediating between communities and the non-Indian state. Although Bolívar's liberal decrees abolished corporate tenure and tributary obligation, the *varayoqs* kept them alive in practice and inflected them with republican egalitarianism. By resisting the privatization of community lands and aggressively paying tribute in money and collective labour to make the state recognize corporate tenure, they contested liberal understandings of the republic (Platt 1982, Thurner 1997: 39). Citizenship was to be based on community membership and to promote egalitarian collectivism, not private accumulation. Tellingly, *republica* became the name of collective labour tribute to the state: this labour epitomized Andean notions of civic obligation and order (Thurner 1997: 30, 34, 51–2). Although superficially colonial and clearly at odds with liberal ideology, this subaltern citizenship universalized Andean commoners' social position and so was a hegemonic bid, one that continues into the present.

This study owes much to these authors for clarifying the political context in which the mountain spirits arose. By showing how mountain spirits helped articulate community-based anti-colonialisms and nationalisms in the Andes, this study also corrects some of their shortcomings. Despite their careful attention to Andean institutions, these authors often treat them negatively and schematically as 'non-liberal' or 'communal' (i.e., non-individual). By deriving modern Andean communities from the colonial *ayllu*'s breakdown as an ancestor-worshipping unit of indirect rule, this study shows where their egalitarianism came from. Commoners' labour-tribute, rotating community service and ritual obligations were not new but an established subaltern component of divine kingship, often recorded on *quipus* (knotted cord records) as Salomon's brilliant study (2004) shows. Their elite counterpart was the duty to protect and ensure prosperity. As *curacas* systematically broke this contract, commoners stopped sacralizing them through ancestor worship and transferred their authority to mountain spirits, who personified the new community-based republicanism. Yet

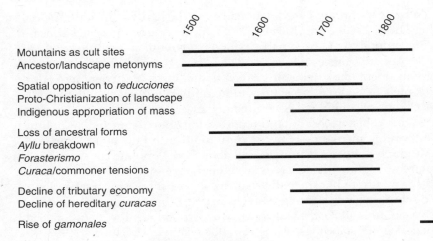

Figure 7.2 Mountain Spirit Analytics over Time

commoners still demanded protection and prosperity from such spirits and the republican states they came to represent. To that extent, Andean people imposed the old social contract of divine kinship on new republican regimes (cf. Scott 1985: 335–40). Yet they also made important changes: the new political imaginary of mountain spirits sacralized subaltern values and practices in ways that mummy worship had not. Mountain spirits appear as blond-haired, blue-eyed men, but they participate in the same political forms as commoners, and so project them onto national life.

We will further explore these developments in the next chapter. For now, the important point is to recognize the seismic political shift that occurred when older forms of *ayllu* ancestor worship broke down and newer forms of mountain worship took their place. Such changes were always a possibility under earlier *ayllu* regimes, thus we have had halting and partial glimpses of them since chapter 5 (see figure 7.2). They became generalized and systematic only in the second half of the eighteenth century, however, when *curacas'* authority over (and solidarity with) their *ayllus* reached terminal crisis. Thereafter, mountains definitively replaced mummies as ancestral deities. This fundamental historical fact vindicates a functionalist linkage of mummy worship to *curacas'* authority. Yet the rise of the mountain spirits and their recycling of localized divine kingship also challenges such a functionalism.

Precisely because it redeployed an older ancestral ideology in new circumstances and to new effects, it shows that the earlier articulation of *ayllus* through mummies did not indelibly fix the meaning of Andean ancestor worship as a cultural practice. Still using the language of divine kingship, Andean people made radical social changes, sacralizing new forms of direct democracy and rotating authority through older hierarchical rituals. Those social changes gave a new and more egalitarian meaning to Andean divine kingship, but also extended its life through the new cultural vehicle of mountain spirits and the continuities with the past that they maintained.

8 Ancestral Reconfigurations in the Ethnographic Record

When mountain spirits displaced mummies as ancestral deities, they systematically reorganized Andean ideas about landscape, mummies, and the dead. This chapter treats the ethnographic record as an extension of that historical process, one that embodied these systematic changes and partly resolved the long colonial struggles documented above. Yet ethnography also records contemporary Andean people's views of their own past. It is not just this history's provisional point of arrival but the living tip of a cultural tradition, one with its own agenda. Since document-based histories and contemporary Andean people both address what is ostensibly the same past, how should we approach their differences? We cannot expect a perfect correspondence between folk and analysts' views. Still, I join many other Andean scholars (notably Wachtel 1990 and Abercrombie 1998) in rejecting their dichotomization as myth and history, respectively. My alternative is to resume the intercultural dialogue on ancestorhood that this study has documented by finding areas of shared concern. Contemporary Andean people still discuss the fate of mummies that once qualified as ancestors. By listening to them and relating their recurring themes and preoccupations to the historical processes discussed above, we can approach culture as a precipitate of history, one that registers lengthy collective experiences like the extirpation of idolatry. More important still, we can discover the understandings and strategies that Andean people culturally institutionalized as they reconstructed their earlier ancestral devotions. The historical record gives us some interesting clues about what emerged from this long process, but ethnography makes clear and categorical what is only faintly visible in the documents: that a long-term transformation of mummy worship into mountain worship occurred. It does so by fleshing out the scant details on mountain worship in the historical record, and by robustly contrasting them with a previous regime of mummies.

Differentiating the Ancestral: Mountain Spirits and *Gentiles*

Contemporary Andean people differentiate mountain spirits from another category of ancestral beings, variously known as the *gentiles* (pagans), *machus* (grandfathers), or *chullpas* (tomb dwellers). These are their most common names for the mummified dead that still exist in mortuary caves and monuments across the Andes.[1] Whether such mummies pre- or post-date the Extirpation is an interesting question that deserves case-by-case investigation. No such question arises for contemporary Andean people, however, who consistently associate such mummies with archaeological remains.[2] They see these mummies as denizens of a past, pre-Christian era.[3]

Let us begin with Fuenzalida's classic ethnographic account of the *gentiles* from Moya in Huancavelica. Moyanos see them as survivors of a primordial epoch, that of God the Father, as opposed to our subsequent epoch, that of God the Son. They lived before the Incas (whom the Sun made afterwards) and were tall and skinny, with blond hair. Strong and hard-working, they invented agriculture and weaving. In these basic ways they resemble the *huaris* and *viracochas* of earlier Andean moiety regimes: hispanicized primordial others. They lived on the mountains and in gullies in oven-shaped houses, and their numbers grew over time since they did not die until food became scarce. In the words of an informant, 'The *gentiles* were covetous. They were witches and did evil to each other. Many sins they committed, and adulteries. They cohabited with their parents. They cohabited with their children. And so [there was incest] among family members: mothers with sons, fathers with daughters, between brothers and daughters in-law, between siblings, between cousins, between *compadres*, with their mothers, with their fathers. There came to be a great many people since they lived like that among family members.' These immoral ways undid the *gentiles*. God became angry and wiped them out. First he sent a flood that drove them to mountain tops, then he scorched them with two suns, one from the east and another from the west: 'Those *gentiles*, God punished them for idolatry, for adultery, ordering two suns to burn them. Due to heat [they died]. Their God was the Eternal Father. But they did not worship the Father, the Sun. They [God and the Sun] punished them because they were getting the better of God: they were adulterers and evil. Many sins. They were the grandfathers, the *awkis* they also call them.' Thus, the account initially concludes that 'this race was consumed' (Fuenzalida 1977: 61–3).

Yet like earlier primordial humanities, the *gentiles* survived despite their defeat by the sun. No sooner does the Moya account describe their demise than it mentions how some lingered on the earth by hiding in caves and *chullpas* (mortuary monuments): 'Even now the *gentiles* are alive. At night, all their bones join together and form a person. They can never die. The *gentiles* even now, they say, arise at night and go to parties. But only until the cock's crow, until two or three in the morning at the latest. After this hour they disappear. They cohabit with young women who have their children. They are born looking just like the *gentil*, with their teeth already in, asking for boiled corn' (Fuenzalida 1977: 64, cf. Flores 1973: 48–9). This proclivity to penetrate contemporary human bodies is not entirely sexual, since people diagnose certain human diseases as the result of intrusive *gentil* bones. Such invasions express the *gentiles*' desire to regain the fully embodied status that contemporary humanity now enjoys. Towards this end, they engage in some initially puzzling behaviour: 'They say that the *gentiles* talk at night in the mountains. They want to talk, they begin but they don't finish. If they finish, they say the moon will fall. When the moon wanes, at that moment they say they begin to talk. Then everyone, everyone hears this: 'iñique ... iñique ... iñique ...' they say. They want to say it but they do not finish. Rather, they say 'iñe ..., iñe ..., iñe ...' and no more' (Fuenzalida 1977: 65). As Casaverde Rojas' ethnography of Kuyo Grande shows, the words the *gentiles* struggle to finish are 'I believe,' the opening of the Christian credo, and if they managed to recite it they would recover their preeminence on the earth and displace humanity (1970: 162, 166). Their inability to profess Christianity therefore marginalizes them during the current age.[4]

Oscar Núñez del Prado reproduces a Q'ero version of the *gentil* myth that lacks overt Christian content, but arguably remains the same story. Roal, the creator spirit and chief of the *apus*, engendered the *ñaupa machus*, who could make rocks move at will and turn mountains into plains. One day, Roal asked if they would like to inherit his power, to which they arrogantly replied that they needed only their own. Irritated, Roal created the sun and sent it on its path, which blinded the *ñaupas* and drove them to their houses for refuge, where they became dehydrated without completely dying. The earth was empty, so the *apus* created a new humanity, starting with Inkarí and Qollari. They told Inkarí to throw a golden bar and build a city where it entered the ground. The first time he threw the bar it bounced off the ground, and the second time it landed obliquely, and there he created Q'ero. The *apus*, seeing that Inkarí had disobeyed them, allowed *ñaupas* to take on new life: their first desire was to exterminate Inkarí, so they rolled stones down the mountain to crush him. He fled to Titicaca but eventually returned to found Cuzco. When his labour was complete, he went about the realm teaching people and passed through Q'ero again before disappearing into the jungle (Núñez del Prado 1964: 275–6). In this version, Roal occupies the role of God the Father and the *apus* that of God the Son or Christ, who creates the Incas,[5] the second iteration of humanity who displaced the *ñaupa machus*. Although not so obviously Christian as the two previous versions, this tale still shares with them two key features. First, it disparages the mummified *ñaupa machus* and does not treat them as contemporary Andean people's ancestors but malevolent denizens of a previous era. Second, it identifies the decisive historical break as that between the Incas and the *ñaupas*, and thus invokes the providential view of the Incas as precursors of the contemporary (i.e., Christian) era. Neither trait makes sense if we view this 'indigenous' version as somehow 'pure' and miraculously free of missionary influence. Instead, we must conclude that Christianity pervades this narrative so thoroughly that it no longer matters whether God the Father and God the Son figure as protagonists or lend their names to the epochs in question. Thus, the Q'ero myth reproduces the same prejudices and periodizations present in other Andean localities. Apparently we are dealing with a widespread and consistent aspect of contemporary Andean culture, one that articulates a broadly shared historical experience central to the self-conception of those who tell it. That historical experience was evangelization.

Collectively these accounts show that Andean people internalized the extirpators' basic teachings decisively, and integrated them into subsequent versions of 'their culture.' Andean people now avoid any mummified bodies that remain in their localities, bodies their ancestors would have venerated. In consigning them to a previous era, calling them pagans and using the vocabulary of idolatry, heresy, and sin to describe their behaviour, contemporary Andean people clearly invoke Christianity to differentiate themselves from this earlier humanity. An informant described this epochal shift to Mendizábal in terms that explicitly recall the extirpation of idolatry: 'Inspectors [*visitadores*] came to examine all of our minds [*interiores*] ... they [the *gentiles*] did not tremble but scratched their heads [and] took away earth from other people's fields and brought it to their own. Whatever. They fought among themselves. This is why the inspectors came' (1966: 66). This passage reads like a memory of the Extirpation, in which conflict eventually replaced idolatry as an explanation of what brought these inspectors. Arguably all these accounts also remember the Extirpation by transposing the extirpators' burning of mummies into the Sun's scorching of the *gentiles*. More important, however, they internalize the Extirpation's perspective. If, as Taylor (1980: 53) suggests, ancestral mummies were the extirpators' *bête noir* and primary object, they successfully stigmatized them to their former descendants. Thus, some contemporary Andean people take offence at the notion, which researchers often advance, that they descend from the mummified *chullpas* found on their landscape (Abercrombie 1998: 117). By rejecting these mummies, stripping them of their ancestral functions, and identifying them with a previous epoch, Andean people conformed to the fundamental requirements of missionary 'conversion': accepting Christianity but also rejecting 'idolatry.' Precisely because we must qualify this 'conversion' scenario so extensively below, it is worth lingering first on how Andean people fulfilled it. They gave up something important when they reclassified their mummies, which previously epitomized everything worth keeping from their past, as malevolent *gentiles*. As we have seen, extirpators did not win this concession quickly or lightly, yet win it they did. This colonial policy's transformation into a fundamental and widespread premise of contemporary Andean culture testifies to their success. Yet it is equally clear that this internalization of the Extirpation occurred in fundamentally Andean terms, through the retention of the past as a subordinate lower moiety (Gose 1996a).

When Andean people deepened their identification with Christianity by rejecting mummy worship, they did not thereby abandon the moiety logic that had earlier organized their polities, cosmologies, and responses to Spaniards' presence. Rather, they rearticulated that moiety logic through Christianity, whose opposition between heaven and hell neatly mapped onto earlier distinctions between 'upper' and 'lower.' We saw this process under way in the Andean appropriation of Santiago and the identification of lightning-worshipping ancestors as saints in chapters 4 and 5, but the rejection of those mummified ancestors compounded and transformed that earlier revision. Whereas earlier, Christianity entered a moiety framework still defined in relatively autonomous Andean terms, later it became the central principle of dual articulation itself, eliminating many ancestral traces that allowed its initial incorporation. Henceforth, Christian concepts and practices that emphasized the opposition to paganism displaced, marginalized, or reorganized dual socio-political organization as the basis of moiety-like distinctions in Andean cosmology and temporal periodization. Christianity became more fully Andean in the process, in contrast to triumphalist Christianizing accounts (Armas Medina 1953, Marzal 1983, Estenssoro 2003), but it also transformed Andean sociocultural dualism, making its continuity across this change less robust than transhistorical Andean essentialisms would have it. Both tendencies are further evident in these accounts.

Fuenzalida's narrative continues by noting that after the *gentiles* died in this judgment, the Inca King emerged from Lake Titicaca and went about opening roads, rocks, and mountains (1977: 66). He established a dynasty of fourteen rulers, but during the reign of the last, Juan Atawallpa, the Spaniards came to seize the Inca's mines. They captured the Inca, who raised a room full of gold and silver as a ransom, so the Spaniards saw his power and had to kill him. The Inca's power did not entirely disappear, however, but went to the *wamani*, or mountain: 'He had more power than the Wamani, because the Inca King walked throughout all Peru. The Wamani does not walk. He has his places. Rather, the Inca King had power. Now, since he is no longer here, only the Wamani inherited his power or all that is left of it. The wamanis guard it. That is why they are worshipped' (Fuenzalida 1977: 66). A comparable narrative (Roel Pineda 1965: 25) specifies that the Inca created the mountain spirits, without inserting this act in the epochal framework that concerns us here. If we can combine these accounts legitimately, the mountain spirits, like the Inca, would belong to God the Son's Christian era, a point to which we will return below.

Fuenzalida's narrator then crucially observes that 'when the Spaniards came they engendered us' (1977: 67). We can understand this assertion in many ways. First, it underlines the epochal distancing from the indigenous *gentiles* discussed above. As Christians, contemporary Andean people trace their filiation to Spaniards, not to representatives of the primordial indigenous past. In so doing, the narrator implicitly challenges the idea that he and his ilk are to be taken for 'Indians' or defined by their putatively indigenous ancestry. Instead, he accurately draws attention to how Andean people incorporated initially intrusive Spaniards as ancestors, both biologically and culturally. This observation obviously takes its significance against a historical background of racist exclusion, in which 'Indian' and 'Christian' were opposed terms. Second, this observation recalls earlier Andean alliance strategies based on reciprocal ancestor worship between intrusive and indigenous groups. Ancestry no longer articulates separatist or racist 'identity' but is performative and oriented towards inter-group accommodation and assimilation such that each group partially becomes the other through participating in its practices. That Spaniards repeatedly failed to admit their own indigenousness did not stop Andean people from claiming Spanish ancestry and defining the current epoch by the succession of Incas to Spaniards, not Spaniards alone.

Perhaps this epochal narrative's most important feature is that it treats the Incas' arrival, not the Spaniards', as the defining moment (cf. Harris 1995: 9–11). The sun that wipes out the *gentiles* becomes the Incas' primary deity. One account names the sun Huaynacapac, after the last Inca to die in power (Delran 1974: 15). In worshipping the Sun, the Incas acted not as idolaters but as precursors of the true faith, for it is the sun as a medium of divine retribution against the miscreant *gentiles* that inaugurates the current era of God the Son. A variant of this narrative explicitly connects Christ and the sun through a figure named Jesucristu-Tatalantix or Tatala:

> Tatala and the Supay-Chullpas were enemies. The Chullpas chased Tatala, a foreign old man, and finally were able to kill him because they were many and he only one. They buried him in the earth and put thorns on top. They waited, then went away. Later they discovered that he had escaped. They caught him and buried him again, this time putting a large stone on top. They waited and waited, but when they left, again he escaped. They went after him. While following his trail, the Chullpas asked some people if they had seen the fleeing old man. These people pointed out the ashes of his cooking fire, and from their appearance the Chullpas believed he was long gone. [Here the teller explains that this is a deceit in which the ashes (*sak'a sunchu*) only appear to be old.] Exactly at this point, the Chullpas become frightened. They learn [or remember] that the old man would conquer them if he got away. They frantically build strong houses, with their doors facing east, to protect themselves from the heat and light of Tatala's fire. Tatala rises into the sky as the sun from the east, and the Chullpas die in their houses, burned and dried up by the heat. To this day, one can see their remains, and the sun, Tata Awatiri, continues to travel across the sky. Some of the Chullpas, however, managed to

escape, by diving under the water of Lake Poopo. These became the present day Chullpa people. (Dillon and Abercrombie 1988: 56)

The references to the resurrection and the (crown of) thorns confirm that Tatala is indeed at least partially equated with Christ, although his age may also suggest God the Father.

Similar mergings of the Christian God and the sun can be found throughout the ethnographic record, and were clearly part of the Catholicism that Spanish missionaries brought to Andean people (Abercrombie 1998: 326). Platt describes Corpus Christi in Macha, where people use traditional Catholic solar representations of the Holy Sacrament in monstrances to confirm the connection between the sun, God the Father, and the body of Christ: 'At dawn on Corpus Thursday the musicians for the Holy Sacrament returned to the church door to play for the rising sun: "Our Father" (tatanchej), "Lord Sun" (tata inti), "Holiest Father" (tata santisimo). As his rays burst over the horizon all doffed their hats and genuflected towards the East' (1987: 160, cf. 140, 149). Cuzco's Qoyllur Rit'i pilgrimage, which happens just before Corpus, similarly venerates the rising sun (Sallnow 1987: 231, 237). This symbolic merging of the sun and the body of Christ derives partially from Corpus's approximate correspondence to the June solstice, when the Incas' Festival of the Sun (*Inti Raymi*) occurred (Gow 1974: 58–9). Contemporary Andean people Christianize the sun that vanquished the *gentiles*, but it is clearly pre-Columbian, and at times explicitly Inca.[6]

Arguably this periodization builds on providential understandings of the Incas from earlier in the colonial period. It explicitly differentiates retrograde *gentil* idolaters from the religiously 'progressive' Incas who followed them, and presents this succession, not the Spanish invasion, as the epochal watershed. The Spaniards have their historical role, but it is not as conquerors. In Fuenzalida's version, Spaniards arrive to complete the triumph over idolatry that the Incas and the Sun initiated, but Christianity, understood as obedience to God the Father, had already begun. Thus, Spaniards succeeded the Incas but also allied with them to define the current epoch as a struggle against the idolatry that *gentiles* personified. Dillon and Abercrombie's version omits the Incas and represents Tatala as foreign, but not Spanish. The tale recalls earlier wandering apostle narratives, and like them it asserts that primordial Andean humanity martyred Christ or one of his Apostles. As Dillon and Abercrombie insist, however, contemporary tellers of this story in K'ulta do not see themselves as descendants of *chullpa* idolaters, and take insult at the very suggestion (1988: 51, cf. Delran 1974: 17). Like Fuenzalida's narrator, they identify with the Christian era, which originated after the episode narrated above.

Even the Chipaya, perhaps the only Andean group that claims descent from *chullpas*, recount their origins similarly. Their *chullpa* ancestors lived before the sun's appearance in a world without colours, which a perpetually full moon illuminated. When the sun rose in the east, it caused a 'judgment' that wiped out the *chullpas*, except those who hid in Lake Ajllata, from whom Chipayas trace descent (Wachtel 1990: 216–17). Then Tata Sabaya led the Aymaras into the area to construct Sabaya's church tower. At night, the *chullpas* secretly came out of Lake Ajllata to help and finished walls on three successive nights, on the last of which the Aymaras tried to surprise and capture them. They caught only one and tried to interrogate him, but he did not speak their language. So they let him go with a string tied to his leg, and traced him to his hiding place in Lake Ajllata. The following night, the Aymaras captured and baptized all the *chullpas* there. For helping them construct their church tower, Sabaya's four Aymara *ayllus* offered the *chullpas* four different mountains. When the *chullpas* abandoned them and returned to Lake Ajllata, the Aymara fished them out again. So they migrated south and established the Capilla Perdida, before settling in Santa Ana de Chipaya, where they founded the Torre Mallku, a church tower of their own (Wachtel 1990: 220–1). This story differs from previous versions by depicting the Aymara, not the Incas, as Christianity's indigenous agents and those *chullpas* who survived the 'judgment' as willing converts to Catholicism. Otherwise, it retains all the main thematic emphases of other epochal narratives: particularly that Christianity separates the contemporary age from that of the *chullpas*, and that this faith is endogenous to the Andes, not a Spanish import.

The Chipaya version of this epochal narrative introduces another crucial theme: the founding role of church towers (and mountains) bearing the ancestral title *mallku* (literally 'condor') in the new Christian regime. As Wachtel shows, the Chipaya see Sabaya's Torre Mallku as the 'father' of their own church tower, which is in turn 'father' to the tumulus shrines of Chipaya's eight lineages (1990: 221–2). Wachtel notes that this segmentary chain resembles archaic *pacarinas* (1990: 61), but since church towers define human settlements and subgroupings, it clearly incorporates the experience of *reducción*, and reveals the arrangement to be mid-colonial or later in origin. Better than any other epochal account, this one defines contemporary humanity's Christian origins through these church towers. Of particular interest, therefore, are the lineage shrines. They are up to two metres tall and have a 'mouth' through which their resident deities, also called *mallkus*, receive offerings (Wachtel 1990: 57). *Mallkus* are male deities, but have their accompanying spouse, *t'allas*, who reside in the same monument: lineage rites address both entities. The neighbouring Aymara also have *mallkus* and *t'allas* but they are mountain spirits, the terms' standard referent. Thus, Wachtel concludes that Chipaya shrines represent miniature mountains simulated to compensate for lack of the real thing in their flat, lacustrine landscape (1990: 57–8). The narrative itself underlines this connection: after baptizing the Chipaya, the Aymara of Sabaya send them to four mountains from which they return to the lake and then migrate south to construct their own *torre mallku* and subsidiary lineage shrines. Instead of identifying with mummified ancestors, then, the Chipaya claim origin from these shrines, which resemble both the church tower and the mountains, and reveal an important interaction between these entities in the contemporary Christian epoch. As the abodes of *mallkus*, both are indigenous and ancestral but also register and incorporate Christianity, and so break from the idolatrous *chullpas'* earlier world.

This fusion of mountain and church tower strongly suggests the mountain spirits' Christianity. For some, the affiliation is direct because the *apus* 'were created by God, who put them as guardian spirits for the towns and communities. They can talk to God, and according to various informants of Urpay, "they meet with Him three times a year, but especially during Holy Week"' (Marzal 1971: 250). Salazar Soler's peasant informants corroborate these statements, insisting that God or Christ created the *wamanis* (2002: 183). She notes that they frequently syncretize with various saints, most notably Santiago, and like them are patrons of local communities or advocates of particular activities who act as intermediaries with God. They frequently assemble in groups of twelve, like the Apostles (Salazar Soler 2002: 184–6). Quispe shows that *wamanis* often have an indigenous name and a saint's name, such that Waytarino and Saint Matthew refer to the same entity (1969: 87).[7] Throughout the southern Andes, people equate sacrificial offerings for the mountain spirits with Church mass, their officiants with Catholic priests, and their shrines with altars. Saintly images and *retablos* (altarpieces) may preside over these altars, or crosses of reeds or straw.[8] Quite likely, these affinities between mountain spirits and saints also extend to miraculous apparitions of Christ, since the latter typically occur on mountains and bear the honorific title of *tayta* or *taytacha* (father or little father, see Sallnow 1987: 54), as mountains often do. These shared features implicitly group mountains, saints, and Christ as patrons of the current order. Much indirect evidence also links the mountain spirits to Christianity. *Wamanis* inhabit crosses, usually those on mountain peaks, and chapels above church-based settlements so that people think they own the church's cattle (Isbell 1978: 59, 152–3). To celebrate the Finding of the Holy Cross on May 3, people bring large crosses called *calvarios* that overlook high mountain passes to church for blessing, along with other crosses that guard the fields (Isbell 1978: 141–51, cf. Quispe 1969: 87–9). Andean people often call the mountains directly above valley towns Mount Calvary (Cerro Calvario, see Gose 1994: 83), thereby Christianizing their spirits. Finally, the Q'eros narrative states that the *apus* created both the sun that destroyed the *gentiles* and the new humanity that replaced them (Núñez del Prado 1964: 276). Thus, Andean ethnology broadly supports these narratives' implication that the mountain spirits define the current Inca/Christian order and not a primordial past.

Of course this ethnographic evidence proves only that contemporary Andean people strongly differentiate mummies and mountain spirits, and assign them to different epochs. To argue that mountain spirits succeeded mummies as objects of ancestral devotion, one must still marshal the historical record, as have the preceding chapters. Yet for all their differences, ethnographic accounts of the *gentiles* and this document-based history fundamentally agree with and complement each other. Each asserts in its own way that mountain spirits displaced mummies and established a new religious regime in the Andes. The *gentil* narratives do so categorically, since they consign mummies to a previous epoch that ended in a solar cataclysm. In comparison, the transitions from mummies to mountain spirits that I showed in geographically localized runs of documentation are much more gradual and equivocal. *Gentil* narratives boldly express a repudiation of mummies that emerges only haltingly, with much ambivalence and many reversals, from the historical record. Thus, they condense and simplify a more complex history but also crystallize its outcome more intelligibly than the documentary record. This is no small service, as it articulates a firm cultural point of arrival for the long historical processes discussed here, one that idolatry documents alone do not provide. Conversely, the documentary record allows us to identify the conditions under which the sensibility behind the *gentil* narratives emerged.

Clearly the extirpation of idolatry laid the groundwork for these narratives and provided much of their language and thematic orientation. Yet it also covered its historical tracks and seldom appears overtly in them. Knowing the historical conditions from which these narratives arose greatly aids any understanding of the indigenous Christianity they proclaim. Each perspective therefore complements the other, while retaining its own specificity. Andean social memory and document-based history are not simply irreconcilable, as Abercrombie (1998: 16) suggests but are partially commensurable and can address and incorporate each other, without effacing their mutually illuminating differences.

In their own way, *gentil* narratives join this document-based history in contesting the common scholarly view that mountain spirits are primordial, something that Andean people have always recognized and worshipped. By treating mountain spirits as a Christian innovation, Andean people assert that they are a contemporary phenomenon, not a survival like the malevolent but also somewhat laughable *gentiles*. As an ethnographer who learned his craft during the era of high Andeanism, which routinely asserted continuities between pre-Columbian and contemporary Andean cultures, I value *gentil* narratives' insistence on epochal separation as a guide to history. They helpfully (if inadvertently) reveal the rhetoric of scholarly primordialism, the inappropriately universalized romantic assumption that landscapes embody memories of ancient and enduring pasts.[9] Ironically, this primordialism is itself a recent nationalist invention that tries to eternalize connections between territories and political communities. By contrast, contemporary Andean telluric imagery emphasizes cataclysm and intrusive outsiders' destruction of earlier orders. Mountains represent upheaval, not enduring order, and are poor candidates for the benchmark of a Western romantic 'identity' that Andean people may or may not have maintained over time.

The convergence of purpose between *gentil* narratives and this historical analysis is limited, however, and Abercrombie is right to reject any complete reconciliation between them (1998: 118, 129–32). *Gentil* narratives express only an epochal disjunction between mummy- and mountain-based religious regimes, and suppress the continuities between them, which are also essential to my argument. Obviously the extirpation of idolatry, which provides the basic historical motive for rejecting the *gentiles* as ancestors, also explains this suppression of religious continuities with their epoch. In articulating these continuities below, I do not aim to violate Andean peoples' own sense of their past or to reinstate a static view of Andean culture within the scholarly community. Rather, I argue that the missionary experience subsumed and transformed earlier versions of Andean culture, which became new but remained recognizable and traceable to a renounced past. All living traditions practice such critical editing and rearticulation, which, far from negating continuity, actually allow it. As we turn to the ethnography of mountain spirits, I will further consolidate this argument by exploring their similarities and differences with earlier mummy cults.

The Ethnographic Mountain in Historical Perspective

Modern mountain spirits invite comparison with earlier *pacarinas* because both define landscape regimes. *Huaris'* upward burrowing or *llacuazes'* downward deposition by lightning strike created mountains as *pacarinas*. Mountains contained access points to both the celestial and the subterranean world, without connoting one more than the other. Contemporary mountain spirits continue to mediate between the subterranean and the celestial, but these domains' coding changed significantly under Christianity. The celestial realm became heaven or *hanaq pacha*, place of God and the saints. The subterranean or interior world (*ukhu pacha*) became hell, place of devils and demonically inspired ancestral deities and, of course, the *gentiles*. As the evaluation of these realms shifted, mountains could no longer remain neutral in their mediating role. To be morally acceptable, they had to emphasize their heavenly connections, and so allied closely with Santiago, whom Andean people recast early in the colonial period as a thunder and lightning deity (Silverblatt 1988). They also had to downplay mountains' infernal connections, and did so by focusing on the upward-facing surface of the earth, not perforations leading into it. The result was a relative 'sealing-off,' in which people emphasized mountains' surfaces and profiles on the horizon over their lingering conduits to the interior world. This alteration made mountain spirits into scalable entities on the divisible surface of the earth. Their height emerged as a basic hierarchical attribute in relation to other mountains. Finally, their silhouette against the sky gave them a unitary character. All these surficial features are key to the modern landscape regime of mountain spirits, and distinguish it from earlier *pacarina* regimes, in which perforation was the corresponding emphasis.

Nonetheless, similarities between these regimes persist. The landscape's segmentary subdivision remains, although altitude articulates it, not ancestral journeys. Contemporary Andean people allow that mountain spirits live inside their mountains, and thus that they traffic with the demonic interior world. They may also state that underground tunnels connect various distant landscape features, much as they did in *pacarina* narrative's subterranean ancestral journeys. Their alpacas emerge from springs or caves (sometimes called *paqarinas*) and graze in swamps because they want to return to them.[10] Such continuities pointedly exclude ideas about human origins, however, and therefore only underline the massive changes that occurred in relations between ancestors and landscape. As the last chapter argued, *pacarina* and mountain spirits landscapes are far from identical: the identification of ancestral 'lord' and landscape in the mountain spirit is an innovation that became generalized only after the mid-eighteenth century.

Mountain spirits have other manifestations that build on this primary identification with the landscape. They may inhabit stone cairns and wood or straw crosses that crown mountain tops and accentuate peaks as mountains' defining feature (Isbell 1978: 152; Mendizábal 1966: 68, 71). Certain accounts identify the coarse *ichu* grass that grows at high altitudes as another embodiment of the mountain spirit.[11] Others stress his association with wild creatures: people say that foxes are his dogs, pumas his cats, vicuñas his mules, skunks his pigs, eagles his chickens, and so on (Morote Best 1956: 293; Salazar Soler 2002: 179). By living above and beyond human settlements, consorting with wild animals, and above all in his forays as a wild bull from the mountain's interior, the mountain spirit reveals himself as undomesticated (Harris 1980: 80; Gose 1994: 217; Salazar Soler 2002: 178). Earlier Andean ancestors inhabited tomb-communities above their living descendants' settlements (Isbell 1997: 264), whereas contemporary mountain spirits live farther outside society. This expresses their historical marginalization, but also underlines that their power is unpredictable and escapes human control: features that set it apart as extra-mundane, even sacred. As master of a wild vitality independent of human stewardship, the mountain spirit gives the domesticated world fertility, particularly water, a resource that it otherwise lacks.[12]

Although mountain spirits lie outside human cultivation and habitation, they patronize these activities and channel their undomesticated power into them. Agriculture, in particular, would be unthinkable without the rain that mountain spirits distribute. In many areas, people believe that crosses on mountains' summits or flanks guard the crops as they grow. To inaugurate the harvest, they festoon such crosses with produce and bring them into church. This association between crosses and crops leads to a highly elaborated identification of the crops with Christ, one that asserts the Christianity of Andean agricultural production (Gose 1994: 83–4, 165–70, 186, 227, 229). By participating intimately in this process, and above all by their identification with crosses, the mountain spirits further affirm their own Christianity. Yet they do so from a decidedly peripheral position to church- and valley-based towns, one that the extirpation of idolatry inadvertently but enduringly re-sacralized by placing crosses in such localities. Andean people sometimes call the wild power that mountain spirits offer humanity *niñu*, after the Christ child (Harris 1982: 65, Gose 1994: ch. 5). Apparently they assimilated Christian blessing into an older scheme that identified power and fertility with places beyond agricultural settlements' control, including the horizon and large bodies of water (Gose 1993). Thus, the mountain spirit's power presupposes that he is a stranger to the valley towns established under *reducción*.

Mountain spirits underline their association with high altitude by commonly appearing as condors and hawks. Beyond denoting lordship, many of their titles, such as *wamani* (hawk), *mallku* (condor) and *condor mamani* (condor-hawk), are avian. As birds, mountain spirits clearly belong to the celestial realm, from which they omnisciently survey their earthly territories. Thus, when people consult them in seances, they arrive to the sound of flapping wings (Arguedas 1956: 236–7; Morote Best 1956: 290, 302), and in one locality always address their devotees as 'Christians' (Platt 1997: 201). The mountain spirits' avian forms further link them to the Christian heaven, abode of the saints and God, with whom they are known to consult, and to the Holy Ghost, in whose coming epoch people will approach pure spirit by living as birds (Delran 1974: 15–16; Salazar Soler 2002: 222). This connection is particularly strong with Santiago and Santa Barbara, the Catholic saints whom Andean people associate with thunder and lightning (Roel Pineda 1965: 29; Salazar Soler 2002: 185–8). As Apo Parato's chicken legs showed in chapter 7, Andean ancestors had an avian aspect long before they became Christianized mountain spirits. Their bird forms allowed them to communicate with Illapa, the thunder-and-lightning deity, and act as weather makers then, much as they do with Santiago now. Thus, mountain spirits' avian form articulates two of their most important features: their Christianity and their control over rainfall. By giving these two features a common celestial coding, mountain spirits reconcile Christianity with the ancestors' fundamental role as bestowers of fertility.

As idealized ruler-proprietors who use their power to adjudicate agrarian fertility and their subjects' health, mountain spirits update earlier Andean scripts of ancestorhood and divine kingship. Andean people offer them sacrifices to cure human illnesses and for the fertility of their crops and herds. Building on these tutelary and protective qualities, many accounts identify mountain spirits as ancestors of particular human groups or communities.[13] They do all the important supernatural tasks that ancestral mummies previously did, and so succeeded them not only in title but also in function. Yet they now appear as republican political authorities, whose hierarchies parallel national administrative structures, with departments, provinces, districts, and their respective prefects, mayors, town councils, and aldermen.[14] People call mountain spirits that 'regulate the health of humans, cattle and plants under their jurisdiction' *cabildos*, or town councils.[15] Thus, they meet in assemblies over such matters as the state of the crops or the mines, land disputes between communities, or the progress of communal labour projects (Salazar Soler 2002: 175–6). In Yura, rotating communal authorities possess staffs that they sacralize and conceptualize very much like mountain spirits. Only by hearing mass is their power activated, however, and titles such as 'young Viracocha' include them in the history of posthumously Christianized ancestors recounted above (Rasnake 1988: 217–24). The link between the mountain spirits and communal Christianized ancestral authority is therefore particularly close, and extends into support of communities' claims to the land against the depredations of *haciendas* and mining companies (Gose 1994: 240–4). By rearticulating ancestral functions around communal assemblies and town councils, Andean people gave the mountain spirits a democratic inflection that mummies lacked. This shift directly registers the historical overturning of *curacas'* local rule discussed in the previous chapter and consigns it to the epoch of the *gentiles*. Thus, the mountain spirits deeply express Andean society's democratic transformation from the late colonial period onward: they not only arose in that process but consolidated its institutional and cultural outcome. They represent a specifically republican form of Andean divine kingship, not just a specifically Andean form of republicanism.

The mountain spirits' tutelary relation to community-based democracy has limits, however. When they take human form, it is usually as a *gringo* or a *misti:* a man with white skin, blond hair and blue eyes.[16]

Some accounts further specify that he is tall, thin, has long hair and a beard, rides a white horse, wears silver spurs and a vicuña wool poncho or the clothes of a *hacendado* (powerful land owner).[17] These guises of racial other and class enemy complicate the mountain spirits' status as a collective representation of Andean communal democracy. Yet they are also relative, since mountain spirits may be female and indigenous, particularly attractive or ferocious women who present a more Andean but equally predatory face of power.[18] As white males, such spirits have splendid palaces inside their mountains, furnished in gold and silver, with many riches, sometimes including livestock and fields.[19] They reputedly take women from their territories into these palaces to live with them as concubines, and men to serve them as labourers.[20] The mountain's interior produces precious metals, sometimes organically like growing potatoes and other times industrially, through machines that extract them from sacrificial offerings (Earls 1969: 70). Using vicuñas as pack animals, the mountain spirits deliver these metals to other higher-ranking mountains: this tributary allegiance establishes their hierarchies, which ultimately finance the government in Lima. Intense rivalries also exist among different branches of this hierarchy. One group of mountains may despoil another through mining.[21] Paradoxically, then, the mountain spirits appear as the very white *hacendados* and miners against whom they also protect their Andean descendants.

That Andean people maintain an ancestral relation with such white oppressors seems to embarrass many modern commentators. They either ignore it entirely when discussing Andean racial formation (Weismantel 2001) or invoke the theory of ideology to dismiss it as alienation or false consciousness (Zorilla 1978: 123; Ansion 1987: 134). Sometimes it may have been either, but as yet no detailed ethnographic study shows exactly how. Meanwhile, much evidence proves that Andean people repeatedly extended their ancestral relation with mountain spirits into political struggles over the land, using them to articulate successful alliances with the state and regain land lost to *hacendados* (Gose 1994: ch. 8). In these and more routine agrarian contexts, Andean people clearly relate to mountain spirits as ancestral advocates, and do not worship white domination through them. Yet the mountain spirits are ostentatiously white, and it would be equally problematic to view their power as merely analogous to that of the white landowners they resemble, but not substantively connected to it. Such structuralist approaches misconstrue the politico-symbolic processes underlying the mountain spirits, who act as idealized intermediaries precisely because they participate simultaneously in the powers of whiteness and the agrarian world so commonly racialized as Indian. By embodying the state's 'alien' power and making it available to Andean commoners, mountain spirits act as their ancestral protectors. That the mountain spirit is both white and the 'Indians'' ancestor is, for these analysts, an insuperable paradox. We can overcome it, however, by recognizing that no racially essentialized notion of 'identity' underwrites mountain spirits' appearance as white political authorities. A different dynamic is at work: Andean people invoke the image of these white political authorities only to subject them to their own forms of sociality, and thereby ideally remake them into a power that is no longer alien, one that they can live with (Gose 1994: 243–4). The history discussed above adds several levels to this argument.

The most obvious is that Andean people have long given ancestral status to intrusive outsiders. This was the standard strategy by which the conquered made peace and coexisted with conquerors (Duviols 1973). By incorporating them into local forms of sociality, indigenes hoped to domesticate them and convert relations of conquest into relations of agrarian complementarity, but also to participate in and even appropriate intrusive power through reciprocal ancestor worship. Very similar strategies characterize contemporary Andean peoples' relation to their mountain spirits, through whom they assert claims to land, inclusion, and recognition from the nation state. A second point is that the early missionary effort reinforced these strategies and so gave them a degree of intercultural validation. Spaniards saw wandering apostles in Andean ancestral narratives, and represented themselves as sons of Viracocha. To this extent, they conformed to Andean norms of reciprocal ancestor worship, although they violated them in almost every other way. In the process, however, they inadvertently whitened and Christianized Andean ancestors, a move that native peasantries and intellectuals were already exploiting by the early seventeenth century. Beyond these Hispanic features, Andean people also gave their ancestors newly relevant cultural skills. Arriaga mentions the belief that mummified ancestors could act as lawyers (1621: 202) for their descendants, one that made litigation in colonial courts the occasion of extensive sacrifices and oracular consultations (Duviols 1986: 144, 165–6, 176, 208, 228). When Spaniards blocked this ancestral transformation by refusing to baptize mummies, Andean people eventually invented mountain spirits, new ancestral forms that incorporated the necessary revisions. Andean people affiliate with the contemporary order, not the *gentiles*, precisely because they have an ancestral relation to mountain spirits who are white and Christian. From a long-term perspective, then, the mountain spirits continue traditional Andean strategies of incorporating the other as ancestor to promote intergroup accommodation and empowerment.

Nonetheless, the various historical documents reviewed in the preceding chapter pointedly do not specify that the emerging mountain spirits were white. Only in contemporary ethnography does this feature emerge. If people already thought of mountain spirits as rich white gentlemen by the late eighteenth century, the idolatry documents in question fail to report it. Probably the emphasis on whiteness emerged only in republican times, after the relevant documentation ends. During this period, scientific racist ideologies found their way into the Andes and displaced earlier forms of inquisitorial racism, whose primary concern was not skin colour but religious orientation. With the colonial state's collapse and the rise of republicanism, a new form of rural domination called *gamonalismo* emerged, which reasserted 'Indians" servile and tributary status and often deprived them of their land. These developments generally occurred illegally in isolated rural areas, but took form and justified themselves under modernizing racist ideologies, which presupposed 'white' superiority. Since mountain spirits appear specifically as *hacendados* or *gamonales* dressed in riding gear and mounted on horses, they probably did not take on these traits until the nineteenth century, when such figures became salient in Andean people's social experience.

By claiming an ancestral relation to such figures, Andean people refused to relinquish their claim to the otherwise racializing forms of power wielded against them during this period. Above all, they refused to identify themselves as 'Indian' victims and, fighting fire with fire, staked their own claims to white power through the mountain spirits. Thus, they continued to identify with the present order and struggled vigorously to include themselves in it, repeatedly contesting their difference and subordination in principle and in practice. When Andean people conferred racialized power on their mountain spirits, it was precisely to appropriate them as ancestors, and so to counteract the racializing subordination to which they were subjected. In so doing, they resurrected their proven strategy of incorporating the other as ancestor. Andean peoples' long historical experience of racism gave their incorporative alliance strategies renewed meaning and urgency, since they spoke as pointedly to republican strategies of exclusion as they had to their colonial counterpart. In short, the racial and the ancestral significance of the mountain spirits were not in contradiction but shared a tightly logical strategic relationship.

Inevitably, this reiterated ancestral appropriation challenged the republican meaning of whiteness. Salazar Soler (2002: 175) uses the word 'ashen' rather than 'white' to describe the mountain spirit's skin, which could suggest death more than race. As my introduction noted, indigenous people worldwide interpreted Europeans as returning dead, probably because of their pallid complexions. Andean people also liken white mountain spirits to the dead:

> When he shows himself to people, particularly in dreams, the *Wamani* always appears as a very tall individual, thin and almost emaciated. His skin is pale and parchment-like. He has long brown hair which falls down his back over a vicuña-wool poncho. His teeth, which stick out of his mouth permanently, make people say that 'the Wamani always smiles, even when he is furious'.
>
> This description has the peculiarity of corresponding quite exactly to that of the pre-Hispanic mummies that are interred in various places in the zone (Laiwe, Chanki, etc.), inside artificial or natural caves. If one considers the fact that these funerary sites are all situated on the flanks of mountains known to be important *Wamanis*, and that the *Wamanis* are all linked to descent groups, one is led to envision a 'wamani complex' under the aspect of a religion of ancestors or the senior dead. (Favre 1967: 137)

Here, the mountain spirits' cadaverous appearance signifies ancestorhood, and whiteness seems to mark mortality more than race. More important, these disparate meanings interact to give the mountain spirits their peculiar character as 'foreign' ancestors. To appreciate this subtlety, however, we must first acknowledge that non-European, non-racial understandings of whiteness exist (Bonnet 1998). Only then can we avoid reductive approaches to their interaction.

Favre's observation reopens the relationship between mountain spirits and the *gentiles*. Whereas the narratives discussed above clearly assigned them to two catastrophically differentiated epochs, this account fuses them into a single, continuous ancestral category. Here, the metonymic relation between mountain top and *chullpa* burials appears to motivate the association. Yet this is hardly the only location that the *gentiles* and the mountain spirits share. The mountain's interior, often described as a fabulous palace, is also where the *gentiles* fled from the sun to assume their shadowy life in the current era. Like their caves and springs of refuge, the mountain spirit's abode belongs to *ukhu pacha*, or the interior world. Missionaries successfully equated this domain with hell, but it remains a source of animal and vegetable life and mineral wealth in Andean peoples' view. Similarly, its denizens remain crucial to human life despite their demonic stigma. As ancestors, mountain spirits control this fertile inner world and mediate contemporary humanity's access to it. There, they necessarily consort with the *gentiles*, and their orientations interact. Sometimes the mountain spirit succumbs to the *gentiles'* malevolence and acts demonically towards contemporary humanity, but at other times the *gentiles* may adopt the mountain spirits' benevolent ancestral stance and momentarily overcome their habitual jealousy of the living.

Covert rehabilitations of the *gentiles* as ancestors occur in several Andean localities. Allen reports that in Sonqo people generally view mummified 'grandfathers' (*machulas*) as malevolent and satirize them, but admit that their sickening winds make the potatoes grow. They even recognize 'our old grandfathers' (*machula aulanchis*) as benevolent ancestors despite their inhabiting of *chullpas*, probably because these sepulchres lie on a sacred hill. Sonqeños could not agree whether the benevolent *machula aulanchis* belong to the current age or the previous one, suggesting a very real ambiguity. Allen concludes that all *machulas* form a single category composed of both positive and negative elements (1988: 56–9). Oblitas Poblete (1978: 114–15), Casaverde Rojas (1970: 151, 156–7) and Sallnow (1987: 127–8) describe similar configurations. Ansion (1987: 140) also reports that some commoners of Ayacucho view the *gentiles* as ancestors. People even address one mountain spirit as Machula when it receives offerings (Roel Pineda 1965: 26). Since this is the same name that the *gentiles* generally bear in that region, we must assume that these two categories interact or merge here. When Andean people view the *gentiles* positively, they are likely to recognize them as the guardians of precious metals and the originators of agriculture and pastoralism.[22] As inventors of the techniques and patrimony from which contemporary humanity lives, they would qualify fully as ancestors were it not for their hostility to God.

Mendizábal's data from Huánuco go the furthest in merging mountain spirits and *gentiles*. There, people call mountain spirits *awkillus* (paternal grandfathers) and see them as ancestors who protect livestock and make rain. The *awkillus* appear as white-bearded old men walking with canes, but also as prehistoric mummies (Mendizábal 1966: 62–3, 70–1, 77). In an informant's words, 'the mountain is the bones of the ancient ones who are living.' *Awkillus* are pre-Inca pagans: they date to God the Father's epoch, a time 'when there were no prayers,' so contemporary people recite 'Our Father' and they do not. They eventually faced a judgment when Santa Rosa summoned three suns to send them underground; where they discovered the water of life to stay alive (1966: 63–7). Thus, we see a familiar epochal distinction between mummies and mountain spirits: in an informant's words, 'the mountain is the mountain, the *gentil* is ancient' 'from the time of the Jews, from Judas' (1966: 76). To establish contemporary humanity through Adam and Eve, however, God had to make a contract with the *awkillus*, by which they became a 'second god' that requires sacrificial payments: thus, the mountains shake and stop people from living in peace (1966: 69–70, 76). This contract Christianized the *awkillus:* people say they have their own (church) bells that ring during important Catholic celebrations, that they left their own saintly relics, and have their own temples of worship in archaeological sites (1966: 74).[23] Other Andean localities also have *chullpa* churches and saints (Platt 1997: 220, 222).

These associations rehabilitate the *gentiles* but also demonize the mountain spirits (cf. Salazar Soler 2002: 189). Thus, Ansion notes that *gentil* bones imparted a virulently anti-Christian disposition to a certain mountain spirit (1987: 128–9, 142). Fuenzalida's account describes a mountain as 'of the gentiles' because their bones infuse it (1977: 64). Burial helps determine mountain spirits' disposition, as we will see at length below. Yet mountain spirits and *gentiles* interact in other ways. To the extent that mountain spirits inhabit the interior world, they are categorically diabolical. Earls (1969: 67) reports that mountain spirits may be 'referred to as devils and demons, and are associated with notions of incest and filth.' The mention of incest is particularly suggestive, as Fuenzalida's narrative suggests that was a trait of the *gentiles* during their era on earth. Similarly, others report that God and the mountain spirits are enemies (Marzal 1971: 253), that they cannot live together (Gow and Condori 1976: 25), or reject the suggestion that *wamani* ('hawk,' mountain spirit) is just another name for Christ (Szeminski and Ansion 1982: 126). Ansion notes that in many stories the *wamani* is a fallen angel, and some add that *wamanis* were sent to earth for rebelling against God. He further adds that some stories treat them' as gods of the 'ancestors' (presumably the *gentiles*), perhaps because they led this rebellion. Nonetheless, his informants continued to stress that the *wamanis* are also Christian, and in some parts of Ayacucho they differentiated between demonic and Christian mountain spirits to resolve their ambiguous character (1987: 127–9). Similar affirmations of the mountain spirits' ambiguity abound in the literature,[24] and present a significant analytical challenge.

One explanation of the similarities between mountain spirits and *gentiles* might be that they were never as fully differentiated as the epochal narratives suggest. Abercrombie, who has most insisted on these narratives' importance, ironically implies this in arguing that the mountain spirits unambiguously associate with the interior world and oppose the saints' celestial world (1998: 364, 385, 415–16, cf. Harris 1982: 66). If so, the K'ulta case he presents would contrast with all those mentioned above, which give the mountain spirits at least a part-time place in the Christian world of sun and sky. Abercrombie reinforces the notion that people in K'ulta lump the mountain spirits and the *chullpas* together as primordial beings defeated and driven underground by Christianity by contrasting public Christian worship with private worship of non-Christian deities (1998: 375, 384–6, 415–16). As Platt observes, however, Christianity's rehabilitation of the sun as God shows that it did not drive all 'indigenous' deities underground (1987: 169). Even if the *chullpas* and the mountain spirits shared this fate, their distinction within this infernal domain requires further explanation. Elsewhere, Abercrombie gives a structuralist partial answer: the mountain spirits occupy an elevated position in the interior world, analogous to that of the sun outside it (1998: 330–1). He does not specify what (beyond height) qualifies the mountain spirits for this exalted position, but surely it must be participation in the celestial Christian world that height and the sun signify in this cosmology. If so, the mountain spirits would partly escape the interior world's confines. From the historical perspective developed here, Abercrombie's analysis raises additional questions. If both the *chullpas* and the mountain spirits were primordial beings displaced by Christianity, why do the narratives of divine solar vengeance and underground exile focus exclusively on the *chullpas?* Why would people in K'ulta (or elsewhere in the Andes) have developed mountain spirits in the first place if they were just another category of repudiated ancestors?

My preferred explanation of these troubling similarities is that the repudiation of mummies is sincere and categorical, but becomes relative because the mountain spirits hierarchically encompass the interior world and so operate part-time within it, where they associate with the *gentiles* and other 'demonic' beings. Since mountain spirits retain a Christian association with the sky (*hanan pacha*) that *gentiles* lack entirely, however, their differentiation remains primary. They also dominate the earth's surface (*kay pacha*) as *gentiles* once did, but now attempt only in their limited nocturnal forays. Only their shared location in the interior world (*ukhu pacha*) weakens their differentiation (cf. Salazar Soler 2002: 183). In short, mountain spirits operate throughout the morally coded vertical dimension of the Andean cosmos, whereas God confines the *gentiles* to its bottom end. There the two metonymically share many associations as their respective qualities 'rub off' on each other, partially undoing their differentiation in the ways we have just explored. The *gentiles* may influence the mountain spirits to attack contemporary humanity, or to join them in directing the interior world's generative powers to humanity's benefit. These interactions assume each category's primary orientation, however, and so do not neutralize their initial differentiation. Moiety logic, which is hierarchical and encompassing, not the absolutely differential logic of 'identity,' underwrites the nature of this distinction.

Other facets of Andean ethnography clarify this redemptive channelling of the interior worlds' demonic fertility. Platt shows that the Macha value rooted vegetation for drawing life from the interior world and projecting it towards the sky. They attribute roots to other entities from which they wish similar mediations, such as the church tower (Torre Mayku), Calvary shrines, and various crosses in their locality (1987: 145–6, cf. Abercrombie 1998: 333, 343–4). Of particular interest is the Christianity of the entities that connect the inner world (*ukhu pacha*), the surface of the earth (*kay pacha*), and the sky (*hanan pacha*). They participate in the life of the interior world and its devils, but send it upward towards the Sun and God, and so are Christian. Similar conclusions derive from the widespread association between crops and crosses throughout the Andes. My own ethnographic research revealed that people in Huaquirca metaphorically equated the growing maize with Christ in an elaborate sequence of agricultural rituals (Gose 1994: chs. 4– 6). By attributing Christianity to all the things that draw life into this world from below, then, Andean people in effect assert the hegemonic or encompassing quality of the celestial or upper Christian realm in relation to those realms that exist below it. Their heavenly orientation defines these forms of life, not their origins in the demonic interior world.[25] The same holds for the mountains themselves. The upward, 'pumping' action they exert on the interior world morally elevates the forces they traffic in there, although the opposite 'sucking' dynamic may also occur, and characterizes the mountain spirits' worst punishment: their extraction of hearts from living people (Arguedas 1956: 235).

These aspects of Andean ethnography have massive historical significance. Not only do they fully register the long historical experience that this book describes, but they also specifically speak to the extirpators' standard practice of placing a cross on the ancestral shrines they destroyed. As Mills (1994b: 104–12) argues, this gesture of destruction and superimposition was inevitably ambiguous to Andean people. On the one hand, it clearly declared Christian primacy, but on the other, it partially rehabilitated the subordinated ancestors by relating them to the cross. In Andean eyes, the cross not only proclaimed Christian victory but also promised to communicate with and uplift the ancestral forces it vanquished when it grounded itself in their interior world. Thus, the extirpators' actions had profoundly unexpected consequences. Their planting of crosses and promotion of celebrations such as the Exaltation (September 14) and Finding (May 3) of the Holy Cross allowed Andean people to invest the cross with the traditional ancestral function of guarding the crops within the new Christian order. By making the growing crops into a manifestation of Christ himself, they did not domesticate the interior world's uncontrollable forces entirely but at least gave them an acceptable outlet.

In conclusion, these secondary interactions between mountain spirits and *gentiles* do not fully contradict or nullify their epochal differentiation. Mountain spirits conserve a Christian dimension that *gentiles* never had, but share with them an ancestral relation to contemporary Andean people, one that is by turns benevolent and malevolent, and stems from their shared occupation of the interior world, where the ancestral gifts of life and wealth originate. Although the Christian recoding of the mountain into heavenly and infernal components now organizes this ambivalence, it does so according to a moiety logic derived from earlier ancestor cults. In previous chapters, we saw that mummified Andean ancestors never uniformly supported their descendants, but also punished them with sickness or drought for moral or ritual laxity. Descendants therefore interpreted epidemics and other calamities as expressions of intense ancestral displeasure that could call their mutual loyalties into question. Over time, these moments of doubt promoted Andean peoples' acceptance of Christianity. To the extent that the ancestors no longer backed them, then, Andean people could accept that ancestors might be devils, as the missionaries and extirpators claimed. Like all Christians, however, they still had to deal with their faith's rejection of carnal life and wealth, precisely the values their form of divine kingship had celebrated as the most tangible sign of ancestral blessing. That Christianity and Andean ancestor worship took such opposed views of worldly prosperity and fertility was surely a stumbling block to 'conversion,' but it also helped it in backhanded ways. Precisely because they addressed wealth and the flesh, Andean ancestor cults were a ready-made supplement to Christianity. In this sense, Christianity itself, with its characteristic refusals, was a powerful force for retaining Andean ancestor cults. The two became complementary. By rehabilitating the ancestors' benevolent aspect in a Christian form, and partially merging them with the saints, Andean people consolidated this religious alliance or division of labour. To appease Christian sensibilities, Andean people had to disown mummy cults and acknowledge a dark side to the mountain spirits, who could not transfigure the (under-) worldly without continuing to traffic in it. Thus, the mountain spirits' moral ambiguity is both traditionally Andean and specifically Christian in character. By treating mountain spirits as holy to the extent that they are celestial, and demonic to the extent that they are subterranean, Andean Christians spatialized and overdetermined their already firm understanding that ancestral power is ambiguous.

The Ethnography of Death

Ethnographies of death in the Andes also confirm these long-term historical changes. Burial was a major colonial flashpoint between Andean people and their priests, so its contemporary form speaks to those struggles' ultimate resolution. Chapters 4 and 6 showed that mummy cults tightly subsumed mortality within *ayllus*. How did the transfer of ancestral status from mummies to mountains alter mortuary practices and beliefs? Do mountain spirits preside over death as mummies did in the seventeenth century? By attending to these final pieces of the puzzle, we can reach systematic conclusions about these long and complex historical transformations.

Modern Andean people bury their dead in graveyards, usually on the periphery of their settlements. No ethnography that I know of describes interment in raised tombs outside settlements, in caves, or any of the other locations that the extirpators of idolatry mention. Possibly some mummies still found in caves throughout the Andes are colonial in origin, but we have already seen that Andean people do not claim descent from them. Contemporary Andean people seldom if ever claim that they once employed such burial practices, which would amount to admitting that they descend from non-Christians. In short, there is little cultural memory of pre-extirpation interment practices. The same, however, is largely true of the practice of church burial that the extirpators tried so hard to enforce. My own ethnographic research provides an exception: people in Huaquirca told me that the bones in the church's crypt were of earlier generations of notables and *curacas* who paid for burial inside the church (Gose 1994: 119). Otherwise, however, the ethnographic record seems silent about this practice, which probably declined during the eighteenth century. Elsewhere in Latin America, church burial came under attack for reasons of 'public health' and reformed piety starting in the late eighteenth century (Voekel 2002), and we have already seen that similar discourses condemned Andean secondary reburial practices as of then (Gentile 1994). Apparently the Church insisted that Andean people bury their dead in churches only while *reducción* and the extirpation of idolatry prevailed as ideological initiatives. Thereafter, it reverted to the standard Catholic practice of reserving burial *ad sanctos* for the most devout and providing graveyards for the rest. This pattern, in turn, gave way to burial exclusively in graveyards with the waning of baroque piety and the banning of church burial in 1787.

The normative emergence of graveyard burial in the Andes ensures precisely the decomposition of bodies that so offended seventeenth-century Andean people and their carefully mummified dead. Descriptions of contemporary burial note that graves are reused once the living no longer remember the current occupant (Harris 1982: 51; Gose 1994: 119). The excavation of new graves therefore disturbs old burials, sometimes quite dramatically when a pick crashes through a skull. During my ethnographic research, the exposed bones received no special care, and often went into the backfill of the new burial. Over time, the repeated disturbance of older burials ensures that skeletons become broken and disarticulated, as their bones intermix with others. Some commentators suggest that this mixing and remixing of bones collectivizes individual deaths, as does the celebration of All Saints' (Harris 1982: 55–6; Gose 1994: 119, 144–6). Clearly this emphasis is nearly opposite to the earlier keeping of the body intact through mummification. By promoting the corpse's decomposition and dearticulation, Andean people further repudiated mummy worship at a basic material level.

The single most important consequence of graveyard burial is that unlike in mortuary cave or even church-floor interment, the body is no longer ritually available to its living kin. This change therefore precluded the elaborate *ayllu* rituals, described in chapters 4 and 6, in which the living physically interacted with the dead. Since those rituals articulated the *ayllu* as an ancestor-worshipping corporate kin group, their termination was bound to alter it. Contemporary rites diverge significantly from those that the extirpators described in their assignment of all important ritual duties to affines: they notify distant kin, wash and invigilate the body for five days before burial, dig the grave, inter the body, wash those clothes of the deceased that are to be retained, burn the rest, and prepare a meal for the community after burial.[26] During the seventeenth century, each *ayllu*'s ritual specialists performed such duties, and non-kin merely attended a meal that the *ayllu* prepared following the corpse's interment. Such changes reflect the extinguishing of *ayllus* as corporate kin groups and their transformation into egocentric bilateral kindreds derived from individual marriages. Consanguines' loss of ritual control over death also corresponds to the decline of *ayllu*-specific burial caves or chambers. Now interment occurs in a mortuary space that the entire community shares. In effect, the parish supplanted the *ayllu* as the relevant mortuary unit. That Andean parishioners have so thoroughly forgotten these changes proves that they themselves came to identify with the Church's position in the fierce earlier colonial struggles over burial, probably as part of their later colonial repudiation of *curacas* and mummy worship. Modern Andean mortuary ritual both reflects and helps articulate the egalitarian co-residential community that emerged during late-colonial and early-republican times.

The details of death ritual and lore vary from place to place in the Andes, yet also have a widely shared core. Most accounts suggest that Andean people view death as a process marked by a series of separations, of which the cessation of life is only the first. Andean people frequently represent death as the definitive separation of souls whose interaction maintained the person in life. There are varying opinions about the number, character, and names of these souls,[27] but nearly all include an entity called the *alma* (Spanish: 'soul'), which records the physical appearance and moral conduct of the deceased. It is this soul that funerary rites and beliefs address. The living must persuade the *alma*, often against its will, to abandon the body, its kin, and possessions and journey to the afterlife, where it will face judgment. Initially, however, it lingers around its dead body and the places the person frequented in life. In many areas of the Andes, mourners observe wakes of five days and nights, during which they assume that the *alma* is still present. At night, non-kin play divination games that prognosticate on the *alma*'s journey and fate, and may require the players to help it with prayers.[28] All present attempt to keep vigil during the wake to show solidarity with the *alma* and its living kin. They may sprinkle ashes outside the house where the wake is in progress, and inspect them in the morning for tracks, to see which people or animals the *alma* will inhabit as it tries to remain in this world, or which it wants to take into the next. The assumption is that it covets its former possessions and does not want to leave them behind. Similarly, it does not wish to leave its kin, whose extended lamentations and sobbing songs to the cadaver (*aya taki*) during the wake underscore their ongoing mutual connection.

On the morning of the burial, women assemble at the deceased's house and the daughters-in-law lead them in cooking a meal for all who will attend the funeral. Men also arrive, some to dig the grave and others to wash and burn the deceased's clothing at a specially designated stream. Burial and clothes washing occur simultaneously in mid or late morning, and sons-in-law direct both events. When men dig the grave, others bring the body from the house in a poncho and lay it in the ground. In some areas, they imitate a yoke of bulls in their manner of carrying the corpse (Harris 1982: 51–2). The non-kin attending the funeral then throw dirt on the body to fill the grave. This moment of separation makes the *alma* desperate to remain in this world. It may 'seize' one of its living kin, who may try to jump into the grave themselves, and are therefore closely supervised and restrained if necessary (Harris 1982: 53; Gose 1994: 119). If there is not enough dirt to create a small mound over the grave, people may say that the *alma* wishes one or more of its living kin to join it in death (Flores 1979: 63; Harris 1982: 52). The mourners then pass by the grave to offer prayers and final words before retiring to the gate of the cemetery to await the clothes washers' arrival. They pass the time by pouring libations in the name of the deceased. This practice is called 'doing *ayni* [mutual aid] with the dead.' Meanwhile, the clothes washers have gone to the stream to sort the deceased's clothes, removing ragged items and washing the rest. When they are done, they burn the ragged clothes and a selection of the deceased's favourite foods while pouring libations for the soul. Finally, they may take a cord of white-and-black woollen strands spun to the left, and suspend it over the stream, or sacrifice a black dog – acts intended to help the *alma* on its journey to the afterlife.[29] Then the supervising son-in-law cuts a switch and, telling them not to look back, drives the washers back into town at a trot, carrying the sodden clothes. Arriving at the cemetery gate, they remain apart from the other mourners, but all go to the deceased's house to eat a meal that the daughters-in-law have prepared and to comfort the deceased's kin.

Several of these details also appear in extirpators' accounts more than three centuries earlier: the spreading of ashes to look for tracks, five-day wakes featuring divination games, and a sorting of the deceased's clothes for washing and burning, capped by killing a black dog.[30] Today's accounts lack extirpators' descriptions of women calling the deceased's soul from its old haunts at night during the wake. Yet modern mourners clearly expect it to linger similarly, and probably try to expel it more adamantly. These details suggest that cosmological continuities could occur when people did not implicate them fully in death's changing social organization across the centuries. They do not alter contemporary Andean mortuary observances' consistent overall emphasis on expelling the dead *alma*, primarily by burying its body, washing its traces from some clothes, and burning the rest along with its favourite foods. By stressing severance and expulsion, these rites contrast significantly with earlier, *ayllu*-based mummy worship, which not only conserved the body locally in the company of its kin but also the deceased's primary soul or *camaquen*, leaving only the secondary and shadowy *upani* to journey into the afterlife (Duviols 1978, Gose 1993).

Modern accounts of the *alma*'s journey to the afterlife generally describe a long westward trek towards an imposing mountain whose details vary regionally. Sometimes the *alma* passes through Dog Town, where dogs' souls reside and punish human souls that mistreated them in life. Nearly all accounts agree that at a certain point, usually just after this encounter with dog souls, the *alma* reaches a body of water it must cross but cannot.[31] For the living, this may be a mere stream, but for the *alma* it appears as a seething and intimidating ocean. It can pass only by getting a black dog to carry it across or by a suspension bridge that the living construct.[32] These notions clearly rationalize sacrificing a black dog and constructing such bridges over the stream during funerary clothes washing. Once across, the *alma* resumes its journey, climbing the slopes of the mountain whose interior it will inhabit during the afterlife. During this ascent, the soul may pass through Cat Town, Chicken Town, Guinea Pig Town, and Pot Town, where each of these beings further punishes the *alma* for mistreating them in life (Valderrama and Escalante 1980: 258–60; Gose 1994: 125). Finally it reaches the summit, where God or a saint judges it[33] and will deny it entry if it has committed heinous sins such as incest. In that case, the *alma* must live in its rotting body as a *condenado* (condemned one) in this world. Otherwise it passes into the world of the dead, often described as a hot and miniaturized land (Casaverde Rojas 1970: 208; Harris 1982: 62–3), where it remarries and cultivates the land, much as during life. Many accounts state that day and night, the dry season and the rainy season, and power relations between notables and commoners reverse as one enters the land of the dead from the land of the living.[34]

Beyond the varying specific localizations of the mountain of the dead, two attributes emerge as near constants: first, that it is in the west, the direction of the setting sun, and second, that the dead inhabit the interior of this mountain. As Abercrombie (1998: 335–7) observes, these basic coordinates of death refer to the differentiation of the cosmos caused by the rise of the sun and the banishing of the *chullpas*. The dead's descent into the interior world follows the sun's path, and thus remains Christian, but also takes them into the infernal world of those who refused to convert. Let us explore this apparent contradiction. This interior world clearly correlates in part with the Christian hell, so people reclassify *almas* as 'devils' once they arrive there (Harris 1982: 58). Similarly, only children too young to sin escape this journey to the infernal interior world: they ascend straight to heaven (Harris 1982: 63–4; Mariño Ferro 1989: 43). Apparently Andean people took to heart the missionary message that as sinners and idolaters they were going to hell. But contemporary Andean descriptions of the afterlife hardly reveal a place of eternal torment. The *alma* enjoys an afterlife that is existentially comparable to its previous life on this earth. Some accounts add that relations of domination between Indians and *mistis* are reversed, a definite bonus. In the interior world, the meek inherit the earth and may even act benevolently as ancestors to their living descendants. Thus, certain accounts stipulate that Andean people deify their dead, petition them, and offer them libations (Mariño Ferro 1989: 29–30; Gose 1994: 145), much as they would any other ancestral deity. The interior world remains a source of ancestral renewal and is far from an unqualified hell. Similarly, the dead's demonization is only partial, and merely expresses the negative dimension of the characteristically mixed ancestral package. Initially they may be jealous of the living and wish to reclaim their place in life. Like the *gentiles*, they may even enter their kins' bodies, but unlike them they ultimately accept their new life in the interior world and marry there instead of returning to seduce and sicken the living. Thus, the Christian dead and the *gentiles* both have an aggressive nostalgia for life, and both may also act as ancestral benefactors to the living. Yet the *gentiles* are more likely to display both behaviours than the Christian dead: how do we explain their more polarized disposition towards the living?

The answer lies in their lingering presence near the earth's surface, on the landscapes that contemporary humanity inhabits. Whereas the Christian dead undertake a long westward journey that removes them from the localities they once inhabited, the *gentiles* remain in place, hiding in their old territories' springs and caves. Such proximity makes them simultaneously more competitive with and more available to contemporary humanity. Like the mountain spirits with whom they partially merge, the *gentiles* can act either benevolently or malevolently towards the living, but always through their connection to a specific locality. Since the Christian dead go to the cosmos' far-western edge, they lose local influence. Once they leave the place they inhabited, they can no longer indulge their covetous passions or 'seize' the living. Generally the combination of burial and clothes washing is enough to expel them, but they may resist and require a specialist's services. Such problems are rare and minor compared to those caused by the *gentiles*, however.

If correct, this analysis implies that the mountains of the dead are not ordinary places but lie outside the inhabited world. Much evidence corroborates such an inference. In certain Andean regions, the mountain of the dead is an abstract five-tiered entity with no name or position in this world (Zuidema and Quispe 1968: 367). In southern Bolivia, people call it Mundo or Muntu. Abercrombie's discussion (1998: 72–3, 357, 502) shows that it is not a place in the world of the living, but a separate domain where the sun goes after it sets in this world. Mariño Ferro reports that it is a known ice-capped mountain two days' journey west of Chaquilla, which is off-limits to the living, who cannot visit it and survive (1989: 55–8). Thus, it has extraterritorial status in the world of the living. The Laymi say that the dead go to Tacna, a town on the Pacific coast that they represent as already beyond this world and part of the interior world far to the west (Harris 1982: 62–3). Throughout southern Peru, Andean people identify Qoropuna, a large snow-capped volcano in the Department of Arequipa, as the abode of the dead.[35] To many, it is a known geographical landmark separated from points east by a small but cosmologically important stream called the Map'a Mayo (Dirty River), which issues from the foot of Qoropuna (Valderrama and Escalante 1980: 258–9, Gose 1994: 123–4). This is the stream that the journeying *alma* crosses on a suspension bridge or a black dog's back. Thus, Qoropuna lies beyond the most significant barrier between life and death during the *alma*'s journey: it is out of this world, although plainly visible from it. Like Mundo (Mariño Ferro 1989: 56), Qoropuna is the highest-ranking mountain spirit in its region, a place that encompasses all other places, and partly transcends them in another dimension.

These details of the afterlife also have seventeenth-century precedents. Arriaga and Noboa report that one of the dead's souls journeyed to the *upaymarca*, or town of the shades, usually equated with a higher-level aquatic *pacarina* but sometimes with important mountains such as Qoropuna (Guaman Poma 1615: 294). This journey reversed that of the founding ancestors, ending where they originated, usually far away from the territories they founded. In earlier times, then, the abode of the dead also lay at or near the top of a segmentary territorial system, so that the journeying soul left the locality it inhabited during life. En route, it also had to cross an intimidating body of water on a black dog's back or a suspension bridge of hair.[36] The nature of this soul, however, was different under earlier ancestral regimes, which retained mummified bodies within the locality. Then, the journeying soul (*upani*) was a weakly embodied entity associated with shadow, water, and perhaps the vitality lost at death. Another soul, the *camaquen*, stayed behind in the mummified body, anchored there by the founding ancestors, who qualified as such by staying in the territories they established and not drifting back to their remote origins (Gose 1993: 498–9). Thus, the *camaquen* was localized and dry because of its association with the mummy, while the *upani* was mobile and wet, departing the desiccated body for distant aquatic *pacarinas*. Death implied a local loss of water and its accumulation around the *upaymarca* to form the barrier that the *upani* had to cross to reach this final destination (Gose 1993: 495–500). The continuities are remarkable, since contemporary Andean people also treat death and the dead as the cosmological sources of water through which an agricultural regeneration of life occurs (Harris 1982; Gose 1994: chs. 4–5). Water, then, is the vestige of life extracted on death. Mummification elegantly expressed this understanding, but it is entirely compatible with contemporary emphasis on the body's subterranean decomposition. The difference is that modern Andean people no longer conserve *malquis*, seed-like mummies, and so rely exclusively on agricultural practices to mediate the hydraulic life cycle. Agriculture also articulated earlier forms of ancestor worship, but not to the extent that it does contemporary Andean Christianity, which makes the crops into exclusive ancestral mediators.

These regenerative expectations reveal that Andean people still have an ancestral orientation. Their relation with the deceased does not end on death but gradually shifts its focus from kinship and friendship to a shared relation to the earth, in which agricultural fertility is the paramount common interest. In the modern Andes, celebrations of All Saints' and the Day of the Dead play a particularly important role in effecting this transition. On these days, households that have experienced a death in the past year expect that soul to return for a visit, and they prepare elaborately for it.[37] On All Saints' Eve (1 November) they assemble an 'altar': a small table with some clothes washed during the funeral, a photograph, a selection of distinctive foods that may include bread babies, and two lit candles of unequal diameter.[38] These objects receive an all-night vigil similar to the one on death, in some areas with the same games of chance and participation of non-consanguines, and in other areas without them (Mariño Ferro 1989: 59–60; Gose 1994: 142). Affines usually attend, but instead of directing proceedings, as during the funeral, they may openly mock mourners' continuing attachment to the returning dead (Harris 1982: 60). In other areas, a cowled figure called the Paqpako visits all the households conducting vigils, does a song and dance of condolence, but then steals part of the food offerings from the altar before retiring to the graveyard, where he and his entourage dance and drink until dawn. In so doing, he purportedly provides for the returning dead who have nobody left to remember them (Gose 1994: 142).

On the Day of the Dead, all households, not just those with a recent death, may prepare a midday meal for returning souls and serve them food at the table. Some say that the *almas* return as flies (Bastien 1978: 179), so it is forbidden to kill them, particularly if they land on the food set out. After this meal, people go to the cemetery to lay flower wreathes on the graves of those they wish to remember. They may also place food on the graves to attract and nourish the dead.[39] Those who can say prayers in Latin over the graves receive lavish rewards in cane alcohol for their services. Soon everyone begins to pour libations on the graves, and heavy drinking follows. In some areas, people then break and distribute bread babies or bury them whole so worms will eat them instead of newly buried bodies (Mariño Ferro 1989: 62). By mid-afternoon, rain or advanced drunkenness usually send the mourners home, where they resume their vigils, and may boil dried whole cobs of maize to make an evening meal called *phatawa*. That evening, the returning souls return to Qoropuna without facing the obstacles of their initial journey (Gose 1994: 143).

Harris (1982: 55–6) stresses that All Saints' collectivizes the randomness of individual deaths, and harnesses them into a more predictable and productive regime, in which the presence of the dead defines the rainy season and its intense agricultural growth. Since All Saints' typically correlates with the onset of heavy rains and the intensification of agricultural labour, the argument is well taken. As we have seen, the earlier seasonal rituals of *pocoymita* and *caruamita* also subsumed individual deaths, and drew them into an ancestral collectivity with an agriculturally mediated relation to its living descendants. Yet important differences also exist. Those earlier collective death rituals marked transition into the dry season and the rainy season respectively, but the contemporary ritual of All Saints' lacks such a dry season counterpart.[40] In that earlier regime, the dead could articulate both the wet and the dry seasons, whereas now people invoke them only for water. This shift correlates with that between mummification (in which the dead gave off water but also remained as dry, seed-like life forms) and burial (in which their bodies simply decompose and give off water). Within the historical continuity, then, lies a discontinuity, which again consists of rejecting mummy worship, and a refusal to retain the dead above ground as dry life forms.

Occasionally, All Saints' observances address the fate of the body and its wetness/dryness. In certain highland towns of Moquegua in southern Peru, the 'foreman of souls' (*mayordomo de almas*) may re-open the graves of those interred long enough for the flesh to have disintegrated by All Saints.' He hires a priest to give the bones a mass and re-burial, identical in its details to the first, on the Day of the Dead. This second burial marks the soul's definitive liberation from the body (and presumably, of its journey to the afterlife), in the classic pattern of double burial (Hertz 1960). People call it the 'sendoff' (*despacho*), implying that the soul will not return in subsequent years (Rojas Zolezzi 1995: 224–7). We encountered similar rites during the eighteenth century. Other ethnographers describe ossuaries in churches and homesteads that receive attention on the Day of the Dead, which suggests that similar practices may once have been more widespread.[41] The retention of these bones is significant, and is the closest contemporary approximation of both mummification and church burial as described during the seventeenth century. It suggests a lingering attempt to deify the dead by conserving and honouring their transformed bodies, one that Andean people may also express in words (Mariño Ferro 1989: 30; Gose 1994: 145).

These reports seem to minimize the differences between contemporary and previous mortuary regimes, but others reassert that distinction. The Laymi call the returning dead devils (Harris 1982: 58). This does not mean that they wish to harm the living: on the contrary, their presence during the rainy season brings much-needed agricultural growth. Rather, their demonic designation identifies them with the interior world in a Christian, morally coded three-layered vertical cosmos. From this perspective, what matters about the dead is that people bury them. They subsequently return during the rainy season as another partially rehabilitated subterranean force like the mountain spirits and *gentiles*. As Dillon and Abercrombie note, the rainy season is a time of weaker differentiation between the interior world and the earth's surface (1988: 64). During this time, the dead can rise to their former abode, along with the waters they bring. None of this changes their primary identification with the interior world, however, or that they must undergo physical decomposition to benefit their descendants as ancestors.

Burial of the dead also plays a crucial role in Christianizing the Andean landscape. We have seen how certain mountain spirits are anti-Christian because *gentil* bones animate them. Are most mountain spirits Christian because Christian bones animate them? I strongly suspect it to be so, but know of no elaborate informants' statements to that effect in the literature. By regularly interring Christians in the ground, and sending their souls on long lateral journeys to the interior world, bringing them back on All Souls' only to send them off again, the contemporary mortuary regime creates a significant Christian traffic across the landscape that necessarily infuses it with their religious affiliation. As Christian bodies and souls descend into the interior world, they also modify its demonic character and promote the recuperation of its productive forces for their descendants. Since people revere mountain spirits for exactly this ancestral function, we must assume that the Christian dead orient and act with them in this regard. Together, they elevate the interior world's fertility to the earth's surface, and so reconcile ancestorhood with Christianity.

Water is the medium by which the dead return their life to this world.

The land of the dead expels water back into the land of the living, and water separates the two. Such water derives from the underworld's heat and the separation of flesh from bones. When this water returns to the earth's surface, only the crops can recuperate its vitality. Living people fear that contact with it will cause malaria in men and monstrous pregnancies in women (Gose 1994: 132–3). Although water is the ancestral gift of life, it retains the sinister qualities of the interior world. Thus, the crops become a crucial mediation between the living and the dead. Not only do they convert the vitality of the dead into the staff of life, they do so in an eminently Christian manner. The growing crops, particularly maize, are rooted like crosses in the interior world, but draw its regenerative forces upward to fruition under the Christian sun. My ethnographic research documented the systematic equation between the growing maize and the life of Christ, starting with the sowing as immaculate conception, its growth through Christmas as comparable to that of the Christ child, and its death in the killing frosts of April as the crucifixion of Easter (Gose 1994: chs. 4–6). Prominent in this data was a notion of salvation that referred to an expenditure of the self into the crops. For the dead, this meant providing water, and for the living, it meant labour. To work hard in the fields was 'to save one's self' by investing one's life in the maize, as an embodiment of Christ. Thus, death became a metaphor of labour not only in the sense of consuming the body but also as spiritual judgment. The cultivation of maize thereby became a kind of Christian communion, one in which grace circulated between the living and the dead as a form of *ayni*, by which commoners affirm social equality through the reciprocal exchange of labour, and the growing maize became the body of Christ. Through such understandings, Andean peasantries have given sacramental significance to the basic processes of life and livelihood, and identify themselves as Christian, even more Christian than the Hispanicized overlords who ostensibly taught them the faith.

An instructive contrast to the crops' indirect recuperation of life from the dead can be found in both the cannibalism and immortality that contemporary Andean people frequently attribute to the *gentiles*. Whereas the latter refused to die, and so ended up eating each other, contemporary Andean people accept death, and give their lives to the crops that their descendants can eat. Mummification, specifically the refusal to let the flesh rot and separate from the bones, correlates here with the refusal to surrender life in death, specifically by providing water to the crops. Cannibalism is the consequence of that refusal. More than a trace of it remains in the communion achieved through the crops as the body of Christ, but its mediated nature is significant, and enough to establish a new moral era. From this perspective, the waters surrendered by the dead represent a kind of generalized baptism, in which people die to the flesh, only to be reborn in spirit as Christianized crops. Thus, bonds of spiritual co-parenthood (*compadrazgo*) constantly affirm relations of agricultural cooperation in the Andes, particularly those of *ayni* in which people alternate between working on others' land for food and drink and acting as host-proprietor when others work on their land. As Rostworowski notes (1977), and as we saw in chapter 4, the hierarchical one-way exchange of food for labour called *mink'a* was the predominant Andean relation of production well into the colonial period. *Ayni*'s subsequent emergence as the practice that most defines commoners' social position in the Andes (Gose 1994: 7–16) is almost certainly another facet of Andean culture's complex egalitarian transformation starting in the second half of the eighteenth century. Instead of eating each other's children, the *gentiles*' form of *ayni*, contemporary Andean people help raise each other's crops as spiritualized child surrogates. In so doing, they once again prove the thoroughly Christian character of their livelihood and culture.

In summary, the ethnographic record dramatically confirms that Andean people rejected mummy worship for a more Christian and republican articulation of their local communities through mountain spirits. Andean Christianity revised the subject position from which ancestral notions were formulated, replacing *curacas* and their mummified predecessors with peasants and their agrarian life activities. In the process, Andean communities became more egalitarian, and the ancestral vehicles that articulated them took the new and ultimately republican form of mountain spirits. People did not forget the mummified past, however, but conserved it as a malignant subterranean force, largely (though not entirely) stripped of its ancestral functions. This dis-identification built on earlier Andean recognitions that ancestral power is ambivalent, and earlier moiety strategies of conserving vanquished ancestral orders under new regimes. To see only continuity here, however, is to miss the break with the past that Andean people themselves avow, and develop so creatively in the new, Christianized ancestral order we have just explored. The extirpation of idolatry formulated the accusatory questions to which this new ancestral regime is a response, and some traces of those questions arguably remain in Andean peoples' eagerness to proclaim their Christianity. Yet this ancestral transformation was far more complex than an internalized domination, and far more substantial than religious conversion. Less overtly, but just as surely, it consisted of a social levelling. As *curacas* disappeared, community-based democratic institutions such as the *cabildo* inherited their ancestral authority. *Ayni* increasingly articulated divine kingship's traditional emphasis on agrarian fertility. Within that received framework, republican ancestor worship valorized working the land in new, class-like ways that resonated with the larger project of subaltern, community-based democracy. Thus, a truly post-colonial order took form through a transformation that superficially resembles a final colonial capitulation.

Conclusion

Such a *longue durée* history seemingly explodes the questions of cultural hybridity raised at the outset. Christianity and Andean ancestor worship engaged in wave upon wave of mutual appropriations, each emanating from a particular subject position and engaging others in a struggle of evaluative accents, only to sediment into the basis for new historical initiatives and revisions. Now that we have traced through their cumulative interpenetration, there can be no going back to a pseudo-history of origin-bound elements and 'cultural mixtures,' whatever the vocabulary in which they are couched. Properly historical consideration of these issues gives us the positive grounding of a critical anti-essentialist sensibility, namely an appreciation of the rich interaction, succession, and layering of politico-cultural projects over time. The hegemonic dynamics involved turn out to be the real story, the source of all the surprises, indeterminacy, and drama. Outright struggle and strategic capitulation, partial subsumption and alignment, the emergence of inter-cultural formations subject to refraction, critique and reappropriation in an endless stream of initiatives each with unintended consequences: these dynamics encompass the 'cultural mixtures' that inevitably result and give perspective to this otherwise flat notion. They are hybridity's only theoretically interesting feature, and the best hope in avoiding its ubiquitous misinterpretation.

Within these hegemonic dynamics, however, we still have to account for the persistence of the subject positions involved, no matter how transformed they may have become by these cultural innovations. Some tendencies towards fixity must also have been at work. Here, it is tempting to invoke class and critical race analysis at their least nuanced: we can still speak of Andean people at the end of such a long history because tributary subsumption and racializing exclusion have marked them throughout. While this has not been a history of these phenomena per se, they have been present all along, and I reaffirm their structuring role. To leave the matter there, however, implies that the Andean orientations discussed here are no more than an externally imposed indigeneity that those thus stigmatized would abandon at the first opportunity. Many in fact did so throughout this history, but others remained committed enough to the subject positions involved to renegotiate them in more dignified republican terms. My primary concern has been to document that fact, and to explore its positive internal constitution in relation to external constraint.

A reiteration of the ancestral is key to both the internal and external maintenance of the Andean throughout this history. Externally, the ancestral has signified Andean people's difference, initially as idolaters, later as race and culture, with substantial slippage between these frameworks throughout. Internally, however, Andean people have striven to overcome or at least manage that difference by incorporating the Hispanicized outsider as ancestor, initially through the Viracocha attribution and later via the mountain spirits. Beyond these historically shifting vehicles and what they reveal about their conjunctures of use, however, is the more fundamental and enduring ancestral orientation itself. The most remarkable continuity that this history reveals is the stranger-king model of localized sovereignty, in which the ancestor figure (whether mummy or mountain) founds local groups on a relation to the outside. As in the classic pattern of divine kingship, it is only by bringing vitality in from the outside that the ancestor-ruler's local power is established. Politico-ritual mediation is therefore the core activity that articulates this framework. Around it, the subject position of Andean ruler took form. Even when it fell apart at the end of the colonial period, commoners immediately re-created it through mountain spirits, who continued to act as ancestor-rulers. That such a hegemony survived the demise of those who exercised it proves that it had thoroughly infiltrated other practices and subject positions in this society. Commoner descendants had always recognized ancestral power through sacrifice, which implicated them in a cosmological circulation of life that flows both inwardly and outwardly through ancestral channels. Since this sacrificial circulation articulated and subsumed the agrarian practices that were the peasantry's lot in life, these activities could sustain a decapitated version of divine kingship 'from below.' Thus, the remarkable continuity of this framework spanned an impor-

tant historical displacement of its primary site of articulation from ruling to subaltern subject positions. Nonetheless, peasant livelihood
continues to generate the ancestor-ruler figure as a kind of ghost limb in
the phantasmal presence of the mountain spirits. In effect, the class
habitus of Andean commoners became the repository of the ancestral,
and the source of its continuing reiteration.

Such a hasty invocation of practice theory, however, tends to smooth
over a transition that was almost certainly lived as turbulent. As
Tambiah (1985: 165–6) argues, repetition of a received practico-ritual
formula eventually provokes a disjunctive crisis with its broader sociocultural conditions of existence: either the formula loses meaning or it
undergoes reform and revival. The transition from mummies to mountains as objects of ancestor worship clearly exemplifies the latter. Yet
chapter 6 describes a moment when ancestor worship entered crisis but
was not yet reinvented, and could have disappeared entirely. Reiteration of received devotions in altered circumstances takes us up to this
point of crisis, but cannot specify whether abandonment or reform will
be its resolution. This is an indeterminate and ultimately political matter that requires more than Tambiah's relatively formal semiotic discussions (or those of Derrida 1982), helpful as they are. Questions of
agency inevitably arise: how people assess the situation and its strategic possibilities, where their loyalties fall, their resourcefulness and
determination, and so on. We see this dramatically with Hernando Carhuachin, Juana Ycha, Pasqual Haro, and Pedro Alanya, but thousands
of other priests and communities must have faced 'to be or not to be'
moments with their received ancestral rituals. Habit is the one thing
that cannot explain their strikingly varied responses. When pushed to
the brink, they had to do something different and improvise towards a
liveable future with all the reflexive, analytical, and performative powers at their disposal.

We know retrospectively from the ethnographic record that a widespread reconstruction of the ancestral occurred in the Andes, but late
colonial sources give only a few glimpses of how it actually happened.
Without them, we could easily view the ethnographic record as essentially continuous with the previous ancestral regime invested in
mummies, marked only by a replacement of the relatively arbitrary
figurehead of an otherwise unmodified pattern of divine kingship. Yet
as we have seen, that shift in ancestral form was anything but arbitrary.
The egalitarian levelling involved was a major editing of the past, one
that was in no sense habitual and cannot have been any less deliberate

than the other radical decisions that Andean people took when they scuttled or abandoned the entire ancestral framework. Hence, these continuities count as Tambiah's conscious reform and reconstruction, as an energized rearticulation of the ancestral past and of devotees' relation to it. Such revitalization instantiates Gadamer's more general point that cultural traditions and their endless constituent process of self-adjustment and self-appropriation presuppose a fundamental expectation of meaning from the past (1975: 282–95). Yet that expectation is also conditional and can become frail or die, permutations that are very much a part of this history.

Even the reiteration of localized divine kingship as a framework (distinct from its shifting ancestral focuses) contains an internal trajectory of change. During the early colonial period, it generated a range of political responses to the Spanish presence, ranging from collaborationist alliance to outright resistance. With the onset of the Extirpation, it became more defensive but nonetheless remained remarkably open to Catholicism, and consistently refused to accept the boundaries that extirpators drew around it. From the late-colonial collapse of indirect rule onward, it became progressively more subaltern as commoners appropriated the functions of external mediation that *curacas* had previously monopolized. Far from becoming aggressively separatist in the process, however, as subaltern theory would predict, localized divine kingship centred even more resolutely on mediation in its commoner articulation. It reimposed the 'pact of reciprocity' on the republican state, forcing it to recognize communal tenure in return for labour tribute, and continued to fend off various *gamonales*, agrarian reform officials, and armed guerrilla groups that interposed themselves between Andean people and the state. In short, the most pitched forms of resistance during republican times have been against those who tried to encapsulate Andean people and usurp their connections to the state. Localized divine kingship still contains a strategic repertoire, but over time it has focused ever more exclusively on mediation with the outside, particularly with the collapse of the internal power relations it once sustained.

To argue that Andean divine kingship became progressively more invested in strategies of external mediation is not to essentialize it but rather to draw attention to the relational space in which it took form historically. That space includes centuries of pre-Columbian indirect colonial rule, which promoted external mediation as a key political practice. Nearly three centuries of Spanish colonialism further entrenched this orientation, not only as the basis of indirect rule but also as an Andean response to their treatment as a separate and inferior racial group by Spaniards. Under these circumstances, strategies that blurred ancestral difference were key to social inclusion. When mounting mercantile extraction threatened *ayllus* in the eighteenth century, they largely responded by reasserting the tributary economy from below, replacing their own hereditary leaders with commoners when necessary. In the process, localized Andean divine kingship acquired a complex relation to globalizing liberal republicanism. On the one hand, the egalitarian revision of this Andean framework that began in the 1740s opened the way for the Creole independence movements of the nineteenth century and fortified their democratic leanings. On the other hand, it contrasted and still contrasts markedly with liberalism, particularly as boundary-oriented possessive individualism. This contrast is most obvious in the sacrificial idiom that links communal tenure to state tribute in the Andean 'pact of reciprocity,' whose consubstantial emphasis powerfully counteracts liberalism's unconditional notions of individual and national 'identity.' By insisting that the state materially absorb the life forms that they administer, Andean people force it to participate in their localized tradition of divine kingship, and judge it by the standards of fertility and justice involved. This stance continues the earlier emphasis on political mediation, but also responds to the colonial experience of racism, and its fortified reformulation under liberal notions of identity. Andean sacrifice pointedly denies racist proclamations of substantialized social difference and, in this sense, has an important critical function. Thus, the historical experiences of racialized subalternity and globalizing liberalism promoted and amplified tendencies that were already well developed in earlier versions of Andean culture, and gave them new meaning.

Such a relational context precludes seeing these developments as simply 'internal' to Andean culture. We view them better as symptoms of an atrophied inter-cultural dialogue that modernizing liberal elements in the Andean countries and beyond have largely abandoned, letting the labour of mediation fall primarily to Andean people. A racializing essentialism that reclassifies rituals of inter-group mediation as markers of cultural backwardness is clearly the other half of this story. Despite its better intentions, contemporary cultural theory conspires with this racism when it reduces these mediating strategies into statements of 'identity' on the implicit model of ethnicity under modern nation state and global market regimes. Modernist ethnicity differs from Andean moiety strategies by promoting atomistic differentiation, not organic solidarity. This contrast arises directly from that between divine kingship and political-economic liberalism as the overarching social frameworks within which group differentiation occurs. Whereas divine kingship promotes complementary group formation to effect a circulation of life, liberalism deflects interdependence into the economic idiom of the market. Commodities circulate in ideological separation from their producers and interrelate them 'objectively.' These producers become individuals who may initiate transactions but remain in principle separate from and prior to them. As Handler (1988: 153, 1994, cf. Brubaker and Cooper 2000) argues, this model of individuality writ large defines national and ethnic groups, whose differentiation becomes a matter of unconditional 'identity' and is divested of any complementary relation with like units. Within this framework, 'culture' becomes the privileged guarantor of collective individuality: the notion ceases to function anthropologically as 'a total way of life' and is reduced to a marker of difference. Since modern individualists have already universalized the liberal political-economic framework within which they operate, they cease to view it as cultural. Rather, they separate political economy as an objective domain from 'culture' as a subjective remainder, which nonetheless defines transactors' individuality within the supposedly culture-free arenas of the market and nation state. What this diacritical notion of 'culture' loses in scope it recuperates in intensity: even as it verges on stereotype, it claims a romantic authenticity against the supposedly homogenizing qualities of the market and the nation state, whose imagined neutrality only heightens the demand for essentializing particularity.

In contrast to the above, Andean culture has reproduced its differences from Western possessive individualism primarily as an alternative political-economic framework and only secondarily as a marker of ethnic difference. When Andean people differentiate social entities they tend to do so according to their logic of moieties, not the Western model of 'cultural identity.' No matter how violently they may sometimes assert difference, they do so relationally so that it becomes a prelude to a productive relationship within a larger unity. Instead of demanding recognition for their cultural difference in an essentializing fashion, Andean people have demanded inclusion in (and their right to modify) the broader formations of Christendom and republicanism. Ironically, then, it is precisely because Andean people do not assert radical cultural difference that they are culturally different from those in the grip of neoliberal identity discourses. Their strategy of overtly appropriating the colonizer via the logic of localized divine kingship subverts notions of essential cultural difference, which proves that it truly is a different strategy. Unlike bellicose but ultimately hollow assertions of 'strategic essentialist' difference, this deeper cultural difference is more cunning than it is obvious. It continues a pitched but underground hegemonic struggle, not at the level of boundaries and resistance but over the logic of the whole.

Primordialism is another major issue over which Andean moiety strategies and those of Western ethnicity differ. As we have seen, Andean people have increasingly refused to identify with the past as a standard of cultural authenticity in the manner that so typifies modernist ethnicity. By treating Spaniards as *viracochas*, Andean people identified them as useful representatives of a submerged past order, but affiliated themselves with a dominant present that quickly encompassed Santiago and the Christian heaven as 'upper' elements. Thus, they included themselves in the new overarching order of Christendom on favourable terms, and denied that they had been conquered. In a later colonial moment, Andean people intensified these strategies by rejecting ancestral mummies as representatives of an earlier, pre-Christian epoch, and identifying with white, Christianized mountain spirits as founding ancestors of the present. Contemporary Andean peoples' denial that they are 'Indians' is part of this further transformation. While occasional bouts of Inca revivalism may seem to contradict this forward-looking orientation, we must understand the Incas too as Christianized founding ancestors of the present, much like mountain spirits. Far from representing a kind of historical sour grapes, in which Andean people disavowed aspects of 'their culture' that outsiders would have taken from them in any event, we must acknowledge that they often initiated these changes when they did not have to, and did so for their own strategic reasons. This desire to address and partially incorporate the other, instead of adopting an isolationist minoritarianism, stems from Andean people's identification with the progressive orientation of the 'upper' position in their moiety systems. While the past has a place in these systems, it is 'lower' and encompassed, and so does not orient the whole. From this perspective, Western modernists' intense identification with the past makes us *viracochas* at best, but more probably mere *gentiles*.

Andean assimilative strategies are so out of step with contemporary Western identity politics that they do not register as strategies at all.

When judged by recent commentators' expectations of 'resistance' or 'strategic essentialism' they can only appear as failure. Yet by any less ethnocentric standard they have been a remarkable success, promoting their inclusion in broader political formations, the critical egalitarian revision of their own tradition from within, and regaining control over their agricultural land, to name only the most obvious victories. If Andean culture's decolonization is not complete, that is not because it has failed to adopt boundary-oriented liberal strategies of resistance and identity. If anything, it is faring better because of its distinctive response. To evaluate this Andean strategy by the standards of 'strategic essentialism' is not only arrogant but itself a further act of colonization, one whose epistemic violence is entirely comparable to that of the missionary project analysed in this book. Both have sought to impose racializing notions of bounded cultural tradition on Andean strategies of mediation, inclusion, and assimilation. Thus, Andean 'strategic assimilationism' reveals Western 'strategic essentialism' for what it is: a process by which resistance to colonization is itself colonized, and evacuated of any distinctive cultural logic.

Yet it is precisely because these Andean strategies have assimilated such violence before that they have enduring power and relevance to us. Andean people have already absorbed Western attempts to make them 'resistant' defenders of a culture that they did not conceive as separate or bounded. Colonial subsumption and the attendant experience of racialized subordination gave new meaning to already existing Andean strategies for claiming recognition and inclusion. Those strategies survived largely because they effectively addressed the difficult realities of a shared history. Their persistence exposes the peculiarity of Western liberalism's commitment to bounded individuality and partially compensates for its chronic neglect of such alternative values as recognition, inclusion, and solidarity. Moreover, this relationship to liberalism is internal to Andean society, whose 'mestizo' elements have long since adopted but also inflected Western individualist orientations. Yet sadly, none of the important recent studies of Andean *mestizaje* addresses if or how it embodies any of the strategies documented here. Similarly, research on the various social movements currently contesting neoliberalism in the Andes seldom asks if they draw on established Andean political strategies (cf. Goodale 2006: 635–6). For all their exhaustion, received universalizing scripts of 'modernization' and 'revolution' continue to block such inquiry.

Those of us who want a different discussion can begin by recognizing that the Andean strategies documented here address us. They remind us that alternative social values come not only from independent social groundings, cultures, and historical experiences but also from hegemonic subsumption and shared frameworks. Above all, they invite us to resume the truncated intercultural conversation over ancestry with which this shared history began, now as part of an attempt to widen our own cultural repertoire. In the finest tradition of Andean reciprocal ancestor worship, that dialogue's goal need not be a definitive fusion of horizons as much as a mutual participation in them, to transform violence (both militarist and epistemic) into more productive modes of coexistence. To become adequate interlocutors, we should admit that we have something to learn, something that demands we reformulate our own cultural tradition as critically and meaningfully as Andean people reformulated theirs. Such a transformation can only occur relationally, however, and will demand that we elaborate (among many other things) more generous forms of cultural analysis than those we practise today.

Notes

1. Introduction

1 For Africa, see MacGaffey (1968: 173–5, 1972: 51–7), Lan (1985: 173) and Cole (1982: 206–7). For Oceania, see Bashkow (2000: 314), Kempf (1994: 121–2) and Sahlins (1995: 177–89).

2 Some refer to these groupings as 'ethnic' polities or kingdoms, a phrase that privileges the perspective of a centralized state and obscures the internal 'ethnic' differences that often existed within these units. Since *ayllu* organization has persisted and transformed over time (Isbell 1997: 98, 126–7), note that I refer here to the form it took in the seventeenth century and earlier, which differs significantly from what is described in the more recent ethnographic record.

3 See Molina (1574: 51), also Betanzos (1551: chs. 1–2), Cobo (1653: 151), Duviols (1984: 197), Pachacuti Yamqui (1613: 199), Polo (1571: 53–4), and Sarmiento (1572: 106–7).

4 See Duviols (1986: 202–3, 245, 486–7, 489–90). Note that Hernández Príncipe also describes an *ayllu* that was founded by a *llacuaz* ancestor and a *huari* ancestress (Duviols 1986: 495).

5 See Duviols (1986: 52, 59, 89–90, 343, 479–81, 488, 491, 497).

6 See Duviols (1986: 60, 140, 161, 173, 202–3, 278–9, 486).

7 See 'Sobre el estatuo de limpieza de la Sancta Iglesia de Toledo,' Biblioteca Nacional de Madrid (hereafter BNM), ms. 13267, f. 279v (cf. Medina 1887 II: 129).

8 Letter of don Antonio Olea to king, 9/9/1606. Archivo General de Indias, Audiencia de Lima, Legajo 330 (hereafter AGI Lima 330).

9 See 'Sobre el estatuo de limpieza de la Sancta Iglesia de Toledo,' Biblioteca Nacional de Madrid (hereafter BNM), ms. 13267, f. 284v–285v, Medina (1887 II: 28–9).

332   Notes to pages 25–48

10 See Estete (nd: 281, 295, 299, 302–3, 313), Mena (1534: 153–4, 158–9), H.
   Pizarro (1533: 176–7), Sancho (1534: 331), Xérez (1534: 90, 104, 123–4, 127,
   132, 136), also Archivo Arzobispal de Lima, Hechicerías e Idolatrías, Legajo
   11 Expediente 7 (hereafter AAL Idolatrías 11/7), Checras 1724, ff. 29v, 34v.
11 In discussing Guha's work, Spivak argued that he deployed a 'strategic
   essentialism' of resistance to construct subaltern subjects. Her account of
   subject formation largely coincides with hegemony theory except in its
   assumption that any articulation of a subject position is necessarily essentialist (1985: 338–345). See Colebrook (2001: 570) for a useful discussion.
12 The term has since been appropriated to describe cosmopolitan writers'
   incorporation of regional and indigenous realities during the 'boom' of the
   Latin American novel (Rama 1976, 1983) and Latin American postmodern-
   ism (Zavala 1999).

2. Viracochas: Ancestors, Dieties, and Apostles

1 See Estete (nd.: 297–8, 300, 307–8), Mena (1534: 140–1, 148–9, 168), Sancho
  (1534: 305–8, 319) and Xérez (1534: 59–60).
2 See Cieza (1553: 232–274), Estete (n.d.: 279–290), Mena (1534: 135–9), Anonymous (1534: 174–7), Trujillo (1571: 192–200), Xérez (1534: 61–102).
3 See Betanzos (1551: chs. 20–3), Cieza (1553: 274–9), Estete (n.d.: 290–9), Mena
  (1534: 140–150), H. Pizarro (1533: 168–72), Urteaga (1920: 4), Anonymous
  (1534: 178–80), Trujillo (1571: 200–3) and Xérez (1534: 103–122).
4 See Betanzos (1551: 247–86), Cieza (1553: 279–92), Estete (nd.: 299–307),
  Jiménez de la Espada (1965: 227, 238), Mena (1534: 151–167), Murúa (1613:
  chs. 61–3), H. Pizarro (1533: 172–9), P. Pizarro (1571: 58–9, 126), Urteaga
  (1920: 27–31), Anonymous (1534: 181–2), Sancho (1534: 278–81), Trujillo
  (1571: 203–4), and Xérez (1534: 125–55).
5 See Cieza (1553: 293–315), Estete (nd.: 307–8), Mena (1534: 167), Murúa
  (1613: chs. 64–5), Urteaga (1920: 32–4), Sancho (1534: 281–315), Titu Cusi
  (1570: 23), Trujillo (1571: 204–6), Xérez (1534: 156–7).
6 See Anonymous (1539), Betanzos (1551: 287–301), Cieza (1553: 325–346),
  Estete (nd.: 309–319), Murúa (1613: chs. 66–73), P. Pizarro (1571: 141),
  Urteaga (1920: 33–42), Anonymous (1534: 183), Sancho (1534: 285–325), and
  Molina (1553: 87–92).
7 See Santillán (1553: 51), Jiménez de la Espada (1965: 178), Polo (1561: 144),
  Matienzo (1567: ch. 7).
8 See Cieza (1553: 152), Molina (1553: 73), and Sarmiento (1572: 109): Cabello
  Valboa (1586: 296–7) and de la Vega (1609: 301) rightly contest this latter ety-
  mology.

9 Betanzos (1551: 137, 200, 208), Zárate (1555: 478), Pachacuti Yamqui (1613: 252–3), and Guaman Poma (1615: 262) attribute similarly foreboding prophecies to Huayna Capac. Only de la Vega follows the Quipucamayocs in linking this prophecy to the identification of Spaniards as Viracochas. Like Las Casas (1561 VIII: 1560), he argued that the first Inca to foretell the end of their empire was Viracocha and that Huayna Capac merely publicized the prophecy. Spaniards were called Viracochas because they fulfilled Viracocha's prophecy by overthrowing the Incas (de la Vega 1609: 319). Pedro Pizarro attributes a similar prophecy to the oracle Apurimac (1571: 241).

10 Minimally, these emendations and supplements include the document's introduction, which refers in the preterite tense to the time of Vaca de Castro (Urteaga 1920: 3), mention of Paullo's death in 1551 (Urteaga 1920: 47), and the document's terminal date of March 11, 1608, which clearly relates to Melchor Carlos Inca's litigation (Urteaga 1920: 53). Beyond these obvious chronological clues, it is difficult to determine if and where Melchor Carlos Inca's subsequent claim modified an earlier stratum of this document. A physical examination of the original document might reveal clues about its 'stratified' production, but I could not locate it. Urteaga (1920: v) states that Jiménez de la Espada found this manuscript in Legajo J, No. 133 of the Biblioteca Nacional de Madrid, but it does not appear in Paz' inventory (1933). It is *not* part of the Melchor Carlos Inca documents that the BNM currently holds (ms. 20193), but may once have belonged to that assemblage.

11 See BNM ms. 20193, f. 12.

12 See Cieza (1553: 150–1), Las Casas (1561 7: 874), Sarmiento (1572: 102), Molina (1574: 51–5), Cabello Valboa (1586: 297), Acosta (1590: 314–5, 421) and Cobo (1653: 151). De la Vega makes similar arguments for Pachacamac as an alternative Andean instantiation of the Judaeo-Christian 'creator god' (1609: 70–3).

13 Not all chroniclers who entertained these ideas necessarily agreed with Las Casas (1561) that indigenous religions prepared Indians to receive the true faith. By recasting them in an implicitly monotheistic manner, however, they facilitated such arguments.

14 Viracocha exterminated earlier eras of humanity, and comparably primordial ancestors such as Huallallo Carhuincho and Huari were cannibals (Salomon and Urioste 1991: 43, 67; Duviols 1986: 119–120), thus the Spaniards might be Viracochas and still have such proclivities.

15 Like Betanzos, Cieza deploys *supay* in its colonial sense to demonize the Spaniards retrospectively. Suspicious as this shared phrasing may be, neither chronicler necessarily authored it: each may have heard it from his Inca

informants in Cuzco, who were busy reformulating their notions of the past during the 1540s, as they adjusted to colonial rule.

16 See Polo (1561: 154), Acosta (1590: 425), de la Vega (1609: 300), and Ramos Gavilán (1621: 18).

17 Only superficially does this confirm Obeyesekere's analysis, for the problem is that this 'reasonable' explanation comes from a sixteenth-century European, who ought to be promoting apotheosis by any means possible.

18 See Acosta (1590: 422), Betanzos (1551: 32–3), Cabello Valboa (1586: 298–301), Cieza (1553: 194–6), Cobo (1653; 74–5, 156, 161–2), de la Vega (1609: 242–9, 289–305), Las Casas (1561 VIII: 1522–4), Polo (1571: 5, 49–50), Pachacuti Yamqui (1613: 217–21) and Sarmiento (1572: (164–73).

19 Cabello Valboa reports that Inca Viracocha organized a strong military coalition of these aboriginal groups under Yupanqui's command to defeat the Chancas, only to turn on them afterwards (1586: 299–300). His account describes the arrival of reinforcements in the battle with the Chancas, but does not specify that they were *pururaucas*, which suggests a certain interchangeability between aboriginal allies and the *pururaucas* in these accounts.

20 A more accurate translation in this vein would be 'powerful ones of the sea,' but the term more commonly referred to human sacrificial victims, which is how Atahuallpa may well have intended to treat them.

21 Note that the 1984 Spanish edition of Cieza's complete works omits from this description the word 'white,' which appears in other editions. Virtually the same phrase appears in Las Casas' description of Quetzalcoatl (1561 VII: 879), which appears to substantiate Las Casas' hypothesized access to Cieza's manuscripts, but might also reflect their shared reliance on Domingo de Santo Tomas as a source (Pease 1995: 196–7). These (along with Betanzos 1551: 137, 201) are also among the earliest Spanish uses of whiteness as a social marker in the Americas: at this stage, Christianity and paganism were far more commonly invoked to characterize colonial social boundaries, but also had racializing overtones due to Spanish theories of 'purity of blood.'

22 Estenssoro's derivation of this myth from missionary accounts of fallen angels (2003: 126–7) would be more viable if combined with the Andean sources of the moiety logic involved.

3. Diseases and Separatism

1 See Millones (1990: 61, 63, *passim*), AGI Lima 136: 'Ysidro Sánchez de la Mota y Aguilar presenta una información hecha por su parte ante un alcalde

de corte cerca de la general reformación de los naturales de los indias', 1589, ff. 4v, 10r, 19v.

2 By his own admission, Titu Cusi was only a regent for his younger brother Tupac Amaru, whom Sayre Topa appointed as his successor (Guillén 1994: 299). Vilcabamba accepted Titu Cusi as titular Inca, however, and he assigned Tupac Amaru to priestly care of their mummified father (Murúa 1613: 268), a situation that changed when hard-line militarists who initially backed Titu Cusi switched their support to Tupac Amaru in 1570.

3 Varón, who questions the Taqui Oncoy's connection to Vilcabamba (1990: 346–7), inexplicably ignores Sotelo as a source. A single dismissive comment (there were others: see AGI, Lima 92, Ramo 18. No. 136, Monzon to King, 22/12/1566; Ramo 19. No. 142, Monzón to King, 26/2/1567) leads him to doubt the very existence of a planned native uprising in 1565–6 (Varón 1990: 383–4), despite the solid and diversified evidence Mogrovejo (1987) assembles.

4 See AGI Lima 472, king to viceroy, 2/1/1569, f. 2v.

5 Ramos rejects such syntheses for ignoring how the Taqui Oncoy was progressively 'constructed' in Albornoz' successive accounts, allegedly to capitalize on the changing ideological climate under Toledo (1992: 140, 149–53). In fact, the Taqui Oncoy's discursive 'construction' began with Guerrero and Sotelo well before Toledo's arrival, and changed very little in response to it. Since Ramos is unaware of these two earliest sources on the movement, she mistakenly assumes that the Taqui Oncoy first appeared in the historical record in Albornoz' 1570 report of merits and services. She makes much of its absence from his 1569 report, implying that only with the viceroy's arrival at the end of that year could Albornoz claim his extirpation of the Taqui Oncoy as a credential. A simpler and more plausible explanation of this absence is that when Albornoz filed his request for promotion in January of 1569, only two months into his assignment in Huamanga, neither he nor his superiors were aware of the Taqui Oncoy. Even if he had been extirpating the movement since his arrival in December 1568, he would not have been ready to present his activities by the following month, nor would there have been witnesses available in Cuzco to comment on them. Chronology explains this absence far more economically and reliably than Ramos' misinformed 'symptomatic reading.' After all, the Augustinian account of 1561 shows that the conditions for denouncing and extirpating idolatry existed well before the arrival of Toledo and helped set the stage for his interventions. Had Albornoz been able to cite activities against the Taqui Oncoy in his request of early 1569, he might well have done so. In short, Ramos' efforts suffer not only from the same

inattention to chronological detail she criticizes in other scholars, but also from the broader anti-realist malaise of colonial discourse analysis, whose critical distain for the historical record reduces the Taqui Oncoy to a discursive fabrication. Her convoluted denial that she denied the existence of the 'so-called Taqui Oncoy' (2002: 139–41) is self-refuting. The byline for her 1992 article on the cover of *Revista Andina* (for which she worked at the time), 'Taqui Oncoy: ¿Rebelión andina o superchería?' is at least frank in its scepticism.

6 Varón omits oracular possession as one of the movement's 'Andean roots' (1990), whereas Ramos dismisses it as an invention of Christian discourses on demonic possession (1992: 153–4, 159), displaying a remarkable ignorance of this important Andean cultural form.

7 Millones (1964: 88) initially assumed that Juan Chocne and the two Marías were the three principal preachers to whom Molina referred, but the published documents (Millones 1990: 181, 225, Yaranga 1978: 168) specify that two of these preachers were male and one female, invalidating this hypothesis.

8 Despite its Andean appearances, Estenssoro holds that 'an exegesis of the catechism [w]as the basis of the Taki unquy' (2003: 133). He takes Sotelo's report of attempts to revive Pachacamac out of the larger documentary context that pairs this *huaca* with Titicaca, and argues that Pachacamac actually refers to the Christian God who, after thirty-three years on earth following the conquest of 1532, had expired in 1565, only to revive and bring all the pagan souls out of hell with him as the disembodied *huacas* (2003: 128–34). The argument is ingenious and tempting, especially if taken as one possible layer of a complex phenomenon, not the complete explanation Estensso intends. Yet it fails not only in the details (the movement began in 1564 or earlier, not 1565; *huacas* were distinct from demonized *supays*, etc.), but above all to provide a coherent basic raison d'etre for the Taqui Oncoy: why all the militance if the goal was merely to assimilate early evangelical messages? Since Estenssoro's commitment is to prove Andean peoples' full and early Christianity, however, he feels no need to address the many data on the Taqui Oncoy that disallow such a reading. The hermeneutical violence involved reaches missionary proportions and discredits what could have been a useful and original contribution.

9 Other evidence also suggests a final date of 1571. Molina states that the Taqui Oncoy 'began ten years ago, more or less' (1574: 129) and lasted 'more than seven years' (1574: 132). Assuming a starting date of 1564 would make 1571 its seventh year.

10 See Archivo del Cabildo Metropolitano de Lima, Acuerdos Capitulares,

tomo 2, ff. 52r–v, 53v, 56r. I thank Alan Durston for kindly drawing my attention to this source.

11 The mountain and idol in question probably corresponded to the modern mountain of P'iste (see Gose 1986: 304), located on the border of Antabamba and Aymaraes. A parish named Picti also existed in nearby Cotabambas, however (Villanueva 1982: 54–6).

12 See Arriaga (1621: 219–220, 224), Duviols (1986: 74, 76, 94, 97, 98, 99, 100, 125–6, 145, 156, 174, 180, 189, 196, 204, 206, 211, 215, 218, 221, 226, 227, 234, 237, 239, 265, 272–3, 280, 282, 284, 297–8) and Polia (1999: 276, 302–3, 333–5, 367–8, 380, 389, 392–3, 400, 443–4, 453–4, 474, 503, 510, 518, 532).

4. *Reducción* and the Sruggle over Burial

1 *Reducir* and *reducción* have long been approximately cognate with 'to reduce' and 'reduction' in English, but their range of meaning in both languages was much broader in the sixteenth and seventeenth centuries than it is now. The oldest Spanish dictionary has the following entry: 'reducirse is to become convinced. Reducido, convinced and returned to better order.' (Covarrubias 1611: 854). Other uses of the term more specifically denote conversion and incorporation into Catholicism, for example, Pope Alexander VI's stipulation that 'se procure la salvación de las almas y las naciones bárbaras sean reducidas a la fe cristiana' (Levillier 1919: 7, cf. 8, 12, 14). The sense of incorporation and order denoted by *reducción* was significantly (and sometimes primarily) religious. Elsewhere the term referred to an obedience that was both political and religious, as in Toledo's account of how armed men 'rreduxeron estas prouincias a dios y a la corona real' (Levillier 1921–6 IV: 72, cf. III: 82, 309; IV: 352). It might also designate a purely political subjugation, as when a conquistador 'los redujeron a la obedienzia y señorio y corona real de castilla' (Levillier 1921–6 IV: 116, cf. III: 98, 150, 270; IV: 127, 326).

2 See Millones (1990: 209, 212, 220, 224, 231, 233, 235, 239, 244, 248, 250–1).

3 See *Obras publicadas en el Concilio de Alcala de año 1481 presidido en nombre de don Alfonso Carrillo por don Vasco de Ribera Arcediano de Talavera*. BNM, Ms. 13021, ff. 129–46.

4 See *Confirmación del Cardenal Arzobispo de Toledo don Pedro González de Mendoza de lo resuelto en la Congregación que celebró en Alcala don Juan de Torres Arcediano de Medina y suspensión de la censuras fulminados por algunas constituciones de don Alfonso Carrillo a 13 de noviembre de 1483*. BNM, Ms. 13021, ff. 153–6. The Council of Granada effectively reinstated the decree of 1481 when in 1565 it ordered that both new and old Christians be buried in

churches (see Eire 1995: 91–2). In 1591, Philip II ordered 'that all Moriscos be buried in churches, regardless of local customs' (Eire 1995: 94).

5 See AAL Capellanías 7/6, 8/1.

6 See Levillier (1918–22 I: 373), Lissón y Cháves (1943–7, II: 609, 661, 767, 784), AGI Lima 300, letter from bishop of Quito to king, 4/8/1571, letter of licenciado Joan de Obando to king, 25/5/1572.

7 See AGI Lima 136, 'Ysidro Sánchez de la Mota y Aguilar presenta una información hecha por su parte ante un alcalde de corte cerca de la general reformación de los naturales de las indias,' 3/3/1603, ff. 6r–v, 7r, 8r–v, 15v.

8 Ibid. ff. 5v, 6v, 7v, 12v,13r–v.

9 Ibid. ff. 4v–5r,

10 Ibid. ff. 8v, 11v, 21r–v, 23v.

11 See AAL Capítulos 1/9, 2/13, 2/16, 3/11, 3/14, 6/1, 8/8, 9/13, 12/6, 13/7, 17/8, 18/7, 19/4, 22/1, 22/5, 22/8, 28/9.

12 See AGI Lima 136, 'Ysidro Sánchez de la Mota y Aguilar presenta una información hecha por su parte ante un alcalde de corte cerca de la general reformación de los naturales de las indias,' 3/3/1603, ff. 4v–5r, 9v, 18v.

13 Ibid. f. 19r.

14 Ibid. ff. 4v, 6r, 9v, 10v, 13v–14r, 16r–v, 18v, 19v–20r 22r.

15 Ibid. ff. 4v, 7r, 10r, 15v, 22r.

16 See AGI Lima 33, f. 35r–v, letter of Velasco to king, 10/4/1597, ff. 13v–14r, Lima 44, Parecer del Tribunal de Cuentas, 6/5/1633, f. 95r–v, Parecer de Juan de Arriola y Peñarrieta, s/f, ff. 128r–130r, 135r, Levillier (1921–6 XIV: 76, 171), Málaga Medina (1974: 163).

17 See AGI Lima 44, Parecer del Capitán García Tamayo, Escribano Mayor de la Caja Real de Lima, 18/4/1633, f. 144v.

18 See BNM Ms. 2989 *Provisiones reales para el gobierno de Indias*, p. 96, letter from king, Tordesillas, 12/6/1600.

19 See British Library, Miguel de Monsalve, *Redvción Vniversal de todo el Piru, y demas Indias, con otros muchos Auifos, para el bien de los naturales dellas, y en aumento de las Reales Rentas*, 1604, ff. 4v, 6r, 9v, 11r, 24v, 31v.

20 See AGI Indiferente 428, L. 33, f. 18v–19v.

21 See AGI Lima 301, letters from Lobo Guerrero to king dated 15/3/1610, 20/3/1610, 3/4/1617, 15/4/1619, Lobo Guerrero (1613: 237).

22 See AGI Lima 301, letter from Lobo Guerrero to king, 3/4/1617.

23 See AGI Lima 35, Copias de cartas que escrivio el Marqués de Montesclaros en raçon de la reduciones en 25 de agosto, 25/8/[1609?], ff. 39r–40r; AGI, Lima 44 Parecer del Tribunal de Cuentas, 6/5/1633, f. 99r–v; Wightman (1990: 26).

24 See AAL Idolatrías 1/3, Margos 1615.

25 See AAL Papeles Importantes 3/13, San Francisco de Callaguaya, 1616.
26 Betanzos (1551: 285–6) reports similar wrangling over the dead body of the Inca Atahuallpa by Cuxi Yupangue and Rumiñagui in a struggle of succession.
27 See AAL Idolatrías 1/15, Mangas 1605.
28 Arriaga (1621: 198) locates this shrine in a cave 'en un monte aspero,' one league from the town of San Cristobal de Rapaz.
29 See AGI Lima 327: the document is is a notarized copy of the original inquest records from 1614, included in Avendaño's *relación de servicios y méritos* of March 27, 1618.
30 Ibid. f. 3v.

5. Strategies of Coexistence

1 See AGI Lima 44, Parecer de la Real Audiencia de la Plata, 1/11/1632, f. 80v.
2 See AGI Lima 302, letter of archbishop to king, 8/10/1626; AGI Lima 304, letters of archbishop to king dating 20/11/1664, 19/3/1670, 31/1/1693.
3 See Duviols (1984: 206–214), Jiménez de la Espada (1965: 222, 231, 242, 330, 346, 358–9), Arriaga (1621: 201–2, 248, 273), Lobo Guerrero (1613: 38), Polia (1999: 227, 260, 285, 302–3, 318, 350, 358, 380, 405, 418, 440, 433–4, 458, 463, 472, 473, 497, 508, 519).
4 See Guaman Poma (1615: 268–9, 282), Polia (1999: 275, 302–8) and Salomon and Urioste (1991: 75, 94).
5 Pariacaca's sons are distinct from his brothers except for Paria Carco, who is described as both (Salomon and Urioste 1991: 68, 92). Note that these seven conquering sons do not figure in the order of six sons and six daughters that Pariacaca said he would create prior to conquest (Salomon and Urioste 1991: 67). I suspect that the latter represents a Yunga territorial structure that the invaders were to occupy, not their own sibling group.
6 Chaupi Ñamca's segmentary personality comprised five subdivisions, one of which personified the whole, which further confirms her structural equivalence to Pariacaca (Salomon and Urioste 1991: 85–6). That her subdivisions did not articulate a political order, as did Pariacaca's, expressed her group's subordination.
7 See AAL Idolatrías 1/2: 2r–7v.
8 See AAL Idolatrías 11/7 (García Cabrera 1994: ch. 16).
9 See AAL Idolatrías 1/4: 2r–3r.
10 "Su señor serro y su yaya:" see AAL Idolatrías 1/11: 2v–3r. Two published transcriptions of this document exist (Anonymous 1923: 659–66; Mills 1992).
11 Adorno improbably suggests that Guaman Poma did not actually believe in

his own creation but offered it to his European readers as a satire meant merely to deflate the pretensions of providential writings (1986: 130, 141–3). This analysis conforms nicely to the notion of colonial mimicry but very badly to Guaman Poma's relentlessly serious tone.

12 See AGI Lima 40, letter to king from viceroy, 24/3/1625.

13 See AGI Lima 302, letter of Guadalcazar to *corregidor* of Huamalies, 11/8/1625, copied to king 3/10/1625, letter to king from viceroy, 18/7/1626, letter to king from archbishop, 15/10/1626.

14 See AGI Lima 302, letter of Campo to king, 8/10/1626, ff. 1r–2r.

15 See AGI Lima 302, letter from Campo to king, 15/10/1626, 6 ff.

16 See AGI Lima 302, letter of Campo to king, 8/10/1626, ff. 2r–6r.

17 See AGI Lima 302, letter of Campo to king, 15/10/1626, ff. 1r–2v.

18 AGI Lima 302, collated testimony with terminal date of 28/9/1626, ff. 6v–7r.

19 AGI Lima 302, collated testimony with terminal date of 28/9/1626, ff. 8r–10r, 11v, 12v, 15r, 16r,16v, 19r.

20 See AGI Lima 44, Conde de Chinchón to king, 8/10/1633, ff. 70r–71r, and the position papers in ff 72r–159r.

21 See AGI Lima 302, letter of Arias Ugarte to king, 3/5/1633, ff. 1r–v, and other letters to king dated 20/5/1630, 20/5/1631.

22 See AGI Lima 44, Parecer del Arzobispo de Lima, 4/4/1633, ff. 72r–73v.

23 See AGI Lima 44, Parecer del Tribunal de Cuentas, 6/5/1633, 95r, 96v, 101r, Parecer de P. Ruiz de Navarro, provincial mercedario, 20/3/1633, f. 120v, Parecer de D. de Torres, vice-provincial jesuita, 16/4/1633, f. 121r, Parecer de Juan de Arriola y Peñarrieta, contador, s/f, f. 127v.

24 See AGI Lima 44, Parecer de M. Aroztegui, provincial franciscano, 28/3/1633, ff. 109v–110r, Parecer del Capitán García Tamayo, Escribano Mayor de la Caja Real de Lima, 18/4/1633, f. 142v.

25 See AGI Lima 45, Conde de Chinchón to king, 21/3/1634, f. 39r–v.

26 See AGI Lima 44, Parecer de la Real Audiencia de Lima, 11/4/1633, ff. 75r–76r.

27 See Polia (1999: 463, 506–7, 509–10, 517–19), AAL Capítulos 22/8: 37r–38v, 50v–52v, 72v–73r

28 See AAL Cofradías 34/2, 1613; 34/3, 1614; 34/4, 1629.

29 See AAL Sepulturas 1/9, quote from f. 10r, also Sepulturas 2/18, 1647, Recuay, for a similar case.

30 See AAL Cofradías 46/3.

31 See AAL Cofradías 46/9, quote from f. 3r.

32 See AAL Cofradías 46/13: 7r, 11v–12r, 37r–38r, 42v–43r, 56v, 59r, 65r, 66r.

33 See AAL Cofradías 46/12, quote from f. 7r.

34 See AAL Capítulos 17/11: The verdict is this case does not survive, but

Mena seemed to be losing up to where the documentation breaks off, and therefore introduced new witnesses and questionnaires to bolster his case.

35 See AAL Cofradías 46/15, quote from f. 1v.
36 See AAL Sepulturas 3/5 and 3/12.
37 See AAL Cofradías 46/15: 1v, 2v, 3v, 5r, 7r.
38 See AAL Cofradías 46/14: 3r–v.
39 See *Constituciones synodales deste Obispado de Guamanga; ordenadas por el Reverendismo Señor don Francisco de Verdugo del Consejo de Su Magestad obispo de la misma ciudad; y publicadas en cinco y seis de agosto de 1629 años*, AGI Lima 308, ff. 11 r–12r.
40 See *Constituciones Sindodales de Arequipa*, 1638, BNM Ms. 723, ff. 10r–v.
41 See Ibid. f. 73r.
42 See Ibid. ff. 71v–75r, 94v–99v.
43 See, for example, AAL Derechos Paroquiales 4/13, 4/14; Causas Criminales 29/2.
44 See AAL Capítulos 3/11, 5/2, 5/4, 5/13, 8/2, 10/10, 11/4, 12/6, 13/7, 15/5, 15/7, 17/8, 17/11, 18/7, 19/4, 20/8, 21/7, 22/1, 22/2, 22/5, 22/8, 23/8, 25/6, 25/9, 25/12, 26/1, 26/3, 28/9; Derechos Paroquiales 2/35, 2/41, 3/16, 3/20, 3/22, 4/2, 4/27, 4/34, 4/38, 4/39, 4/44, 4/45; Causas Criminales 33/9.
45 See AAL Capítulos. 10/10: 1r–3v.
46 See AAL Capítulos 11/4: 37v.
47 See AAL Capítulos 17/8: 22v; 17/11, f. 1r; 22/1, f. 2v.
48 See AAL Capítulos 15/7, and Marzal's discussion (1983: 376).
49 See AAL Capítulos 18/7: 231r.
50 See AAL Capítulos 21/7: 7r–8v.
51 See AAL Capítulos 22/5: 1r.
52 See AAL Capítulos 25/6: 1r, 32r.

6. Ayllus in Transition

1 See AAL Testamentos 21/5A: 22r–23r, 2r–21r, 35r–72r.
2 See AAL Idolatrías 2/7: 1r, 7r–8r.
3 Ibid. ff. 34r–35v, 37r–41r, 48r–72r.
4 See the following documents in AGI Lima 303: a notarized copy of several documents with a covering letter from Valenzuela dated 4/5/1651, letters of Villagómez to king of 3/9/1650, 20/8/1651, 16/8/1654, Juan Bautista Saenz to king, 30/8/1653, and the "Informe del Dr. Don Juan de Solórzano sobre lo que contienen las cartas inclusas del Arcobispo de Lima," 8/30/1653.
5 See letter of Padilla to king 15/10/1654 (Vargas Ugarte 1966–71 III: 391–420)

and commentaries by Garcia Cabrera (1994: 56–61) and Marzal (1983: 119–71).

6 See AGI Lima 303, "Medios en servicio de su magestad, para que la reducción general de los Indios del Reyno del Peru a sus pueblos, se pueda hazer con efecto en breve tiempo sin costa de la Real hazienda," no date, 9ff. The John Carter Brown Library also has a copy of this document, and dates it to 1662. Marzal's (1983: 86–8) summary of this document is reasonable, but follows Villagómez' response to it more closely than it does the original.

7 Ibid, ff. 1r–2v.

8 See AGI Lima 303, letter of Villagómez to king, 26/7/1663, 16 ff. Although Marzal (1983: 86–8) treats Pedro de Loma as the coauthor of Ugarte's treatise, the latter bears only Ugarte's name, and folio 1r of Villagómez' reply specifies that he received two papers, a letter and a treatise, from these two persons. The letter does not appear in this *legajo*, but it would be logical to assume that Pedro de Loma wrote it.

9 Ibid. ff. 4v–6v, ff. 13v–14v.

10 See Duviols (1986: 23–5, 27, 80, 107–8, 126–7).

11 See Duviols (1986: 9–10, 12–13, 15–16, 26, 30–1, 33, 63–4).

12 See Guiance (1998: 62) and Marzal (1983: 424–5), also Pedro de Villagómez, *Constituciones Sindodales de Arequipa*, 1639, BNM Ms. 723, f. 74r.

13 See Duviols (1986: 8–10, 13, 16, 19, 25–8, 64–5, 72)

14 See Duviols (1986: 8, 23, 28–9, 34–5, 54, 60–2, 64–5, 71).

15 See AAL Idolatrías 2A/2: 182r.

16 See Duviols (1986: 16–20, 28–38). Doyle (1988: 124) states that Ricari instructed people to represent pagan bodies as Christian rather than the reverse, an interpretation that is consistent with early testimony but that subsequent more detailed accounts contradict.

17 See Duviols (1986: 62–3, 72, 86–7, 90, 92–3, 98–9, 111–12, 130).

18 See Duviols (1986: 19, 28–38, 50, 72, 87, 106, 115).

19 See AAL Idolatrías 2A/2: 223v.

20 Although see Duviols (1986: 266).

21 See AAL Idolatrías 2A/2: 223v–224r.

22 See Duviols (1986: 8, 25, 100, 120, 161, 173, 204, 304, 344, 362, 455). Other Catholic feasts such as Our Lady of the Assumption, Our Lady of the Nativity, and the Exaltation of the Holy Cross also coincided with sacrificial rites for the ancestors (Duviols 1986: 10, 29, 32, 59).

23 See Duviols (1986: 145, 155–6, 164, 167, 176–7, 180–1, 200, 211, 212, 219, 222, 244, 277).

24 See Duviols (1986: 146, 161, 179, 188–9, 240, 277).

25 See AAL Idolatrías 7/14: 6r.

26 See AAL Idolatrías 7/14: 2r–v, 4v, 10v, 12r, 13v–14v, 16v, 17v, 18v–19r, 20v–21v, 23r, 24v, 26v, 28r–v, 30r–v, 32v–33r, 34r, 35v, 40v–41r.

27 See AAL Idolatrías 7/14: 2v, 4r–v, 5r–v, 30v–31r. 34r–v, 37v–38r, 41r–v, 43v, 44v.

28 See AAL Idolatrías 7/14: 3v–4r, 5r, 6r, 11r, 17r, 19r–v, 21r–v, 23r, 24r, 25r–v, 26v, 28v, 29v, 31r–v, 36r–v, 43r.

29 See AAL Idolatrías 7/14: 3r–4v, 5v, 34r–36v, 41v, 42v, 44r.

30 See AAL Idolatrías 7/14: 3r, 4r–v, 5v, 36v, 41v, 42v.

31 See AAL Idolatrías 7/14: 3v, 4r, 36r–v, 42v, 50v.

32 See AAL Capítulos 22/5: 1r–v; 22/8: 3r–28v; 22/8: 50r, 51r, 55v, 98r, 100v, 109r, 111v, 114v–115r, 117r–v, 151 r–v.

33 See AAL Idolatrías 11/7: 3r–5v; Capítulos 28/7, 28/9: 22r–26r, 33r–34v, 38r–v.

34 See AAL Idolatrías 11/7: 5v–9r, 10r–12r.

35 See AAL Idolatrías 11/7: 21r–29r, 30r, 35r, 41v.

36 See AAL Capítulos 28/9: 14r, 33v, 55v.

37 See AGI Lima 40, letter of Viceroy Guadalcazar to king, 24/3/1625.

38 See AGI Lima 412, letters and reports of viceroy to king, 26/10/1728, 19/10/1728.

7. The Rise of the Mountain Spirits

1 Earls (1969: 77), Favre (1967: 121–3, 139–140), Gose (1986: 299), Isbell (1997: 131).

2 See Betanzos (1551: 18), Cieza (1553: 150, 153), Sarmiento (1572: 123), Duviols (1986: 172), Salomon and Urioste (1991: chs. 6, 8), (Polia 1999: 347–8).

3 Thus, mountains were not categorically associated with lightning or the upper realm, as Silverblatt (1988: 178) implies. Her study also overemphasizes connections between the mountains and Santiago. Summarizing the 1689 idolatry trial of don Carlos Apoalaya in Jauja, she states that "when an indigenous healer from another central highland village appealed to his mountain god for help, it was Santiago who appeared" (Silverblatt 1988: 184). In the passage she cites, people actually summoned Santiago directly and counterposed the mountains to him as an alternative source of healing power (AAL Idolatrías 8/2, ff. 86r–87r).

4 See AAL Idolatrías 1/2: 2v–3r, 4r–v, 6r, 7r–v.

5 Ansion (1987: 115), Earls (1969: 66), Morote Best (1956: 290), Mendizábal (1966: 71).

6 Arguedas (1956: 235), Isbell (1978: 59), Salazar Soler (2002: 182)

7 See Betanzos (1551: 19), Cieza (1553: 155), Sarmiento (1572: 128, 133), Duviols (1978; 1986: 154, 172, 279, 443–4, 464–7), Salomon and Urioste (1991: 58–9, 63, 78, 121, 125–6, 134).

8 Arriaga mentions that *pacarinas* might be addressed as *camac* or creator (1621: 219–20) and Albornoz (Duviols 1984: 197) also metonymically conflates ancestral creator with the site of creation. Doyle suggests that this conflation was commonplace (1988: 91–4), but cites only one case from Maray in 1677 that actually illustrates her claim.

9 See Álvarez (1588: 81, 87), Salomon and Urioste (1991: 77) and Polia (1999: 304–5, 443–4, 508).

10 See Duviols (1986: 341, 343, 403), Polia (1999: 218, 232–2, 262, 307–9, 317, 351–2, 469, 486–7, 497–8, 508, 515–6).

11 See Álvarez (1588: 74–5, 87), Polia (1999: 207, 208, 220, 222–3, 236, 253, 262, 271–2, 275, 280, 304–5, 315, 366, 409, 429–30, 430, 431, 442, 486–7, 488–9, 507–8, 513, 517, 519–21, 534–5, 545).

12 See Duviols (1984: 207, 211–2), AAL Idolatrías 3/10: 26r; 4/14; 11/1 ff. 29r–v, 119r.

13 See Anonymous Jesuit (1590: 159), Polia (1999: 216, 243, 247–8, 252, 272, 280, 304, 305, 306, 318–9, 368, 385–6, 508, 539–41, 545).

14 See Agustinos (1561: 22, 27–9), Duviols (1984: 205–14), Álvarez (1588: 74–5, 77), Guaman Poma (1615: 268–9, 282), (Arriaga 1621: 196, 227).

15 See Álvarez (1588: 82), Duviols (1986: 154, 279, 452, 467), Polia (1999: 207, 252, 259, 262, 306, 307, 324, 436, 506, 517–18, 539, 544, 545, 547, 555).

16 Griffiths (1996: 292) briefly cites most of the 1660 documents, including one (bearing the old signature of Legajo I, Expediente 1; see Huertas Vallejos 1981: 121) that is clearly relevant to this discussion, but has since disappeared from the Archivo Arzobispal de Lima.

17 See Guaman Poma (1615: 268–9, 282), Polia (1999: 275, 302–8) and Salomon and Urioste (1991: 75, 94).

18 See AAL Idolatrías 1/6: 4r, 6r–v, 13r–14r.

19 See AAL Idolatrías 1/6: 4r, 6v, 13v–16r.

20 See AAL Idolatrías 4/22.

21 See AAL Idolatrías 3/13: 1v–2r, 4r, 7v.

22 See AAL Idolatrías 3/14: 3r, 5r, 17v–18v, 30r–32r, 34v–37v, 42r–43r, 56v–57r, 62v.

23 See AAL Idolatrías 3/19: 1v–2r, 4r, 5r, 8r–10v, 11v.

24 See AAL Idolatrías 4/25: 5r–11v, 23r–v.

25 See also another document of 1660 for Omas: AAL Idolatrías 3/20: 1r.

26 See AAL Idolatrías 3/1: 2r–3v, 4v–5v, 6v–25r.

27 See AAL Idolatrías 3/1: 7v, 9r–v, 10v, 12r–v, 13r, 18r.

28 For Julcan, see text below. Cochayoc is described on f. 29v of the document as a lake atop the second mountain, but I suspect that this is one of the many cases where the notary garbles what Ycha said, and that the name actually refers to the mountain itself, since it could appropriately be called Cochayoc, which means "having lake," whereas the lake could not.

29 See AAL Idolatrías 3/1: 15v, 30r.

30 See AAL Idolatrías 3/2: 4r–8r.

31 See AAL Idolatrías 3/2: 2r, 4v.

32 See AAL, Idolatrías 3/9, 1656, ff 6r–8v, and Mills's precis (1997: 39–45). Note the distinction between ancestors and landscape: the most important ancestor, Chontabilca, could also be called Guaracani, as was the mountain where his shrine lay, but the two did not merge conceptually. The ancestor had a name, Chontabilca, that the mountain did not share. Moreover, the mountain also housed Mother Nurturer and Creator's statue and shrine, and the *pacarina*/mortuary site/*huaca* called Marca Aura, neither of which it subsumed in name.

33 See AAL Idolatrías 3/9: 4v–6r, 8r, 15v.

34 See AAL Idolatrías 3/9: 11v–12r.

35 See AAL Idolatrías 3/9: 16r–v, also 10/7, 1697 f. 11r for another case of an ancestral "devil" appearing on a mule and in the clothes of a Spaniard.

36 See AAL Idolatrías 3/9: 3v–4r, 9v, 10v.

37 See AAL Idolatrías 3/9: 1r, 11r, 13v, 14r, 15r–16r, 17r–19v.

38 See AAL Amancebados 5/5, 1658; 5/16, 1659.

39 See AAL Visitas Pastorales 23/30: 9r–v.

40 See AAL Idolatrías 5/4: 14r.

41 See AAL Amancebados 5/36, 1664.

42 See AAL Idolatrías 5/4, 1664, ff. 32r–v, 33v, 35r, 38r, 39r. Folio 23v of this document states that Carua Capcha testified in earlier *capítulos* against don Rodrigo, as indeed he did in the concubinage charges above, but neither he nor Menacho figure in Idolatrías 3/9.

43 See AAL Amancebados 5/36: 1r–v.

44 See AAL Capítulos 21/1, 1673; Idolatrías 3/9, 1656, f. 19r–v; 10/3, 1697, ff. 1v, 17r.

45 See AAL Idolatrías 7/17, 1678.

46 See AAL Idolatrías 3/9: 3v–4r, 9v, 12r–v.

47 See AAL Idolatrías 3/9: 8r, 9r.

48 See AGI Lima 31, "Relación del Cerro Guamaní" 1586 and AGI Lima 329, Relación de méritos y servicios de don Francisco Marmolejo, f. 29v

49 AGI Lima 308, letter from Bishop Francisco to king, 10/07/1656.

50 More potentially relevant idolatry documents exist in the Archivo Arzo-

bispal de Arequipa but were not available at the time of my research. I hope that changes in personnel and policy will eventually allow scholars access to those documents.

51 Duviols' speculation that Sorimana the idol was the mountain's double (1966: 201) is dubious. As he himself subsequently showed (1978), ancestral mummies and Inca rulers commonly had idols or statues that acted as their doubles, but they were surrogate ancestral bodies, not personifications of the landscape.

52 See Archivo Arzobispal de Arequipa, juicio penal contra Gregorio Taco, 293 ff., document not classified, and the studies by Salomon (1987) and Marzal (1988).

53 See Biblioteca Nacional del Perú, Manuscritos, C4284.

54 See Guaman Poma (1615: 294), Arguedas (1956), Valderrama and Escalante (1980), Gose (1994).

8. Ancestral Reconfigurations in the Ethnographic Record

1 Additional names for males include *soq'a machu*, *ñawpa machu*, *machula*, *awki*, and *awicho* and for females, *soq'a paya*, *awlay*, *paya*, and *awicha* (Flores 1973: 47).

2 Casaverde Rojas (1970: 151), Martínez (1983: 88), Szeminski and Ansion (1982: 221), Valderrama and Escalante (1997: 180–1).

3 Casaverde Rojas (1970: 151), Flores (1973: 47), Gow and Condori (1976: 27), Szeminski and Ansion (1982: 221),

4 Salazar Soler's research on peasants and miners, also in Huancavelica, confirms and develops most of Fuenzalida's points (2002: 220–2).

5 Roel Pineda's version reverses this relationship and has the Inca creating the *apus* (1965: 25). Although this may be significant for certain purposes, for those at hand it only underlines that Incas and *apus* are intimately associated, opposed to the *gentiles*, and belong to the contemporary era.

6 Note, however, that certain contemporary Andean accounts may also classify the Incas as belonging to the same age as the *gentiles*, so there is not absolute consensus here (see Delran 1974: 14; Gow and Condori 1976: 26).

7 One of Quispe's informants Christianizes mountain spirits differently: "the mountain is the angel seraphim" (1969: 39, cf. Ansion 1987: 128).

8 See Flores (1998), Gose (1986: 299; 1994: 197), Isbell (1978: 158–60) and Quispe (1969: 34–7, 65, 72; 1984: 610–13).

9 Even scholars as careful as Sallnow (1987: 128) and Abercrombie (1998: 377) articulate this position.

10 Flores (1977: 219; 1979: 84), Gow and Gow (1975: 142), Roel Pineda (1965: 27, 30). Martínez (1983: 94) mentions a *pacarina*-like "agujero creacional" called a *juturi* from which all livestock are thought to emerge.

11 Mendizábal (1966: 62), Morissette and Racine (1973: 170), Salazar Soler (2002: 179).

12 Arguedas (1956: 226, 229), Gose (1994: 194, 203, 217), Morissette and Racine (1973: 170), Salazar Soler (2002: 179), Valderrama and Escalante (1988: 97).

13 Ansion (1987: 132), Earls (1969: 68, 1970: 91), Favre (1967: 123), Mendizábal (1966: 62, 71), Morissette and Racine (1973: 174), Morote Best (1956: 290), Sallnow (1987: 130).

14 Ansion (1987: 138–9), Earls (1969: 68–9), Favre (1967: 140), Gose (1986: 299–300), Isbell (1978: 151), Morissette and Racine (1973: 171), Morote Best (1956: 303), Salazar Soler (2002: 180–1).

15 Gelles (2000: 83–5), cf. Morote Best (1956: 303), Gose (1986: 300).

16 Ansion (1987: 124), Arguedas 1956 (235–6), Earls (1969: 67), Gose (1986: 299), Gow and Condori (1976: 52), Isbell (1978: 59), Morissette and Racine (1973: 170), Rasnake (1988: 257), Salazar Soler (2002: 175–6)

17 Earls (1969: 67), Gose (1986: 299), Isbell (1978: 59), Salazar Soler (2002: 175–6)

18 Ansion (1987: 129), Earls (1969: 67), Mendizábal (1966: 68), Roel Pineda (1965: 25–6), Gelles (2000: 170–1), Salazar (2002: 179), Sallnow (1987: 130).

19 Arguedas (1956: 236), Earls (1969: 68), Isbell (1978: 59), Salazar Soler (2002: 175–6)

20 Favre (1967: 134), Fuenzalida (1980: 161), Morote Best (1956: 295–6), Salazar Soler (2002: 183).

21 Morote Best (1956: 293–4), Earls (1969: 69–70), Fuenzalida (1980: 161), Gose (1986: 304), Salazar Soler (2002: 176–7, 182).

22 See Delran (1974: 14), Fuenzalida (1977: 62), Gow and Condori (1976: 26), Valderrama and Escalante (1997: 180).

23 During my fieldwork of 1981–83, people called one of Huaquirca's three abandoned pre-*reducción* towns Iglesiapotaqa, and insisted that it contained the ruins of a Catholic church, although I could never find them. This may qualify as a similar Christianization of the *gentiles*.

24 Salazar Soler (2002: 183), Sallnow (1987: 130–1).

25 Thus, the Incas are once again rehabilitated as Christian: Delran produces a contemporary Andean narrative in which they are high, in that they can be seen only from Mount Ccaniguay, whereas *machus* are low or subterranean (1974: 17).

26 See Mayer (1977: 78), Valderrama and Escalante (1980: 250), Harris (1982: 53), Skar (1982: 194) and Gose (1994).

27 See Carter (1968: 246–7), Casaverde Rojas (1970: 188), Bastien (1978: 45),

Ossio (1980: 260), Valderrama and Escalante (1980: 252), Gose (1994: 115) and Orta (1999: 872).

28 See Valderrama and Escalante (1980: 237), Harris (1982: 51), Gose (1994: 117–18).

29 See Valderrama and Escalante (1980: 238–40, 258–9), Mariño Ferro (1989: 46, 50–1), Gose (1994: 120).

30 See Arriaga (1621: 216, 220, 226) and Noboa (Duviols 1986: 151, 171, 184, 208, 213, 241, 276, 330, 499).

31 See Stein (1961: 307), Ossio (1978: 381), Valderrama and Escalante (1980: 259), and Harris (1982: 55), Gose (1994: 123–4).

32 See Valderrama and Escalante (1980: 259), Harris (1982: 62), Mariño Ferro (1989: 55), Gose (1994: 124).

33 Arguedas (1956: 266) mentions San Francisco, Valderrama and Escalante (1980: 266) mention San Pedro, whereas Gose (1994: 125) mentions St. John the Baptist.

34 See Stein (1961: 312–13), Ortiz (1973: 14), Bastien (1978: 53), Valderrama and Escalante (1980: 259–60), Harris (1982: 62), Gose (1994: 125) and Abercrombie (1998: 72–3).

35 See Arguedas (1956: 265–6), Roel Pineda (1965: 27–8), Valderrama and Escalante (1980) and Gose (1994: 123–5).

36 See Arriaga (1621: 220) and Duviols (1986: 63, 200, 205, 212, 268–9, 274, 276, 499).

37 See Harris (1982: 54), Mariño Ferro (1989: 58–9) and Gose (1994: 141–2).

38 See Bastien (1978: 179–80), Buechler (1980: 80), Harris (1982: 56), Mariño Ferro (1989: 58–9) and Gose (1994: 142).

39 See Hartman (1973: 180–4), Flores (1979: 64) and Mariño Ferro (1989: 61).

40 Of course there are important rituals at this time of year in the contemporary Andes, but they are not addressed primarily to the dead.

41 See Harris (1982: 61), Sallnow (1987: 128), Gose (1994: 143).

Bibliography

Abercrombie, T. 1998. *Pathways of Memory and Power: Ethnography and History among an Andean People*. Madison: University of Wisconsin Press.

– 2002. 'La perpetuidad traducida: del "debate" al Taki Onqoy y una rebelión comunera peruana,' pp. 79–120 in (ed.) J.J. Decoster *Incas e indios cristianos. Elites indígenas e identidades cristianas en los Andes coloniales*. Cusco: Centro de Estudios Rurales Andinos 'Bartolomé de las Casas,' Asociación Kuraka, IFEA.

Abu Lughod, L. 1990. 'The Romance of Resistance: Tracing Transformations of Power through Bedouin Women.' *American Ethnologist* 17/1: 41–55.

Acosta, J. de. 1576 [1984]. *De procuranda indorum salute, tomo 2*. Madrid: Consejo Superior de Investigaciones Científicas.

– 1590 [1987]. *Historia natural y moral de las indias*. Madrid: Historia 16.

Adorno, R. 1986. *Guaman Poma: Writing and Resistance in Colonial Peru*. Austin: University of Texas Press.

Agustinos. 1561 [1992]. *Relación de los Agustinos de Huamachuco*. Lima: Pontificia Universidad Católica del Perú.

Allen, C. 1988. *The Hold Life Has: Coca and Cultural Identity in an Andean Community*. Washington: Smithsonian.

Alonso, M. (ed.). 1943. 'Sentencia que Pedro Sarmiento, asistente de Toledo, y el común de la ciudad dieron en el año 1449 contra los conversos,' pp. 357–65 in A. de Cartagena, *Defensorium unitatis christianae*. Madrid: Consejo de Investigaciones Científicas.

Álvarez, B. 1588 [1998]. *De las costumbres y conversión de los indios del Perú: Memorial a Felipe II (1588)*. Madrid: Ediciones Polifemo.

Anonymous 1534 [1968]. 'Relación francesa de la conquista del Perú,' pp. 173–88 in *El Perú a través de los siglos*, vol. 1. Lima: Editores Técnicos Asociados.

Anonymous. 1539 [1968]. 'Relación del sitio del Cuzco,' pp. 515–612 in *El Perú a través de los siglos*, vol. 2. Lima: Editores Técnicos Asociados.

Anonymous. 1923. 'Idolatrías de los indios Wancas.' *Inca* 1: 651–67.

Anonymous Jesuit. 1590 [1968]. *Relación de las costumbres antiguas de los naturales del Pirú*, pp. 153–77 in *Biblioteca de Autores Españoles*, vol. 209. Madrid: Ediciones Atlas.

Ansion, J, 1987. *Desde el rincon de los muertos: El pensamiento mítico en Ayacucho*. Lima: GREDES.

Antze, P., and M. Lambek. 1996. *Tense Past: Cultural Essays in Trauma and Memory*. New York: Routledge.

Arguedas, J.M. 1956 [1964]. 'Puquio, Una Cultura en Proceso de Cambio,' pp. 221–72 in (ed.) J.M. Arguedas, *Estudios sobre la Cultura Actual del Perú*. Lima: Universidad Nacional Mayor de San Marcos.

– 1975. *Formación de una Cultura Nacional Indoamericana*. Mexico City: Siglo XXI.

Arias Ugarte, F. 1636 [1987]. *Constituciones Sinodales del Arçobispado de los Reyes en el Perv*, pp. 247–86 in B. Lobo Guerrero and F. Arias Ugarte, *Sínodos de Lima de 1613 y 1636*. Madrid: Consejo Superior de Investigaciones Científicas, Centro de Estudios Históricos.

Armas Medina, F. 1953. *Cristianización del Perú, 1532–1600*. Seville: Escuela de Estudios Hispano-Americanos.

Arriaga. J. de. 1621 [1968]. *Extirpación de la idolatría en el Pirú*, pp. 191–277 in *Biblioteca de Autores Españoles*, vol. 209. Madrid: Ediciones Atlas.

Avendaño, H. de. 1649. *Sermones de los misterios de nuestra Santa Fe Católica en lengua castellana y la general del Inca. Inpúgnanse los errores particulares que los indios han tendio*. Lima: Jorge López de Herrera.

Ávila, F. de. 1648. *Tratado de los Evangelios que nuestra madre la Iglesia propone en todo el año desde la primera dominicana de adviento hasta la última missa de difuntos Santos de España y añadidos en el nuevo rezado*. Lima: Publisher unknown.

Barth, F. 1969. 'Introduction,' pp. 9–38 in (ed.) F. Barth, *Ethnic Groups and Boundaries: The Social Organization of Cultural Difference*. London: George Allen and Unwin.

Bashkow, I. 2000. '"Whitemen" Are Good to Think With: How Orokaiva Morality Is Reflected on Whitemen's Skin.' *Identities* 7/3: 281–332.

Bastien, J. 1978. *Mountain of the Condor: Metaphor and Ritual in an Andean Ayllu*. St. Paul: West Publishing Co.

Benito Ruano, E. 1957. 'El memorial contra los conversos del bachiller Marcos García de Mora.' *Sefarad* 17: 314–51.

Betanzos, J. de. 1551 [1987]. *Suma y Naración de los Incas*. Madrid: Ediciones Atlas.

Beverley, J. 1999. *Subalternity and Representation: Arguments in Cultural Theory.* Durham: Duke University Press.

Bhabha, H. 1994. *The Location of Culture.* London: Routledge.

Bonnet, A. 1998. 'Who Was White? The Disappearance of Non-European White Identities and the Formation of European Racial Whiteness.' *Ethnic and Racial Studies* 21/6: 1029–55.

Bouysse-Cassagne, T. 1988. *Lluvias y cenizas: Dos pachacuti en la historia.* La Paz: Hisbol.

– 1997. 'De Empédocles a Tunupa: Evangelización, hagiografía y mitos,' pp. 157–21 in (ed.) T. Bouysse-Cassagne, *Saberes y memorias en los andes: In memorium Thierry Saignes.* Lima: CREDAL-IFEA.

Brown, P. 1981. *The Cult of the Saints: Its Rise and Function in Latin Christianity.* Chicago: University of Chicago Press.

Brubaker, R., and F. Cooper. 2000. 'Beyond "Identity."' *Theory and Society* 29/1: 1–47.

Buechler, H. 1980. *The Masked Media.* The Hague: Mouton.

Burga, M. 1988. *Nacimiento de una utopía: Muerte y resurrección de los Incas.* Lima: Instituto de Apoyo Agrario.

Bynum, C.W. 1995. *The Resurrection of the Body in Western Christianity, 200–1336.* New York: Columbia University Press.

Cabello Valboa, M. 1586 [1951]. *Miscelánea Antárctica.* Lima: Universidad Nacional Mayor de San Marcos.

Calancha, A. de la. 1638 [1972]. *Crónicas Agustinianas del Perú,* vol. 1. Madrid: Consejo de Investigaciones Científicas Instituto 'Enrique Florez.'

Carrasco, D. 1982. *Quetzalcoatl and the Irony of Empire: Myths and Prophecies in the Aztec Tradition.* Chicago: University of Chicago Press.

Carrillo de Huete, P. 1946. *Crónica del halconero de Juan II, Pedro Carrillo de Huete (hasta ahora inédita).* Madrid: Espasa-Calpe.

Carter, W. 1968. 'Secular Reinforcement in Aymara Death Ritual.' *American Anthropologist* 70/2: 238–263.

Casaverde Rojas, J. 1970. 'El mundo sobrenatural en una comunidad.' *Allpanchis* 2: 121–243.

Castañeda, P., and P. Hernández. 1989. *La Inquisición de Lima, tomo 1 (1570–1635).* Madrid: Editorial Deimos.

Castro-Klarén, S. 2000. 'A Genealogy for the "Manifesto antropófago," or the Struggle between Socrates and the Caraïbe.' *Nepantla* 1/2: 295–322.

Cavero, R. 2001. *Los dioses vencidos: Una lectura antropológica del Taki Onqoy.* Ayacucho: Escuela de Posgrado de la Universidad Nacional de San Cristóbal de Huamanga (Perú)- Centro de Pesquisa en Etnología Indígena (Unicamp, Brazil).

Celestino, O., and F. Meyers. 1981. *Las cofradías en el Perú: región central*. Frankfurt: K.D. Vervuert.

Christian, W. 1981. *Apparitions in Late Medieval and Renaissance Spain*. Princeton: Princeton University Press.

Cieza de León, P. de. 1553 [1984]. *La Crónica del Perú*, Parts 1 and 2, in *Obras Completas*, vol. 1. Madrid: Consejo Superior de Investigaciones Cientificas, Instituto Gonzalo Fernández de Oviedo.

Cobo, B. 1653 [1956]. *Historia del Nuevo Mundo*, Biblioteca de Autores Españoles, vol. 92. Madrid: Ediciones Atlas.

Colebrook, C. 2001. 'Certeau and Foucault: Tactics and Strategic Essentialism.' *South Atlantic Quarterly* 100/2: 543–74.

Cole, H. 1982. *Mbari: Art and Life among the Owerri Igbo*. Bloomington: Indiana University Press.

Cole, J. 1984. 'Viceregal Persistence versus Indian Mobility: The Impact of the Duque de la Palata's Reform Program on Alto Peru, 1681–1692.' *Latin American Research Review* 19/1: 37–56.

– 1985. *The Potosí Mita 1573–1700: Compulsory Indian Labor in the Andes*. Stanford: Stanford University Press.

Conrad, J., and A. Demarest. 1984. *Religion and Empire: The Dynamics of Aztec and Inca Expanisonism*. Cambridge: Cambridge University Press.

Covarrubias, S. 1611 [1995]. *Tesoro de la Lengua Castellana o Española*. Madrid: Editorial Castalia.

Curatola, M. 1989. 'Suicidio, holocausto y movimientos religiosos de redención en los andes (SS. XVI–XVII).' *Antropología* 7: 233–62.

Delran, G. 1974. 'El sentido de la historia.' *Allpanchis* 6: 13–28.

Derrida, J. 1982. 'Signature, Event, Context,' pp. 307–30 in J. Derrida, *Margins of Philosophy*. Chicago: University of Chicago Press.

Díaz del Castillo, B. 1575 [1984]. *Historia verdadera de la conquista de la Nueva España*. Madrid: Historia 16.

Dillon, M., and T. Abercrombie. 1988. 'The Destroying Christ: An Aymara Myth of Conquest,' pp. 50–77 in (ed.) J. Hill, *Rethinking History and Myth*. Chicago: University of Illinois Press.

Doyle, M.E. 1988. *The Ancestor Cult and Burial Ritual in Seventeenth and Eighteenth-Century Central Peru*. Ann Arbor: UMI Dissertation Services.

Durston, A. 2007. *Pastoral Quechua: The History of Christian Translation in Colonial Peru, 1550–1650*. Notre Dame: University of Notre Dame Press.

Duviols, P. 1966. 'Un procès d'idolatrie. Arequipa, 1671.' *Fenix* 16: 198–211.

– 1971. *La lutte contre les religions autochtones dans le Pérou coloniale (L'extirpation de l'idolatrie entre 1532 et 1660)*. Lima: Institut Français d'Études Andines.

- 1973. 'Huari y Llacuaz: Agricultores y Pastores. Un dualismo prehispánico de oposición y complementariedad.' *Revista del Museo Nacional* 39: 153–91.
- 1977. 'Los nombres quechua de viracocha, supuesto "Dios creador" de los evangelizadores.' *Allpanchis* 10: 53–63.
- 1978. 'Un symbolisme Andin du double: La lithomorphose de l'ancêtre.' *Actes du XLIIe Congrès International des Américanistes*, vol. IV: 359–64.
- 1979. 'Datation, paternité et idéologie de la "Declaración de los quipuca-mayos a Vaca de Castro" (Discurso de la descendencia y gobierno de los Ingas),' pp. 583–91 in *Les cultures Ibéique en devenir: Essais publiés en hommage à la mémoire de Marcel Batallon (1895–1977)*. Paris: Fondation Singer-Polignac.
- 1984. 'Albornoz y el espacio ritual andino prehispánico.' *Revista Andina* 3: 169–222.
- 1986. *Cultura Andina y Represión: Procesos y Visitas de Idolatrías y Hechicerías, Siglo XVII*. Cusco: Centro de Estudios Rurales Andinos 'Bartolomé de las Casas.'
- 1993. 'Estudio y comentario etnohistórico,' pp. 11–126 in J. Pachacuti Yamqui *Relación de antiguedades deste reyno del Piru*. Lima: Institut Français d'Études Andines / Centro de Estudios Regionales Andinos Bartolomé de las Casas.
Earls, J. 1969. 'The Organization of Power in Quechua Mythology.' *Steward Journal of Anthropology* 1: 63–82.
- 1970. 'The Structure of Modern Andean Social Categories.' *Steward Journal of Anthropology* 2: 69–106.
Eire, C. 1995. *From Madrid to Purgatory: The Art and Craft of Dying in Sixteenth-Century Spain*. Cambridge: Cambridge University Press.
Espinoza, W. 1971. 'Los Huancas, aliados de la conquista.' *Anales científicos [de la Universidad Nacional del Centro del Perú]* 1: 3–407.
- 1973. 'Un Movimiento Religioso de Libertad y Salvación Nativista,' pp. 143–52 in (ed.) J. Ossio, *Ideología Mesiánica del Mundo Andino*. Lima: Ignacio Prado Pastor.
Estenssoro, J.C. 2003. *Del paganismo a la santidad: La incorporación de los indios del Perú al catholicismo, 1532–1750*. Lima: IFEA/Insitutio Riva-Agüero.
Estete, M. de. 1535 [1924]. Noticia del Perú. In *Colección de libros y documentos referentes a la historia del Perú*, vol. 8. H. Urteaga and C. Romero, eds. Pp. 3–56. Lima: Imprenta y Librería Sanmarti.
- nd. 'El descubrimiento y la conquista del Perú,' pp. 253–319 in (eds.) A. Salas, M. Guérin, and J.L. Moure, *Crónicas iniciales de la conquista del Perú*. Buenos Aires: Editorial Plus Ultra.
Favre, H. 1967. 'Tayta Wamani: Le culte des montagnes dans le centre sud des Andes péruviennes,' pp. 121–40 in *Colloque D'Études Péruviennes*, Publica-

tions des Annales de la Faculté des Lettres, N.S. 61. Aix-en-Provence: Éditions Ophrys.

Ferguson, J. 2002. 'Of Mimicry and Membership: Africans and the "New World Society."' *Cultural Anthropology* 17/4: 551–69.

Flores, J. 1973. 'La Viuda y el Hijo del Soq'a Machu.' *Allpanchis* 5: 45–55.

– 1977. 'Aspectos mágicos del pastoreo: Enqa, enqaychu, illa y khuya rumi,' pp. 211–38 in (ed.) J. Flores, *Pastores de Puna: Uywamichiq Punarunakuna.* Lima: Instituto de Estudios Peruanos.

– 1979. *Pastoralists of the Andes: The Alpaca Herders of Paratía.* Philadelphia: Institute for the Study of Human Issues.

– 1998. 'La misa andina,' pp. 99–115 in *Actas del IV Congreso Internacional de Etnohistoria,* vol. 3. Lima: Pontificia Universidad Católica del Perú.

Fraser, V. 1990. *The Architecture of Conquest: Building in the Viceroyalty of Peru, 1535–1635.* Cambridge: Cambridge University Press.

Fuenzalida, F. 1977. 'El mundo de los gentiles y las tres edades de la creación.' *Revista de la Universidad Católica* 2: 59–84

– 1980. 'Santiago y el wamaní: Aspectos de un culto pagano en Moya.' *Debates en Antropología* 5: 155–88.

Gadamer, H.G. 1975. *Truth and Method.* New York: Continuum.

García Cabrera, J.C. 1994. *Ofensas a Dios, pleitos e injurias: Causas de idolatrías y hechicerías, Cajatambo, Siglos XVII–XIX.* Cusco: Centro de Estudios Rurales Andinos 'Bartolomé de las Casas.'

Gelles, P. 2000. *Water and Power in Highland Peru: The Cultural Politics of Irrigation and Development.* New Brunswick: Rutgers University Press.

Gentile, M. 1994. 'Supervivencia colonial de una ceremonia prehispánica.' *Bulletin de l'Institut Français d'Études Andines* 23/1: 69–103.

Gillespie, S. 1989. *The Aztec Kings: The Construction of Rulership in Mexica History.* Tucson: University of Arizona Press.

Gilroy, P. 1993. *The Black Atlantic: Modernity and Double Consciousness.* London: Verso.

González, J. 1989. *El huanca y la cruz.* Lima: IDEA/Tarea.

Goodale, M. 2006. 'Reclaiming Modernity: Indigenous Cosmopolitanism and the Coming of the Second Revolution in Bolivia.' *American Ethnologist* 33/4: 634–49.

Gose, P. 1986. 'Sacrifice and the Commodity Form in the Andes.' *Man* 21/2: 296–310.

– 1993. 'Segmentary State Formation and the Ritual Control of Water under the Incas.' *Comparative Studies in Society and History* 35/3: 480–514.

– 1994. *Deathly Waters and Hungry Mountains: Agrarian Ritual and Class Formation in an Andean Town.* Toronto: University of Toronto Press.

– 1995a. 'Les momies, les saints et les politiques d'inhumation au Perou, au XVIIe siècle.' *Recherches Amérindiennes au Québec* 25/2: 35–51.
– 1995b. 'Contra Pascual Haro: Un proceso de idolatrías, Cuzco 1697.' *Ciencias Sociales* 1/1: 203–18.
– 1996a. 'The Past Is a Lower Moiety: Diarchy, History, and Divine Kingship in the Inka Empire.' *History and Anthropology* 9/4: 383–414.
– 1996b. 'Oracles, Mummies, and Political Representation in the Inka State.' *Ethnohistory* 43/1: 1–33.
– 2000. 'The State as a Chosen Woman: Brideservice and the Feeding of Tributaries in the Inka Empire.' *American Anthropologist* 102/1: 84–97.
– 2003. 'Converting the Ancestors: Indirect Rule, Settlement Consolidation, and the Struggle over Burial in Colonial Peru, 1532–1614,' pp. 140–74 in (eds.) K. Mills and A. Grafton, *Conversion: Old Worlds and New*. Rochester: University of Rochester Press.
– 2006. 'Mountains Historicized: Ancestors and Landscape in the Colonial Andes,' pp. 29–38 in (ed.) P. Dransart, *Kay Pacha: Cultivating Earth and Water in the Andes*. Oxford: BAR.
Gow, D. 1974. 'Taytacha Qoyllur Rit'i.' *Allpanchis* 7: 49–100.
Gow, D., and R. Gow. 1975. 'La alpaca en el mito y el ritual.' *Allpanchis* 8: 141–74.
Gow, R., and B. Condori. 1976. *Kay Pacha*. Cusco: Centro de Estudios Rurales Andinos Bartolomé de las Casas.
Gramsci, A. 1971. *Selections from the Prison Notebooks*. New York: International Publishers.
Greenblatt, S. 1991. *Marvelous Possessions: The Wonder of the New World*. Chicago: University of Chicago Press.
Griffiths, N. 1996. *The Cross and the Serpent: Religious Repression and Resurgence in Colonial Peru*. Norman: University of Oklahoma Press.
Guaman Poma de Ayala, F. 1615 [1936]. *Nueva corónica y buen gobierno*. Paris: Université de Paris.
Guha, R. 1983 [1999]. *Elementary Aspects of Peasant Insurgency in Colonial India*. Durham: Duke University Press.
– 1989. 'Dominance without Hegemony and Its Historiography.' *Subaltern Studies* 6: 210–309.
Guiance, A. 1998. *Discursos sobre la muerte en la castilla medieval (siglos VII–XV)*. Valladolid: Consejería de Educación y Cultura.
Guibovich, P. 1991. 'Cristóbal de Albornoz y el Taki Onqoy.' *Histórica* 15/2: 205–36.
Guillén, E. 1974. *Versión inca de la conquista*. Lima: Editorial Milla Batres.
– 1984. 'Tres documentos inéditos para la historia de la guerra de reconquista inca.' *Bulletin de l'Institut Français d'Études Andines* 13/1–2: 17–46.

– 1994. *La guerra de reconquista inka. Vilcabamba: Epílogo trágico del tawantinsuyo*. Lima: Ediciones e.i.r.1.

Guilmartin, J. 1991. 'The Cutting Edge: An Analysis of the Spanish Invasion and Overthrow of the Inca Empire, 1532–1539,' pp. 40–69 in (eds.) K. Andrien and R. Adorno, *Transatlantic Encounters: Europeans and Andeans in the Sixteenth Century*. Berkeley: University of California Press.

Haefeli, E. 2007. 'On First Contact and Apotheosis: Manitou and Men in North America.' *Ethnohistory* 54/3: 407–43.

Hamlin, W. 1994. 'Attributions of Divinity in Renaissance Ethnography and Romance, or, Making Religion of Wonder.' *Journal of Medieval and Renaissance Studies* 14/3: 415–47.

Handler, R. 1988. *Nationalism and the Politics of Culture in Quebec*. Madison: University of Wisconsin Press.

– 1994. 'Is "Identity" a Useful Cross-Cultural Concept?,' pp. 27–40 in (ed.) J. Gillis, *Commemorations: The Politics of National Identity*. Princeton: Princeton University Press.

Harris, O. 1980. 'The Power of Signs: Gender, Culture and the Wild in the Bolivian Andes,' pp. 70–94 in (eds.) C. MacCormack and M. Strathern, *Nature, Culture and Gender*. Cambridge: Cambridge University Press.

– 1982. 'The Dead and the Devils among the Bolivian Laymi,' pp. 45–73 in (eds.) M. Bloch and J. Parry, *Death and the Regeneration of Life*. Cambridge: Cambridge University Press.

– 1995. '"The Coming of the White People": Reflections on the Mythologization of History in Latin America.' *Bulletin of Latin American Research* 14/1: 9–24.

Hartman, R. 1973. 'Conmemoración de Muertos en la Sierra Ecuatoriana.' *Indiana* 1: 179–97.

Hertz, R. 1960. *Death and the Right Hand*. Oxford: Oxford University Press.

Huertas Vallejos, L. 1981. *La Religión en una Sociedad Rural Andina (Siglo XVII)*. Ayacucho: Universidad Nacional de San Cristóbal de Huamanga.

Huntington, R., and P. Metcalf. 1979. *Celebrations of Death*. Cambridge: Cambridge University Press.

Isbell, B.J. 1978. *To Defend Ourselves: Ecology and Ritual in an Andean Village*. Austin: University of Texas Press.

Isbell, W. 1997. *Mummies and Mortuary Monuments: A Postprocesual Prehistory of Central Andean Social Organization*. Austin: University of Texas Press.

Iwasaki, F. 1984. 'Idolatrías de los indios checras.' *Historia y Cultura* 17: 75–90.

Jiménez de la Espada, M. 1965. *Relaciones geográficas de Indias*, vol. 1. Madrid: Ediciones Atlas.

Kamen, H. 1965. *The Spanish Inquisition*. New York: New American Library.

– 1997. *The Spanish Inquisition: An Historical Revision*. London: Nicholson and Weidenfeld.

Kaplan, M., and J. Kelly 1994. 'Rethinking Resistance: Dialogues of "Disaffection" in Colonial Fiji.' *American Ethnologist* 21/1: 123–51.

Kempf, W. 1994. 'Ritual, Power, and Colonial Domination: Male Initiation among the Ngaing of Papua New Guinea,' pp. 108–26 in (eds.) C. Stewart and R. Shaw, *Syncretism/Anti-Syncretism: The Politics of Religious Synthesis*. London: Routledge.

Kertzer, D. 1988. *Ritual, Politics and Power*. New Haven: Yale University Press.

Laclau, E., and C. Mouffe. 1985. *Hegemony and Socialist Strategy: Towards a Radical Democratic Politics*. London: Verso.

Lan, D. 1985. *Guns and Rain*. Berkeley: University of California Press.

Las Casas, B. 1561. *Apologética Historia Sumaria* in B. de las Casas, *Obras Completas*. Madrid: Editorial Alianza.

Leavitt, S. 2000. 'The Apotheosis of White Men?: A Reexamination of Beliefs about Europeans as Ancestral Spirits.' *Oceania* 70: 304–23.

Levillier, R. 1919. *Organización de la iglesia y órdenes religiosas en el virreinato del Perú en el siglo XVI*. Madrid: Sucesores de Rivadeneyra.

– 1921–6. *Gobernantes del Perú*, 14 vols. Madrid: Imprenta de Juan Pueyo

Lienhard, M. 1997. 'La matriz colonial y los procesos culturales en América Latina' *Universidad de La Habana* 247: 62–74.

Lissón y Cháves, E. 1943–7. *La iglesia de España en el Perú*, 5 vols. Seville.

Lobo Guerrero, B. 1613 [1987]. *Liblro [sic] primero de las constituciones synodales de este Arzobispado de los Reyes del Perù*, pp. 29–209 in B. Lobo Guerrero and F. Arias Ugarte, *Sínodos de Lima de 1613 y 1636*. Madrid: Consejo Superior de Investigaciones Científicas, Centro de Estudios Históricos.

Lockhart, J. 1992. *The Nahuas after the Conquest: A Social and Cultural History of the Indians of Central Mexico, Sixteenth through Eighteenth Centuries*. Stanford: Stanford University Press.

Lohmann Villena, G. 1941. 'El Inca Titu Cusi Yupanqui y su entrevista con el oidor Matienzo (1565).' *Mercurio Peruano* 166: 3–18.

– 1957. *El corregidor en indios en el Perú bajo los austrias*. Madrid: Ediciones Cultura Hispánica.

– 1967. 'Etude préliminaire,' pp. v-lxix in J. de Matienzo, *Gobierno del Perú*. Lima: Institut Français d'Études Andines.

MacCormack, S. 1991. *Religion in the Andes: Vision and Imagination in Early Colonial Peru*. Princeton: Princeton University Press.

MacGaffey, W. 1968. 'Kongo and the King of the Americans.' *Journal of Modern African Studies* 6/2: 171–81.

– 1972. 'The West in Congolese Experience,' pp. 49–74 in (ed.) P. Curtin, *Africa and the West: Intellectual Responses to European Culture.* Madison: University of Wisconsin Press.

Málaga Medina, A. 1974. 'Las reducciones en el Perú.' *Historia y Cultura* 8: 141–72.

Mallon, F. 1983. *The Defense of Community in Peru's Central Highlands: Peasant Struggle and Capitalist Transition 1860–1940.* Princeton: Princeton University Press.

– 1994. 'The Promise and Dilemma of Subaltern Studies: Perspectives from Latin American History.' *The American Historical Review* 99/5: 1491–1515.

– 1995. *Peasant and Nation: The Making of Postcolonial Mexico and Peru.* Berkeley: University of California Press.

Manrique, N. 1993. *Vinieron los saracenos ... El universo mental de la conquista de america.* Lima: DESCO.

Mariño Ferro, X. 1989. *Muerte, religión y simbolos en una comunidad Quechua.* Santiago de Compostela: Universidade de Santiago de Compostela.

Martínez, G. 1983. 'Los dioses de los cerros en los Andes.' *Journal de la Société des Américanistes* 69: 85–115.

Martínez Cereceda, J. 1995. *Autoridades en los andes, los atributos del señor.* Lima: Pontificia Universidad Católica del Perú.

Marzal. M. 1971. *El mundo religioso de Urcos.* Cusco: Instituto de Pastoral Andina.

– 1983. *Transformación religiosa peruana.* Lima: Pontificia Universidad Católica del Perú.

– 1985. *El sincretismo iberoamericano: Un estudio comparativo sobre los quechuas (Cusco), los mayas (Chiapas) y los africanos (Bahía).* Lima: Pontificia Universidad Católica del Perú.

– 1988. 'La religión andina persistente en Andagua a fines del Virreinato.' *Histórica* 12/2: 161–81.

Mateos, F. 1944. *Historia general de la Companía de Jesus en la provincia del Perú.* Madrid: Consejo Superior de Investigaciones Científicas, Instituto Gonzalo Fernández de Oviedo.

Maticorena, M. 1974. *Sobre el concepto de cuerpo de nación en el siglo XVIII.* Lima: Universidad Nacional Mayor de San Marcos.

Matienzo, J. de. 1567 [1967]. *Gobierno del Perú.* Lima: Institut Français d'Études Andines.

Mayer, E. 1977. 'Beyond the Nuclear Family,' pp. 60–80 in (eds.) R. Bolton and E. Mayer, *Andean Kinship and Marriage.* Washington DC: American Anthropological Association.

Medina, J.T. 1887 [1956]. *Historia del tribunal de la Inquisición de Lima (1569–1820),* 2 vols. Santiago: Fondo Histórico y Bibliográfico J.T. Medina.

Mena, C. 1534 [1968]. 'La conquista del Perú,' pp. 135–69 in *El Perú a través de los siglos*, vol. 1. Lima: Editores Técnicos Asociados.

Mendizábal, E. 1966. 'El awkillu entre los descendientes de los Chupachos.' *Cuadernos de investigación, Facultad de Letras y Educación, Universidad Nacional Hermilio Valdizan* 1: 61–79.

Millones, L. 1964 [1973]. 'Un movimiento nativista del Siglo XVI: El Taki Onqoy,' pp. 83–94 in (ed.) J. Ossio, *Ideología Mesiánica del mundo Andino*. Lima: Ignacio Prado Pastor.

– 1975. 'Economía y ritual en los condesuyos de Arequipa.' *Allpanchis* 8: 45–66.

– 1978. 'Los ganados del Señor: Mecanismos de poder en las comunidades andinas, Arequipa, siglos XIII-XIX.' *Historia y Cultura* 11: 7–43.

– 1979. 'Religion and Power in the Andes: Idolatrous Curacas of the Central Sierra.' *Ethnohistory*: 26/3: 243–63.

– 1984. 'Shamanismo y política en el Perú colonial: Los curacas de Ayacucho.' *Histórica* 8/2: 131–49.

– 1990. *El retorno de las huacas: Estudios y documentos del siglo XVI*. Lima: IEP/ SPP.

Mills, K. 1992. 'Persistencia religiosa en Santiago de Carhuamayo (Junín), 1631,' pp. 222–31 in (ed.) M. Leinhard, *Testimonios, cartas y manifiestos indígenas (época colonial y primer periódo republicano)*. Caracas: Biblioteca Ayacucho.

– 1994a. *An Evil Lost to View? An Investigation of Post-Evangelization Andean Religion in Mid-Colonial Peru*. Liverpool: Institute of Latin American Studies.

– 1994b. 'The Limits of Religious Coercion in Mid-Colonial Peru.' *Past and Present* 145: 84–121.

– 1997. *Idolatry and Its Enemies: Colonial Andean Religion and Extirpation, 1640–1750*. Princeton: Princeton University Press.

– 2004. 'A Very Subtle Idolatry': Estanislao de Vega Bazán's Authentic Testimony of Colonial Andean Religion,' pp. 157–73 in (eds.) M. Valdes and D. Kadir, *Literary Cultures of Latin America: A Comparative History* vol. 3. Oxford: Oxford University Press.

Mogrovejo, J. 1987. 'La fracasada rebelión de 1565: Un documento histórico.' *Boletín de Lima* 52: 13–19.

Molina, C. de (el Almagrista). 1553 [1968]. 'Relación de muchas cosas acaescidas en el Perú,' pp. 56–95 in *Biblioteca de autores españoles*, vol. 209. Madrid: Ediciones Atlas.

Molina, C. de. 1574 [1988]. *Relación de las fabulas y ritos de los Ingas* ... pp. 47–134 in (eds.) H. Urbano and P. Duviols, *Fábulas y mitos de los Incas*. Madrid: Historia 16.

Moore, S.F. 1958. *Power and Property in Inca Peru*. New York: Columbia University Press.

Morote Best, E. 1956. 'Espíritus de montes.' *Letras* 56/7: 288–306.

Morissette J., and L. Racine, 1973. 'La hiérarchie des wamaní: Essai sur la pensée classificatoire Quechua.' *Recherches Amérindiennes au Québec* 3/1–2: 167–88.

Mróz, M. 1991. 'Los viracochas de la conquista: Entre un mito andino y un prejuicio cristiano,' pp. 91–107 in (ed.) M. Ziolkowski, *El culto estatal del imperio Inca*. Warsaw: University of Warsaw, Centro de Estudios Latinamericanos.

Murra, J. 1980. *The Economic Organization of the Inca State*. Greenwich: JAI Press.

Murúa, Martín de. 1613 [1987]. *Historia general del Perú*. Madrid: Historia 16.

Negro, S. 1996. 'La persistencia de la visión andina de la muerte en el virreinato del Perú.' *Antropológica* 14: 121–42.

Netanyahu, B. 1995. *The Origins of the Inquisition in Fifteenth Century Spain*. New York: Random House.

Nowack, K. 2004. 'Las provisiones de Titu Casi Yupangui.' *Revista Andina* 38: 139–79.

Núñez del Prado, O. 1964. 'El hombre y la familia: Su matrimonio y organización politico-social en Q'ero,' pp. 273–97 in (ed.) J. Arguedas, *Estudios sobre la cultura actual del Perú*. Lima: Universidad Nacional Mayor de San Marcos.

Obeyesekere, G. 1992. *The Apotheosis of Captain Cook: European Mythmaking in the Pacific*. Princeton: Princeton University Press.

Oblitas Poblete, E. 1978. *Cultura Callawaya*. La Paz: Ediciones Populares Camarlinghi.

Odriozola, M. 1872. *Documentos históricos del Perú*, vol. 3. Lima: Imprenta del Estado.

O'Phelan, S. 1997. *Kurakas sin succesiones: Del cacique al alcalde de indios, Perú y Bolivia 1750–1835*. Cuzco: Centro de Estudios Rurales Andinos Bartolomé de las Casas.

Orta, A. 1999. 'Syncretic Subjects and Body Politics: Doubleness, Personhood, and Aymara Catechists.' *American Ethnologist* 26/4: 864–89.

Ortiz, A. 1973. *De Adaneva a Inkarrí*. Lima: Retablo de Papel.

Ortiz, F. 1940 [1947]. *Cuban Counterpoint: Tobacco and Sugar*. New York: A.A. Knopf.

Ortiz de Zúñiga, I. 1562 [1967–1972]. *Visita de la Provincia de León de Huánuco en 1562*, 2 vols. Huánuco: Universidad Nacional Hermilio Valdizán.

Ortner, S. 2006. *Anthropology and Social Theory: Culture, Power and the Acting Subject*. Durham: Duke University Press.

Ossio, J. 1978. 'El Simbolismo del Agua y la representación del tiempo y el espacio en la fiesta de la Acequia de la comunidad de Andamarca,' pp.

377–95 in *Actes du XLIIe Congrès International des Américanistes*, vol. 4. Paris.

– 1980. 'La estructura social de las comunidades Andinas,' pp. 203–377 in *Historia del Perú*, vol. III. Lima: Mejía Baca.

Pachacuti Yamqui, J. 1613 [1993]. *Relación de antigüedades deste reyno del Piru*. Lima: Institut Français d'Études Andines / Centro de Estudios Regionales Andinos Bartolomé de las Casas.

Pagden, A. 1982. *The Fall of Natural Man: The American Indian and the Origins of Comparative Ethnology.* Cambridge: Cambridge University Press.

Paz, J. 1933 [1992]. *Catálogo de manuscritos de América existentes en la Biblioteca Nacional.* Madrid: Ministerio de Cultura.

Pease, F. 1974. 'Un movimiento mesiánico en Lircay, Huancavelica (1811).' *Revista del Museo Nacional* 40: 221–52.

– 1995. *Las crónicas y los andes.* Mexico City: Fondo de Cultura Económica.

Pietschman, R. 1910. 'Bericht des Diego Rodríguez de Figueroa über seine Verhandlungen mit dem Inka Titu Cusi Yupanqui in den Anden von Villcapampa,' pp. 79–122 in *Aus den Nachrichten der K. Gessellschaft der Wissenschaften zu Göttingen. Philologisch-historische Klasse*. Göttingen: Unnamed publisher.

Pizarro, F. de. 1926. 'Encomenderos y encomiendas.' *Revista del Archivo Nacional del Perú* 4/1: 1–21.

Pizarro, H. 1533 [1920]. *A los señores oydores de la Audiencia Real de su Magestad*, pp. 167–180 in (ed.) H. Urteaga, *Informacions sobre el antiguo Perú*, Colección de libros y documentos referentes a la historia del Perú, vol. 2 (2a series). Lima: Imprenta y Libreria Sanmarti y Ca.

Pizarro, P. 1571 [1978]. *Relación del Descubrimiento y Conquista de los Reinos del Perú.* Lima: Pontificia Universidad Católica del Perú.

Platt, T. 1982. *Estado boliviano y ayllu andino: Tierra y tributo en el Norte de Potosí.* Lima: IEP

– 1987. 'The Andean Soldiers of Christ. Confraternity Organization, the Mass of the Sun and Regenerative Warfare in Rural Potosí (18th-20th Centuries).' *Journal de la Société des Américanistes* 73: 139–192.

– 1988. 'El pensamiento político aymara,' pp. 365–443 in (ed.) X. Albó, *Raízes de américa: El mundo aymara.* Madrid: Alianza Editorial.

– 1997. 'The Sound of Light: Emergent Communication through Quechua Shamanic Dialogue' pp. 196–226 in (ed.) R. Howard-Malverde, *Creating Context in Andean Cultures.* Oxford: Oxford University Press.

Platt, T., T. Bouysee-Cassagne, and O. Harris. 2006. *Qaraqara-Charka: Mallku, Inka y Rey en la provincia de Charcas (siglos XV-XVII).* Lima: Instituto Francés de Estudios Andinos.

Polia, M. 1999. *La cosmovisión religiosa andina en documentos inéditos del Archivo Romano de la Compañía de Jesus 1581–1752.* Lima. Pontificia Universidad Católica del Perú.

Polo de Ondegardo, J. 1561 [1940]. 'Informe del Licenciado Juan Polo de Ondegardo al Licenciado Briviesca de Muñatones sobre la perpetuidad de las ecomiendas en el Perú.' *Revista Histórica* 13: 125–200.

– 1571 [1916]. *Relación de los fundamentos acerca del notable daño que resulta de no guardar a los indios sus fueros,* pp. 45–188 in *Informaciones acerca de la Religión y Gobierno de los Incas,* vol. 1. Lima: Imprenta y Libreria Sanmarti.

Prescott, W. 1847. *History of the Conquest of Peru* (2 vols.). New York: Harper and Brothers Publishers.

Quispe, U. 1969. *La Herranza en Choque Huarcayo y Huancasancos.* Lima: Instituto Indigenista del Perú, Monograph Series 20.

– 1984. 'La 'Chupa': Rito Ganadero Andino.' *Revista Andina* 2/2: 607–28.

Radcliffe-Brown, A.R. 1952. *Structure and Function in Primitive Society.* London: Routledge.

Rama, A. 1976 [1989]. *Transculturación narrativa en américa latina.* Montevideo: Arca Editorial.

– 1983. 'Literatura y cultura en américa latina,' *Revista de Crítica Literaria Latinoamericana* 9/2: 7–35.

Ramos, G. 1992. 'Política eclesiástica y la extirpación de la idolatría: Discursos y silencias en torno al Taqui Oncoy.' *Revista Andina* 19: 147–69.

– 2002. 'Política eclesiástica, culture e historia: Cristóbal de Albornoz y el Taqui Onqoy, otra vez.' *Colonial Latin American Review* 11/1: 139–45.

Ramos Gavilán, A. 1621 [1976]. *Historia de nuestra Señora de Copacabana.* La Paz: Academia Boliviana de la Historia.

Rasnake, R. 1988. *Domination and Cultural Resistance: Authority and Power among an Andean People.* Durham: Duke University Press.

Redfield, R. 1941. *The Folk Culture of the Yucatan.* Chicago: University of Chicago Press.

Reinhard, J. 1983. 'High Altitude Archaeology and Andean Mountain Gods.' *American Alpine Journal* 25: 54–67.

Restall, M. 2003. *Seven Myths of the Spanish Conquest.* Oxford: Oxford University Press.

Robles Mendoza, R. 1982. *Quipu y mashas en la comunidad de Mangas.* Lima: Universidad Nacional Mayor de San Marcos, Seminario de Historia Rural Andina.

Roel Pineda, J. 1965. 'Creencias y prácticas religiosas en la provincia de Chumbivilcas.' *Historia y Cultura* 2: 25–32.

Rojas Zolezzi, M. 1995. 'Segundas exequias en el mundo andino y la noción de alma.' *Antropológica* 13: 221–36.

Romero, C. 1918. 'Idolatrías de los Indios Huachos y Yauyos.' *Revista Histórica* 6: 180–97.

Rostworowski, M. 1977. 'Reflexiones sobre la reciprocidad andina.' *Revista del Museo Nacional* 42: 341–354. .

Sahlins, M. 1981. *Historical Metaphors and Mythical Realities: Structure in the Early History of the Sandwich Islands kingdom.* Ann Arbor: University of Michigan Press.

– 1985. *Islands of History.* Chicago: University of Chicago Press.

– 1995. *How 'Natives' Think, about Captain Cook, for Example.* Chicago: University of Chicago Press.

Said, E. 1978. *Orientalism.* New York: Vintage.

Saignes, T. 1984. 'Las etnías de Charcas frente al sistema colonial (siglo XVII). Ausentismo y fugas en el debate sobre mano de obra indígena, 1595–1665.' *Jahrbuch für Geschichte von Staat, Wirtschaft und Gesellsch ft Lateinamerikas* 21: 27–75.

Sala i Vila, N. 1990. 'Alianzas y enfrentamientos regionales. Consideraciones sobre la representación de un ritual andino en Lircay, 1794–1814.' *Historia y Cultura* 20: 221–42.

Salazar Soler, C. 2002. *Anthropologie de mineurs des andes: Dans les entrailles de la terre.* Paris: L'Harmattan.

Sallnow, M. 1987. *Pilgrims of the Andes.* Washington: Smithsonian Institution Press.

Salomon, F. 1987. 'Ancestor Cults and Resistance to the State in Arequipa, ca. 1748–1754,' pp. 148–65 in (ed.) S. Stern, *Resistance, Rebellion, and Consciousness in the Andean Peasant World: 18th to 20th Centuries.* Madison: University of Wisconsin Press.

– 1995. '"The Beautiful Grandparents": Andean Ancestor Shrines and Mortuary Ritual as Seen through Colonial Records,' pp. 315–53 in (ed.) T.D. Dillehay, *Tombs for the Living: Andean Mortuary Practices.* Washington DC: Dumbarton Oaks Research Library and Collection.

– 2004. *The Cord Keepers: Khipus and Cultural Life in a Peruvian Village.* Durham: Duke University Press.

Salomon, F., and J. Urioste. 1991. *The Huarochirí Manuscript.* Austin: University of Texas Press.

Sancho de la Hoz, P. 1534 [1968]. 'Relación para Su Majestad de lo sucedido en la conquista y pacificación de estas provincias de la Nueva Castilla ...,' pp. 275–343 in *Biblioteca Peruana: El Perú a través de los siglos*, vol. 1. Lima: Editores Técnicos Asociados.

Santillán, Hernando de. 1553 [1927]. *Relación del origen, descendencia, politica y gobierno de los Incas* in (ed.) H. Urteaga. *Historia de los Incas y relación de su gobierno*, Colección de Libros y documentos referentes a la historia del Perú, vol. 9. Lima: Imprenta y Libreria Sanmarti.

Santo Tomás, D. de. 1560 [1951]. *Lexicon o vocabulario de la lengua general del Peru*. Lima: Universidad Nacional Mayor de San Marcos.

Sarmiento de Gamboa, P. 1572 [1942]. *Historia de los Incas*. Buenos Aires: Biblioteca Emecé.

Scott, J. 1985. *Weapons of the Weak: Everyday Forms of Peasant Resistance*. New Haven: Yale University Press.

– 1990. *Domination and the Arts of Resistance: Hidden Transcripts*. New Haven: Yale University Press.

Sempat Assadourian, C. 1994. *Transiciones hacia el sistema colonial andino*. Lima: IEP/El Colegio de México.

Serlunikov, S. 2003. *Subverting Colonial Authority: Challenges to Spanish Rule in Eighteenth-Century Southern Andes*. Durham: Duke University Press.

Sicroff, A. 1960. *Les controverses des statuts de pureté de sang en Espagne du XVe au XVIIe siècle*. Paris: Librairie Marcel Didier.

Silverblatt, I. 1987. *Moon, Sun, and Witches: Gender Ideologies and Class in Inca and Colonial Peru*. Princeton: Princeton University Press.

– 1988. 'Political Memories and Colonizing Symbols: Sanitago and the Mountain Gods of Colonial Peru,' pp. 174–84 in (ed.) J. Hill, *Rethinking History and Myth*. Chicago: University of Illinois Press.

Skar, H. 1982. *The Warm Valley People: Duality and Land Reform among the Quechua Indians of Highland Peru*. Oslo: Universitetsforlag.

Solórzano de Pereyra, J. de. 1648 [1972]. *Politica Indiana*, 5 vols. Madrid: Ediciones Atlas.

Spalding, K. 1984. *Huarochirí: An Andean Society under Inca and Spanish Rule*. Stanford: Stanford University Press.

Spivak, G. 1985. 'Subaltern Studies: Deconstructing Historiography.' *Subaltern Studies* 3: 330–63.

– 1988. 'Can the Subaltern Speak?' pp. 217–313 in (eds.) C. Nelson and L. Grossberg, *Marxism and the Interpretation of Culture*. Urbana: University of Illinois Press.

– 1989. 'In a Word. Interview.' *Differences* 2/1: 124–56.

– 1990. *The Post-Colonial Critic: Interviews, Strategies, Dialogues*. New York: Routledge.

Stein, W. 1961. *Hualcán: Life in the Highlands of Peru*. Ithaca: Cornell University Press.

Stern, S. 1982. *Peru's Indian Peoples and the Challenge of Spanish Conquest.* Madison: University of Wisconsin Press.

Szeminski, J., and J. Ansion. 1982. 'Dioses y hombres de Huamanga.' *Allpanchis* 9: 177–92.

Tambiah, S. 1985. *Culture, Thought, and Social Action.* Cambridge, Mass.: Harvard University Press.

Taylor, G. 1974–76. '*Camay, Camac* et *Camasca* dans le manuscrit Quechua de Huarochirí.' *Journal de la Société des Américanistes* 63: 231–44.

– 1980. 'Supay.' *Amerindia* 5: 47–63.

Taylor, W. 1996. *Magistrates of the Sacred: Priests and Parishioners in Eighteenth-Century Mexico.* Stanford: Stanford University Press.

– 2005. 'Two Shrines of the Cristo Renovado: Religion and Peasant Politics in Late Colonial Mexico.' *American Historical Review* 110/4: 945–74.

Thomas, N. 1994. *Colonialism's Culture: Anthropology, Travel and Government.* Princeton: Princeton University Press.

Thomson, S. 2002. *We Alone Will Rule: Native Andean Politics in the Age of Insurgency.* Madison: University of Wisconsin Press.

Thurner, M. 1997. *From Two Republics to One Divided: Contradictions of Postcolonial Nationmaking in Andean Peru.* Durham: Duke University Press.

Tineo Morón, M. 1992. *La fe y las costumbres: Catálogo de la sección documental de Capítulos (1600–1898) Archivo Arzobispal de Lima.* Cusco: Centro de Estudios Rurales Andinos Bartolomé de las Casas.

Titu Cusi. 1570 [1916]. *Relación de la conquista del Perú y hechos del Inca Manco II.* Colección de libros y documentos referentes a la historiac del Perú, vol. 2. Lima: Imprenta y Libreria Sanmarti y Ca.

Toledo, F. de. 1975. *Tasa de la visita general de Francisco de Toledo.* Lima: Universidad Nacional Mayor de San Marcos.

– 1986. *Francisco de Toledo: Disposiciones Gubernativas para el Virreinato del Perú, 1569–1574.* Sevilla: Escuela de Estudios Hispano-Americanos.

– 1989. *Francisco de Toledo: Disposiciones Gubernativas para el Virreinato del Perú, 1575–1580.* Sevilla: Escuela de Estudios Hispano-Americanos.

Torres, B. de. 1657 [1972]. *Crónicas agustinianas del Perú,* vol. 2. Madrid: Consejo Superior de Investigaciones Científicas, Instituto 'Enrique Florez.'

Trujillo, D. de 1571 [1987]. 'Relación del descubrimiento del reino del Perú que hizo Diego de Trujillo en compañía del gobernador don Francisco Pizarro y otros capitanes, desde que llegaron a Panama el año de 1530, en que refiere todas derrotas y sucesos, hasta 15 de abril de 1571,' pp. 191–206 in F.de Xérez, *Verdadera relación de la conquista del Perú.* Madrid: Historia 16.

Tylor, E.B. 1871 [1956]. *Religion in Primitive Culture, Part II of 'Primitive culture.'* New York: Harper and Brothers Publishers.

Urbano, H. 1990. 'Cristóbal de Molina, el Cuzqueño. Negocios eclesiásticos, mesianismo y Taqui Oncoy.' *Revista Andina* 15: 265–83.

– 1996. 'Rituales andinos y discurso anti-idolátrico (s. XVI-XVII),' pp. 137–52 in (eds.) B. Schmelz and N. R. Crumrine, *Estudios sobre el sincretismo en América Central y en los Andes*. Bonn: Holos.

– 1997. 'Sexo, pintura de los Incas y Taqui Oncoy. Escenas de la vida cotidiana en el Cuzco del siglo XVI.' *Revista Andina* 29: 207–246.

Urteaga, H. 1920. *Informaciones sobre el antiguo Perú*, Colección de libros y documentos referentes a la historia del Perú, vol. 3 (2a series). Lima: Imprenta y Libreria Sanmarti y Ca.

Valderrama, R., and C. Escalante 1980. 'Apu Qorpuna (Visión del Mundo de los Muertos en la Comunidad de Awkimarca).' *Debates en Antropología* 5: 233–64.

– 1988. *Del tata mallku a la pachamama: Riego, sociedad y ritos en los andes peruanos*. Lima: DESCO.

– 1997. *La doncella sacrificada: Mitos del Valle de Colca*. Arequipa: Universidad Nacional San Agustín de Arequipa/Instituto Francés de Estudios Andinos.

Vargas-Hidalgo, R. 1996. 'El Perú de 1590 visto por el provincial de los jesuitas.' *Revista Andina* 27: 107–19.

Vargas Ugarte, R. 1951. *Concilios Limenses (1551–1772)*, 3 vols. Lima: Juan Cardenal Guevara, Arzobispo de Lima.

– 1953–62. *Historia de la iglesia en el Perú*, 5 vols. Lima, Imprenta Santa María (vol. 1), Burgos: Imprenta de Aldecoas (vols. 2–5).

– 1956. *Historia del culto de Maria en Ibero-America y de sus imagenes y santuarios mas celebrados*, 2 vols., 3rd ed. Madrid : Talleres Gráficos Jura.

Varón, R. 1990. 'El Taki Onqoy: las raíces andinas de un fenómeno colonial' pp. 331–405 in (ed.) L. Millones, *El retorno de las huacas: Estudios y documentos del siglo XVI*. Lima: IEP/SPP.

Vega, G. de la. 1609 [1991]. *Comentarios reales de los Incas*, 2 vols. Mexico City: Fondo de Cultura Económica.

Vega, J.J. 1974. 'Prólogo,' pp. 5–18 in Collapiña, Supno y otros Quipucamayos, *Relación de la descendencia, gobierno y conquista de los Incas*. Lima: Ediciones de la Biblioteca Universitaria.

– 1978. *La guerra de los viracochas*. Lima: Ediciones Peisa.

Villagómez, P. de. 1649 [1919]. *Carta pastoral de exhortación e instrucción contra las idolatrías de los indios del arzobispado de Lima*, in (eds.) C. Romero and H. Urteaga, *Colección de libros y documentos referentes a la historia del Perú*, vol. 12. Lima: Sanmartí.

Villanueva, H. 1982. *Cuzco 1689: Economía y sociedad en el sur Andino*. Cusco: Centro de Estudios Rurales Andinos Bartolomé de las Casas.

Voekel, P. 2002. *Alone before God: The Relgious Origins of Modernity in Mexico.* Durham: Duke University Press.

Voloshinov, V. 1973. *Marxism and the Philosophy of Language.* New York: Seminar Press.

Wachtel, N. 1971 [1977]. *The Vision of the Vanquished: the Spanish Conquest of Peru through Indian Eyes, 1530–1570.* New York: Barnes and Noble.

– 1990. *Le retour des ancêtres: Les indiens Urus de Bolivie, XXe–XVIe siècle.* Essai d'histoire régressive. Paris: Édition Gallimard.

Walker, C. 1999. *Smouldering Ashes: Cuzco and the Creation of Republican Peru, 1780–1840.* Durham: Duke University Press.

Weismantel, M. 2001. *Cholas and Pishtacos: Stories of Race and Sex in the Andes.* Chicago: University of Chicago Press.

Wightman, A. 1990. *Indigenous Migration and Social Change: The* Forasteros *of Cuzco, 1520–1720.* Durham: Duke University Press.

Xérez, F. de. 1534 [1987]. *Verdadera relación de la conquista del Perú.* Madrid: Historia 16.

Yaranga, A. 1978. 'Taki Onqo ou la vision des vaincus au XVIe siècle,' pp. 119–79 in *Les mentalités dans la Péninsule ibérique et en Amérique latine aux XVIe et XVIIe siècle.* Tours: Publications de l'Université de Tours.

Young, R. 1995. *Colonial Desire: Hybridity in Theory, Culture and Race.* London: Routledge.

Zárate, A. de. 1555 [1995]. *Historia del descubrimiento y conquista del Perú.* Lima: Pontificia Universidad Católica del Perú.

Zavala, I. 1999. 'La transculturación, la paradoja y el enigma.' *Quimera* 185: 58–67.

Zorilla, J. 1978. 'Sueño, mito y realidad en una comunidad ayacuchana.' *Debates en Antropología* 2: 119–24.

Zuidema, R.T. 1964. *The Ceque System of Cuzco.* Leiden: Brill.

– 1965. 'Observaciones sobre el Taki Onqoy.' *Historia y Cultura* 1: 137.

– 1973. 'Kinship and Ancestor Cult in Three Peruvian Communities: Hernández Príncipe's Account in 1622.' *Boltín de l'Institut Français d'Études Andines* 2/1: 16–33.

Zuidema, R., and U. Quispe. 1968 [1973]. 'A Visit to God: The Account and Interpretation of a Religious Experience in the Peruvian Community of Choque-Huarcaya,' pp. 358–74 in (ed.) D. Gross, *Peoples and Cultures of Native South America.* New York: Doubleday.

Index

Abercrombie, T., 28, 81, 121–2, 282,
  286, 289, 293, 304–5, 312–13, 317,
  346, 348
abstinence, ritual, 95, 179, 215, 233,
  235–6
acllas, 39, 61, 77, 132–4, 188, 226, 231–
  2, 236, 253, 268–9
Acobamba, Treaty of, 87–90, 92–3
Acosta, J. de, 25–7, 71, 80, 127, 139,
  142, 162, 164, 333–4
Acosta, T. de, 209, 227
Adorno, R., 187, 339–40
Africa, 4, 331
agency, 8, 30, 33, 35, 180, 184, 230, 323
agriculture, 18–20, 143–4, 152, 158–9,
  162–3, 171–3, 177, 185, 215–16, 218,
  225–9, 233–5, 242, 256–7, 263, 266–
  7, 269, 274, 295–9, 302, 305–6, 315–
  20, 322, 328
Alanya, P., 266–7, 323
Alba, Conde de, 210
Albornoz, C. de, 88–9, 91–6, 101–2,
  105–8, 112, 115, 123, 165–7, 264,
  268, 335, 344
Alcalá, Council of, 126
Alexander VI, Pope, 27, 44, 337
Allen, C., 302

alma, 309–17
Almagro, D., 40, 42, 68, 187
altar, 112, 125, 127, 151–2, 161–2, 196,
  198, 201–2, 235, 262, 274–5
All Saints,' 225, 266, 308, 315–17
Alvarado, P., 42
Álvarez, B., 94–6, 107–8, 111, 135,
  140–5, 151, 157, 159, 166, 204, 344
Ampato, 165
ancestors: as enemies, 103, 109–10,
  112, 114–16, 220, 248, 252–3, 255–7,
  261, 312–13; as saints, 28, 167, 267,
  270, 275, 299; conquering, 18–20,
  169–73, 175, 177–8, 218–19; Europeans as, 3–6, 301; founding, 18–
  20, 141, 156, 159, 208, 215, 221–2,
  228–31, 246, 270, 314, 327; malquis,
  154–5, 159, 208, 220–4, 228, 230,
  315; mountain spirits as, 180, 247,
  297–303, 306, 317; mummies, 3, 11,
  28, 41, 72, 97, 114, 141–3, 146, 151–
  4, 156, 158, 169, 177, 180, 208–9,
  218–22, 224–8, 231, 234–5, 237,
  239–43, 245, 247–51, 254, 256, 263–
  5, 268–72, 274–8, 280–3, 285–6,
  291–3, 297, 299, 301, 303, 306–9,
  314–19, 322–3, 327, 346; —, bap-

tized, 148, 154, 219–23, 275, 299; —,
unbaptized, 148, 154, 219–23; narratives of, 17–20, 66, 69, 73–5, 103,
105, 159, 166, 177–8, 181–2, 184,
218, 223, 228–30, 240, 245, 255, 299;
petrified, 18, 159, 171, 178–9, 215,
226, 228–31, 242–3, 245, 274; political authority and, 16, 108, 143,
149–50, 202, 224, 237, 242, 261–2,
270, 280, 297, 322–3; rejection of,
11–12, 112, 248, 316, 319, 327; Spaniards as, 3, 6–7, 19, 49–51, 54, 58,
64–6, 69, 74–5, 177, 185–6, 188, 218–
19, 226, 257–8, 287, 299, 322, 327;
statues of, 97, 114, 142–3, 165–6,
169, 180, 224, 226–7, 229, 231, 235–
6, 239, 241–3, 245–8, 250, 254–5,
263, 265, 268–70, 272, 274, 277, 346;
stone monoliths as, 62, 158, 184,
228–32, 234–7, 248–9, 251, 254–5,
257–8, 263, 270, 274; worship of, 7,
11, 14–15, 17, 72, 82, 97–9, 101–2,
113–16, 127, 143–4, 151–4, 174–5,
179–80, 209, 215–16, 221–2, 225–31,
234–7, 239–43, 248–9, 253, 255,
261–2, 264, 268–70, 275, 277–81,
306–9, 316, 319–23; —, reciprocal,
17, 20, 103, 114, 174–5, 187, 216,
218, 222, 288, 299, 329
Anconcaua, 143, 166
Andagua, 269–72
Andahuaylas, 106
Andahuaylillas, 201
Andajes, 152–3, 175, 213, 236
Apachi, Santo Domingo de, 153–5
apo (apu), 179, 186, 209, 217, 224, 231,
233–6, 239, 241, 251–5, 258, 260,
263, 284–5, 291–2, 296, 343, 346
apotheosis, 4, 48, 55, 57, 60, 64, 179,
242

Arequipa, 83, 91, 94, 108, 165, 167,
202, 268–73, 275, 313, 341–2, 346
Arguedas, J.M., 241, 296, 306, 343,
346–8
Arias Ugarte, H., 194–5, 202–3, 207,
209, 340
Arriaga, J.P. de, 20, 26, 138, 153, 156–
60, 179, 190, 212, 234, 240, 243, 262,
264, 273–5, 299, 314, 337, 339, 344,
348
Atabillos, 240
Atahuallpa, 37–41, 46, 48–9, 51–2, 58,
60–1, 63–4, 68, 70–1, 82, 184, 287,
334
Atunchuca, 174, 178
Augustinians, 73–6, 78, 80, 88, 109,
335
Aullagas, 83, 140–5, 155, 166
Australia, 4
Avendaño, F. de, 152–6, 175, 191–2,
207, 219, 226, 230, 236, 339
Ávila, F. de, 148, 156, 197, 207, 245–6,
248–9
Ayacucho, 165, 302, 304
Ayaranga, San Pablo de, 153–5
ayllu, 14–20, 84, 114, 118, 132, 143–6,
148, 150, 152, 155–9, 161, 163, 165–
6, 169, 179, 186, 212–31, 234, 236–
43, 246–7, 250, 252–6, 261–4, 268–
71, 273, 275, 277–81, 290, 307, 309,
311, 325, 331
Aymaraes, 83, 85, 114–5, 262, 337
ayni, 310, 318–20

Betanzos, J. de, 48, 56–60, 66, 68–70,
72, 331–4, 339, 343–4
Bhabha, H., 7–8, 12, 29
Blasphemy, 56, 197
Bombom, 174, 178, 192
Bourbons, 238, 276–7

Bouysse-Cassagne, T., 73, 167
brideservice, 130–4
Burga, M., 173, 227, 241
burial, 303, 307; church floor, 124–7,
    135, 140–1, 144–6, 150–1, 156–7,
    160, 196–205, 209, 213, 219, 224,
    226, 275–6, 308–9, 317;pagan, 24,
    134–5, 140–2, 144, 146, 150–1, 156–
    7, 186, 202, 213, 219, 224, 226, 309

Cabanas, 166
Cabello Valboa, M., 77–9, 185, 332–4
cabo de año, 214–15, 217, 225, 271
Cacha, 77, 186
Cajamarca, 37–9, 52, 58–9, 64, 68, 70,
    120, 181
Cajamarquilla, 212–13
Cajatambo, 146, 175, 212–13, 216,
    220, 222, 225–7, 232, 237, 240, 248,
    270, 273, 275
Calancha, A. de la, 113
Callaguaya, San Francisco de, 139,
    339
Callan, Carlos (and brothers), 146–9
Caltama, 166
camachicos, 15, 212–13, 215, 219, 221–
    2, 225–7, 234.
Camaquenes, 225, 311, 314
Campo, G. de, 191–4, 211, 340
Cañaris, 39, 42, 46, 63
Canas, 56
Cañete, 83–4
Cañete, Marqués de, 136
Canin, 231
Canta, 19, 175, 213, 237, 251–62
capacochas, 49, 64, 105
Carabuco, Cross of, 78, 80, 182, 186
Carhuachin, H., 255–9, 261–2, 278,
    323
Carhuamayo, 175, 179, 213

Carhuamita, 214, 225, 316
Carhuayacolca, 19, 229, 231
Carhuaz, 200
Carua Capcha, J., 260–1, 345
Casaverde Rojas, J., 284, 302, 312,
    346–7
Castro, L.G. de, 67, 84, 86–8, 93, 118,
    128
Cauri, San Miguel de, 174–6, 181,
    213, 219, 240
caves, mortuary, 139, 145–6, 148,
    150–1, 156–7, 159, 202, 212–5, 219–
    24, 256, 272, 275, 283, 301, 309
Chachapoyas, 39, 42, 58, 83, 85, 108–9
Chalcochima, 40
Chancas, 62, 184
Chancay, 152, 175, 213
Charcas, 83–4, 195
Charles III, King, 276
Charles V, King, 43, 120, 188
Chaupi Ñamca, 173, 339
Chaupis Yauri, A., 216, 218
Checa, 169, 172–3
Checras, 152, 156, 175, 209, 222, 227,
    270, 332
Chichas, 268
Chimborazo, 83, 105
Chinchaycocha, 174–81, 213, 255,
    275
Chinchón, Conde de, 194, 211, 340
Chipaya, 289–91
Chocne, J., 92, 98, 115, 336
Chono, J., 92
Christians: new, 23–6, 26–7; old, 23–
    5, 126–7, 187
Chucho Liviac, J., 163
Chupachos, 178
Chupas, Battle of, 43
Chuquisaca, 79, 83, 94, 108
Churin, 213, 233–6

Cieza de León, P., 45–6, 57, 60–5, 68–9, 70, 72, 332–4, 343–4

Ciquinchara, 58–61, 66

civil war, 43, 45, 56, 66, 76, 81, 187

class, 15, 45, 221, 298, 320–3

Cochabamba, 275–6

Cocharcas, Virgin of, 164, 167

Cochas, 138–9, 205

Collaguas, 166

Collao, 43, 83, 186

colonialism, 3, 30, 240, 324, 328; as alliance, 3–5, 10, 19–20, 28, 36–37, 43–8, 66, 78, 81, 84, 187, 222, 288, 300, 307, 324;as assimilation of colonizers, 3, 6, 19–20, 33–4, 218, 300, 322, 327; as binary differentiation, 7–8, 11–13, 29, 31, 33, 103, 144–5, 151, 155, 159–60, 163–5, 236, 270; as conquest and violence, 4–5, 10, 19–20, 23, 26–7, 32–7, 41, 43–7, 52, 63, 73–5, 81, 101, 188, 190, 217–19, 242; as hegemony, 5, 14, 47; as intergroup coexistence and solidarity, 4, 6, 13, 19–20, 28, 101–3, 114, 161, 171–4, 187–90, 196, 218, 222, 288, 299–300, 329; as missionary enterprise, 27, 52, 69, 71, 82, 87, 102–3, 123, 299; as reform, 3, 11, 118–20, 122, 129, 134, 137–8, 161, 188, 194, 207, 211–2, 275; as extraction and servile labour, 4, 33–4, 47, 134; contradictions of, 3, 8, 10–12, 28; Inca, 5, 48, 62, 66; indigenous collaboration with, 5, 45, 81–2, 278, 324; inter-cultural character of, 3, 8, 13, 28, 31–3, 37, 48–9, 70, 78, 101–3, 114, 176, 181, 187–90, 222, 282, 299; pre-Inca, 17–20, 73–5, 102, 161, 167–74, 177, 188, 190, 217–19, 222, 242

commerce, 130, 162–3, 270

commoners, Andean, 7, 12, 15, 133, 155, 198, 221, 232, 239, 260, 275, 279–80, 302, 319, 322–5

community, geographically based, 12, 241–2, 278–9, 319–20

Concha, 171–3

Conchucos, 109

concubines, 61, 132, 141, 143, 149, 188, 193, 207, 259–60, 298

confessions: Catholic, 135, 141, 205; Andean, 143, 150, 152, 158, 215, 229, 256

confraternities, 127, 160, 197–200, 225–7, 232–3, 269, 276

conquest denial, 52–3, 67–8, 187–90, 327

conversion, 10–11, 23–4, 26, 69, 70, 96, 102, 111, 116–20, 122–3, 126, 129, 145, 184, 199, 286, 307, 312, 320, 337

Cook, Captain J., 4, 48

Copacabana, Virgin of, 164, 199

corn beer, 37, 40–1, 95, 132–3, 143, 158, 226, 234–5, 245–6, 258, 268, 275

Coropuna (Qoropuna), 165, 263, 272, 313–14, 316

Corpus Christi, 115, 144, 150, 158, 225, 289

corregidor, 86, 88, 113, 115, 118, 128–30, 133, 135–8, 140, 166, 188, 191–3, 195, 199, 208, 234–5, 258, 263, 269, 277

corruption, 12, 56, 118, 121, 128–38, 161, 188, 190, 195, 198, 204–6, 209, 211–2, 228, 274, 277

Council of the Indies, 73, 84, 88, 118, 128, 136–7, 191, 210, 212

Counter-Reformation, 82, 118, 122, 124, 203, 206

crosses: as ancestral, 274, 292, 306; *calvarios*, 274, 292, 305

Cuenca, J., 86, 130, 140

curacas, 3, 5, 10–12, 15, 23, 39–40, 43–46, 66, 70, 78–9, 81, 84–7, 95, 111, 114–15, 120, 123, 127–36, 139, 141–4, 146, 151, 155, 158, 163, 166, 176, 179, 181–2, 184, 187–8, 191–2, 194–5, 197–8, 200, 202, 207–9, 218–19, 221, 224–7, 232, 235, 237, 239, 241–2, 245, 248, 251–2, 258–64, 268–9, 271, 275, 277–80, 297, 308–9, 319–20, 324

Cuzco, 39–43, 51, 54, 56–7, 60–3, 70, 77, 84–7, 91–4, 105–6, 108, 115, 136, 149, 183, 262–3, 273, 275, 278, 285, 289, 334–5

democracy, 278, 281, 297–8, 320, 325

Derrida, J., 323

Devil (and demons), 27, 55, 58, 60–1, 67–8, 75–7, 79, 85, 110, 115, 127, 142, 149, 151–2, 163–4, 167, 186, 197, 240, 251–2, 256–8, 294, 302–7, 312, 317, 336, 345

discourse, 7–8, 11–14, 29–30, 33, 44, 69, 74, 82, 102, 129, 134, 138, 144, 149, 161, 194, 204, 207, 209, 232, 238, 327, 336

disease, 96, 98–101, 103, 109–16, 136, 149, 151, 176, 222, 234, 248–9, 306

disinternment, 124, 139–41, 145–6, 148–52, 154–7, 203, 209, 212–3, 219–22, 275–6

divine kingship, 16, 23, 28, 61, 63, 114, 176, 242, 278–81, 297, 307, 320, 322–7

doctrine, 79, 115, 122, 141, 145, 151, 153, 202–4, 206, 209

Dominicans, 128, 137

Doyle, M.E., 18, 155, 214–16, 222–3, 230–1, 342, 344

Durkheim, E., 17

Durston, A., 51, 337

Duviols, P., 19, 54, 78, 143, 153, 156, 172, 176–7, 184, 216, 272–3, 299, 311, 344, 346

egalitarianism, 278–9, 281, 319–20, 323, 325, 328

eggs, 73, 167, 217

Eliade, M., 223

encomenderos, 8, 10–11, 43–5, 54, 68, 70, 81, 84–5, 87, 118–19, 121–2, 128, 130, 187–8, 191, 211

Enríquez, M., 128

epidemics. *See* disease

Espinoza, W., 43–5, 66, 114

Esquivel Y Aguilar, J. de, 228–32

essentialism, 6, 28–31, 114, 287, 321, 324–8; strategic, 28, 30, 327–8

Estenssoro, J.C., 10–11, 48, 55, 60, 75, 81, 104, 181, 287, 334, 336

Estete, M. de, 41, 61, 72, 332

ethnicity, 28, 33, 325–7, 331

ethnography, 28, 240, 251, 271–2, 282–319, 323; in extirpator's writings, 76, 140, 143, 149, 153, 157, 159, 161

Flores Caxamalqui, R., 207–10

forasteros, 136–7, 161, 188, 191, 195–6, 199, 202, 210, 239, 242, 262–4, 278, 280

Foucault, M., 13, 30, 103, 122

Fuenzalida, F., 283–4, 289, 291, 303, 346–7

Gadamer, H.G., 324

gamonales, 280, 300, 324

García, M., 88
Gasca, P. de la, 43
gentiles, 218, 269, 283–94, 297, 300–5, 312–13, 317–19, 327, 346–7
Gose, P., 14–16, 19–20, 28, 63, 97, 104, 106, 131–3, 177, 215–16, 226, 229, 239, 241, 249–50, 262, 268, 271–2, 286, 295–9, 305, 308, 310–9, 337, 343, 346–8
grace, 23, 28, 125, 127, 139, 161–2, 176, 196, 200, 266–7, 318
Griffiths, N., 149, 190, 209, 231, 240, 248, 252, 261, 344
Guadalcázar, Marqués de, 190–1, 194–5, 340, 343
Gualcagualca, 166
Guaman Poma de Ayala, F., 47–8, 63, 67, 96, 130–1, 161, 181, 185–90, 218, 264, 314, 333, 339–40, 344, 346
guamani (*wamani*), 84, 239, 241, 264–5, 267, 287, 291–2, 296, 301, 303, 345
Guamri, 216, 223
Guaquis, 245–7, 250
Guerrero, 82–5, 92, 94, 335
Guha, R., 5, 8, 12–13, 31–2, 332
Guibovich, P., 84, 91, 106
Guillén, E., 43, 45, 49, 86, 89–90, 107, 335

Hacas, San Pedro de, 18–19, 205, 213, 229
Hacas Poma, H., 225.
haciendas (and *hacendados*),138, 162, 298, 300
hanaq pacha, 176, 218–9, 294, 304–5, 307
Handler, R., 29, 326
Hapsburgs, 238
Haro, P., 262–4, 278, 323

Harris, O., 48, 288, 295–6, 304, 308, 310, 312–17, 347–8
Haquira, 262–4
Hawaii, 4–5, 62
hegemony, 5–7, 30–5, 47, 279, 305, 321–3, 327, 329
Holy Cross; exaltation of, 274–5, 306, 342; finding of, 274, 292, 306
Holy Week, 87, 93, 270, 291
horses, 46, 58–9, 64, 94
huaca, 56, 82–4, 92, 94–106, 109, 111, 114–16, 134–5, 140–4, 146, 149–52, 154–5, 157–9, 165–6, 171–2, 177–9, 183, 185, 209, 233, 243, 255–7, 261, 263–4, 273, 336
Huachos, 149, 176
Huacra, 151
Huallallo Carhuincho, 168, 172, 244, 333
Huamachuco, 73–6, 82, 99, 109
Huamalies, 340
Huamanga, 65, 83–5, 91–4, 105–8, 112–13, 149, 201, 264–5, 273, 341
Huamantanga, 255–62
Huancas, 39, 42, 46, 69, 84
Huancavelica, 129, 149, 163, 263–4, 283
Huánuco, 83–5, 109–10, 178, 193, 302–3
Huaquirca, 114, 305, 308, 347
Huaraz, 198–200
huaris, 19, 159, 184–5, 216–18, 222–3, 227, 265, 283, 294, 331, 333
Huarihuillca, 42
Huarochirí, 148, 174, 247
Huarochirí manuscript, 18, 167–74, 183, 187, 217–18, 243–5, 247, 273
Huascar, 37, 39–40, 46, 49, 51, 60–3, 68, 70–1, 184, 187
Huaylas, 175

Huayna Capac, 37, 40–1, 51–2, 54, 67, 288
hybridity, 7, 10, 13, 29103, 117, 321

identity, 3–4, 10, 29–32, 293, 299, 305, 325–8
idolatry, 3, 26–7, 55, 69, 72–3, 75–6, 84, 88, 94, 102, 109, 112–13, 115–16, 118, 121–3, 127, 129, 132, 134–5, 137–8, 140–2, 144–5, 149–53, 158, 160–5, 176, 180–1, 183–8, 190–7, 204–10, 218, 220, 226–8, 230–6, 246, 249–50, 253, 257–62, 265–7, 269–70, 272–4, 283, 285–6, 288–9, 292, 300, 312, 322, 345; extirpation of, 11–12, 26, 73, 75–6, 80, 84, 86, 88, 99–100, 102, 107, 122, 137–9, 149, 151–2, 154–6, 159–60, 165, 167, 173, 179–81, 190–6, 199–204, 206–12, 220, 224, 226, 228, 230–2, 235–7, 240, 243, 247–9, 255, 259–60, 262, 265, 267–8, 272–4, 282–3, 285–6, 293, 296, 306–9, 311, 319, 324, 335
Incas, 5, 14, 16, 37, 41, 45–6, 49, 54, 56, 60, 62–3, 66–8, 73, 75, 77–8, 82, 84–5, 87–8, 94, 97, 102, 104–7, 110–12, 116, 128, 131–3, 142, 152, 165–6, 183–4, 186–8, 238, 240, 264, 283, 285, 287, 289, 327, 333, 335, 346
incest, 149, 193, 207, 259, 283, 303
India, 5, 35
indirect rule, 3, 5–6, 11–12, 29–30, 33, 66, 76, 78, 81, 118, 128–9, 134, 161, 173, 184, 227, 237–9, 277–9, 324–5
individualism, 7, 29, 325–6, 328
Inquisition, 25, 27, 55, 73, 103, 113, 118, 123, 126–7, 140, 192, 300
Isbell, W., 14, 239, 295, 331, 343

Jauja, 40, 83–5, 87, 108, 197, 343

Jesuits, 25–6, 75–6, 78–80, 110–11, 113, 115, 128, 149, 151–3, 156–7, 167, 191, 210, 240
Jews, 23–4, 26–7, 113, 125–6, 159, 197, 234–5, 303
Judgment Day, 156
Julí, 83, 110
Jurado, B., 228, 230

kay pacha, 305, 313
Kuyo Grande, 284

landscape, 164–8, 179–81, 183, 223, 226, 230–1, 241–3, 245, 247–50, 253–5, 265, 273–6, 278, 280, 282, 286, 291, 293–5, 313, 317, 346
La Paz, 83, 94, 269
Las Casas, B. de, 27, 52, 71–3, 75–8, 129, 333–4
Leavitt, S., 5–6
liberalism, 6, 23, 29, 278–9, 325–8
Libiac Cancharco (Yanaraman), 152–3, 174–5, 177, 217, 233–6
lightning, 18, 77, 79, 151, 174–6, 180, 216–19, 228, 247, 286, 294, 296, 343
Lima: archbishopric of, 26, 84, 137, 149, 155–6, 160, 190–1, 194, 203, 210, 228, 232, 236–7, 273, 336; Audiencia (High Court) of, 136, 140, 195, 210, 340; city of, 42, 83, 94, 108–9, 134, 153, 157, 196–7, 208, 236, 250, 256, 258, 298; First Council of, 124, 139, 154, 204; Second Council of, 118, 203–4; Third Council of, 124, 203–4
Lircay, 266–7, 275
litters, 8–9, 38, 41, 63, 188
llacuaz, 19, 184, 216–19, 222–3, 229, 265, 294, 331
Llibiac Binac Vilca, 174–6

Lobo Guerrero, B., 124, 137, 153, 163, 190, 196–7, 200–1, 208, 211, 338–9
Loma, P. de, 211, 342
Lono, 4–5
Lucanas, 39, 111

maca, 96
Macha, 289
Mallon, F., 14, 279
mallku, 143, 239, 290–1, 296; Torre Mallku, 290–1, 305
Manco Inca, 40–3, 52, 54, 63, 67–8, 84, 87
Mangas, San Francisco de, 145–9, 175, 209, 213, 216–17, 224, 241, 275, 339
Maray, Santiago de, 209, 213, 227–32, 235–7, 249, 344
Margos, 138–9, 338
marriage, 24, 115, 130–4, 158, 171–4, 188, 241–2, 270
Martínez Cereceda, J., 16
Marzal, M., 28–30, 160, 204, 287, 291, 303, 341–2, 346
mass, 38, 89, 109–10, 125, 128, 135, 146, 162–3, 180, 193, 205, 266–7, 275, 280, 291, 297
Matienzo, J. de, 86–7, 118, 332
Mayobamba, 213, 231–2
Medina, F. de, 207–8, 210, 220, 226
Melanesia, 4–6
Melchor Carlos Inca, 54, 333
Mena Godoy, J., 199–200
Menacho, M., 260–1, 345
Mendizábal, E., 285, 295, 302, 343, 347
mercantilism, 277, 325
Mercedarians, 191–2
mesa, 266, 270
metonymy, 230, 243, 273, 280, 301, 305, 344

Mexía, C., 259–61
Mexico, 4, 62, 77, 176, 211
Millones, L., 82, 143, 264, 271, 336
Mills, K., 13–14, 155, 246, 248, 252, 274, 339, 345
mimicry, 7–8, 29, 34, 69, 340
mink'a, 15, 132, 199, 251, 319
miracles, 80, 113, 164, 167, 186, 265, 276
Mito, 197, 200
mocha, 16, 114, 158
Mogrovejo, T., 139
moieties, 14, 19–20, 50, 63, 65–6, 73–5, 79, 104, 171–4, 176–7, 181, 188–90, 218–9, 222–3, 234, 265, 283, 286–7, 293, 303–7, 319, 326–7, 334
Molina, C. de, 57, 70, 92–6, 99–101, 105, 107–8, 111–12, 331–3, 336
monotheism, 51, 55, 57, 68, 160, 185–6
Monsalve, M. de, 137, 338
Monterrey, Conde de, 136
Montesclaros, Marqués de, 138, 191, 338
Moors, 23–4, 26–7, 76, 125–6, 159
Moquegua, 316
moro oncoy, 114, 262
mortuary ritual, 14, 16, 124, 126, 134–5, 140–2, 145, 149–50, 152–3, 155–7, 159–60, 202, 204, 213–15, 219, 225–6, 229, 235, 271, 275–6, 307–11
mountains, 112, 114–15, 140, 143, 149, 151–2, 164–9, 174, 177–81, 223–4, 229–31, 233, 239–43, 245–51, 253–6, 262–6, 268–9, 271–6, 282–3, 287, 290–5, 301, 303, 305, 307, 313–14, 323, 337, 343, 345
mountain spirits, 12, 179–81, 231, 239–45, 247, 250–1, 254–5, 263–5, 267–8, 271–3, 275–6, 278–81, 282–5,

291–307, 313–14, 317, 319, 322–3, 327
Moya, 283–4
Moyobamba, 109
Mróz, M., 48, 55
Musca, San Francisco de, 153–4

nationalism (and nations), 4, 6, 19–20, 23–5, 32–3, 35–6, 44, 67, 114, 242, 279, 293, 297, 299, 325–6
neoliberalism. *See* liberalism
New Laws, 43
Ninacaca, San Pedro de, 175, 179, 213
Noboa, B. de, 163, 203, 212–14, 216, 219–21, 224, 226, 275, 314, 348
Núñez del Prado, O., 284–5, 292
Núñez Vela, B., 43, 85

Obeyesekere, G., 4–5, 48, 62, 334
obrajes, 87, 162, 197
Ocros, 207, 213
old towns, 121, 123, 132–4, 137, 159, 163, 191, 223, 234–6, 265, 268
Olvera, L. de, 82, 84–5, 91–3, 97, 101, 108
Omas, 247–50, 344
Omate, 167, 268
oracles (and oracular possession), 82–3, 88, 95–8, 100–1, 105–6, 113–16, 127, 142–4, 150, 166–7, 232–5, 248–9, 261, 263, 265–8, 270–1, 299, 336
orthodoxy, 203, 222
orthopraxy, 203–4, 206, 225
Ortiz, F., 32
Ortiz, D., 88–90
Ortner, S., 8, 31
Otuco, 163, 175, 212–13, 215–8, 220–5, 239

pacarinas, 18, 20, 50, 56–7, 84, 102, 105, 111, 116, 143, 152, 159, 165–6, 169, 174–5, 179–81, 183, 215, 222–4, 230–1, 239, 243–5, 247, 249, 254–5, 264–5, 268, 272–3, 275, 290, 294–5, 314, 344, 347
Pachacamac, 39–40, 49, 82–3, 85, 94, 104–5, 336
pachacuti, 51, 62, 65, 75, 82, 94, 104, 167
Pachacuti Yamqui, J., 161, 181–6, 190, 331, 333
pachamama, 77, 143
Pachangara, 213, 233–6
Pacific Ocean, 18–19, 56, 64, 66, 94, 104, 240, 249, 258
Padilla, J. de, 210, 212, 341
Palata, Duque de, 237–8
Pando, M., 89
Pararin, 205
Pariac, 212, 219–20
Pariacaca, 149, 167–73, 243–7, 255, 264–5, 339
Parinacochas, 82–5, 106
Paullo Inca, 42–3, 54
Pease, F., 48, 55, 57, 66, 70–1, 334
Pérez Bocanegra, J., 201–2
Philip II, King, 135, 338
Philip IV, King, 210
Pimachi, 212–13, 219–21, 223
Pizarro, F., 36–40, 42–4, 46, 59–60, 64, 68, 70, 82, 94, 99, 176, 187
Pizarro, G., 42–3, 54, 85
Pizarro, H., 37, 39–40, 42, 332
Platt, T., 7, 20, 28, 166, 279, 289, 296, 303–5
pocoymita, 214, 225, 316
Polo, J., 44, 48, 70, 140, 331–2, 334
polygyny, 15, 88, 133
Pomacocha, 251–5

Porco, 166
post-colonial theory, 7–10, 12–14
Potosí, 129, 163, 182, 190–1, 237, 269
power/knowledge, 13–14, 32, 44, 209
Prado, P., 149–52, 160
priests: Andean, 15, 88, 101, 106–7,
   111, 113–14, 132, 144, 150, 152–3,
   155, 157–8, 179–81, 197, 213–15,
   224–5, 228–30, 233–5, 245–6, 254,
   323; Spanish, 11, 14, 77, 88, 121,
   123, 129–30, 132–4, 136, 140, 142–3,
   146, 162, 166, 187–8, 192, 195, 197,
   199–200, 203–6, 209–11, 234, 251–3,
   257–8, 265, 269, 276–7
primordialism, 293, 327
Protestantism, 124
providentialism, 27, 50, 52, 54, 69,
   71–2, 75–8, 82, 113, 182, 184, 187,
   212, 289, 340
provincial Andean polities, 5, 10, 14–
   17, 65–6, 111, 114
Puñon, 231–3
purgatory, 125, 196, 198, 200, 205
pururaucas, 62–3, 184, 334
Putina, 165, 167

Q'ero, 284–5, 292
Quetzalcoatl, 4, 334
Quiñones, P., 233–6
Quipucamayocs, 51–2, 54–5, 57, 67
quipus, 279
Quiru Machan, 178
Quito, 42, 63, 77, 83–4, 87, 195, 338
Quizquiz, 59

race (including racism, purity of
   blood), 3, 4–6, 23–8, 33, 36, 47–8,
   127, 142, 159, 162, 188, 196–8, 200,
   288, 297–301, 321–2, 325, 327–8,
   331, 334

Raco, 174–5, 179, 213, 215–6
Radcliffe-Brown, A.R., 17
Ramos, G., 81, 94, 102, 144, 335–6
Ramos Gavilán, A., 109, 112, 334
Rapaz, San Cristóbal de, 339
realism, 13, 44, 76, 145, 336
Reconquest of Spain, 23, 25, 44, 125,
   127, 176
Recuay, 194, 340
reducción, 11, 13, 107, 118–40, 159–66,
   181, 188, 190–6, 210–12, 217, 223,
   237, 247, 257, 265, 269, 273–6, 278,
   280, 290, 308, 337, 342, 347
repartos, 238, 277
resistance, 31–4, 52, 67, 89, 92, 103–4,
   106–9, 111–12, 114–17, 145, 200,
   206, 225, 324, 328
Restall, M., 36, 45, 47
resurrection of the dead, 72, 89, 125–
   6, 154, 157
Ribera, F. de, 191–2.
Ricari, A., 212–13, 219–21, 342
Rodríguez de Figueroa, D., 86–7
Rupaychagua, R., 258–62, 345

sacrifice, 7, 17, 20, 95, 97–8, 101, 106,
   109–10, 114–15, 142–4, 146, 150–1,
   154, 158, 167, 179, 192, 214–15, 226–
   9, 232–3, 235, 239, 245–6, 248–50,
   258, 262–3, 265–6, 268–70, 275, 297,
   299, 303, 310–11, 322, 325, 342
Sahlins, M., 4–5, 8, 48, 62, 331
Said, E., 7, 12, 29
saints, 246, 291; ancestral quality of,
   7, 28, 167, 175–6, 181, 218–19, 224–
   5, 263, 265–7, 270, 275, 286, 292;
   Andrés, 275; Bartholomew, 72, 186;
   celestial location of, 175–6, 181,
   218–19, 235–6; communion of, 23,
   124–7, 196–7, 200, 202–3, 275, 318–

19; Cristóbal, 224, 275; cult of, 7, 23, 125, 176; Francisco, 167, 275, 348; John the Baptist, 348; Lázaro, 144; María, 101, 115, 336; María Magdalena, 101, 115, 336; mountains as, 167, 224, 275, 291–2; Pedro, 348; relics, 125, 303; Rosa, 303; Thomas, 72, 77–8, 182–4

Salazar Soler, C., 291, 295–7, 301, 305, 343, 346

Salinas, Battle of, 42

Salomon, F., 171, 239, 245, 279, 346

Salvatierra, Conde de, 210

Sánchez, Y., 132–6, 334–5, 338

San Miguel, 37–8, 58

Santiago: as ancestor, 150–1, 176–7, 188, 218–9, 240, 270, 286, 296, 327; as thunder/lightning deity, 150–1, 176, 188, 219, 247, 294, 296; battle-cry, 38, 176; relation to mountain spirits, 240, 265–7, 291, 343

Sarasara, 165

Sarmiento de Gamboa, P., 57, 70, 73, 331, 334, 343–4

Sarmiento de Vivero, J., 247–50, 259–60

Sayre Topa, 87

Scott, J., 31, 280

segmentation, political, 14–16, 19–20, 28, 169, 220–1, 223, 246, 290, 295

separatism, 20, 89, 91–2, 96, 99–100, 102–3, 110–13, 115–16, 129, 151, 154–5, 176, 188, 196, 198, 219, 221–2, 224–5, 236, 262, 267, 288, 324, 328

Serulnikov, S., 7, 275, 277–8

Silverblatt, I., 176, 240, 252, 294, 343

simony, 199, 204–5, 231–2

slaughtering of Indians for fat, 94, 100–1

Solimana (Sorimana), 165, 268, 346

Sotelo, G. de, 85–7, 90–4, 108–9, 335–6

Soto, H. de, 38, 40

Spalding, K., 10, 44, 81, 118, 131, 242, 249, 277

Spivak, G., 8, 12–13, 31–2, 332

Stern, S., 10, 44, 82, 101, 118

subalternity, 7–8, 13–14, 30–5, 279, 323–5

suffrages, 125, 127, 159, 198, 200–1, 208, 219

Sun: as deity, 41, 49, 59, 61, 77, 88, 104, 216, 228, 256, 258, 283–4, 288–9, 292, 304–5, 312, 318; Temple of, 39, 41, 61–2, 77, 105

supay, 58, 60–1, 67–8, 333, 336

syncretism, 28–9, 176, 219, 291, 321

Taco, G., 269–72, 346

Tambiah, S., 323–4

taquies, 10, 18, 134, 188

Taqui Oncoy, 81–6, 88–116, 118, 123, 173, 176, 262, 335–6

Tarma, 193, 213

Taylor, G., 60, 127, 142, 286

Teruel, L. de, 208, 210, 264

Thomas, N., 8, 11, 31

Thurner, M., 279

Tiahuanaco (Tiwanaku), 16, 56, 65, 83, 182

Ticllos, 212–13

t'inkas, 250, 271–2

Titicaca, Lake, 16, 18, 56, 62, 64–5, 78–9, 82–3, 94, 104–5, 182–3, 216, 285, 287, 336

Titu Cusi, 40, 67–71, 81, 84–6, 88–93, 107–9, 111, 332, 335

Toledo (city of), 24–5, 126, 337

Toledo, F. de, 70, 73, 106–7, 118–23, 128–33, 136, 140, 162–3, 182, 185, 191–4, 335, 337

Thomson, S., 275, 277–8
Tongos, 209, 213
Torres, B. de, 113
transculturation, 32–5
Trent, Council of, 118
tribute, 6, 33, 120–2, 128–38, 188, 191,
    193, 195, 210–12, 234, 237–9, 263–4,
    269–71, 275, 277, 279–80, 300, 322,
    325; as 'pact of reciprocity,' 7, 277,
    324–5; labour, 15, 130–2, 249, 271,
    279, 324; *mita*,129, 131, 136, 163,
    190, 195, 211, 237, 263; sacrifice as,
    7, 270, 325; *tasa*, 129–33
Tumayhananpa, 177, 179–80
Tumayricapa, 177–80
Tumbéz, 187
Tupac Amaru I, 87, 89–90, 106–8,
    111
Tupac Amaru rebellion, 12, 239, 271,
    277–8
Tupac Huallpa, 40
Tutay Quiri, 169–71

Ugarte, F. de, 210–11, 342
ukhu pacha, 294, 301–7, 312, 317–19
upani, 249, 311, 314
upaymarca, 152–3, 215–16, 314
Urbano, H., 81, 102, 144

Vaca de Castro, C., 43, 51, 54, 333
Valenzuela, F., 210, 212, 341
Valverde, V., 38, 59
varayoq, 279
Varón, R., 81–2, 94, 96, 107, 111,
    335–6
vecochina, 214, 216, 225
Vega, J. J., 43, 48–9
Vega Bazán, E., 165
Velasco, L., 136–7, 157, 338
Verdugo, F. de, 201, 203, 341

Vilcabamba, 42, 81, 83–4, 86–92, 94,
    101, 104, 106–8, 111–12, 335
Vilcashuaman, 40, 82–3, 111, 112,
    265
Villacongo, 40
Villagómez, P. de, 26–7, 199, 202–3,
    207–8, 210–12, 228, 274, 342
Viracocha, 48, 50–1, 182, 297; as
    ancestral category, 36, 48–51, 55,
    57, 59–60, 62–3, 65–6, 69–70, 78,
    185–6, 283, 333; as apostle, 36–7,
    50–1, 72–80, 181–4, 218, 289, 299; as
    crypto-Christian deity, 36, 48–51,
    55–9, 61, 63, 67–72, 77–8, 183, 186;
    as Inca, 62, 77–8, 183–4, 334; as
    Spaniard, 49–51, 54–75, 77–8, 177,
    185–6, 188, 218, 283, 322
visita general, 106–7, 120, 122, 128
vomit, 23, 113, 143

Wachtel, N., 282, 290–1
wamani. See guamani

Xaquixahuana, 40, 93
Ximénez, C., 93, 101, 108

Yacopoma, C., 207–8
yanaconas, 237
Yanahuara, 83, 112–14, 262–3
Yanamates, 178
Yanaraman. *See* Libiac Cancharco
Yarupaja, 216, 240
Yauyos, 64, 149, 169, 176, 244–51; eth-
    nic group, 39, 46
Ycha, J., 251–4, 323, 345
yungas, 169, 171–3, 219, 339
Yura (Arequipa), 271–2
Yura (Bolivia), 297

Zuidema, R.T., 14, 16, 104, 313

ANTHROPOLOGICAL HORIZONS

Editor: Michael Lambek, University of Toronto

Published to date:

1 *The Varieties of Sensory Experience: A Sourcebook in the Anthropology of the Senses* / Edited by David Howes
2 *Arctic Homeland: Kinship, Community, and Development in Northwest Greenland* / Mark Nuttall
3 *Knowledge and Practice in Mayotte: Local Discourses of Islam, Sorcery, and Spirit Possession* / Michael Lambek
4 *Deathly Waters and Hungry Mountains: Agrarian Ritual and Class Formation in an Andean Town* / Peter Gose
5 *Paradise: Class, Commuters, and Ethnicity in Rural Ontario* / Stanley R. Barrett
6 *The Cultural World in Beowulf* / John M. Hill
7 *Making It Their Own: Severn Ojibwe Communicative Practices* / Lisa Philips Valentine
8 *Merchants and Shopkeepers: A Historical Anthropology of an Irish Market Town, 1200–1991* / Philip Gulliver and Marilyn Silverman
9 *Tournaments of Value: Sociability and Hierarchy in a Yemeni Town* / Ann Meneley
10 *Mal'uocchiu: Ambiguity, Evil Eye, and the Language of Distress* / Sam Migliore
11 *Between History and Histories: The Production of Silences and Commemorations* / Edited by Gerald Sider and Gavin Smith
12 *Eh, Paesan!: Being Italian in Toronto* / Nicholas DeMaria Harney
13 *Theorizing the Americanist Tradition* / Edited by Lisa Philips Valentine and Regna Darnell
14 *Colonial 'Reformation' in the Highlands of Central Sualwesi, Indonesia, 1892–1995* / Albert Schrauwers
15 *The Rock Where We Stand: An Ethnography of Women's Activism in Newfoundland* / Glynis George
16 *Being Alive Well: Health and the Politics of Cree Well-Being* / Naomi Adelson
17 *Irish Travellers: Racism and the Politics of Culture* / Jane Helleiner
18 *Writing and Colonialism in Northern Ghana: The Encounter Between the LoDagaa and the 'World on Paper,' 1892–1991* / Sean Hawkins
19 *An Irish Working Class: Explorations in Political Economy and Hegemony, 1800–1950* / Marilyn Silverman
20 *The Double Twist: From Ethnography to Morphodynamics* / Edited by Pierre Maranda

21 *Of Property and Propriety: The Role of Gender and Class in Imperialism and Nationalism* / Edited by Himani Bannerji, Shahrzad Mojab, and Judith Whitehead

22 *Guardians of the Transcendent: An Ethnography of a Jain Ascetic Community* / Anne Vallely

23 *The House of Difference: Cultural Politics and National Identity in Canada* / Eva Mackey

24 *The Hot and the Cold: Ills of Humans and Maize in Native Mexico* / Jacques M. Chevalier and Andrés Sánchez Bain

25 *Figured Worlds: Ontological Obstacles in Intercultural Relations* / Edited by John Clammer, Sylvie Poirier, and Eric Schwimmer

26 *Revenge of the Windigo: The Construction of the Mind and Mental Health of North American Aboriginal Peoples* / James B. Waldram

27 *The Cultural Politics of Markets: Economic Liberalization and Social Change in Nepal* / Katherine Neilson Rankin

28 *A World of Relationships: Itineraries, Dreams, and Events in the Australian Western Desert* / Sylvie Poirier

29 *The Politics of the Past in an Argentine Working-Class Neighbourhood* / Lindsay DuBois

30 *Youth and Identity Politics in Pre-Apartheid South Africa, 1990–1994* / Sibusisiwe Nombuso Dlamini

31 *Maps of Experience: The Anchoring of Land to Story in Secwepemc Discourse* / Andie Diane Palmer

32 *Beyond Bodies: Rainmaking and Sense Making in Tanzania* / Todd Sanders

33 *We Are Now a Nation: Croats between 'Home' and 'Homeland'* / Daphne N. Winland

34 *Rural Nostalgias and Transnational Dreams: Identity and Modernity among Jat Sikhs* / Nicola Mooney

35 *Kaleidoscopic Odessa: History and Place in Contemporary Ukraine* / Tanya Richardson

36 *Invaders as Ancestors: On the Intercultural Making and Unmaking of Spanish Colonialism in the Andes* / Peter Gose